Lecture Notes in Computer Science　13727

Founding Editors

Gerhard Goos

Juris Hartmanis

More information about this series at https://link.springer.com/bookseries/558

Fei Fang · Haifeng Xu · Yezekael Hayel
Editors

Decision and Game Theory for Security

13th International Conference, GameSec 2022
Pittsburgh, PA, USA, October 26–28, 2022
Proceedings

 Springer

Editors
Fei Fang (ID)
Carnegie Mellon University
Pittsburgh, PA, USA

Haifeng Xu
University of Chicago
Chicago, IL, USA

Yezekael Hayel
Université d'Avignon
Avignon, France

ISSN 0302-9743 ISSN 1611-3349 (electronic)
Lecture Notes in Computer Science
ISBN 978-3-031-26368-2 ISBN 978-3-031-26369-9 (eBook)
https://doi.org/10.1007/978-3-031-26369-9

This Springer imprint is published by the registered company Springer Nature Switzerland AG
The registered company address is: Gewerbestrasse 11, 6330 Cham, Switzerland

Preface

The concept of security goes beyond narrowly-defined infrastructure security and cyber security. For example, when machine learning systems are being developed and deployed, they can be under the threat of adversarial attacks, which induce the systems to generate wrong predictions or estimations. How to improve the robustness of such systems and make them more resilient against attacks is an important topic regarding security. Also, artificial intelligence-based algorithms have been used to help address a variety of real-world problems involving many decision-makers, such as driver dispatching and pricing in ridesharing platforms and assigning papers to reviewers in peer-reviewed conferences. However, self-interested decision-makers may exploit these algorithms to benefit themselves. A group of drivers may collusively pretend that they are not available to create a demand-supply imbalance, which will trigger the pricing algorithm to increase trip prices. A reviewer could lie about their preferences over papers in the paper bidding phase, causing the paper assignment algorithm to assign a specific paper to them. How to protect these algorithms from such undesirable behavior can be viewed as a security problem. Game theory provides mathematical foundations for these security problems as they all involve strategic interactions among multiple decision-makers.

GameSec 2022, the 13th Conference on Decision and Game Theory for Security, tried to encourage and attract contributions to game theory for security, broadly construed. GameSec 2022 received 39 submissions. The reviewing process was single-blind, although the authors could choose to make their submissions anonymized. Each paper received at least 3 reviews, with a few papers receiving up to 6 reviews where additional reviewers were needed to make a better evaluation of the submission. Each PC member reviewed 1 to 6 papers, with an average review load of 3 papers. After extensive discussions among the Technical Program Committee (TPC) chairs and the general chair, 15 papers were accepted. In addition to the 6 papers on traditional GameSec topics such as game-theoretic models for infrastructure security and cyber security, GameSec 2022 featured 3 papers on adversarial learning and optimization, 3 papers on planning and learning in dynamic environments, and 3 papers on novel applications and new game models. This volume contains all the papers accepted to GameSec 2022. We hope that readers will find this volume a useful resource for their security and game theory research.

GameSec 2022 was held in Pittsburgh, Pennsylvania, USA, during October 26–28, 2022. The conference was held in person, but due to the long-tailed impact of COVID-19, some attendees participated remotely. Several organizations supported GameSec 2022. We are particularly grateful to the Carnegie Mellon CyLab Security and Privacy Institute.

The GameSec conference series was inaugurated in 2010 in Berlin, Germany. Over 13 years, GameSec has become an important venue for interdisciplinary security research. The previous conferences were held in College Park (USA, 2011), Budapest (Hungary, 2012), Fort Worth (USA, 2013), Los Angeles (USA, 2014), London (UK, 2015), New York (USA, 2016), Vienna (Austria, 2017), Seattle (USA, 2018), Stockholm (Sweden,

2019), College Park (USA/virtual conference, 2020), Prague (Czech Republic/virtual conference, 2021).

October 2022

Fei Fang
Haifeng Xu
Yezekael Hayel

Organization

General Chair

Fei Fang   Carnegie Mellon University, USA

Technical Program Committee Chairs

Haifeng Xu   University of Chicago, USA
Yezekael Hayel   University of Avignon, France

Publicity Chair

Tiffany Bao   Arizona State University, USA

Travel Grant Chair

Quanyan Zhu   New York University, USA

Web Chair

Chun Kai Ling   Carnegie Mellon University, USA

Workflow Chair

Steven Jecmen   Carnegie Mellon University, USA

Steering Board

Tansu Alpcan   University of Melbourne, Australia
John S. Baras   University of Maryland, USA
Tamer Başar   University of Illinois at Urbana-Champaign, USA
Anthony Ephremides   University of Maryland, USA
Radha Poovendran   University of Washington, USA
Milind Tambe   Harvard University, USA

Advisory Committee

Fei Fang   Carnegie Mellon University, USA
Tiffany Bao   Arizona State University, USA
Branislav Bosansky   Czech Technical University in Prague,
  Czech Republic
Stefan Rass   Johannes Kepler University Linz, Austria
Manos Panaousis   University of Greenwich, UK
Quanyan Zhu   New York University, USA

Program Committee

Palvi Aggarwal   University of Texas, El Paso, USA
Isabel Amigo   IMT Atlantique, France
Bo An   Nanyang Technological University, Singapore
Konstantin Avrachenkov   National Institute for Research in Digital Science
  and Technology (Inria), France
Carlos Barreto   KTH Royal Institute of Technology in Stockholm,
  Sweden
Svetlana Boudko   Norsk Regnesentral, Norway
Jakub Cerny   Nanyang Technological University, Singapore
Andrew Clark   Worcester Polytechnic Institute, USA
Edward Cranford   Carnegie Mellon University, USA
Yinuo Du   Carnegie Mellon University, USA
Zhili Feng   Carnegie Mellon University, USA
Jiarui Gan   University of Oxford, UK
Andrey Garnaev   Rutgers University, USA
Jens Grossklags   Technical University of Munich, Germany
Minbiao Han   University of Chicago, USA
Eduard Jorswieck   Technical University of Braunschweig, Germany
Charles Kamhoua   Army Research Lab, USA
Murat Kantarcioglu   University of Texas at Dallas, USA
Mohammad M. Khalili   University of Delaware, USA
Christopher Kiekintveld   University of Texas at El Paso, USA
Tomas Kroupa   Czech Technical University in Prague,
  Czech Republic
Aron Laszka   Pennsylvania State University, USA
Yee Wei Law   University of South Australia, Australia
Christian Lebiere   Carnegie Mellon University, USA
Chuanhao Li   University of Virginia, USA
Jian Lou   Amazon Research, USA

Spiros Mancoridis   Drexel University, USA
Stephanie Milani   Carnegie Mellon University, USA
Katerina Mitrokotsa   Chalmers University of Technology, Sweden
Shana Moothedath   Iowa State University, USA
Parinaz Naghizadeh   Ohio State University, USA
Thanh Nguyen   University of Oregon, USA
Mehrdad Nojoumian   Florida Atlantic University, USA
Miroslav Pajic   Duke University, USA
Sakshyam Panda   University of Greenwich, UK
Bhaskar Ramasubramanian   Western Washington University, USA
Alexandre Reiffers   IMT Atlantique, France
Arunesh Sinha   Rutgers University, USA
Zimeng Song   Tsinghua University, China
Fnu Suya   University of Virginia, USA
Alejandro Villalba   Carnegie Mellon University, USA
Jayneel Vora   University of California, Davis, USA
Yevgeniy Vorobeychik   Washington University in St. Louis, USA
James Wright   University of Alberta, Canada
Jibang Wu   University of Chicago, USA
Fan Yao   University of Virginia, USA
Zhicheng Zhang   Carnegie Mellon University, USA
Quanyan Zhu   New York University, USA
Jun Zhuang   State University of New York at Buffalo, USA

Sponsors

Carnegie Mellon CyLab Security and Privacy Institute
Springer

Contents

Deception in Security

The Risk of Attacker Behavioral Learning: Can Attacker Fool Defender
Under Uncertainty? 3
   Thanh Hong Nguyen and Amulya Yadav

Casino Rationale: Countering Attacker Deception in Zero-Sum
Stackelberg Security Games of Bounded Rationality 23
   Ryan Gabrys, Mark Bilinski, Justin Mauger, Daniel Silva,
   and Sunny Fugate

Cyber Deception Against Zero-Day Attacks: A Game Theoretic Approach 44
   Md Abu Sayed, Ahmed H. Anwar, Christopher Kiekintveld,
   Branislav Bosansky, and Charles Kamhoua

Planning and Learning in Dynamic Environments

On Almost-Sure Intention Deception Planning that Exploits Imperfect
Observers 67
   Jie Fu

Using Deception in Markov Game to Understand Adversarial Behaviors
Through a Capture-The-Flag Environment 87
   Siddhant Bhambri, Purv Chauhan, Frederico Araujo, Adam Doupé,
   and Subbarao Kambhampati

Robust Moving Target Defense Against Unknown Attacks:
A Meta-reinforcement Learning Approach 107
   Henger Li and Zizhan Zheng

Security Games

Synchronization in Security Games 129
   Stefan Rass and Sandra König

Multiple Oracle Algorithm to Solve Continuous Games 149
   Tomáš Kroupa and Tomáš Votroubek

Optimal Pursuit of Surveilling Agents Near a High Value Target 168
    Shivam Bajaj and Shaunak D. Bopardikar

Adversarial Learning and Optimization

On Poisoned Wardrop Equilibrium in Congestion Games 191
    Yunian Pan and Quanyan Zhu

Reward Delay Attacks on Deep Reinforcement Learning 212
    Anindya Sarkar, Jiarui Feng, Yevgeniy Vorobeychik, Christopher Gill,
    and Ning Zhang

An Exploration of Poisoning Attacks on Data-Based Decision Making 231
    Sarah Eve Kinsey, Wong Wai Tuck, Arunesh Sinha, and Thanh H. Nguyen

Novel Applications and New Game Models

A Network Centrality Game for Epidemic Control 255
    Olivier Tsemogne, Willie Kouam, Ahmed H. Anwar, Yezekael Hayel,
    Charles Kamhoua, and Gabriel Deugoué

Optimizing Intrusion Detection Systems Placement Against Network
Virus Spreading Using a Partially Observable Stochastic Minimum-Threat
Path Game 274
    Olivier Tsemogne, Yezekael Hayel, Charles Kamhoua,
    and Gabriel Deugoué

Voting Games to Model Protocol Stability and Security of Proof-of-Work
Cryptocurrencies 297
    Sanjay Bhattacherjee and Palash Sarkar

Author Index 319

Deception in Security

The Risk of Attacker Behavioral Learning: Can Attacker Fool Defender Under Uncertainty?

Thanh Hong Nguyen[1(✉)] and Amulya Yadav[2]

[1] University of Oregon, Eugene, OR 97403, USA
thanhhng@cs.uoregon.edu
[2] Pennsylvania State University, University Park, PA 16802, USA
amulya@psu.edu

Abstract. In security games, the defender often has to predict the attacker's behavior based on some observed attack data. However, a clever attacker can intentionally change its behavior to mislead the defender's learning, leading to an ineffective defense strategy. This paper investigates the attacker's *imitative behavior deception under uncertainty*, in which the attacker mimics a (deceptive) behavior model by consistently playing according to that model, given that it is uncertain about the defender's learning outcome. We have three main contributions. First, we introduce a new maximin-based algorithm to compute a robust attacker deception decision. Second, we propose a new counter-deception algorithm to tackle the attacker's deception. We show that there is a *universal* optimal defense solution, regardless of any private knowledge the defender has about the relation between his learning outcome and the attacker deception choice. Third, we conduct extensive experiments, demonstrating the effectiveness of our proposed algorithms.

Keywords: Security games · Behavior models · Deception · Uncertainty

1 Introduction

In many real-world security domains, security agencies (defender) attempt to predict the attacker's future behavior based on some collected attack data, and use the prediction result to determine effective defense strategies. A lot of existing work in security games has thus focused on developing different behavior models of the attacker [20, 24, 27]. Recently, the challenge of playing against a deceptive attacker has been studied, in which the attacker can manipulate the attack data (by changing its behavior) to *fool* the defender, making the defender learn a wrong behavior model of the attacker [18]. Such deceptive behavior by the attacker can lead to an ineffective defender strategy.

A key limitation in existing work is the assumption that the defender has full access to the attack data, which means the attacker knows exactly what

© The Author(s), under exclusive license to Springer Nature Switzerland AG 2023
F. Fang et al. (Eds.): GameSec 2022, LNCS 13727, pp. 3–22, 2023.
https://doi.org/10.1007/978-3-031-26369-9_1

the learning outcome of the defender would be. However, in many real-world domains, the defender often has limited access to the attack data, e.g., in wildlife protection, park rangers typically cannot find all the snares laid out by poachers in entire conservation areas [8]. As a result, the learning outcome the defender obtains (with limited attack data) may be different from the deception behavior model that the attacker commits to. Furthermore, the attacker (and the defender) may have imperfect knowledge about the relation between the deception choice of the attacker and the actual learning outcome of the defender.

We address this limitation by studying the challenge of attacker deception given such uncertainty. We consider a security game model in which the defender adopts Quantal Response (QR), a well-known behavior model in economics and game theory [15, 16, 27], to predict the attacker's behavior, where the model parameter $\lambda \in \mathbb{R}$ is trained based on some attack data. On the other hand, the attacker plays deceptively by mimicking a QR model with a different value of λ, denoted by λ^{dec}. In this work, we incorporate the deception-learning uncertainty into this game model, where the learning outcome of the defender (denoted by λ^{learnt}) can be any value within a range centered at λ^{dec}.

We provide the following key contributions. First, we present a new maximin-based algorithm to compute an optimal robust deception strategy for the attacker. At a high level, our algorithm works by maximizing the attacker's utility under the worst-case of uncertainty. The problem comprises of three nested optimization levels, which is not straightforward to solve. We thus propose an alternative single-level optimization problem based on partial discretization. Despite this simplification, the resulting optimization is still challenging to solve due to the non-convexity of the attacker's utility and the dependence of the uncertainty set on λ^{dec}. By exploiting the decomposibility of the deception space and the monotonicity of the attacker's utility, we show that the alternative relaxed problem can be solved optimally in polynomial time.

Second, we propose a new counter-deception algorithm, which generates an optimal defense function that outputs a defense strategy for each possible (deceptive) learning outcome. Our key finding is that there is a *universal* optimal defense function for the defender, regardless of any additional information he has about the relation between his learning outcome and the deception choice of the attacker (besides the common knowledge that the learning outcome is within a range around the deception choice). Importantly, this optimal defense function, which can be determined by solving a single non-linear program, only generates two different defense strategies despite the infinite-sized learning outcome space.

Third, we conduct extensive experiments to evaluate our proposed algorithms in different game settings. Our results show that (i) despite the uncertainty, the attacker still obtains a significantly higher utility by playing deceptively; and (ii) the defender can substantially diminish the impact of the attacker's deception when following our counter-deception algorithm.

2   Related Work

Parameterized models of attacker behavior such as Quantal Response, and other machine learning models have been studied for SSGs [1, 8, 13]. These models provide general techniques for modeling the attacker decision making. Prior work assumes that the attacker always plays truthfully. Thus, existing algorithms for generating defense strategies would be vulnerable against deceptive attacks by an attacker who is aware of the defender's learning. Our work addresses such a strategic deceptive attacker by planning counter-deception defense strategies.

Deception is widely studied in security research [3,5,6,10,11,28]. In SSG literature, a lot of prior work has studied deception by the defender, i.e., the defender exploits his knowledge regarding uncertainties to mislead the attacker's decision making [9,21,22,26]. Recently, deception on the attacker's side has been studied. Existing work focuses on situations in which the defender is uncertain about the attacker type [4,7,19]. Some study the attacker behavior deception problem [17,18]. They assume that the attacker knows exactly the learning outcome while in our problem, the attacker is uncertain about that learning outcome.

Our work is also related to poisoning attacks in adversarial machine learning in which an adversary can contaminate the training data to mislead ML algorithms [2,12,23,25]. Existing work in adversarial learning uses prediction accuracy as the measure to analyzing such attacks, while in our game setting, the final goals of players are to optimize their utility, given some learning outcome.

3 Background

Stackelberg Security Games (SSGs). There is a set of $\mathbf{T} = \{1, 2, \ldots, T\}$ targets that a defender has to protect using $L < T$ security resources. A pure strategy of the defender is an allocation of these L resources over the T targets. A mixed strategy of the defender is a probability distribution over all pure strategies. In this work, we consider the no-scheduling-constraint game setting, in which each defender mixed strategy can be compactly represented as a coverage vector $\mathbf{x} = \{x_1, x_2, \ldots, x_T\}$, where $x_t \in [0, 1]$ is the probability that the defender protects target t and $\sum_t x_t \leq L$ [14]. We denote by $\mathbf{X}$ the set of all defense strategies. In SSGs, the defender plays first by committing to a mixed strategy, and the attacker responds against this strategy by choosing a single target to attack.

When the attacker attacks target t, it obtains a reward R_t^a while the defender receives a penalty P_t^d if the defender is not protecting that target. Conversely, if the defender is protecting t, the attacker gets a penalty $P_t^a < R_t^a$ while the defender receives a reward $R_t^d > P_t^d$. The expected utility of the defender, $U_t^d(x_t)$ (and attacker's, $U_t^a(x_t)$), if the attacker attacks target t are computed as follows:

$$U_t^d(x_t) = x_t R_t^d + (1 - x_t) P_t^d \qquad U_t^a(x_t) = x_t P_t^a + (1 - x_t) R_t^a$$

Quantal Response Model (QR). QR is a well-known behavioral model used to predict boundedly rational (attacker) decision making in security games [15,16,27]. Essentially, QR predicts the probability that the attacker attacks each target t using the following softmax function:

$$q_t(\mathbf{x}, \lambda) = \frac{e^{\lambda U_t^a(x_t)}}{\sum_{t'} e^{\lambda U_{t'}^a(x_{t'})}} \qquad (1)$$

where λ is the parameter that governs the attacker's rationality. When $\lambda = 0$, the attacker attacks every target uniformly at random. When $\lambda = +\infty$, the attacker is perfectly rational. Given that the attacker follows QR, the defender and attacker's expected utility is computed as an expectation over all targets:

$$U^d(\mathbf{x}, \lambda) = \sum_t q_t(\mathbf{x}, \lambda) U_t^d(x_t) \tag{2}$$

$$U^a(\mathbf{x}, \lambda) = \sum_t q_t(\mathbf{x}, \lambda) U_t^a(x_t) \tag{3}$$

The attacker's utility $U^a(\mathbf{x}, \lambda)$ was proved to be increasing in λ [18]. We leverage this monotonicity property to analyze the attacker's deception. In SSGs, the defender can learn λ based on some collected attack data, denoted by λ^{learnt}, and find an optimal strategy which maximizes his expected utility accordingly:

$$\max_{\mathbf{x} \in \mathbf{X}} U^d(\mathbf{x}, \lambda^{\text{learnt}})$$

4 Attacker Behavior Deception Under Uncertainty

We first study the problem of imitative behavior deception in an uncertainty scenario in which the attacker is uncertain about the defender's learning outcome. Formally, if the attacker plays according to a particular parameter value of QR, denoted by λ^{dec}, the learning outcome of the defender can be any value within the interval $[\max\{\lambda^{\text{dec}} - \delta, 0\}, \lambda^{\text{dec}} + \delta]$, where $\delta > 0$ represents the extent to which the attacker is uncertain about the learning outcome of the defender. We term this interval, $[\max\{\lambda^{\text{dec}} - \delta, 0\}, \lambda^{\text{dec}} + \delta]$, as the *uncertainty range* of λ^{dec}. We are particularly interested in the research question:

Given uncertainty about learning outcomes, can the attacker still benefit from playing deceptively?

In this section, we consider the scenario when the attacker plays deceptively while the defender does not take into account the prospect of the attacker's deception. We aim at analyzing the attacker deception decision in this no-counter-deception scenario. We assume that the attacker plays deceptively by mimicking any λ^{dec} within the range $[0, \lambda^{max}]$.[1] The value λ^{max} represents the limit to which the attacker plays deceptively. When $\lambda^{max} \to \infty$, the deception range of the attacker covers the whole range of λ. We aim at examining the impact of λ^{max} on the deception outcome of the attacker later in our experiments. Given uncertainty about the learning outcome of the defender, the attacker attempts to find the optimal $\lambda^{\text{dec}} \in [0, \lambda^{max}]$ to imitate that maximizes its utility in the worst case scenario of uncertainty, which can be formulated as follows:

$$(\mathbf{P}^{\text{dec}}) : \max_{\lambda^{\text{dec}}} \min_{\lambda^{\text{learnt}}} U^a(\mathbf{x}(\lambda^{\text{learnt}}), \lambda^{\text{dec}})$$

---

[1] In this work, we consider $\lambda \geq 0$ as this is the widely accepted range of the attacker's bounded rationality in the literature.

$$\text{s.t. } \lambda^{\text{dec}} \in [0, \lambda^{max}]$$
$$\max\{\lambda^{\text{dec}} - \delta, 0\} \leq \lambda^{\text{learnt}} \leq \lambda^{\text{dec}} + \delta$$
$$\mathbf{x}(\lambda^{\text{learnt}}) \in \underset{\mathbf{x}' \in \mathbf{X}}{\operatorname{argmax}} \, U^d(\mathbf{x}', \lambda^{\text{learnt}})$$

where $\mathbf{x}(\lambda^{\text{learnt}})$ is the defender's optimal strategy w.r.t his learning outcome λ^{learnt}. The objective $U^a(\mathbf{x}(\lambda^{\text{learnt}}), \lambda^{\text{dec}})$ is essentially the attacker's utility when the defender plays $\mathbf{x}(\lambda^{\text{learnt}})$ and the attacker mimics QR with λ^{dec} to play (see Eqs. (1–3) for the detailed computation).

4.1   A Polynomial-Time Deception Algorithm

($\mathbf{P}^{\text{dec}}$) involves three-nested optimization levels which is not straightforward to solve. We thus propose to limit the possible learning outcomes of the defender by discretizing the domain of λ^{learnt} into a finite set $\Lambda^{\text{learnt}}_{\text{discrete}} = (\lambda_1^{\text{learnt}}, \lambda_2^{\text{learnt}}, \ldots, \lambda_K^{\text{learnt}})$ where $\lambda_1^{\text{learnt}} = 0$, $\lambda_K^{\text{learnt}} = \lambda^{max} + \delta$, and $\lambda_{k+1}^{\text{learnt}} - \lambda_k^{\text{learnt}} = \eta, \forall k < K$ where $\eta > 0$ is the discretization step size and $K = \frac{\lambda^{max} + \delta}{\eta} + 1$ is the number of discrete learning values.[2] For each deception choice λ^{dec}, the attacker's *uncertainty set* of defender's possible learning outcomes λ^{learnt} is now given by:

$$\Lambda^{\text{learnt}}_{\text{discrete}}(\lambda^{\text{dec}}) = \Lambda^{\text{learnt}}_{\text{discrete}} \cap [\lambda^{\text{dec}} - \delta, \lambda^{\text{dec}} + \delta]$$

For each $\lambda_k^{\text{learnt}}$, we can easily compute the corresponding optimal defense strategy $\mathbf{x}(\lambda_k^{\text{learnt}})$ in advance [27]. We thus obtain a simplified optimization problem:

$$(\mathbf{P}^{\text{dec}}_{\text{discrete}}) : \max_{\lambda^{\text{dec}} \in [0, \lambda^{max}]} U$$
$$\text{s.t. } U \leq U^a(\mathbf{x}(\lambda_k^{\text{learnt}}), \lambda^{\text{dec}}), \text{ for all } \lambda_k^{\text{learnt}} \in \Lambda^{\text{learnt}}_{\text{discrete}}(\lambda^{\text{dec}})$$

Remark on Computational Challenge. Although ($\mathbf{P}^{\text{dec}}_{\text{discrete}}$) is a single-level optimization, solving it is still challenging due to (i) ($\mathbf{P}^{\text{dec}}_{\text{discrete}}$) is a non-convex optimization problem since the attacker's utility $U^a(\mathbf{x}(\lambda_k^{\text{learnt}}), \lambda^{\text{dec}})$ is non-convex in λ^{dec}; and (ii) the number of inequality constraints in ($\mathbf{P}^{\text{dec}}_{\text{discrete}}$) vary with respect to λ^{dec}, which complicates the problem further. By exploiting the decomposability property of the deception space $[0, \lambda^{max}]$ and the monotonicity of the attacker's utility function $U^a(\mathbf{x}(\lambda_k^{\text{learnt}}), \lambda^{\text{dec}})$, we show that ($\mathbf{P}^{\text{dec}}_{\text{discrete}}$) can be solved optimally in a polynomial time.[3]

Theorem 1 (Time complexity). *The problem ($\mathbf{P}^{dec}_{discrete}$) can be solved optimally in a polynomial time.*

---

[2] We use a uniform discretization for the sake of solution quality analysis (as we will describe later). Our approach can be generalized to any non-uniform discretization.

[3] All of our detailed proofs are in online appendix: https://www.dropbox.com/s/frebqe6etjns6c6/appendix.pdf?dl=0.

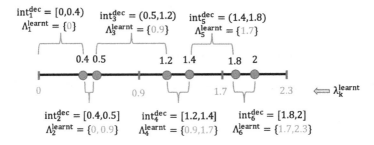

Fig. 1. An example of discretizing λ^{learnt}, $\Lambda^{\text{learnt}} = \{0, 0.9, 1.7, 2.3\}$, and the six resulting attacker sub-intervals and corresponding uncertainty sets, with $\lambda^{max} = 2, \delta = 0.5$. In particular, the first sub-interval of deceptive λ^{dec} is $int_1 = [0, 0.4)$ in which any λ^{dec} corresponds to the same uncertainty set of possible learning outcomes $\Lambda_1^{\text{learnt}} = \{0\}$.

Overall, the proof of Theorem 1 is derived based on (i) Lemma 1—showing that the deception space can be divided into an $O(K)$ number of sub-intervals, and each sub-interval leads to the same uncertainty set; and (ii) Lemma 2—showing that $(\mathbf{P}^{\text{dec}}_{\text{discrete}})$ can be divided into a $O(K)$ sub-problems which correspond to the decomposability of the deception space (as shown in Lemma 1), and each sub-problem can be solved in polynomial time.

Lemma 1 (Decomposability of deception space). *The attacker deception space $[0, \lambda^{max}]$ can be decomposed into a finite number of disjointed sub-intervals, denoted by int_j^{dec} where $j = 1, 2, \ldots,$ and $int_j^{\text{dec}} \cap int_{j'}^{\text{dec}} = \emptyset$ for all $j \neq j'$ and $\cup_j int_j^{\text{dec}} = [0, \lambda^{max}]$, such that each $\lambda^{\text{dec}} \in int_j^{\text{dec}}$ leads to the same uncertainty set of learning outcomes, denoted by $\Lambda_j^{\text{learnt}} \subseteq \Lambda_{\text{discrete}}^{\text{learnt}}$. Furthermore, these sub-intervals and uncertainty sets $(int_j^{\text{dec}}, \Lambda_j^{\text{learnt}})$ can be found in a polynomial time.*

An example of the deception-space decomposition is illustrated in Fig. 1. Intuitively, although the deception space $[0, \lambda^{max}]$ is infinite, the total number of possible learning-outcome uncertainty sets is at most 2^K (i.e., the number of subsets of the discrete learning space $\Lambda_{\text{discrete}}^{\text{learnt}}$). Therefore, the deception space can be divided into a finite number of disjoint subsets such that any deception value λ^{dec} within each subset will lead to the same uncertainty set. Moreover, each of these deception subsets form a sub-interval of $[0, \lambda^{max}]$, which is derived from the following observation:

Observation 1. *Given two deception values $\lambda_1^{\text{dec}} < \lambda_2^{\text{dec}} \in [0, \lambda^{max}]$, if the learning uncertainty sets corresponding to these two values are the same, i.e., $\Lambda_{\text{discrete}}^{\text{learnt}}(\lambda_1^{\text{dec}}) \equiv \Lambda_{\text{discrete}}^{\text{learnt}}(\lambda_2^{\text{dec}})$, then for any deception value $\lambda_1^{\text{dec}} < \lambda^{\text{dec}} < \lambda_2^{\text{dec}}$, its uncertainty set is also the same, that is:*

$$\Lambda_{\text{discrete}}^{\text{learnt}}(\lambda^{\text{dec}}) \equiv \Lambda_{\text{discrete}}^{\text{learnt}}(\lambda_1^{\text{dec}}) \equiv \Lambda_{\text{discrete}}^{\text{learnt}}(\lambda_2^{\text{dec}})$$

The remaining analysis for Lemma 1 is to show that these deception sub-intervals can be found in polynomial time, which is obtained based on Observation 2:

Observation 2. *For each learning outcome λ_k^{learnt}, there are at most two decep-tion sub-intervals such that λ_k^{learnt} is the smallest learning outcome in the cor-responding learning uncertainty set. As a result, the total number of deception sub-intervals is $O(K)$, which is polynomial.*

Since there is a $O(K)$ number of deception sub-intervals, we now can develop a polynomial-time algorithm (Algorithm 1) which iteratively divides the decep-tive range $[0, \lambda^{max}]$ into multiple intervals, denoted by $\{int_j^{\mathrm{dec}}\}_j$. Each of these intervals, int_j^{dec}, corresponds to the same uncertainty set of possible learning outcomes for the defender, denoted by $\Lambda_j^{\mathrm{learnt}}$. In this algorithm, for each $\lambda_k^{\mathrm{learnt}}$, we denote by $lb_k = \lambda_k^{\mathrm{learnt}} - \delta$ and $ub_k = \lambda_k^{\mathrm{learnt}} + \delta$ the smallest and largest possible values of λ^{dec} so that $\lambda_k^{\mathrm{learnt}}$ belongs to the uncertainty set of λ^{dec}. In Algorithm 1, *start* is the variable which represents the left bound of each inter-val int_j^{dec}. The variable *open* indicates if int_j^{dec} is left-open (*open = true*) or not (*open = false*). If *start* is known for int_j^{dec}, the uncertainty set $\Lambda_j^{\mathrm{learnt}}$ can be determined as follows:

$$\Lambda_j^{\mathrm{learnt}} = \{\lambda_k^{\mathrm{learnt}} : \lambda_k^{\mathrm{learnt}} \in [start - \delta, start + \delta]\} \text{ if } int_j^{\mathrm{dec}} \text{ is left-closed}$$
$$\Lambda_j^{\mathrm{learnt}} = \{\lambda_k^{\mathrm{learnt}} : \lambda_k^{\mathrm{learnt}} \in (start - \delta, start + \delta]\} \text{ if } int_j^{\mathrm{dec}} \text{ is left-open}$$

Algorithm 1: Imitative behavior deception — Decomposition of QR parameter domain into sub-intervals

---

1 Input: $\Lambda^{\mathrm{learnt}} = \{\lambda_1^{\mathrm{learnt}}, \lambda_2^{\mathrm{learnt}}, \dots, \lambda_K^{\mathrm{learnt}}\}$;
2 Initialize interval index: $j = 1$; $start = 0$; $open = false$;
   $\Lambda_j^{\mathrm{learnt}} = \{\lambda_k^{\mathrm{learnt}} \in \Lambda^{\mathrm{learnt}} : \lambda_k^{\mathrm{learnt}} \in [start - \delta, start + \delta]\}$;
3 **while** $\Lambda_j^{learnt} \neq \emptyset$ **do**
4   Set the max index: $k_j^{max} = \max_k\{\lambda_k^{\mathrm{learnt}} \in \Lambda_j^{\mathrm{learnt}}\}$;
5   Set the min index: $k_j^{min} = \min_k\{\lambda_k^{\mathrm{learnt}} \in \Lambda_j^{\mathrm{learnt}}\}$;
6   **if** $k_j^{max} < K$ & $lb_{k_j^{max}+1} \leq ub_{k_j^{min}}$ **then**
7   **if** *open* **then** Set $int_j^{\mathrm{dec}} = (start, lb_{k_j^{max}+1})$
8   **else** Set $int_j^{\mathrm{dec}} = [start, lb_{k_j^{max}+1})$
9   Update $start = lb_{k_j^{max}+1}$; $open = false$;
10         $\Lambda_{j+1}^{\mathrm{learnt}} = \{\lambda_k^{\mathrm{learnt}} \in \Lambda^{\mathrm{learnt}} : \lambda_k^{\mathrm{learnt}} \in [start - \delta, start + \delta]\}$;
11   **else**
12   **if** *open* **then** Set $int_j^{\mathrm{dec}} = (start, ub_{k_j^{min}}]$
13   **else** Set $int_j^{\mathrm{dec}} = [start, ub_{k_j^{min}}]$
14   Update $start = ub_{k_j^{min}}$; $open = true$;
15         $\Lambda_{j+1}^{\mathrm{learnt}} = \{\lambda_k^{\mathrm{learnt}} \in \Lambda^{\mathrm{learnt}} : \lambda_k^{\mathrm{learnt}} \in (start - \delta, start + \delta]\}$;
16   Update $j = j + 1$;
17   **return** $\{(int_j^{\mathrm{dec}}, \lambda_j^{\mathrm{learnt}})\}$;

Initially, *start* is set to 0 which is the lowest possible value of λ^{dec} such that the uncertainty range $[\lambda^{\mathrm{dec}} - \delta, \lambda^{\mathrm{dec}} + \delta]$ contains $\lambda_1^{\mathrm{learnt}}$ and *open = false*. Given *start* and its uncertainty range $[start - \delta, start + \delta]$, the first interval int_1^{dec} of λ^{dec} corresponds to the uncertainty set determined as follows:

$$\Lambda_1^{\text{learnt}} = \{\lambda_k^{\text{learnt}} \in \Lambda^{\text{learnt}} : \lambda_k^{\text{learnt}} \in [start - \delta, start + \delta]\}$$

At each iteration j, given the left bound *start* and the uncertainty set $\Lambda_j^{\text{learnt}}$ of the interval int_j^{dec}, Algorithm 1 determines the right bound of int_j^{dec}, the left bound of the next interval int_{j+1}^{dec} (by updating *start*), and the uncertainty set $\Lambda_{j+1}^{\text{learnt}}$, (lines (6–15)). The correctness of Algorithm 1 is proved in the appendix.

Lemma 2 (Divide-and-conquer). *The problem* $(\mathbf{P}_{discrete}^{dec})$ *can be decomposed into* $O(K)$ *sub-problems* $\{(\mathbf{P}_j^{dec})\}$ *according to the decomposibility of the deception space. Each of these sub-problems can be solved in polynomial time.*

Indeed, we can now divide the problem $(\mathbf{P}_{\text{discrete}}^{\text{dec}})$ into multiple sub-problems which correspond to the decomposition of the deception space. Essentially, each sub-problem optimizes λ^{dec} (and λ^{learnt}) over the deception sub-interval int_j^{dec} (and its corresponding uncertainty set $\Lambda_j^{\text{learnt}}$):

$$(\mathbf{P_j^{\text{dec}}}) : \max_{\lambda^{\text{dec}} \in int_j^{\text{dec}}} U^a$$

$$\text{s.t. } U^a \leq U^a(\mathbf{x}(\lambda_k^{\text{learnt}}), \lambda^{\text{dec}}), \forall \lambda_k^{\text{learnt}} \in \Lambda_j^{\text{learnt}}$$

which maximizes the attacker's worst-case utility w.r.t uncertainty set $\Lambda_j^{\text{learnt}}$. Note that the defender strategies $\mathbf{x}(\lambda_k^{\text{learnt}})$ can be pre-computed for every outcome $\lambda_k^{\text{learnt}}$. Each sub-problem $(\mathbf{P_j^{\text{dec}}})$ has a constant number of constraints, but still remain non-convex. Our Observation 3 shows that despite of the non-convexity, the optimal solution for $(\mathbf{P_j^{\text{dec}}})$ is actually straightforward to compute.

Observation 3. *The optimal solution of λ^{dec} for each sub-problem, $\mathbf{P}_j^{dec}$, is the (right) upper limit of the corresponding deception sub-interval int_j^{dec}.*

This observation is derived based on the fact that the attacker's utility, $U^a(\mathbf{x}, \lambda)$, is an increasing function of λ [18]. Therefore, in order to solve $(\mathbf{P}_{\text{discrete}}^{\text{dec}})$, we only need to iterate over right bounds of int_j^{dec} and select the best j such that the attacker's worst-case utility (i.e., the objective of $(\mathbf{P_j^{\text{dec}}})$), is the highest among all sub-intervals. Since there are $O(K)$ sub-problems, $(\mathbf{P}_{\text{discrete}}^{\text{dec}})$ can be solved optimally in a polynomial time, concluding our proof for Theorem 1.

4.2   Solution Quality Analysis

We now focus on analyzing the solution quality of our method presented in Sect. 4.1 to approximately solve the deception problem $(\mathbf{P}^{\text{dec}})$.

Theorem 2. *For any arbitrary $\epsilon > 0$, there always exists a discretization step size $\eta > 0$ such that the optimal solution of the corresponding $(\mathbf{P}_{discrete}^{dec})$ is ϵ-optimal for $(\mathbf{P}^{dec})$.*

Intuitively, let us denote by λ_*^{dec} the optimal solution of ($\mathbf{P}^{\text{dec}}$) and $U_{\text{worst-case}}^a(\lambda_*^{\text{dec}})$ is the corresponding worst-case utility of the attacker under the uncertainty of learning outcomes in ($\mathbf{P}^{\text{dec}}$). We also denote by $\lambda_{\text{discrete}}^{\text{dec}}$ the optimal solution of ($\mathbf{P}_{\text{discrete}}^{\text{dec}}$). Then, Theorem 2 states that:

$$U_{\text{worst-case}}^a(\lambda_*^{\text{dec}}) \geq U_{\text{worst-case}}^a(\lambda_{\text{discrete}}^{\text{dec}}) \geq U_{\text{worst-case}}^a(\lambda_*^{\text{dec}}) - \epsilon$$

Heuristic to Improve Discretization. According to Theorem 2, we can obtain a high-quality solution for ($\mathbf{P}^{\text{dec}}$) by having a fine discretization of the learning outcome space with a small step size η. In practice, it is not necessary to have a fine discretization over the entire learning space right from the beginning. Instead, we can start with a coarse discretization and solve the corresponding ($\mathbf{P}_{\text{discrete}}^{\text{dec}}$) to obtain a solution of $\lambda_{\text{discrete}}^{\text{dec}}$. We then refine the discretization *only* within the uncertainty range of the current solution, $[\lambda_{\text{discrete}}^{\text{dec}} - \delta, \lambda_{\text{discrete}}^{\text{dec}} + \delta]$. We keep doing that until the uncertainty range of the latest deception solution reaches the step-size limit which guarantees the ϵ-optimality. Practically, by doing so, we will obtain a much smaller discretized learning outcome set (aka. smaller K). As a result, the computational time for solving ($\mathbf{P}_{\text{discrete}}^{\text{dec}}$) is substantially faster while the solution quality remains the same.

5   Defender Counter-Deception

In order to counter the attacker's imitative deception, we propose to find a counter-deception defense function $\mathcal{H} : [0, \lambda^{max} + \delta] \rightarrow \mathbf{X}$ which maps a learnt parameter λ^{learnt} to a strategy $\mathbf{x}$ of the defender. In designing an effective $\mathcal{H}$, we need to take into account that the attacker will also adapt its deception choice accordingly, denoted by $\lambda^{\text{dec}}(\mathcal{H})$. Essentially, the problem of finding an optimal defense function which maximizes the defender's utility against the attacker's deception can be abstractly represented as follows:

$$\max_{\mathcal{H}} U^d(\mathcal{H}, \lambda^{\text{dec}}(\mathcal{H}))$$

where $\lambda^{\text{dec}}(\mathcal{H})$ is the deception choice of the attacker with respect to the defense function $\mathcal{H}$ and U^d is the defender's utility corresponding to $(\mathcal{H}, \lambda^{\text{dec}}(\mathcal{H}))$. Finding an optimal $\mathcal{H}$ is challenging since the domain $[0, \lambda^{max} + \delta]$ of λ^{learnt} is continuous and there is no explicit closed-form expression of $\mathcal{H}$ as a function of λ^{learnt}. For the sake of our analysis, we divide the entire domain $[0, \lambda^{max} + \delta]$ into a number of sub-intervals $\mathbf{I} = \{I_1^d, I_2^d, \ldots, I_N^d\}$ where $I_1^d = [\lambda_1^{\text{def}}, \lambda_2^{\text{def}}]$, $I_2^d = (\lambda_2^{\text{def}}, \lambda_3^{\text{def}}]$, $\ldots$, $I_N^d = (\lambda_N^{\text{def}}, \lambda_{N+1}^{\text{def}}]$ with $0 = \lambda_1^{\text{def}} \leq \lambda_2^{\text{def}} \leq \cdots \leq \lambda_{N+1}^{\text{def}} = \lambda^{max} + \delta$, and N is the number of sub-intervals. We define a defense function with respect to the interval set: $\mathcal{H}^{\mathbf{I}} : \mathbf{I} \rightarrow \mathbf{X}$ which maps each interval $I_n^d \in \mathbf{I}$ to a single defense strategy $\mathbf{x}_n$, i.e., $\mathcal{H}^{\mathbf{I}}(I_n^d) = \mathbf{x}_n \in \mathbf{X}$, for all $n \leq N$. We denote the set of these strategies by $\mathbf{X}^{\text{def}} = \{\mathbf{x}_1, \ldots, \mathbf{x}_N\}$. Intuitively, all $\lambda^{\text{learnt}} \in I_n^d$ will lead to a single strategy $\mathbf{x}_n$. Our counter-deception problem now becomes finding an optimal defense function $\mathcal{H}_* = (\mathbf{I}_*, \mathcal{H}_*^{\mathbf{I}})$ that comprises of (i) an optimal interval set

$\mathbf{I}_*$; and (ii) corresponding defense strategies determined by the defense function $\mathcal{H}_*^{\mathbf{I}_*}$ with respect to $\mathbf{I}_*$, taking into account the attacker's deception adaptation. Essentially, $(\mathbf{I}_*, \mathcal{H}_*^{\mathbf{I}_*})$ is the optimal solution of the following optimization problem:

$$\max_{\mathbf{I}, \mathcal{H}^{\mathbf{I}}} U^d(\mathcal{H}^{\mathbf{I}}, \lambda^{\text{dec}}(\mathcal{H}^{\mathbf{I}})) \tag{4}$$

$$\text{s.t. } \lambda^{\text{dec}}(\mathcal{H}^{\mathbf{I}}) \in \underset{\lambda^{\text{dec}} \in [0, \lambda^{max}]}{\operatorname{argmax}} \min_{\mathbf{x} \in \mathbf{X}(\lambda^{\text{dec}})} U^a(\mathbf{x}, \lambda^{\text{dec}}) \tag{5}$$

where $\lambda^{\text{dec}}(\mathcal{H}^{\mathbf{I}})$ is the maximin deception choice of the attacker. Here, $\mathbf{X}(\lambda^{\text{dec}}) = \{\mathbf{x}_n : I_n^d \cap [\lambda^{\text{dec}} - \delta, \lambda^{\text{dec}} + \delta] \neq \emptyset\}$ is the *uncertainty set* of the attacker when playing λ^{dec}. This uncertainty set contains all possible defense strategy outcomes with respect to the deceptive value λ^{dec}.

Main Result. So far, we have not explicitly defined the utility objective function, $U^d(\mathcal{H}^{\mathbf{I}}, \lambda^{\text{dec}}(\mathcal{H}^{\mathbf{I}}))$, except that we know this utility depends on the defense function $\mathcal{H}^{\mathbf{I}}$ and the attacker's deception response $\lambda^{\text{dec}}(\mathcal{H}^{\mathbf{I}})$. Now, since $\mathcal{H}^{\mathbf{I}}$ maps each possible learning outcome λ^{learnt} to a defense strategy, we know that if $\lambda^{\text{learnt}} \in I_n^d$, then $U^d(\mathcal{H}^{\mathbf{I}}, \lambda^{\text{dec}}(\mathcal{H}^{\mathbf{I}})) = U^d(\mathbf{x}_n, \lambda^{\text{dec}}(\mathcal{H}^{\mathbf{I}}))$, which can be computed using Eq. (3). However, due to the deviation of λ^{learnt} from the attacker's deception choice, $\lambda^{\text{dec}}(\mathcal{H}^{\mathbf{I}})$, different possible learning outcomes λ^{learnt} within $[\lambda^{\text{dec}}(\mathcal{H}^{\mathbf{I}}) - \delta, \lambda^{\text{dec}}(\mathcal{H}^{\mathbf{I}}) + \delta]$ may belong to different intervals I_n^d (which correspond to different strategies $\mathbf{x}_n$), leading to different utility outcomes for the defender. One may argue that to cope with this deception-learning uncertainty, we can apply the maximin approach to determine the defender's worst-case utility if the defender only has the common knowledge that $\lambda^{\text{learnt}} \in [\lambda^{\text{dec}}(\mathcal{H}^{\mathbf{I}}) - \delta, \lambda^{\text{dec}}(\mathcal{H}^{\mathbf{I}}) + \delta]$. And perhaps, depending on any additional (private) knowledge the defender has regarding the relation between the attacker's deception and the actual learning outcome of the defender, we can incorporate such knowledge into our model and algorithm to obtain an even better utility outcome for the defender. Interestingly, we show that there is, in fact, a *universal* optimal defense function for the defender, $\mathcal{H}_*$, regardless of any additional knowledge that he may have. That is, the defender obtains the highest utility by following this defense function, and additional knowledge besides the common knowledge cannot make the defender do better. Our main result is formally stated in Theorem 3.

Theorem 3. *There is a* universal *optimal defense function, regardless of any additional information (besides the common knowledge) he has about the relation between his learning outcome and the deception choice of the attacker. Formally, let's consider the following optimization problem:*

$$(\mathbf{P}^{counter}) : \max_{\mathbf{x}, \lambda} U^d(\mathbf{x}, \lambda)$$

$$\text{s.t. } U^a(\mathbf{x}, \lambda) \geq \min_{\mathbf{x}' \in \mathbf{X}} U^a(\mathbf{x}', \lambda^{max})$$

$$0 \leq \lambda \leq \lambda^{max}, \mathbf{x} \in \mathbf{X}$$

Denote by $(\mathbf{x}^*, \lambda^*)$ *an optimal solution of* $(\mathbf{P}^{counter})$, *then an optimal solution of (4),* $\mathcal{H}_*$ *can be determined as follows:*

- *If* $\lambda^* = \lambda^{max}$, *choose the interval set* $\mathbf{I}_* = \{I_1^d\}$ *with* $I_1^d = [0, \lambda^{max} + \delta]$ *covering the entire learning space, and function* $\mathcal{H}_*^{\mathbf{I}_*}(I_1^d) = \mathbf{x}_1$ *where* $\mathbf{x}_1 = \mathbf{x}^*$.
- *If* $\lambda^* < \lambda^{max}$, *choose the interval set* $\mathbf{I}_* = \{I_1^d, I_2^d\}$ *with* $I_1^d = [0, \lambda^* + \delta]$, $I_2^d = (\lambda^* + \delta, \lambda^{max} + \delta]$. *In addition, choose the defender strategies* $\mathbf{x}_1 = \mathbf{x}^*$ *and* $\mathbf{x}_2 \in \operatorname{argmin}_{\mathbf{x} \in \mathbf{X}} U^a(\mathbf{x}, \lambda^{max})$ *correspondingly.*

The attacker's optimal deception against this defense function is to mimic λ^*. *As a result, the defender always obtains the highest utility,* $U^d(\mathbf{x}^*, \lambda^*)$, *while the attacker receives the maximin utility of* $U^a(\mathbf{x}^*, \lambda^*)$.

Corollary 1. *When* $\lambda^{max} = +\infty$, *the defense function* $\mathcal{H}_*$ *(specified in Theorem 3) gives the defender a utility which is no less than his Strong Stackelberg equilbrium (SSE) utility.*

The proof of Corollary 1 is straightforward. Since $(\mathbf{x}^{sse}, \lambda^{max} = +\infty)$ is a feasible solution of $(\mathbf{P}^{counter})$, the optimal utility of the defender $U^d(\mathbf{x}^*, \lambda^*)$ is thus no less than $U^d(\mathbf{x}^{sse}, \lambda^{max})$ ($\mathbf{x}^{sse}$ denotes the defender's SSE strategy).

Now the rest of this section will be devoted to prove Theorem 3. The full proof of Theorem 3 can be decomposed into three main parts: (i) We first analyze the attacker deception adapted to the defender's counter deception; (ii) Based on the result of the attacker adaptation, we provide theoretical results on computing the defender optimal defense function given a fixed set of sub-intervals $\mathbf{I}$; and (iii) finally, we complete the proof of the theorem leveraging the result in (ii).

5.1 Analyzing Attacker Deception Adaptation

In this section, we aim at understanding the behavior of the attacker deception against $\mathcal{H}^{\mathbf{I}}$. Overall, as discussed in the previous section, since the attacker is uncertain about the actual learning outcome of the defender, the attacker can attempt to find an optimal deception choice $\lambda^{dec}(\mathcal{H}^{\mathbf{I}})$ that maximizes its utility under the worst case of uncertainty. Essentially, $\lambda^{dec}(\mathcal{H}^{\mathbf{I}})$ is an optimal solution of the following maximin problem:

$$\max_{\lambda^{dec} \in [0, \lambda^{max}]} \min_{\mathbf{x} \in \mathbf{X}(\lambda^{dec})} U^a(\mathbf{x}, \lambda^{dec})$$

where: $\mathbf{X}(\lambda^{dec}) = \{\mathbf{x}_n : I_n^d \cap [\lambda^{dec} - \delta, \lambda^{dec} + \delta] \neq \emptyset\}$ is the *uncertainty set* of the attacker with respect to the defender's sub-intervals $\mathbf{I}$. In this problem, the uncertainty set $\mathbf{X}(\lambda^{dec})$ depends on λ^{dec} that we need to optimize, making this problem not straightforward to solve.

First, given $\mathcal{H}^{\mathbf{I}}$, we show that we can divide the range of λ^{dec} into several intervals, each interval corresponds to the same uncertainty set. This characteristic of the attacker uncertainty set is, in fact, similar to the no-counter-deception scenario as described in previous section. We propose Algorithm 2 to determine these intervals of λ^{dec}, which works in a similar fashion as Algorithm 1. The

---

Algorithm 2: Counter-deception — Decomposition of QR parameter into sub-intervals

---

1   Input: $\mathbf{I} = \{I_1^d, I_2^d, \ldots, I_N^d\}$ and $\mathbf{X}^{def} = \{\mathbf{x}_1, \ldots, \mathbf{x}_N\}$

2   Initialize attacker interval index $j = 1$;

3   Initialize $start = 0$; uncertainty set $\mathbf{X}_j^{\text{def}} = \{x_n : I_n^d \cap [start - \delta, start + \delta] \neq \emptyset\}$;

4   **while** $\mathbf{X}_j^{def} \neq \emptyset$ **do**

5   Set the max index: $n_j^{max} = \max_n \{x_n \in \mathbf{X}_j^{\text{def}}\}$;

6   Set the min index $n_j^{min} = \min_n \{x_n \in \mathbf{X}_j^{\text{def}}\}$;

7   **if** $n_j^{max} < k$ & $lb_{n_j^{max}+1} \leq ub_{n_j^{min}+1}$ **then**

8         $\lfloor$ Set $end = lb_{n_j^{max}+1}$;

9   **else** Set $end = ub_{n_j^{min}+1}$

10   **if** $j = 1$ **then** Set $int_j^{\text{dec}} = [start, end]$

11   **else** Set $int_j^{\text{dec}} = (start, end]$

12   Update $start = end$; $j = j + 1$;

13      $\lfloor$ Set $\mathbf{X}_j^{\text{def}} = \{x_n : I_n^d \cap (start - \delta, start + \delta] \neq \emptyset\}$;

14 **return** $\{int_j^{\text{dec}}, \mathbf{X}_j^{\text{def}}\}$

---

main difference is that in the presence of the defender's defense function, the attacker's uncertainty set $\mathbf{X}(\lambda^{\text{dec}})$ is determined based on whether the uncertainty range of the attacker $[\lambda^{\text{dec}} - \delta, \lambda^{\text{dec}} + \delta]$ is overlapped with the defender's intervals $\mathbf{I} = \{I_n^d\}$ or not.

Essentially, similar to Algorithm 1, Algorithm 2 also iteratively divides the range of λ^{dec} into multiple intervals, (with an abuse of notation) denoted by $\{int_j^{\text{dec}}\}$. Each of these intervals, int_j^{dec}, corresponds to the same uncertainty set of $\mathbf{x}_n$, denoted by $\mathbf{X}_j^{\text{def}}$. In this algorithm, for each interval of the defender I_n^d, $lb_n = \lambda_n^{\text{def}} - \delta$ and $ub_{n+1} = \lambda_{n+1}^{\text{def}} + \delta$ represent the smallest and largest possible deceptive values of λ^{dec} so that $I_n^d \cap [\lambda^{\text{dec}} - \delta, \lambda^{\text{dec}} + \delta] \neq \emptyset$. In addition, n_j^{min} and n_j^{max} denote the smallest and largest indices of the defender's strategies in the set $\mathbf{X}^{\text{def}} = \{\mathbf{x}_1, \mathbf{x}_2, \ldots, \mathbf{x}_N\}$ that belongs to $\mathbf{X}_j^{\text{def}}$. Algorithm 2 relies on Observations 4 and 5. Note that Algorithm 2 does not check if each interval int_j^{dec} of λ^{dec} is left-open or not since all intervals of the defender I_n^d is left-open (except for $n = 1$), making all int_j^{dec} left-closed (except for $j = 1$).

Observation 4. *Given a deceptive λ^{dec}, for any $n_1 < n_2$ such that $\mathbf{x}_{n_1}, \mathbf{x}_{n_2} \in \mathbf{X}(\lambda^{dec})$, then $\mathbf{x}_n \in \mathbf{X}(\lambda^{dec})$ for any $n_1 < n < n_2$.*

Observation 5. *For any λ^{dec} such that $lb_n < \lambda^{dec} \leq ub_{n+1}$,[4] the uncertainty range of λ^{dec} overlaps with the defender's interval I_n^d, i.e., $I_n^d \cap [\lambda^{dec} - \delta, \lambda^{dec} + \delta] \neq \emptyset$, or equivalently, $\mathbf{x}_n \in \mathbf{X}(\lambda)$. Otherwise, if $\lambda^{dec} \leq lb_n$ or $\lambda^{dec} > ub_{n+1}$, then $\mathbf{x}_n \notin \mathbf{X}(\lambda^{dec})$.*

---

[4] Observation 5 is stated for the general case $n > 1$ when the defender's interval I_n^d is left-open. When $n = 1$ with the left bound is included, we have $lb_n \leq \lambda^{dec} \leq ub_{n+1}$.

Attacker sub-intervals with uncertainty sets

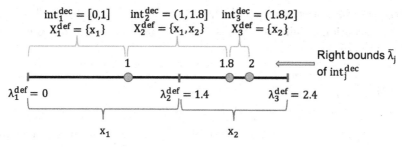

Defender's defense function

Fig. 2. An example of a defense function with corresponding sub-intervals and uncertainty sets of the attacker, where $\lambda^{max} = 2.0$ and $\delta = 0.4$. The defense function is determined as: $I_1^d = [0, 1.4]$, $I_2^d = (1.4, 2.4]$ with corresponding defense strategies $\{\mathbf{x}_1, \mathbf{x}_2\}$. Then the deception range of the attacker can be divided into three sub-intervals: $int_1^{dec} = [0, 1]$, $int_2^{dec} = (1, 1.8]$, $int_3^{dec} = (1.8, 2]$ with corresponding uncertainty sets $\mathbf{X}_1^{def} = \{\mathbf{x}_1\}$, $\mathbf{X}_2^{def} = \{\mathbf{x}_1, \mathbf{x}_2\}$, $\mathbf{X}_3^{def} = \{\mathbf{x}_2\}$. For example, if the attacker plays any $\lambda^{dec} \in int_2^{dec}$, it will lead the defender to play either $\mathbf{x}_1$ or $\mathbf{x}_2$, depending on the actual learning outcome of the defender.

Essentially, this algorithm divides the range of λ^{dec} into multiple intervals, (with an abuse of notation) denoted by $\{int_j^{dec}\}$. Each of these intervals, int_j^{dec}, corresponds to the same uncertainty set of $\mathbf{x}_n$, denoted by $\mathbf{X}_j^{def}$. An example of decomposing the deceptive range of λ^{dec} is shown in Fig. 2.

We denote by M the number of attacker intervals. Given the division of the attacker's deception range $\{int_j^{dec}\}$, we can divide the problem of attacker deception into M sub-problems. Each corresponds to a particular int_j^{dec} where $j \in \{1, \ldots, M\}$, as follows:

$$(\bar{\mathbf{P}}_{\mathbf{j}}^{dec}) : U_j^{a,*} = \max_{\lambda^{dec} \in int_j^{dec}} \min_{x_n \in \mathbf{X}_j^{def}} U^a(x_n, \lambda^{dec})$$

Lemma 3. *For each sub-problem $(\bar{\mathbf{P}}_{\mathbf{j}}^{dec})$ with respect to the deception sub-interval int_j^{dec}, the attacker optimal deception is to imitate the right-bound of int_j^{dec}, denoted by $\bar{\lambda}_j^{dec}$.*

The proof of Lemma 3 is derived based on the fact that the attacker's utility $U^a(\mathbf{x}_n, \lambda^{dec})$ is increasing in λ^{dec}. As a result, the attacker only has to search over the right bounds, $\{\bar{\lambda}_j^{dec}\}$, of all intervals $\{int_j^{dec}\}$ to find the best one among the sub-problems that maximizes the attacker's worst-case utility. We consider these bounds $\bar{\lambda}_j^{dec}$ to be the deception candidates of the attacker. Let's assume j^{opt} is the best deception choice for the attacker among these candidates, that is, the attacker will mimic the $\bar{\lambda}_{j^{opt}}^{dec}$. We obtain the following observations about important properties of the attacker's optimal deception, which we leverage to determine an optimal defense function later.

Our following Observation 6 says that any non-optimal deception candidate for the attacker, $\bar{\lambda}_j^{\text{dec}} \neq \bar{\lambda}_{j^{opt}}^{\text{dec}}$, such that the max index of the defender strategy in the corresponding uncertainty set $\mathbf{X}_j^{\text{def}}$, denoted by n_j^{max}, satisfies $n_j^{max} \leq n_{j^{opt}}^{max}$, then the deception candidate $\bar{\lambda}_j^{\text{dec}}$ is strictly less than $\bar{\lambda}_{j^{opt}}^{\text{dec}}$, or equivalently, $j < j^{opt}$. Otherwise, j^{opt} cannot be a best deception response.

Observation 6. *For any $j \neq j^{opt}$ such that $n_j^{max} \leq n_{j^{opt}}^{max}$, then $\bar{\lambda}_j^{\text{dec}} < \bar{\lambda}_{j^{opt}}^{\text{dec}}$, or equivalently, $j < j^{opt}$.*

Note that we have right bounds of attacker intervals, denoted by $\{\bar{\lambda}_1^{\text{dec}}, \ldots, \bar{\lambda}_M^{\text{dec}} = \lambda^{max}\}$. Our next Observation 7 says that if the max index of the defender strategy $n_{j^{opt}}^{max}$ in the uncertainty set $\mathbf{X}_{j^{opt}}$ is equal to the max index of the whole defense set, N, then $\bar{\lambda}_{j^{opt}}^{\text{dec}}$ has to be equal to the highest value of the entire deception range, that is $\bar{\lambda}_{j^{opt}}^{\text{dec}} = \bar{\lambda}_M = \lambda^{max}$, or equivalently, $j^{opt} = M$.

Observation 7. *If $n_{j^{opt}}^{max} = N$, then $j^{opt} = M$.*

Remark. According to Observations 6 and 7, we can easily determine which deception choices among the set $\{\bar{\lambda}_1^{\text{dec}}, \ldots, \bar{\lambda}_M^{\text{dec}}\}$ cannot be an optimal attacker deception, regardless of defense strategies $\{\mathbf{x}_1, \ldots, \mathbf{x}_N\}$. These non-optimal choices are determined as follow: the deception choice $\bar{\lambda}_j$ can not be optimal for:

- Any j such that there is a $j' > j$ with $n_{j'}^{max} \leq n_j^{max}$
- Any $j < M$ such that $n_j^{max} = N$

For any other choices $\bar{\lambda}_j^{\text{dec}}$, there always exists defense strategies $\{\mathbf{x}_1, \ldots, \mathbf{x}_N\}$ such that $\bar{\lambda}_j^{\text{dec}}$ is an optimal attacker deception.

5.2 Finding Optimal Defense Function $\mathcal{H}^I$ Given Fixed I: Divide-and-Conquer

Given a set of sub-intervals $\mathbf{I}$, we aim at finding optimal defense function $\mathcal{H}^I$ or equivalently, strategies $\mathbf{X}^{\text{def}} = \{\mathbf{x}_1, \mathbf{x}_2, \ldots, \mathbf{x}_N\}$ corresponding to these sub-intervals. According to previous analysis on the attacker's deception adaptation, since the attacker's best deception is one of the bounds $\{\bar{\lambda}_1^{\text{dec}}, \ldots, \bar{\lambda}_M^{\text{dec}}\}$, we propose to decompose the problem of finding an optimal defense function $\mathcal{H}^I$ into multiple sub-problems $\mathbf{P}_j^{\text{counter}}$, each corresponds to a particular best deception choice for the attacker. In particular, for each sub-problem $\mathbf{P}_j^{\text{counter}}$, we attempt to find $\mathcal{H}^I$ such that $\bar{\lambda}_j^{\text{dec}}$ is the best response of the attacker. As discussed in the remark of previous section, we can easily determine which sub-problem $\mathbf{P}_j^{\text{counter}}$ is not feasible. For any *feasible* optimal deception candidate j^{fea}, i.e., $\mathbf{P}_{j^{\text{fea}}}^{\text{counter}}$ is feasible, $\mathbf{P}_{j^{\text{fea}}}^{\text{counter}}$ can be formulated as follows:

$$(\mathbf{P}_{j^{\text{fea}}}^{\text{counter}}) : \max_{\mathcal{H}^I} U^d(\mathcal{H}^I, \bar{\lambda}_{j^{\text{fea}}}^{\text{dec}})$$

$$\text{s.t.} \quad \min_{\mathbf{x} \in \mathbf{X}_{j^{\text{fea}}}^{\text{def}}} U^a(\mathbf{x}, \bar{\lambda}_{j^{\text{fea}}}^{\text{dec}}) \geq \min_{\mathbf{x} \in \mathbf{X}_j^{\text{def}}} U^a(\mathbf{x}, \bar{\lambda}_j^{\text{dec}}), \forall j$$

where $U^d(\mathcal{H}^{\mathbf{I}}, \bar{\lambda}^{dec}_{j_{fea}})$ is the defender's utility when the defender commits to $\mathcal{H}^{\mathbf{I}}$ and the attacker plays $\bar{\lambda}^{dec}_{j_{fea}}$. The constraints in ($\mathbf{P}^{counter}_{\mathbf{j_{fea}}}$) guarantee that the attacker's worst-case utility for playing $\bar{\lambda}^{dec}_{j_{fea}}$ is better than playing other $\bar{\lambda}^{dec}_{j}$. Finally, our Propositions 1 and 2 determine an optimal solution for ($\mathbf{P}^{counter}_{\mathbf{j_{fea}}}$).

Proposition 1 (Sub-problem $\mathbf{P}^{counter}_{\mathbf{j_{fea}}}$). *If $n^{max}_{j_{fea}} < N$, the best defense function for the defender is determined as follows:*

- *For all $n > n^{max}_{j_{fea}}$, choose $\mathbf{x}_n = \mathbf{x}^*_>$ where $\mathbf{x}^*_>$ is an optimal solution of the following optimization problem:*

$$\min_{\mathbf{x} \in \mathbf{X}} U^a(\mathbf{x}, \lambda^{max})$$

- *For all $n \leq n^{max}_{j_{fea}}$, choose $\mathbf{x}_n = \mathbf{x}^*_<$ where $\mathbf{x}^*_<$ is the optimal solution of the following optimization problem:*

$$U^d_* = \max_{\mathbf{x} \in \mathbf{X}} U^d(\mathbf{x}, \bar{\lambda}^{dec}_{j_{fea}})$$
$$s.t. \ U^a(\mathbf{x}, \bar{\lambda}^{dec}_{j_{fea}}) \geq U^a(\mathbf{x}^*_>, \lambda^{max})$$

By following the above defense function, an optimal deception of the attacker is to mimic $\bar{\lambda}^{dec}_{j_{fea}}$, and the defender obtains an utility of U^d_*.

Proposition 2 (Sub-problem $\mathbf{P}^{counter}_{\mathbf{j_{fea}}}$). *If $n^{max}_{j_{fea}} = N$, the best counter-deception of the defender can be determined as follows: for all n, we set: $\mathbf{x}_n = \hat{\mathbf{x}}$ where $\hat{\mathbf{x}}$ is an optimal solution of*

$$\max_{\mathbf{x} \in \mathbf{X}} U^d(\mathbf{x}, \lambda^{max})$$

By following this defense function, the attacker's best deception is to mimic λ^{max} and the defender obtains an utility of $U^d(\hat{\mathbf{x}}, \lambda^{max})$.

Based on Propositions 1 and 2, we can easily find the optimal counter-deception of the defender by choosing the solution of the sub-problem that provides the highest utility for the defender.

5.3 Completing the Proof of Theorem 3

According to Propositions 1 and 2, given an interval set $\mathbf{I}$, the resulting defense function will only lead the defender to play either $\{\mathbf{x}^*_>, \mathbf{x}^*_<\}$ or $\{\hat{\mathbf{x}}\}$, whichever provides a higher utility for the defender. Based on this result, our Theorem 3 then identifies an optimal interval set, and corresponding optimal defense strategies, as we prove below.

First, we will show that if the defender follows the defense function specified in Theorem 3, then the attacker's optimal deception is to mimic λ^*. Indeed, if $\lambda^* = \lambda^{max}$, then since the defender always plays $\mathbf{x}^*$, the attacker's optimal deception is to play $\lambda^* = \lambda^{max}$ to obtain a highest utility $U^a(\mathbf{x}^*, \lambda^{max})$.

On the other hand, if $\lambda^* < \lambda^{max}$, we consider two cases:

Case 1, if $\lambda^{max} - 2\delta \leq \lambda^* < \lambda^{max}$, then the intervals of the attackers are $int_1^{\text{dec}} = [0, \lambda^*]$ and $int_2^{\text{dec}} = (\lambda^*, \lambda^{max}]$. The corresponding uncertainty sets are $\mathbf{X}_1^{\text{def}} = \{\mathbf{x}_1\}$ and $\mathbf{X}_2^{\text{def}} = \{\mathbf{x}_1, \mathbf{x}_2\}$. In this case, the attacker's optimal deception is to mimic λ^*, since:

$$\min_{\mathbf{x} \in \mathbf{X}_1^{\text{def}}} U^a(\mathbf{x}, \lambda^*) = U^a(\mathbf{x}^*, \lambda^*)$$
$$\geq U^a(\mathbf{x}_2, \lambda^{max}) \geq \min_{\mathbf{x} \in \mathbf{X}_2^{\text{def}}} U^a(\mathbf{x}, \lambda^{max})$$

Case 2, if $\lambda^* < \lambda^{max} - 2\delta$, then the corresponding intervals for the attacker are $int_1^{\text{dec}} = [0, \lambda^*]$, $int_2^{\text{dec}} = (\lambda^*, \lambda^* + 2\delta]$, and $int_3^{\text{dec}} = (\lambda^* + 2\delta, \lambda^{max}]$. These intervals of the attacker have uncertainty sets $\mathbf{X}_1^{\text{def}} = \{\mathbf{x}_1\}$, $\mathbf{X}_2^{\text{def}} = \{\mathbf{x}_1, \mathbf{x}_2\}$, and $\mathbf{X}_3^{\text{def}} = \{\mathbf{x}_2\}$, respectively. The attacker's best deception is thus to mimic λ^*, since the attacker's worst-case utility is $\min_{\mathbf{x} \in \mathbf{X}_1^{\text{def}}} U^a(\mathbf{x}, \lambda^*) = U^a(\mathbf{x}^*, \lambda^*)$, and

$$U^a(\mathbf{x}^*, \lambda^*) \geq U^a(\mathbf{x}_2, \lambda^{max}) \geq \min_{\mathbf{x} \in \mathbf{X}_2} U^a(\mathbf{x}, \lambda^* + 2\delta)$$
$$U^a(\mathbf{x}^*, \lambda^*) \geq U^a(\mathbf{x}_2, \lambda^{max}) = \min_{\mathbf{x} \in \mathbf{X}_3} U^a(\mathbf{x}, \lambda^{max})$$

Now, since the attacker's best deception is to mimic λ^*, according to the above analysis, the uncertainty set is $\mathbf{X}_1^{\text{def}} = \{\mathbf{x}_1 = \mathbf{x}^*\}$, thus the defender will play $\mathbf{x}^*$ in the end, leading to an utility of $U^d(\mathbf{x}^*, \lambda^*)$. This is the highest possible utility that the defender can obtain since both optimization problems presented in Propositions 1 and 2 are special cases of ($\mathbf{P}^{\text{counter}}$) when we fix the variable $\lambda = \lambda^{max}$ (for Proposition 2) or $\lambda = \bar{\lambda}_{j^{\text{fea}}}$ (for Proposition 1).

6   Experimental Evaluation

Our experiments are run on a 2.8 GHz Intel Xeon processor with 256 GB RAM. We use Matlab (https://www.mathworks.com) to solve non-linear programs and Cplex (https://www.ibm.com/analytics/cplex-optimizer) to solve MILPs involved in the evaluated algorithms. We use a value of $\lambda^{max} = 5$ in all our experiments (except in Figs. 3(g)(h)), and discretize the range $[0, \lambda^{max}]$ using a step size of 0.2: $\lambda \in \{0, 0.2, \ldots, \lambda^{max}\}$. We use the covariance game generator, GAMUT (http://gamut.stanford/edu) to generate rewards and penalties of players within the range of $[1, 10]$ (for attacker) and $[-10, -1]$ (for defender). GAMUT takes as input a covariance value $r \in [-1, 0]$ which controls the correlations between the defender and the attacker's payoff. Our results are averaged over 50 runs. All our results are statistically significant under bootstrap-t ($p = 0.05$).

Algorithms. We compare three cases: (i) Non-Dec: the attacker is non deceptive and the defender also assumes so. As a result, both play Strong Stackelberg equilibrium strategies; (ii) Dec-δ: the attacker is deceptive, while the defender does not handle the attacker's deception (Sect. 4). We examine different uncertainty ranges by varying values of δ; and (iii) Dec-Counter: the attacker is deceptive while the defender tackle the attacker's deception (Sect. 5).

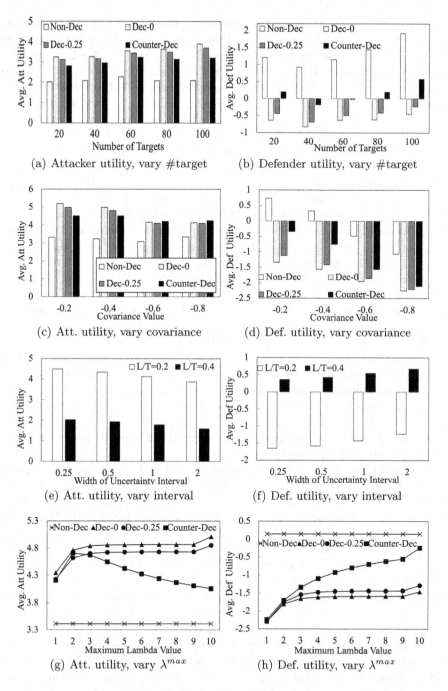

(a) Attacker utility, vary #target

(b) Defender utility, vary #target

(c) Att. utility, vary covariance

(d) Def. utility, vary covariance

(e) Att. utility, vary interval

(f) Def. utility, vary interval

(g) Att. utility, vary λ^{max}

(h) Def. utility, vary λ^{max}

Fig. 3. Evaluations on player utilities

Figures 3(a)(b) compare the performance of our algorithms with increasing number of targets. These figures show that (i) the attacker benefits by playing deceptively (Dec-0 achieves 61% higher attacker utility than Non-Dec); (ii) the benefit of deception to the attacker is reduced when the attacker is uncertain about the defender's learning outcome. In particular, Dec-0.25 achieves 4% lesser attacker utility than Dec-0; (iii) the defender suffers a substantial utility loss due to the attacker's deception and this utility loss is reduced in the presence of the attacker's uncertainty; and finally, (iv) the defender benefits significantly (in terms of his utility) by employing counter-deception against a deceptive attacker.

In Figs. 3(c)(d), we show the performance of our algorithms with varying r (i.e., covariance) values. In zero-sum games (i.e., $r = -1$), the attacker has no incentive to be deceptive [18]. Therefore, we only plot the results of $r \in [-0.2, -0.8]$ with a step size of 0.2. This figure shows that when r gets closer to -1.0 (which implies zero-sum behavior), the attacker's utility with deception (i.e., Dec-0 and Dec-0.25) gradually moves closer to its utility with Non-Dec, reflecting that the attacker has less incentive to play deceptively. Furthermore, the defender's average utility in all cases gradually decreases when the covariance value gets closer to -1.0. This results show that in SSGs, the defender's utility is always governed by the *adversarial* level (i.e., the payoff correlations) between the players, regardless of whether the attacker is deceptive or not.

Figure 3(e)(f) compare the attacker and defender utilities with varying uncertainty range, i.e., δ values, on 60-target games. These figures show that attacker utilities decrease linearly with increasing values of δ. On the other hand, defender utilities increase linearly with increasing values of δ. This is reasonable as increasing δ corresponds to a greater width of the uncertainty interval that the attacker has to contend with. This increased uncertainty forces the attacker to play more conservatively, thereby leading to decreased utilities for the attacker and increased utilities for the defender.

In Figs. 3(g)(h), we analyze the impact of varying λ^{max} on the players' utilities in 60-target games. These figures show that (i) with increasing values of λ^{max}, the action space of a deceptive attacker increases, hence, the attacker utility increases as a result (Dec-0, Dec-0.25 in both sub-figures); (ii) When this λ^{max} is close to zero, the attacker is limited to a less-strategic-attack zone and thus the defender's strategies have less influence on how the attacker would response. The defender thus receives a lower utility when λ^{max} gets close to zero; and (iii) most importantly, the attacker utility against a counter-deceptive defender decreases with increasing values of λ^{max}. This result shows that when the defender plays counter-deception, the attacker can actually gain more benefit by committing to a more limited deception range.

Finally, we evaluate the runtime performance of our algorithms in Fig. 4. We provide results for resource-to-target ratio $\frac{L}{T} = 0.3$ and 0.5. This figure shows that (i) even on 100 target games, Dec-0 finishes in $\sim$5 min. (ii) Due to the simplicity of the proposed counter-deception algorithm, Counter-Dec finishes in 13 s on 100 target games.

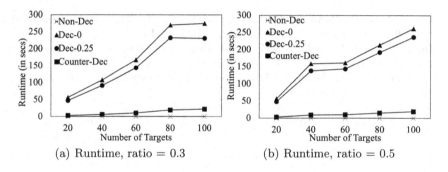

(a) Runtime, ratio = 0.3   (b) Runtime, ratio = 0.5

Fig. 4. Runtime performance

7   Summary

This paper provides a comprehensive analysis of the attacker deception and defender counter-deception under uncertainty. Our algorithms are developed based on the decomposibility of the attacker's deception space and the discretization of the defender's learning outcome. Our key finding is that the optimal counter-deception defense solution only depends on the common knowledge of players about the uncertainty range of the defender's learning outcome. Finally, our extensive experiments show the effectiveness of our counter-deception solutions in handling the attacker's deception.

Acknowledgement. Dr. Yadav was supported in part by ARO Grant No. W911NF-21-1-0047.

References

1. An, B., et al.: A deployed quantal response based patrol planning system for the us coast guard. Interfaces **43**(5), 400–420 (2013)
2. Biggio, B., Nelson, B., Laskov, P.: Poisoning attacks against support vector machines. arXiv preprint arXiv:1206.6389 (2012)
3. Carroll, T.E., Grosu, D.: A game theoretic investigation of deception in network security. Secur. Commun. Netw. **4**(10), 1162–1172 (2011)
4. Estornell, A., Das, S., Vorobeychik, Y.: Deception through half-truths. In: AAAI (2020)
5. Fraunholz, D., et al.: Demystifying deception technology: a survey. arXiv preprint arXiv:1804.06196 (2018)
6. Fugate, S., Ferguson-Walter, K.: Artificial intelligence and game theory models for defending critical networks with cyber deception. **40**, 49–62 (2019). https://doi.org/10.1609/aimag.v40i1.2849. https://www.aaai.org/ojs/index.php/aimagazine/article/view/2849
7. Gan, J., Xu, H., Guo, Q., Tran-Thanh, L., Rabinovich, Z., Wooldridge, M.: Imitative follower deception in stackelberg games. arXiv preprint arXiv:1903.02917 (2019)
8. Gholami, S., Yadav, A., Tran-Thanh, L., Dilkina, B., Tambe, M.: Don't put all your strategies in one basket: playing green security games with imperfect prior knowledge. In: AAMAS, pp. 395–403. AAMAS (2019)

9. Guo, Q., An, B., Bosansky, B., Kiekintveld, C.: Comparing strategic secrecy and stackelberg commitment in security games. In: IJCAI (2017)
10. Han, X., Kheir, N., Balzarotti, D.: Deception techniques in computer security: a research perspective. ACM Comput. Surv. (CSUR) **51**(4), 1–36 (2018)
11. Horák, K., Zhu, Q., Bošanský, B.: Manipulating adversary's belief: a dynamic game approach to deception by design for proactive network security. In: Rass, S., An, B., Kiekintveld, C., Fang, F., Schauer, S. (eds.) GameSec 2017. LNCS, pp. 273–294. Springer, Heidelberg (2017). https://doi.org/10.1007/978-3-319-68711-7_15
12. Huang, L., Joseph, A.D., Nelson, B., Rubinstein, B.I., Tygar, J.D.: Adversarial machine learning. In: AISec, pp. 43–58. ACM (2011)
13. Kar, D., et al.: Trends and applications in stackelberg security games. In: Handbook of Dynamic Game Theory, pp. 1–47 (2017)
14. Kiekintveld, C., Jain, M., Tsai, J., Pita, J., Ordóñez, F., Tambe, M.: Computing optimal randomized resource allocations for massive security games. In: AAMAS, pp. 689–696. AAMAS (2009)
15. McFadden, D., et al.: Conditional logit analysis of qualitative choice behavior (1973)
16. McKelvey, R.D., Palfrey, T.R.: Quantal response equilibria for normal form games. Games Econom. Behav. **10**(1), 6–38 (1995)
17. Nguyen, T.H., Sinha, A., He, H.: Partial adversarial behavior deception in security games. In: IJCAI (2020)
18. Nguyen, T.H., Vu, N., Yadav, A., Nguyen, U.: Decoding the imitation security game: handling attacker imitative behavior deception. In: ECAI (2020)
19. Nguyen, T.H., Wang, Y., Sinha, A., Wellman, M.P.: Deception in finitely repeated security games. In: AAAI (2019)
20. Nguyen, T.H., Yang, R., Azaria, A., Kraus, S., Tambe, M.: Analyzing the effectiveness of adversary modeling in security games. In: AAAI (2013)
21. Rabinovich, Z., Jiang, A.X., Jain, M., Xu, H.: Information disclosure as a means to security. In: AAMAS, pp. 645–653 (2015)
22. Sinha, A., Fang, F., An, B., Kiekintveld, C., Tambe, M.: Stackelberg security games: looking beyond a decade of success. In: IJCAI, pp. 5494–5501 (2018)
23. Steinhardt, J., Koh, P.W.W., Liang, P.S.: Certified defenses for data poisoning attacks. In: NeurIPS, pp. 3517–3529 (2017)
24. Tambe, M.: Security and Game Theory: Algorithms, Deployed Systems, Lessons Learned. Cambridge University Press, Cambridge (2011)
25. Tong, L., Yu, S., Alfeld, S., et al.: Adversarial regression with multiple learners. In: ICML, pp. 4946–4954 (2018)
26. Xu, H., Rabinovich, Z., Dughmi, S., Tambe, M.: Exploring information asymmetry in two-stage security games. In: AAMAS, pp. 1057–1063 (2015)
27. Yang, R., Kiekintveld, C., Ordonez, F., Tambe, M., John, R.: Improving resource allocation strategy against human adversaries in security games. In: IJCAI (2011)
28. Zhuang, J., Bier, V.M., Alagoz, O.: Modeling secrecy and deception in a multiple-period attacker-defender signaling game. Eur. J. Oper. Res. **203**(2), 409–418 (2010)

Casino Rationale: Countering Attacker Deception in Zero-Sum Stackelberg Security Games of Bounded Rationality

Ryan Gabrys[(✉)] [iD], Mark Bilinski[iD], Justin Mauger[iD], Daniel Silva[iD], and Sunny Fugate[iD]

Naval Information Warfare Center Pacific, San Diego, CA, USA
{ryan.c.gabrys.civ,mark.bilinski.civ,justin.m.mauger.civ,
daniel.silva61.civ,sunny.j.fugate.civ}@us.navy.mil

Abstract. In this work, we consider a zero-sum game between an adaptive defender and a potentially deceptive attacker who is able to vary their degree of rationality as a deceptive ruse. Under this setup, we provide a complete characterization of the deception space of the attacker and uncover optimal strategies for adaptive defender against a deceptive attacker. In addition, we consider the setup in which both the attacker and defender are allowed to evolve their strategies over time. In this setting, one of our main results is to demonstrate that allowing the attacker to vary their degree of rationality can significantly impact the game in favor of the attacker.

1 Introduction

Deception has played a critical role in the history of military combat [3], and, more recently, it has been adopted for cyberspace interactions by both offense and defense [11]. It is well understood that cyber attackers make regular and effective use of deceptive strategies (e.g. hiding, masking, bluffing, misdirection). A defender who is unaware of an attacker's presence or misled by attacker misdirection is at a significant disadvantage, often resulting in a defender acting only in response to an attack long after initial damage or compromise has occurred or worse, performing actions that are advantageous to the attacker. The longer or more extensive the ruse, the worse off the defender and the defended systems. While it is a foregone conclusion that attacker goals rely extensively on stealth and subterfuge, the ability of a defender to accommodate malicious deception is relatively unaddressed. In particular, in this work we consider a zero-sum game between a deceiving attacker and defender, exploring the relationship between the rationality of the attacker, the likelihood of deception, the value of defended systems, and study the performance of a deception-aware defender against a learning attacker. This parallels complementary work in [4] which explored the bounds on the learning rate of a defender for inferring attacker preferences.

F. Fang et al. (Eds.): GameSec 2022, LNCS 13727, pp. 23–43, 2023.
https://doi.org/10.1007/978-3-031-26369-9_2

2   Related Work

Previous work on deception in cyber has primarily focused on the setup where there is asymmetric information available to the attacker and defender. Early work in this area considered the use of honeypots usually in a single-round framework [9]. Later works studied the more realistic setup of a turn-based Stackelberg Security Game (SSG) where the defender is able to strategically reveal their information to a potential attacker [7,12,16]. Our goal in this work is to allow for deception on the part of the **attacker** and study efficient strategies for both players in these settings. One of the key steps is the defender attempting to learn parameters that govern the attacker's decision-making process.

Most of the existing literature on learning in security games assumes that the attacker behaves rationally, which is not always a realistic assumption [19]. The problem of formulating a meaningful cognitive model for an attacker in order to better understand efficient defensive strategies has garnered significant interest and several models such as Instance Based Learning (IBL) and Quantal Response (QR) have been proposed [1]. Although recent works such as [4,6,14] have leveraged these cognitive models, their focus was to uncover strategies the defender can use to deceive the attacker. In this work, and similar to [5], we are instead interested in the effects attacker deception can have on a defender.

In an effort to better understand how a defender should respond to attacker deception in a SSG setting, [5] considers a two round game where in the first round the attacker employs a certain amount of deception. The defender observes the actions of this deceptive attacker and then adjusts its defensive strategy in light of these observations (despite the attacker not behaving truthfully). One of the key problems considered in [5] is to determine the deception space of the defender provided a possibly deceitful (yet bounded) attacker.

In this work, we consider a similar setup as [5] except that we assume the reward function of the attacker and defender is zero-sum. Under this setting, we give a complete (and surprisingly) simple characterization of the deception space. Afterwards, we provide explicit expressions for the expected utility of the defender under many settings of interest, which provide insight into which cyber environments are more advantageous to the defender than others. For some of these settings, we are able to characterize the optimal defender strategies. In the second part of this work, we provide simulation results that illustrate the performance of a defender against an attacker that is employing various deceptive strategies that validate our previous analysis. Additionally, we consider a multi-round game extension and evaluate the performance of a deceptive reinforcement learning attacker agent.

3   Model and Preliminaries

In the following, we consider a zero-sum setup similar to [5] where the idea will be to study a SSG given an adaptive defender provided a potentially deceptive attacker. Suppose we are given T targets and suppose $\boldsymbol{x} \in [0,1]^T$ denotes the coverage probability vector so that $x_i \in [0,1]$ denotes the probability target i is protected by the defender. We assume that each target has an associated value $V_i \in \mathbb{R}^+$ that is strictly positive. If the attacker chooses to attack target i and the target is unprotected then the attacker receives a reward of V_i. Otherwise if the attacker attacks target i and it is protected, then the attacker receives a reward of $-(T-1)V_i$. Let $U_i^a(x_i)$ denote the expected utility of an attacker who attacks target i given the parameter x_i and similarly for $U_i^d(x_i)$. Then,

$$U_i^a(x_i) = (1 - Tx_i)V_i \tag{1}$$

$$U_i^d(x_i) = (Tx_i - 1)V_i. \tag{2}$$

We assume the parameters $U_i^a(x_i), U_i^d(x_i)$, and V_i are known to both the attacker and the defender. Our setup is motivated by the scenario where an attacker is familiar with each of the targets in the environment and also has observed the defender for some period of time. This level of insider knowledge is typical in scenarios involving insider threat or advanced persistent threats (APTs) [2], which have been modeled as zero-sum games in the past [13]). Note also that although our setup is zero-sum, we assign more reward/penalty to the event that an attacker attacks a protected target. The motivation for this is to avoid the setup where an attacker's expected reward increases with the number of targets, which isn't necessarily the case in adversarial cyber scenarios [3]. In fact, if the defender plays a random strategy, so that $\boldsymbol{x} = (1/T, 1/T, \ldots, 1/T)$ then the expected reward to both the defender and attacker is zero.

The attacker behaves according to the SUQR model. In particular, the probability the attacker attacks target i is

$$q_i(\boldsymbol{x}, \lambda) := \frac{\exp\left(\lambda U_i^a(x_i)\right)}{\sum_j \exp\left(\lambda U_j^a(x_j)\right)}, \tag{3}$$

where $\lambda \in \mathbb{R}$ is the attacker's degree of rationality.

Since $U_i^a(x_i)$, $U_i^d(x_i)$, and V_i are each known, the only information known to the attacker but not the defender is the degree of rationality, $\lambda \in \mathbb{R}$. The defender uses the observed attack distribution, denoted $\boldsymbol{q} = (q_1', q_2', \ldots, q_T')$, to estimate (or "learn") the learned value of λ, λ^ℓ, using a MLE approach that leverages the cross-entropy loss function given below:

$$\lambda^\ell \in \operatorname{argmax}_\lambda \sum_i q_i' \log q_i(\boldsymbol{x}, \lambda). \tag{4}$$

In an effort to maximize its own utility, the defender responds with the coverage probability vector $\boldsymbol{x}^*$ where

$$\boldsymbol{x}^* = \operatorname{argmax}_{\boldsymbol{x}} \sum_i q_i(\boldsymbol{x}, \lambda^\ell) U_i^d(x_i). \tag{5}$$

Notice that under this setup, the attacker's expected reward guides the attack distribution $(q_1(\boldsymbol{x}, \lambda), q_2(\boldsymbol{x}, \lambda), \ldots, q_T(\boldsymbol{x}, \lambda)$ and that the derived coverage probability depends on *both* the defender and attacker's expected reward.

In [5], the authors studied a more generalized model where the rewards to the defender and attacker were not necessarily of the form of (1) and (2). For their setup, the authors characterized the deception space or the set of possible values for λ^ℓ provided some conditions on the observed distribution q. For our setup, we prove a stronger result and show that for our setup the deception space is either unique[1] or it can be arbitrary[2]. Next, we turn our attention to the problem of maximizing the defender's expected reward. To this end, we show that under certain assumptions when the values of the targets differ enough, the optimum strategy for the defender is to set x^* so that the defender spends *at least* roughly a fraction of $\frac{1}{T}$ of its time defending each of the high value targets and *at most* a fraction of $\frac{1}{T}$ of its time defending each of the low value targets. Afterwards, we consider simple, yet effective, strategies a defender can use to produce accurate estimates for λ^ℓ provided a deceptive attacker.

4   Bounds and Analysis on Optimal Defender Behaviors

This section is organized as follows. We first characterize the range of values for λ^ℓ that can be learned by a defender in our game. Our main result regarding this topic is stated in Theorem 1 where we show that for nearly all choices of parameters, λ^ℓ is unique. In Lemmas 2 and 3, we derive bounds on the expected reward for the defender. Afterwards, we consider game scenarios that improve the defender's expected reward. In particular, in Claim 4, we show that it is possible to strictly improve the defender's expected reward by decreasing the value of low-valued targets. Finally, Theorem 2 characterizes the attacker's optimal strategy x^* in circumstances where the targets differ significantly enough in value.

Lemma 1. *Suppose the defender observes attack distribution* $q = (q_1',$ $q_2', \ldots, q_T')$, *and that there exists an* i, j *such that* $U_i^a(x_i) \neq U_j^a(x_j)$. *Then,* (4) *is unique.*

Proof. The result follows from the fact that under this setup, the second derivative of $\sum_i q_i' \log q_i(x, \lambda)$ with respect to λ is negative so that $\sum_i q_i' \log q_i(x, \lambda)$ is strictly concave and there is a unique global maximum for (4). For shorthand, let $U_i = U_i^a(x_i)$ and denote $q_i = q_i(x, \lambda)$. We have

$$\frac{\partial}{\partial \lambda} \sum_{i \in [T]} q_i' \log q_i(x, \lambda) = \frac{\partial}{\partial \lambda} \sum_{i \in [T]} q_i' \lambda U_i - \frac{\partial}{\partial \lambda} \sum_{i \in [T]} q_i' \log \left(\sum_{j \in [T]} \exp(\lambda U_j) \right)$$

$$= \sum_{i \in [T]} q_i' U_i - \sum_{i \in [T]} q_i' \sum_{j \in [T]} \frac{\exp(\lambda U_j) U_j}{\sum_{k \in [T]} \exp(\lambda U_k)}.$$

Thus,

$$\frac{\partial}{\partial^2 \lambda} \sum_{i \in [T]} q_i' \log q_i(x, \lambda) = -\frac{\partial}{\partial \lambda} \sum_{i \in [T]} q_i' \sum_{j \in [T]} \frac{\exp(\lambda U_j) U_j}{\sum_{k \in [T]} \exp(\lambda U_k)}.$$

---

[1] In other words, the value of λ^ℓ is unique.
[2] By arbitrary, we mean that λ^ℓ can be any real value.

We have

$$-\frac{\partial}{\partial \lambda} \sum_{j \in [T]} \frac{\exp(\lambda U_j) U_j}{\sum_{k \in [T]} \exp(\lambda U_k)} =$$

$$-\frac{\sum_{k \in [T]} \exp(\lambda U_k) \sum_{j \in [T]} U_j^2 \exp(\lambda U_j) - \sum_{j \in [T]} \exp(\lambda U_j) U_j \sum_{k \in [T]} U_k \exp(\lambda U_k)}{\left(\sum_{k \in [T]} \exp(\lambda U_k)\right)^2},$$

and

$$-\left(\sum_{k \in [T]} q_k \sum_{j \in [T]} U_j^2 q_j - \sum_{j \in [T]} q_j U_j \sum_{k \in [T]} U_k q_k\right) = -\frac{1}{2} \sum_{k \in [T]} \sum_{j \in [T]} q_k q_j \left(U_k - U_j\right)^2,$$

which implies the desired result.

For the case where the solution to (4) is not unique it was shown in [5] that there exists an interval $[\lambda_{\min}, \lambda_{\max}]$ whereby λ is a solution to (4) if and only if $\lambda \in [\lambda_{\min}, \lambda_{\max}]$. The interval $[\lambda_{\min}, \lambda_{\max}]$ was termed the **deception space**. For shorthand, we say that the deception space is **simple** if $\lambda_{\min} = \lambda_{\max}$.

The following claim which will be useful in characterizing the deception space.

Claim. For any set of values $V_1, V_2, \ldots, V_T \in \mathbb{R}^+$, there exists an i, j such that $U_i^a(x_i) \neq U_j^a(x_j)$ unless $x_1 = \cdots = x_T = \frac{1}{T}$.

Proof. If $U_1^a(x_1) = U_2^a(x_2) = \cdots = U_T^a(x_T)$, then coverage probability vector $\boldsymbol{x} = \left(x_1, x_2, \ldots, x_{T-1}, 1 - \sum_{j=1}^{T-1} x_j\right)$ satisfies the system of $T - 1$ linear eqs:

$$(1 - Tx_1)V_1 = (1 - Tx_2)V_2$$
$$(1 - Tx_1)V_1 = (1 - Tx_3)V_3$$
$$\vdots$$
$$(1 - Tx_1)V_1 = (1 - Tx_{T-1})V_{T-1}$$

$$(1 - Tx_1)V_1 = \left(1 - T\left(1 - \sum_{j \in [T-1]} x_j\right)\right) V_T.$$

Since $x_1 + x_2 + \cdots + x_T = 1$, by the pigeonhole principle, there exists an i where $x_i \geqslant \frac{1}{T}$. So we assume (without loss of generality) that $i = 1$. We can rewrite the previous set of $T - 1$ equations as:

$$x_2 = \frac{1}{T} + \frac{V_1}{V_2}\left(x_1 - \frac{1}{T}\right)$$

$$x_3 = \frac{1}{T} + \frac{V_1}{V_3}\left(x_1 - \frac{1}{T}\right)$$

$$\vdots$$

$$x_T = \frac{1}{T} + \frac{V_1}{V_T}\left(x_1 - \frac{1}{T}\right)$$

Consider the summation of the T terms $x_1, \ldots, x_T$. The previous equations imply

$$x_1 + x_2 + \cdots x_T \geqslant 1 + V_1 \left(\frac{1}{V_2} + \frac{1}{V_3} + \cdots + \frac{1}{V_T} \right) \left(x_1 - \frac{1}{T} \right).$$

Since $x_1 + x_2 + \cdots x_T \leqslant 1$, this requires $x_1 = \frac{1}{T}$ and also for $x_1 = x_2 = \cdots x_T = \frac{1}{T}$ from the previous set of $T - 1$ equations. Therefore, it follows that if $U_i^a(x_i) = U_j^a(x_j)$ for all $i, j \in [T]$, then $x_1 = x_2 = \cdots = x_T = \frac{1}{T}$ as desired.

The previous two lemmas imply the following.

Theorem 1. *For any set of values $V_1, V_2, \ldots, V_T \in \mathbb{R}^+$, one of the following holds:*

1. *There exists an $i, j \in [T]$, where $U_i^a(x_i) \neq U_j^a(x_j)$. In this case, the deception space is simple.*
2. *For all $i, j \in [T]$, $U_i^a(x_i) = U_j^a(x_j)$ and $x_i = x_j$. Then, λ^ℓ can be any positive real number.*

Proof. The first statement follows from Lemma 1. From Claim 4, if $U_i^a(x_i) = U_j^a(x_j)$ for all $i, j \in [T]$, then $x_i = x_j$. In this case, from (1), (2), and (3), it follows that for any λ', we have $q_i(\boldsymbol{x}, \lambda') = \frac{1}{T}$. Hence, for any $\lambda_1, \lambda_2 \in \mathbb{R}$:

$$\sum_i q_i' \log q_i(\boldsymbol{x}, \lambda_1) = \sum_i q_i' \log \frac{1}{T} = \sum_i q_i' \log q_i(\boldsymbol{x}, \lambda_2),$$

We now consider the possible rewards for the defender under the assumption that $U_1^a(x_1) = U_2^a(x_2) = \cdots = U_T^a(x_T)$ does not hold. Note that since the defender controls the coverage probability vector, it is always possible for the defender to avoid the case where $U_1^a(x_1) = U_2^a(x_2) = \cdots = U_T^a(x_T)$. Suppose that $(q_1', q_2', \ldots, q_T') = (q_1(\boldsymbol{x}, \lambda'), q_2(\boldsymbol{x}, \lambda'), \ldots, q_T(\boldsymbol{x}, \lambda'))$. As a result of our setup (and in particular since the deception space is simple), it follows that $\lambda^\ell = \lambda'$ and where, as a result of the definition of $q_i(\boldsymbol{x}, \lambda)$ in (3), it follows that $\lambda^\ell = \lambda$. We consider the more general case where the observed distribution may not be characterized by the SUQR model according to (3) in the next section[3].

Given λ^ℓ, the next lemma gives an upper bound on the maximum reward possible for the defender. In the following, suppose $0 < V_1 < V_2 < \cdots < V_T$ so that V_T is the maximum reward possible. We begin by recovering bounds for the case of $T = 2$ before considering the case of general T afterwards.

---

[3] In other words, we consider the case where there may not exist a parameter λ' whereby we can write the observed distribution as $(q_1', q_2', \ldots, q_T') = (q_1(x, \lambda'), q_2(x, \lambda'), \ldots, q_T(x, \lambda'))$ in the next section.

Lemma 2. *For $T = 2$ and $\lambda > 0$, we have*

$$\frac{\frac{\exp(-1)}{\lambda} - \frac{V_1}{\lambda V_2}\exp(\frac{V_1}{V_2})}{\exp(-1) + \exp(\frac{V_1}{V_2})} \leqslant \sum_{i \in \{1,2\}} q_i(\boldsymbol{x}^*, \lambda)U_i^d(x_i^*) < \frac{\frac{1}{\lambda}\exp(-1)}{\left(\frac{V_1}{V_2}\right)^{\frac{V_2}{V_1+V_2}}\left(1 + \frac{V_2}{V_1}\right)}.$$

Furthermore, $x_1^{(*)} \leqslant x_2^{(*)}$.

Proof. First, notice that $(2x - 1)\,V\exp\left(\lambda(1 - 2x)V\right) \leqslant \frac{1}{\lambda\exp(1)}$, which is achieved when $x = \frac{1}{2} + \frac{1}{2\lambda V}$. Therefore,

$$\begin{aligned}
&\sum_{i \in \{1,2\}} q_i(\boldsymbol{x}^*, \lambda)U_i^d(x_i^*) \\
&= \frac{\exp\left(\lambda(1 - 2x_2^*)V_2\right)(2x_2^* - 1)V_2 + \exp\left(\lambda(1 - 2x_1^*)V_1\right)(2x_1^* - 1)V_1}{\exp\left(\lambda(1 - 2x_2^*)V_2\right) + \exp\left(\lambda(1 - 2x_1^*)V_1\right)}.
\end{aligned} \tag{6}$$

Since $x_1^* \geqslant \frac{1}{2}$ or $x_2^* \geqslant \frac{1}{2}$ it follows that either $\exp\left(\lambda(1 - 2x_2^*)V_2\right)(2x_2^* - 1)V_2 > 0$ or $\exp\left(\lambda(1 - 2x_1^*)V_1\right)(2x_1^* - 1)V_1 > 0$, but not both, so that

$$\exp\left(\lambda(1 - 2x_2^*)V_2\right)(2x_2^* - 1)V_2 + \exp\left(\lambda(1 - 2x_1^*)V_1\right)(2x_1^* - 1)V_1 \leqslant \frac{1}{\lambda\exp(1)}.$$

Suppose $\delta \geqslant 0$. Then there are two cases to consider. Either (a) $x_1^* \geqslant x_2^*$ so that we can write $x_1^* = \frac{1}{2} + \delta$, $x_2^* = \frac{1}{2} - \delta$, or (b) $x_2^* \geqslant x_1^*$ so that we can write $x_2^* = \frac{1}{2} + \delta$, $x_1^* = \frac{1}{2} - \delta$. If (a) holds, then the denominator of (6) is equal to

$$\exp\left(2\delta\lambda V_2\right) + \exp\left(-2\delta\lambda V_1\right). \tag{7}$$

Otherwise, if (b) holds, then the denominator of (6) is equal to

$$\exp\left(-2\delta\lambda V_2\right) + \exp\left(2\delta\lambda V_1\right). \tag{8}$$

Since $V_2 > V_1$, it follows that (8) is less than or equal to (7). Furthermore, if (a) holds, then the numerator of (6) can be written as

$$-2\delta V_2\exp\left(2\delta\lambda V_2\right) + 2\delta V_1\exp\left(-2\delta\lambda V_1\right). \tag{9}$$

If (b) holds, then the numerator is equal to

$$2\delta V_2\exp\left(-2\delta\lambda V_2\right) - 2\delta V_1\exp\left(2\delta\lambda V_1\right). \tag{10}$$

Since $x\exp(-x) + x\exp(x)$ is increasing when $x \geqslant 0$, (9) $\leqslant$ (10). Hence $x_2^* \geqslant x_1^*$. From (7) and (8),

$$\sum_{i \in \{1,2\}} q_i(\boldsymbol{x}^*, \lambda)U_i^d(x_i^*) \leqslant \frac{\frac{1}{\lambda}\exp(-1)}{\exp\left(-2\delta\lambda V_2\right) + \exp\left(2\delta\lambda V_1\right)}.$$

By taking derivatives, it can be verified that

$$\exp\left(2\delta\lambda V_1\right) + \exp\left(-2\delta\lambda V_2\right)$$

is minimized when $\delta = \frac{\log\frac{V_2}{V_1}}{2\lambda(V_1+V_2)}$, which implies

$$\frac{\frac{1}{\lambda}\exp(-1)}{\exp\left(-2\delta\lambda V_2\right) + \exp\left(2\delta\lambda V_1\right)} \leq \frac{\frac{1}{\lambda}\exp(-1)}{\left(\frac{V_1}{V_2}\right)^{\frac{V_2}{V_1+V_2}}\left(1 + \frac{V_2}{V_1}\right)},$$

which is the stated upper bound.

The lower bound follows by setting $(x_1^*, x_2^*) = (\frac{1}{2} - \frac{1}{2\lambda V_2}, \frac{1}{2} + \frac{1}{2\lambda V_2})$.

From the analysis in the previous lemma, notice that if $\lambda > 0$, both the upper and lower bounds on the reward for the defender increase as the ratio $\frac{V_2}{V_1}$ grows. From the lower bound, a sufficient condition for the defender to win the game is for $\log\left(\frac{V_1}{V_2}\right) + \frac{V_1}{V_2} < -1$, which holds when $\frac{V_1}{V_2} \lesssim .278$. When V_2 is very large, it allows the defender to defend both targets with almost uniform probability, and still obtain a large reward. When $\exp(-1) - \frac{V_1}{V_2}\exp(\frac{V_1}{V_2}) > 0$ the maximum reward possible for the defender is inversely proportional to the attacker's degree of rationality – suggesting that a defender will fare better against a less rational attacker rather than a more rational one. The next lemma generalizes our upper bound to the setup where there are more than two targets.

Lemma 3. *Suppose $T > 2$ and $\lambda > 0$. Then,*

$$\sum_{i \in [T]} q_i(\boldsymbol{x}^*, \lambda) U_i^d(x_i^*) \leq \frac{\frac{T-1}{\lambda}\exp(-1)}{\sum_{j \in \{1,2,\dots,T\}} \frac{V_1}{V_j}},$$

Recall from the discussion after Lemma 2, that both the lower and the upper bounds for the expected utility of the defender increase as the ratio $\frac{V_2}{V_1}$ increases, and the defender has the ability to win the game provided $x_2^{(*)} > \frac{1}{2} > x_1^{(*)}$. For the case where there are more than two targets, a similar trend also holds. Suppose $\boldsymbol{V} = (V_1, V_2, \dots, V_T)$ denotes the values of T targets where V_k denotes the value of target k. Let $\boldsymbol{x} \in [0,1]^T$ denote a coverage probability vector. Then, we denote the expected utility of the defender given $\boldsymbol{V}$ and $\boldsymbol{x}$ as follows:

$$E\left[Q\left(\boldsymbol{V}, \boldsymbol{x}\right)\right] := \frac{\sum_{j \in [T]} \left(Tx_j - 1\right) V_j \exp\left(\lambda(1 - Tx_j)V_j\right)}{\sum_{j \in [T]} \exp\left(\lambda(1 - Tx_j)V_j\right)}. \tag{11}$$

For a coverage probability vector $\boldsymbol{x} = (x_1, \dots, x_T)$, let $x_j = \frac{1}{T} + \delta_j$ so that $\sum_{j \in [T]} \delta_j = 0$. For shorthand, let $\mathcal{J}^+(\boldsymbol{x}) = \{j \in [T] : \delta_j > 0\}$ and $\mathcal{J}^-(\boldsymbol{x}) = \{j \in [T] : \delta_j < 0\}$.

Claim. Let $\boldsymbol{x}^* = \operatorname{argmax}_{\boldsymbol{x}} E\left[Q\left(\boldsymbol{V}, \boldsymbol{x}\right)\right]$ where for $j \in [T]$, $x_j^* = \frac{1}{T} + \delta_j^*$ and $\lambda > 0$. Suppose that $\boldsymbol{V}' = (V_1', \dots, V_T')$ is such that the following holds:

1. For any $j \in \mathcal{J}^+(\boldsymbol{x}^*)$, $V_j' = V_j$.
2. For any $j \in \mathcal{J}^-(\boldsymbol{x}^*)$, $V_j' < V_j$.

If $E\left[Q\left(\mathbf{V}',\boldsymbol{x}^*\right)\right] > 0$ and $E\left[Q\left(\mathbf{V},\boldsymbol{x}^*\right)\right] > 0$, then $E\left[Q\left(\mathbf{V}',\boldsymbol{x}^*\right)\right] > E\left[Q\left(\mathbf{V},\boldsymbol{x}^*\right)\right]$.

Proof. We compare terms in $E\left[Q\left(\mathbf{V}',\boldsymbol{x}^*\right)\right]$ and $E\left[Q\left(\mathbf{V},\boldsymbol{x}^*\right)\right]$. Since $j \in \mathcal{J}^+(\boldsymbol{x}^*)$, $V_j' = V_j$ (by assumption), we only consider terms in the numerator and denominator in (11) that correspond to $\mathcal{J}^-(\boldsymbol{x}^*)$. For terms in the numerator of (11):

$$T\delta_j^* V_j' \exp\left(-\lambda V_j' T \delta_j^*\right) = -T\left|\delta_j^*\right| V_j' \exp\left(\lambda V_j' T \left|\delta_j^*\right|\right)$$
$$> -T\left|\delta_j^*\right| V_j \exp\left(\lambda V_j T \left|\delta_j^*\right|\right) = T\delta_j^* V_j \exp\left(-\lambda V_j T \delta_j^*\right).$$

Similarly, for terms in the denominator of (11):

$$\exp\left(-\lambda V_j' T \delta_j^*\right) = \exp\left(\lambda V_j' T \left|\delta_j^*\right|\right) < \exp\left(\lambda V_j T \left|\delta_j^*\right|\right) = \exp\left(-\lambda V_j T \delta_j^*\right).$$

From the two previous expressions, the result follows.

Our next goal is to characterize the distribution $\boldsymbol{x}^*$ for the defender provided a set of target values $V_1, \ldots, V_T$. The next lemma shows that when $\frac{V_j}{V_i}$ is large enough, the optimal strategy for a defender is to assign $x_j \gtrsim \frac{1}{T}$ and for $x_i \lesssim \frac{1}{T}$.

Lemma 4. *Let* $\mathbf{V} = (V_1, \ldots, V_T)$ *and suppose that* $0 < \beta < 1$ *is a constant and* $\lambda > 0$. *For any pair of indices* $i, j \in [T]$ *if* $\frac{V_j}{V_i} > 1 + \frac{1}{\beta}$, *then unless* $\boldsymbol{x}_j^* \in [\frac{1}{T} - \beta, \frac{1}{T} + \beta]$, *the following cannot hold:*

$$\boldsymbol{x}_i^* > \frac{1}{T} > \boldsymbol{x}_j^*,$$

Proof. For $j \in [T]$, let $x_j^* = \frac{1}{T} + \delta_j$. Assume, on the contrary, that both $\delta_j < -\beta$ and $\boldsymbol{x}_i^* > \frac{1}{T} > \boldsymbol{x}_j^*$ so that $x_i^* = \frac{1}{T} + \delta_i$ where $\delta_i > 0$. We show that if this is the case, then we can increase the expected reward for the defender by swapping x_i^* and x_j^* Let $\boldsymbol{x}' = (x_1', x_2', \ldots, x_T') \in [0,1]^T$ be such that for all $k \in [T] \setminus \{i, j\}$, $x_k' = x_k^*$ and $x_j' = x_i^*$, $x_i' = x_j^*$. For $k \in [T]$, define $\Delta_k = |\delta_k|$. We show under this setup $E\left[Q\left(\mathbf{V}, \boldsymbol{x}'\right)\right] > E\left[Q\left(\mathbf{V}, \boldsymbol{x}^*\right)\right]$.

Our approach is similar to the one taken in the proof of Claim 4 where we consider the numerator and denominator of the expressions for $E\left[Q\left(\mathbf{V}, \boldsymbol{x}'\right)\right]$, $E\left[Q\left(\mathbf{V}, \boldsymbol{x}^*\right)\right]$ when the quantities are written as in (11). First, we show

$$\sum_{j \in [T]} \left(Tx_j' - 1\right) V_j \exp\left(\lambda(1 - Tx_j')V_j\right) > \sum_{j \in [T]} \left(Tx_j^* - 1\right) V_j \exp\left(\lambda(1 - Tx_j^*)V_j\right),$$

which is equivalent to showing $-\Delta_j V_j \exp\left(\lambda V_j T \Delta_j\right) + \Delta_i V_i \exp\left(-\lambda V_i T \Delta_i\right) < \Delta_i V_j \exp\left(-\lambda V_j T \Delta_i\right) - \Delta_j V_i \exp\left(\lambda V_i T \Delta_j\right)$ or

$$\Delta_j V_j \exp\left(\lambda V_j T \Delta_j\right) - \Delta_j V_i \exp\left(\lambda V_i T \Delta_j\right) \tag{12}$$
$$> \Delta_i V_i \exp\left(-\lambda V_i T \Delta_i\right) - \Delta_i V_j \exp\left(-\lambda V_j T \Delta_i\right)$$

Since $\Delta_j > 0$, $V_j \exp(\lambda V_j T \Delta_j) - V_i \exp(\lambda V_i T \Delta_j) \geqslant 0$, and noting $-V_i \exp(\lambda V_i T \Delta_j) \geqslant -V_i \exp(\lambda V_j T \Delta_j)$ implies that the left hand side of (12) is such that

$$\Delta_j \left(V_j \exp(\lambda V_j T \Delta_j) - V_i \exp(\lambda V_i T \Delta_j)\right) \geqslant \beta \left(V_j \exp(\lambda V_j T \Delta_j) - V_i \exp(\lambda V_i T \Delta_j)\right)$$
$$\geqslant \beta \exp(\lambda V_j T \Delta_j)(V_j - V_i).$$

Therefore, since $\Delta_i < 1$ and $\beta \exp(\lambda V_j T \Delta_j)(V_j - V_i) > 0$, in order to show that (12) holds, if suffices to establish that

$$\beta \exp(\lambda V_j T \Delta_j)(V_j - V_i) > V_i \exp(-\lambda V_i T \Delta_i) - V_j \exp(-\lambda V_j T \Delta_i). \tag{13}$$

The right hand side of (13) is maximized when $\Delta_i = \frac{\log(V_j^2/V_i^2)}{\lambda T(V_j - V_i)}$ so that

$$V_i \exp(-\lambda V_i T \Delta_i) - V_j \exp(-\lambda V_j T \Delta_i) \leqslant V_i \left(\frac{V_i}{V_j}\right)^{2\frac{V_i}{V_j - V_i}} - V_j \left(\frac{V_i}{V_j}\right)^{2\frac{V_j}{V_j - V_i}}.$$

Since $\exp(\lambda V_j T \Delta_j) > 1$, from (13) it is enough to show $\beta\left(\frac{V_j}{V_i} - 1\right) > \left(\frac{V_i}{V_j}\right)^{2\frac{V_i}{V_j - V_i}} - \frac{V_j}{V_i}\left(\frac{V_i}{V_j}\right)^{2\frac{V_j}{V_j - V_i}}$, which follows if $\frac{V_j}{V_i} > 1 + \frac{1}{\beta}$ since $\left(\frac{V_i}{V_j}\right)^{2\frac{V_i}{V_j - V_i}} - \frac{V_j}{V_i}\left(\frac{V_i}{V_j}\right)^{2\frac{V_j}{V_j - V_i}} \leqslant \left(\frac{V_i}{V_j}\right)^{2\frac{V_i}{V_j - V_i}} \leqslant 1$.

The next theorem provides a characterization of the defender strategies $\boldsymbol{x}^*$ from (5). It follows as a result of the previous two lemmas.

Theorem 2. *Let $\overline{V} = \{j : V_j \geqslant T_1\}$ and suppose $\underline{V} = \{j : V_j \leqslant T_2\}$ for positive T_1 and T_2 and suppose $\frac{T_1}{T_2} > \frac{1}{\beta} + 1$. Then, for every $j \in \overline{V}$, $x_j^* \geqslant \frac{1}{T} - \beta$, and for every $j \in \underline{V}$, $x_j^* \leqslant \frac{1}{T} + \beta$.*

5 Generalized Multi-round Game of Deception

In this section, we consider the more generalized setup where the defender and a potentially deceptive attacker play a variation of the game described in Sect. 3 for multiple rounds. Similar to [5], we assume that we are dealing with the setup of a constrained attacker. For this setup, $\Delta \in (0, 1)$ is a real number that corresponds to the total amount of deception that is allowed by an attacker. Let $\delta_1, \ldots, \delta_T \in \mathbb{R}^+$ be such that $\sum_{j \in [T]} \delta_j = \Delta$.

Each round of our multi-round game consists of two sub-rounds whereby in the first sub-round, the defender has the initial coverage probability vector $\boldsymbol{x}^{(0)}$, and the defender is able to observe the attack distribution $q_1'(\boldsymbol{x}^{(0)}, \lambda, \delta_1)$, $q_2'(\boldsymbol{x}^{(0)}, \lambda, \delta_2), \ldots, q_T'(\boldsymbol{x}^{(0)}, \lambda, \delta_T)$ where

$$q_i'(\boldsymbol{x}^{(0)}, \lambda, \delta_i) := q_i(\boldsymbol{x}^{(0)}, \lambda)(1 - \Delta) + \delta_i. \tag{14}$$

For shorthand, let $\underline{\delta} = (\delta_1, \ldots, \delta_T)$. The total reward to the defender after the first sub-round is given by:

$$R^1(\boldsymbol{x}^{(0)}, \lambda) = \sum_{i \in [T]} q_i(\boldsymbol{x}^{(0)}, \lambda) U_i^d(x_i^{(0)}). \tag{15}$$

In the second sub-round, and similar to the model from Sect. 3, the defender produces the estimate λ^ℓ according to (4) and uses this estimate to determine its next coverage probability vector $\boldsymbol{x}^{(1)}$ according to (5). The reward for the defender in the second sub-round is equal to

$$R^2\left(\boldsymbol{x}^{(1)}, \lambda\right) = \sum_{i \in [T]} q_i(\boldsymbol{x}^{(1)}, \lambda) U_i^d(x_i^{(1)}). \tag{16}$$

Note that for the case where $\Delta = 0$ and where a single round is played, the game described here is nearly identical that from Sect. 3. The game described in Sect. 3 effectively ignores the reward for the first sub-round (described in (18)), since this reward is highly dependent on the initial coverage probability vector (oftentimes initialized to be a random vector). Our setup is also distinct from that in [5] as we consider an iterative multiple round game instead of a single round – allowing for a much larger action space for both players.

We begin in Sect. 5.1 by first considering the single round version of our game with no deception, which mirrors the setup analyzed in the previous section. For this case, our main result is to illustrate two trends that were first highlighted in the previous section. The first is that the expected reward for the defender appears to increase as the differences between the values of the machines increase. The second trend we demonstrate is that the defender seems to fare better when there are a larger number of targets.

Next, we consider the single-round case where the attacker can employ deception. We analyze the setting where the goal is to maximize $\lambda^\ell - \lambda$ and uncover a simple strategy that allows an attacker to maximize the error in the defender's ML estimate for λ. We evaluate this strategy along with a randomization approach in Sect. 5.2. Finally, in Sect. 5.3, we consider the multi-round setup.

5.1 Single Round, No Deception

First, we assume the attacker is not deceptive and that only a single round of the game is played. In Fig. 1, the rewards for the second sub-round are plotted. For the case of two targets, which is represented by the lowest line in Fig. 1, we are displaying the expected reward for the defender provided $V_1 = 5$ and $|V_1 - V_2|$ is allowed to range between 1.5 and 100 in increments of 0.5. In other words, the lowest line in the figure is showing the expected defender reward when $V_2 = \{6.5, 7.0, 7.5, \ldots, 104.0, 104.5, 105\}$ and $V_1 = 5$. The initial coverage probability vector is set equal to $\left(x_1^{(0)}, x_2^{(0)}\right) = (.49, .51)$.

For the case where there are $T > 2$ targets, we follow a similar strategy to assign values to targets. First we partition the set of targets into two groups denoted G_H and G_L, the set of high and low-valued targets respectively. The targets in G_L are initialized so the lowest-valued target has value $V_1 = 5$, the next has value $V_2 = 10$, and so on. Note that the highest valued target in G_L has value $V_{\frac{T}{2}} = \frac{5T}{2}$. Let D, the difference between the highest and lowest value of the targets, be a positive integer. Then the value of the lowest target in G_H is $V_{\frac{T}{2}+1} = \frac{5T}{2}+D$, the value of the next is $V_{\frac{T}{2}+2} = V_{\frac{T}{2}+1}+5 = 5\left(\frac{T}{2}+1\right)+D$, and so on. Note that the value of the highest valued target is equal to $V_T = 5(T-1)+D$. Figure 1 shows the expected defender reward given that D is allowed to range between 1.5 and 100 in increments of 0.5. For $T = 4, 8, 16$, we set the initial coverage probability vector to be such that $x_1^{(0)} = \cdots = x_{\frac{T}{2}}^{(0)} = \frac{1}{T} - .01$ and $x_{\frac{T}{2}+1}^{(0)} = \cdots = x_T^{(0)} = \frac{1}{T} + .01$. For all values of T, the degree of rationality is set to $\lambda = 1$.

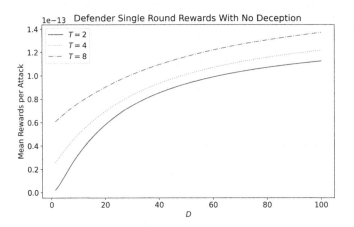

Fig. 1. Expected reward of defender in sub-round 2, no deception, single round

Recall from Sect. 4 the upper bound in Lemma 3, which states that the expected reward to the defender is at most $\sum_{i \in [T]} q_i(\boldsymbol{x}^*, \lambda) U_i^d(x_i^*) \leqslant \frac{\frac{T-1}{\lambda} \exp(-1)}{\sum_{j \in \{1,2,\dots,T\}} \frac{V_1}{V_j}}$. Note that (i) this bound is increasing as the ratio $\frac{V_1}{V_2}$ decreases, and (ii) when $\frac{V_1}{V_j}$ is constant for $j \neq 1$, the bound is increasing in T.

Both these trends appear to be consistent with the result displayed in Fig. 1. For any number of targets, the expected reward increases as D increases. For the case of two targets, allowing $V_2 \gg V_1$ essentially amounts to the setup of a deterministic attacker that will always choose to attack the second (more valuable) target according to (3). Consequently, it seems reasonable that a defender would fare better in such a scenario. In Fig. 1, the defender also performs better when there are more targets. In this case, the defender effectively has more information at its disposal to better estimate the attacker's degree of rationality.

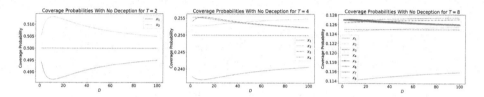

Fig. 2. Coverage probability vector in sub-round 2, no deception, single round

In Fig. 2, we show the coverage probability vectors that were computed by the defender during the second sub-round. For the case $T = 2$, regardless of the value of V_1, V_2, the defender will choose to protect the second, more valuable, target more frequently, which is consistent with Lemma 2. For the case $T > 2$, the coverage probability vector is less simple to describe. However, as can be seen in Fig. 2, the target which was defended with the lowest probability was always the least valued target, while the remaining targets were defended with probabilities concentrated around $\frac{1}{T}$, which is consistent with Theorem 2.

5.2   Single Round, Deception

We now consider the same setup as Sect. 5.1 except that here we no longer assume that $q_i'(\boldsymbol{x}, \lambda, \delta_i) = q_i(\boldsymbol{x}, \lambda)$ in (14). We begin by considering the problem of determining what values of $\delta_1, \delta_2, \ldots, \delta_T$ the attacker should use in order to deceive the defender. We show in Lemma 5 that when the defender determines λ^ℓ according to (4), the best policy for the attacker (which maximizes the error in the defender's estimate of the attacker's degree of rationality, represented by the difference $|\lambda - \lambda^\ell|$) is to set $\delta_{i^*} = \Delta$ where $i^* \in T$ is defined in Lemma 5.

We begin with the following lemma, which motivates the discussion that follows. For the statement in the lemma, we assume that λ^ℓ is a solution to (4) and that this solution is unique.

Lemma 5. *Let* $i^{\min}$ *be such that*

$$i^{\min} = \operatorname{argmin}_i U_i^a(x_i).$$

Then, the quantity $\lambda^\ell - \lambda$ *is maximized when* $\delta_{i^{\min}} = \Delta$.

Proof. In the following, we assume that the conditions from Lemma 1 are satisfied so that λ^ℓ is unique and the function $\sum_i q_i' \log \frac{1}{q_i(\boldsymbol{x}, \lambda)}$ is convex. The unique solution λ^ℓ satisfies:

$$\frac{\partial}{\partial \lambda^\ell} \sum_i q_i' \log \frac{1}{q_i(\boldsymbol{x}, \lambda^\ell)} = 0,$$

(where $\boldsymbol{x} = \boldsymbol{x}^{(0)}$) which implies λ^ℓ is such that

$$\sum_{i \in [T]} q_i(\boldsymbol{x}, \lambda^\ell) U_i^a(x_i) - \sum_{i \in [T]} q_i' U_i^a(x_i) = 0.$$

For shorthand, let

$$F(\lambda, \underline{\delta}) = \sum_{i \in [T]} q_i(\boldsymbol{x}, \lambda^\ell) U_i^a(x_i) - \sum_{i \in [T]} \left(q_i(\boldsymbol{x}, \lambda)(1 - \Delta) + \delta_i \right) U_i^a(x_i),$$

so that under our model of deception λ^ℓ satisfies $F(\lambda^\ell, \underline{\delta}) = 0$.

Suppose $\underline{\delta}^* = (\delta_1^*, \ldots, \delta_T^*)$. For $i \in [T] \setminus i^{\min}$, let $\delta_i^* = 0$. Otherwise, set $\delta_{i_{\min}}^* = \Delta$. Let $\underline{\hat{\delta}} = (\hat{\delta}_1, \ldots, \hat{\delta}_T)$ sequence of positive numbers that satisfies $\sum_{j \in [T]} \hat{\delta}_j = \Delta$. It is not hard to see that under this setup for any λ' we have

$$\sum_{i \in [T]} \left(q_i(\boldsymbol{x}, \lambda')(1 - \Delta) + \hat{\delta}_i \right) U_i^a(x_i) \geqslant \sum_{i \in [T]} \left(q_i(\boldsymbol{x}, \lambda')(1 - \Delta) + \delta_i^* \right) U_i^a(x_i),$$

so that for any λ'

$$F(\lambda', \underline{\delta}^*) \geqslant F(\lambda', \underline{\hat{\delta}}).$$

Since $F(\lambda, \delta)$ is increasing in λ, $\lambda^\ell - \lambda$ is maximized when $\delta = \delta^*$, implying the result.

For shorthand, we will refer to the strategy outlined in Lemma 5 of setting $\delta_{i_{\min}} = \Delta$ as the *min deception* strategy. Figure 4 displays the result of adopting the min deception strategy for the case provided $T = \{2, 4, 8\}$. As a basis for comparison, Fig. 5 shows the result of a random strategy. From Figs. 4 and 5, note that the defender's ranges of expected rewards tend to increase as T increases. For example, when $T = 2$ the attacker's rewards range from roughly -5 to 2 whereas when $T = 8$, the attacker's rewards are no less than -3. In addition, independent of T and D, both strategies tend to result in a lower expected reward for the defender when the parameter Δ – which represents the total amount of deception available to the attacker – increases. Overall, the min deception strategy for the attacker seems to be more effective than the random strategy. In order to more directly see this trend, Fig. 3 displays the setup where $\Delta = .2$ and the attacker uses the min deception vs random strategy.

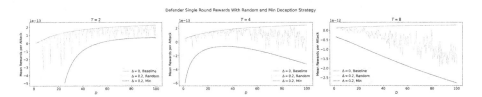

Fig. 3. Expected defender reward. Sub-round 2, min deception strategy and random, single round

The relationship between D and the expected defender reward is less straightforward. For the case of $T = 2$, the general trend is that the defender's expected reward is increasing as a function of D, which is consistent with the results for the case of no deception in the previous subsection. However, for $T = 4$ and $T = 8$, this trend no longer seems to hold, and for both strategies, the defender's expected reward decreases when D becomes large enough.

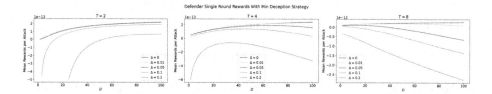

Fig. 4. Expected defender reward. Sub-round 2, min deception strategy, single round

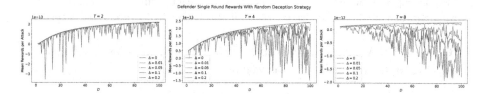

Fig. 5. Expected defender reward. Sub-round 2, random strategy, single round

5.3   Multi-round Game

We now consider the multi-round game setup under the condition that there are exactly two targets. For this setup, we assume our game is played for $N = 10000$ rounds and we will define the game recursively. Recall from the discussion at the start of the section that the reward for the first two sub-rounds is given by (18) and (19). For round $r \in \{2, 3, \ldots, N\}$, we assume that the defender observes the attack distribution $q_1' \left(x^{(r-1)}, \lambda^{(r)}, \delta_1^{(r)} \right)$, $q_2' \left(x^{(r-1)}, \lambda^{(r)}, \delta_2^{(r)} \right)$ where

$$q_i' \left(x^{(r-1)}, \lambda^{(r)}, \delta_i^{(r)} \right) := q_i \left(x^{(r-1)}, \lambda^{(r)} \right) (1 - \Delta) + \delta_i^{(r)}, \qquad (17)$$

and where $\delta_1^{(r)} + \delta_2^{(r)} = \Delta$. The total reward to the defender after the first sub-round is given by:

$$R^{(1,r)} \left(x^{(r-1)}, \lambda^{(r)} \right) = \sum_{i \in [2]} q_i \left(x^{(r-1)}, \lambda^{(r)} \right) U_i^d(x_i^{(r-1)}). \qquad (18)$$

In the second sub-round, the defender produces the estimate $\tilde{\lambda}^{(r)}$ according to (4) and uses it to determine the next coverage probability vector $\boldsymbol{x}^{(r)}$ according to (5). The reward for the defender in the second sub-round is equal to

$$R^{(2,r)}\left(\boldsymbol{x}^{(r)}, \lambda^{(r)}\right) = \sum_{i \in [2]} q_i \left(\boldsymbol{x}^{(r)}, \lambda^{(r)}\right) U_i^d(x_i^{(r)}), \tag{19}$$

and the total reward per round for the defender at round r is

$$R^{(r)} = R^{(1,r)}\left(\boldsymbol{x}^{(r-1)}, \lambda^{(r)}\right) + R^{(2,r)}\left(\boldsymbol{x}^{(r)}, \lambda^{(r)}\right). \tag{20}$$

In the following, we compare 3 strategies that the attacker can use to gain an advantage over the defender. In particular, we will investigate the following:

1. Random δ_1, δ_2, Fixed λ: At each round $r \in \{1, 2, \ldots, N\}$, we randomly pick $\delta_1^{(r)}$ to be a real number between 0 and Δ and we set $\delta_2^{(r)} = \Delta - \delta_1^{(r)}$. For this case, we set $\lambda^{(1)} = \cdots = \lambda^{(N)} = 1$.
2. Min Deception Strategy δ_1, δ_2, Fixed λ: For each round $r \in \{1, 2, \ldots, R\}$, we employ the min deception strategy discussed in Sect. 5.2 to determine $\delta_1^{(r)}, \delta_2^{(r)}$. As before, we fix $\lambda^{(1)} = \cdots = \lambda^{(N)} = 1$.
3. RL δ_1, δ_2, RL λ: For each round $r \in \{1, 2, \ldots, R\}$, we employ reinforcement learning to determine $\delta_1^{(r)}, \delta_2^{(r)}$ as well as $\lambda^{(r)}$.

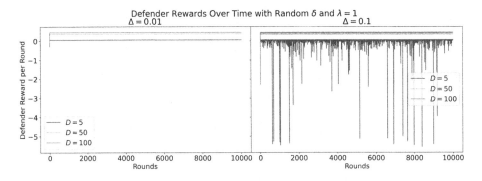

Fig. 6. Expected reward of defender per round using random δs at each round

Figure 6 displays the expected reward of the defender as a function of the round number according to (20) for $N = 10000$ rounds. We again see the trend that the larger the value of D, the larger the expected reward to the defender. In addition, and as expected, we see increasing the amount of available deception (through Δ) potentially decreases the expected reward to the defender.

Figure 7 displays the result of running the min deception strategy under the same setup. We see that, not surprisingly, the min deception strategy almost always results in a lower reward for the defender. The effect of increasing the

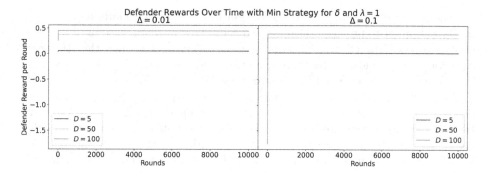

Fig. 7. Expected reward of defender per round using the min deception strategy

amount of deception appears to be correlated with D. For the case where $D = 5$ increasing Δ from 0.01 to 0.1 had little to no effect on the expected reward to the defender. However, when $D \in \{50, 100\}$ increasing the deception had more of an effect towards decreasing the per round defender reward.

Finally, we considered the setup where the attacker is allowed to vary both their degree of rationality as well as δ_1, δ_2. To this end, we implemented an RL agent using tabular q-learning with an epsilon greedy approach with the learning rate $\alpha = 0.1$, decay rate $\gamma = 0.6$, and learning rate $\epsilon = 0.1$. The state space for our attacker agent at round r is equal to the first component of the coverage probability vector from the previous round $x_1^{(r-1)}$. The action space consists of 4 discrete actions: (i) The attacker increments δ_1 and increments λ at the current round so that $\delta_1^{(r)} = \delta_1^{(r-1)} + .001$ and $\lambda^{(r)} = \lambda^{(r-1)} + .001$, (ii) The attacker increments δ_1 and decrements λ so $\delta_1^{(r)} = \delta_1^{(r-1)} + .001$ and $\lambda^{(r)} = \lambda^{(r-1)} - .001$, (iii) $\delta_1^{(r)} = x_1^{(r-1)} - .001$, $\lambda^{(r)} = \lambda^{(r-1)} - .001$, and (iv) $\delta_1^{(r)} = \delta_1^{(r-1)} - .001$, $\lambda^{(r)} = \lambda^{(r-1)} + .001$. For all cases, we ensure that $-q_1\left(x^{(r-1)}, \lambda^{(r)}\right)(1 - \Delta) \leq \delta_1^{(r)} \leq \Delta$ so that if for instance the previous approach attempts to set $\delta_1^{(r)} > \Delta$, then $\delta_1^{(r)} = \delta_1^{(r-1)}$ and similarly when $\delta_1^{(r)} < -q_1\left(x^{(r-1)}, \lambda^{(r)}\right)(1 - \Delta)$.

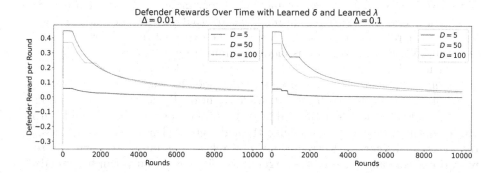

Fig. 8. Expected reward of defender per round using RL attacker agent

The results of running our attacker agent for $N = 10000$ rounds are displayed in Fig. 8. Similar to previous setups, the defender's reward increases as a function of D. However, the effect of increasing D is less dramatic when the RL agent runs for more rounds. In particular, as we approach round 10000, we see that the RL agent achieves a similar reward regardless of the value of D.

Figure 9 compares the 3 strategies in terms of the expected reward to the defender. The random strategy (left) serves as an initial baseline and is typically the least effective compared to the other two. In particular, for all cases under consideration, the min deception strategy (middle) resulted in lower defender rewards than random. Observe from the middle and right plots that by allowing both δ_1, δ_2 and λ to change over time, the RL attacker is able to consistently outperform the min deception attacker by further reducing the defender's expected reward, provided the agent is allowed to play the game for a sufficient number of rounds. Intuitively this makes sense since, by allowing the attacker to alter their degree of rationality, we have effectively increased the attacker's action space thus introducing uncertainty from the defender's point of view.

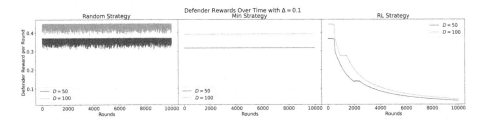

Fig. 9. Expected reward of defender per round comparing random, min deception, and RL strategy (respectively) attack agents

6   Conclusion

In this work we presented a zero-sum game theory model of cyber defense where we explored attacker use of deception. We show that an attacker who is allowed to vary their rationality is able to decrease the expected rewards of a defender over time. We then explored this model in simulation.

Our model and simulations suggest that an attacker with insider knowledge of system value can effectively deceive a defender by varying their rationality over time. This is achieved by the attacker intentionally choosing a non-optimal strategy in respect to the actual value of the systems on the network and learning an optimal degree of rationality through repeated interactions. Although the focus on the current work made several relaxing assumptions regarding the reward function and value of the targets, we believe our results can be extended to more generic setups and believe this is one potential avenue for future work.

In this model the defender is relatively static, but can mitigate the potential risk of poor outcomes by adjusting the number and value of systems present on the network. Sensibly, if the difference in targets is small, attacker learning has little effect on the outcome and a random strategy is more or less optimal. However, if the differences in targets is large, the defender can force an attacker to be deterministic, always attacking the higher-value target. Similarly, the defender also achieves a higher reward when there are a larger number of targets to attack.

An astute reader may note that our work suggests the seemingly impractical notion that a defender can manipulate the defensive environment to impact the rewards of a deceiving attacker. Defensive manipulations such as increasing the number of targets or changing the value of targets in order to increase their expected reward are, in general, untenable. However, such a model may be used to determine a defensively optimal network composition based on a learning attacker model run in simulation – informing how a network is initially deployed.

Alternatively, while dynamically modifying traditional networking environments with changes in system composition seems to fly in the face of practicality, recent explorations of defensive deception provide a straightforward method for manipulating the composition of the network environment. Further, such techniques can also be used to affect the attacker's perception of the value of targeted systems, benefiting a defender and undermining the goals of a deceiving attacker. Notionally, the use of deception to manipulate the value and number of systems would mitigate the profound effects of attacker deception. While we do not explore defensive deception in this work (nor the relationship between performance and real and perceived value), it would be straightforward to extend our models accordingly. Our current exploration suggests that an attacker can deceive defenders with impunity. While this is problematic, the advent of defensive deception techniques suggest that a deceiving defender might be capable of converting an attacker's methodical manipulation into a risky gamble of rationality. Such explorations are left for future work.

A   Proof of Lemma 3

Analogous to the approach in Lemma 2, we note that $(Tx - 1) V \exp(\lambda(1 - Tx)V) \leq \frac{1}{\lambda \exp(1)}$, which is achieved when $x = \frac{1}{T} + \frac{1}{T\lambda V}$. Therefore, $\sum_{i \in \{1,2,\dots,T\}} q_i(\boldsymbol{x}^*, \lambda) U_i^d(x_i^*) \leq \frac{(T-1)\frac{\exp(-1)}{\lambda}}{\sum_{j \in \{1,2,\dots,T\}} \exp(\lambda V_j(1-Tx_j))}$. In order to maximize the previous expression, we seek to minimize the convex function $\sum_{j \in \{1,2,\dots,T\}} \exp(\lambda V_j(1-Tx_j))$. To this end, consider the Lagrangian

$$\mathcal{L}(x_1, x_2, \dots, x_T, \beta) = \sum_{j \in \{1,2,\dots,T\}} \exp(\lambda V_j(1-Tx_j)) + \beta \left(\sum_{j \in \{1,2,\dots,T\}} x_j - 1 \right).$$

For $i \in [T]$, $\frac{\partial \mathcal{L}(x_1, x_2, \dots, x_T, \beta)}{\partial x_i} = 0$ implies that

$$x_i = \frac{1}{T} - \frac{\log \frac{\beta}{T\lambda V_i}}{T\lambda^\ell V_i}. \tag{21}$$

Then, since $\sum_{j \in \{1,2,\ldots,T\}} x_j = 1$, either $\sum_{j \in \{1,2,\ldots,T\}} \frac{\log \frac{\beta}{T\lambda^\ell V_j}}{T\lambda^\ell V_j} = 0$ or $\sum_{j \in \{1,2,\ldots,T\}} \frac{\log \beta}{T\lambda^\ell V_j} = \sum_{j \in \{1,2,\ldots,T\}} \frac{\log T\lambda^\ell V_j}{T\lambda^\ell V_j}$. This implies that $\beta \geqslant T\lambda^\ell V_1$ (recall $V_1 = \min_{j \in [T]} V_j$). From (21), $\sum_{j \in \{1,2,\ldots,T\}} \exp\left(\lambda^\ell V_j (1 - Tx_j)\right) \geqslant \sum_{j \in \{1,2,\ldots,T\}} \frac{\beta}{T\lambda^\ell V_j} \geqslant \sum_{j \in \{1,2,\ldots,T\}} \frac{V_1}{V_j}$, which implies $\sum_{i \in \{1,2,\ldots,T\}} q_i(\boldsymbol{x}^*, \lambda^\ell) U_i^d(x_i^*) \leqslant \frac{(T-1)\frac{\exp(-1)}{\lambda^\ell}}{\sum_{j \in \{1,2,\ldots,T\}} \frac{V_1}{V_j}}$, as desired.

References

1. Abbasi, Y., et al.: Know your adversary: insights for a better adversarial behavioral model. In: CogSci (2016)
2. Alshamrani, A., et al.: A survey on advanced persistent threats: techniques, solutions, challenges, and research opportunities. IEEE Commun. Surv. Tutor. **21**(2), 1851–1877 (2019)
3. Whaley, B.: Stratagem: Deception and Surprise in War. Center for International Studies, Massachusetts Institute of Technology, Cambridge (1969)
4. Bilinski, M., et al.: No time to lie: bounds on the learning rate of a defender for inferring attacker target preferences. In: Bošanský, B., Gonzalez, C., Rass, S., Sinha, A. (eds.) GameSec 2021. LNCS, vol. 13061, pp. 138–157. Springer, Cham (2021). https://doi.org/10.1007/978-3-030-90370-1_8
5. Butler, A.R., Nguyen, T.H., Sinha, A.: Countering attacker data manipulation in security games. In: Bošanský, B., Gonzalez, C., Rass, S., Sinha, A. (eds.) GameSec 2021. LNCS, vol. 13061, pp. 59–79. Springer, Cham (2021). https://doi.org/10.1007/978-3-030-90370-1_4
6. Cranford, E.A., et al.: Toward personalized deceptive signaling for cyber defense using cognitive models. Top. Cogn. Sci. **12**(3), 992–1011 (2020)
7. Guo, Q., et al.: Comparing strategic secrecy and Stackelberg commitment in security games. In: 26th International Joint Conference on Artificial Intelligence (2017)
8. Haghtalab, N., et al.: Three strategies to success: learning adversary models in security games. In: International Joint Conference on Artificial Intelligence (IJCAI) (2016)
9. Mairh, A., et al.: Honeypot in network security: a survey. In: Proceedings of the 2011 International Conference on Communication, Computing and Security, pp. 600–605 (2011)
10. Nguyen, T.H., Wang, Y., Sinha, A., Wellman, M.P.: Deception in finitely repeated security games. In: AAAI (2019)
11. Pawlick, J., et al.: A game-theoretic taxonomy and survey of defensive deception for cybersecurity and privacy. ACM Comput. Surv. **52**(4) (2019)
12. Rabinovich, Z., et al.: Information disclosure as a means to security. In: 14th International Conference on Autonomous Agents and Multi-agent Systems, pp. 645–653 (2015)
13. Rass, S., Zhu, Q.: GADAPT: a sequential game-theoretic framework for designing defense-in-depth strategies against advanced persistent threats. In: Zhu, Q., Alpcan, T., Panaousis, E., Tambe, M., Casey, W. (eds.) GameSec 2016. LNCS, vol. 9996, pp. 314–326. Springer, Cham (2016). https://doi.org/10.1007/978-3-319-47413-7_18

14. Shi, Z.R., et al.: Learning and planning in the feature deception problem. In: GameSec 2020. LNCS, vol. 12513, pp. 23–44. Springer, Cham (2020). https://doi.org/10.1007/978-3-030-64793-3_2

15. Sinha, A., Kar, D., Tambe, M.: Learning adversary behavior in security games: a PAC model perspective. In: AAMAS 2016 (2016)

16. Zhuang, J., Bier, V.M., Alagoz, O.: Modeling secrecy and deception in a multi-period attacker-defender signaling game. Eur. J. Oper. Res. **203**(2), 409–418 (2010)

17. Tambe, M.: Security and Game Theory: Algorithms, Deployed Systems, Lessons Learned. Cambridge University Press, Cambridge (2011)

18. Thakoor, O., Jabbari, S., Aggarwal, P., Gonzalez, C., Tambe, M., Vayanos, P.: Exploiting bounded rationality in risk-based cyber camouflage games. In: Zhu, Q., Baras, J.S., Poovendran, R., Chen, J. (eds.) GameSec 2020. LNCS, vol. 12513, pp. 103–124. Springer, Cham (2020). https://doi.org/10.1007/978-3-030-64793-3_6

19. Zhang, J., Wang, Y., Zhuang, J.: Modeling multi-target defender-attacker games with quantal response attack strategies. **205**, 107165 (2021)

Cyber Deception Against Zero-Day Attacks: A Game Theoretic Approach

Md Abu Sayed[1][(✉)] ⓘ, Ahmed H. Anwar[2][(✉)] ⓘ, Christopher Kiekintveld[1][(✉)] ⓘ,
Branislav Bosansky[3][(✉)] ⓘ, and Charles Kamhoua[2][(✉)] ⓘ

[1] University of Texas at El Paso, El Paso, TX 79968, USA
msayed@miners.utep.edu, cdkiekintveld@utep.edu
[2] US Army Research Laboratory, Adelphi, MD 20783, USA
a.h.anwar@knights.ucf.edu, charles.a.kamhoua.civ@mail.mil
[3] Department of Computer Science, Faculty of Electrical Engineering, Czech
Technical University in Prague, Prague, Czechia
branislav.bosansky@fel.cvut.cz

Abstract. Reconnaissance activities precedent other attack steps in the cyber kill chain. Zero-day attacks exploit unknown vulnerabilities and give attackers the upper hand against conventional defenses. Honeypots have been used to deceive attackers by misrepresenting the true state of the network. Existing work on cyber deception does not model zero-day attacks. In this paper, we address the question of "How to allocate honeypots over the network?" to protect its most valuable assets. To this end, we develop a two-player zero-sum game theoretic approach to study the potential reconnaissance tracks and attack paths that attackers may use. However, zero-day attacks allow attackers to avoid placed honeypots by creating new attack paths. Therefore, we introduce a sensitivity analysis to investigate the impact of different zero-day vulnerabilities on the performance of the proposed deception technique. Next, we propose several mitigating strategies to defend the network against zero-day attacks based on this analysis. Finally, our numerical results validate our findings and illustrate the effectiveness of the proposed defense approach.

Keywords: Cyber deception · Game theory · Zero-day attacks

1 Introduction

The cyber kill chain defines seven stages of cyber attack that end with gaining control of a system/network and infiltrating its data [1]. The first stage is the

Research was sponsored by the Army Research Laboratory and was accomplished under Cooperative Agreement Numbers W911NF-19-2-0150 and W911NF-13-2-0045 (ARL Cyber Security CRA). The views and conclusions contained in this document are those of the authors and should not be interpreted as representing the official policies, either expressed or implied, of the Army Research Laboratory or the U.S. Government. The U.S. Government is authorized to reproduce and distribute reprints for Government purposes notwithstanding any copyright notation herein. Branislav Bosansky was also supported by the Czech Science Foundation (no. 19-24384Y).

ⓒ The Author(s), under exclusive license to Springer Nature Switzerland AG 2023
F. Fang et al. (Eds.): GameSec 2022, LNCS 13727, pp. 44–63, 2023.
https://doi.org/10.1007/978-3-031-26369-9_3

reconnaissance stage in which an adversary collects valuable information regarding the network topologies, structures, node features, and the important assets of the system. To achieve this goal, an attacker may use active sensing techniques and/or passive sensing techniques. The latter can observe traffic between servers and clients to infer information from packet length, packet timing, web flow size, and response delay [2], it is difficult to detect and is invisible to the hosts running the services and can be difficult to be detected by conventional IDS. Active probing attacks send packets to a host and analyze its response. Hence, the attacker learns the system information and vulnerabilities [3]. The active reconnaissance is faster and identifies open and unprotected ports [4]. On the other side, it is more aggressive and intrusive, and hence can be detected. Also, attackers may mix between active and passive attacks during the reconnaissance stage. Game theory provides a suitable framework for modeling attacks and defense against several attacks [5–7].

Cyber Deception: Cyber deception is an emerging proactive cyber defense technology it provides credible yet misleading information to deceive attackers. Deception techniques have been used in the physical space as a classical war technique. However, deception has recently been adopted into cyberspace for intrusion detection and as a defense mechanism [8]. Cyber deception shares some characteristics of non-cyber deception and follows similar philosophical and psychological traits. Successful deception relies on understanding the attacker's intent, tools and techniques, and mental biases. The first step to achieve this deep level of understanding is to act proactively aiming to capture the attacker and exploit the opportunity to monitor her behavior. For that purpose, honeypots are effectively used as fake units in the system/network that deceive the attacker and allow the defender to study her attack strategy, and intent in order to design a better deception scheme.

Honeypots: Among many other techniques, honeypots are widely used for cyber deception. Honeypots are fake nodes that can mislead attackers and waste their resources. They are categorized into two levels, namely low-interaction honeypots and high-interaction honeypots. Low interaction honeypots can memic specific services and are virtualized, and hence they are easier to build and operate than high interaction honeypots. However, they can be detected by adversaries more easily [9].

Attack Graph: An attack graph (AG) is a graph-based technique for attack modeling. Attack modeling techniques model and visualize a cyber-attack on a computer network as a sequence of actions or a combination of events [10]. Attack graphs (trees) are a popular method of representing cyber-attacks. There exist no unique way to instantiate attack graphs, authors in [10] surveyed more than 75 attack graph visual syntax and around 20 attack tree configurations. A key challenge of generating attack graphs is the scalability [11]. None of the existing works has shown that the graph generation tool can scale to the size of an enterprise network. In this work, we consider a simplified attack graph where each node represents a vulnerable host in the network (i.e., it suffers one or more vulnerabilities), and edges on the attack graph represent specific exploits that provide reachability to the attacker from one host to another. In this sense, the graph scale is in the order of the size of the original network. Although this model does not explicitly model each vulnerability in the network, however, it sufficiently illustrates the attack paths that can be exploited by adversaries which are an essential input to generating optimal honeypot allocation policy. However, attack graphs can not directly model zero-day attacks since it remain unknown to the graph generating tool. Therefore, we propose parallel

Zero-Day Attack: The challenge with defending against zero-day attacks is that these attacks exploit a vulnerability that has not been disclosed. There is almost no defense against exploiting such unknown vulnerability [12]. In this work, we leverage attack graphs to model potential zero-day attacks. If the considered network suffers a zero-day vulnerability then the corresponding attack graph will have some edges and hence attack paths that are unknown to the defender. Moreover, zero-day attacks are used for carrying out targeted attacks. To the best of our knowledge, this represents a new framework to proactively defend against zero-day attacks via strategic honeypot allocation based on game theory and attack graphs.

Contributions: In this paper, we propose a cyber deception technique using strategic honeypot allocation under limited deception budget. We consider a game theoretic approach to characterize the honeypot allocation policy over the network attack graph. We then evaluate the deception allocation policy under zero-day attacks by introducing several vulnerabilities to the attack graph and study the sensitivity of the different potential vulnerabilities on the attacker and defender game reward. In our analysis, the defender has no information regarding the zero-day vulnerability. We identify the most impactful vulnerability location and introduce several mitigating strategies to address the possible zero-day attack. The developed game model accounts for the network topology and different importance to each node. We summarize our main contribution below:

- We formulate a deception game between defender and attacker to study the effectiveness of cyber deception against lateral move attacks. The game is played on an attack graph to capture relation between node vulnerabilities, node importance, and network connectivity. We characterize a honeypot allocation policy over the attack graph to place honeypots at strategic locations.
- We evaluate the proposed deception approach against zero-day attack under asymmetric information where the attack graph is not fully known by the defender. We conduct sensitivity analysis to identify critical locations that have major impact on the deception policy in place.
- We present three mitigating strategies against zero-day attacks to readjust the existing honeypot allocation policy based on the conducted analysis.
- Finally, we present numerical results for the developed game model to show the effectiveness of cyber deception as well as the zero-day attack mitigating strategies.

The rest of the paper is organized as follows. We discuss related work in Sect. 2. In Sect. 3, we present the system model, define the game model, and propose our deception approach. In Sect. 5 we present zero-day attack mitigating strategies. Our numerical results is presented in Sect. 6. Finally, we conclude our work and discuss future work in Sect. 7.

2 Related Work

Our research builds upon existing work on cyber deception and games on attack graphs to model zero-day attacks and characterize game-theoretic mitigation strategies.

2.1 Cyber Deception GT

Game theoretic defensive deception [13] has been widely discussed in cybersecurity research. Authors in [14] presented a deception game for a defender who chooses a deception in response to the attacker's observation, while the attacker is unaware or aware of the deception. Authors in [5,15] proposed a signaling game based model to develop a honeypot defense system against DoS attacks. Hypergame theory [16] has been used as an extensive game model to model different subjective views between players under uncertainty. [17] explored hypergames for decision-making in adversarial settings. Authors in [18,19] leveraged hypergames to quantify how a defensive deception signal can manipulate an attacker's beliefs.

2.2 Games on AG

Game Theory (GT) provides a suitable framework to study security problems including cyber deception [20]. Modeling the attacker behavior allows the network admin to better analyze and understand the possible interactions that may take place over cyberspace. Security games are defender-attacker games, the defender allocates a limited set of resources over a set of targets. On other hand, the attacker goal is to attack and gain control over these targets [21]. Resource allocation problems are usually modeled as Stackelberg game where the defender leads the course of play. We consider two-player zero-sum games acting simultaneously, hence the Nash equilibrium of the game coincides with that of the Stackelberg game. Moreover, most of the resource allocation problems considered had no underlying network structure. For the cyber deception problem considered we play a security game on an attack graph which imposes a structure on the players reward function and defines the action space for both players as will be discussed in Sect. 3.

2.3   Zero-Day

A zero-day attack is a cyber attack exploiting a vulnerability that has not been disclosed publicly [12]. Due to the challenges associated with zero-day attacks, authors in [12] conducted systematic study to learn the characteristics of zero-day attacks from the data collected from real hosts and identify executable files that are linked to exploits of known vulnerabilities.

Eder-Neuhauser et al. [22] introduced three novel classes of malware that are suitable for smart grid attacks. Their model provides a basis for the detection of malware communication to predict malware types from existing data. They suggest proper update and segmentation policies for anomaly detection. However, such an approach does not capture the dynamics of zero-day attacks or model its usage in lateral movement attacks.

Al-Rushdan et al. [23] propose zero-day attack detection and prevention mechanism in Software-Defined Networks, prevent zero-days attack based on traffic monitoring. However, in practical zero-day attack incidents alter traffic information to bypass detection systems and traffic monitoring tools. In this work, we take a first step in modeling zero-day attacks in a strategic approach using game theory leveraging the existing work on cyber deception on AGs. We conduct analysis to identify impact of different vulnerabilities and propose zero-day mitigating strategies for several practical scenarios.

3   System Model

We consider a network represented as a graph $G_1(\mathcal{N}, \mathcal{E})$ denote the network graph with a set of nodes $\mathcal{N}$ and edges $\mathcal{E}$. Nodes are connected to each other via edges modeling the reachability and the network connectivity. The defender categorizes the nodes differently according to the node's vitality and functionality. Specifically, there are two distinguishable subsets of nodes, set of entry nodes E and the set of target nodes T, other nodes are intermediate nodes that an attacker needs to compromise along the way from the entry node (attack start node $\in E$) toward a target node $\in T$.

An edge connecting node u and node v, represents an exploitable vulnerability that allows an adversary to launch an attack to reach node v from a compromised node u. In this setting, we adopt a slightly different version of the attack graph introduced in [24]. In other words, in this graph, each node represents a host that suffers one or more vulnerabilities that could be exploited to reach a neighboring node. Hence, the edge models the connecting link that could be used by malicious users to reach the next victim node. A legitimate user at node v, will have the right credentials to reach node u. However, an adversary will only reach u through an exploitable vulnerability. For each node $i \in \mathcal{N}$ we assign a value $v(i)$. Hence, $G_1(\mathcal{N}, \mathcal{E}_1)$ is an attack graph assumed to be known to the defender and the attacker.

A zero-day attack vulnerability is exclusively known to the attacker. The effect of a single zero-day vulnerability is an additional edge. This generates a different attack graph perceived by the attacker solely. Let $G_2(\mathcal{N}, \mathcal{E}_2)$ denote the

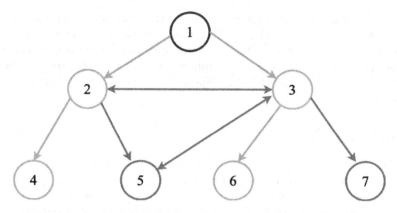

Fig. 1. 7-node tree network topology with single point of entry and two target nodes (5, 7) and zero-day vulnerability (2, 3) and (3, 5).

attack graph induced via zero-day vulnerability e, such that, $\mathcal{E}_2 = \mathcal{E}_1 + e$. The attacker plays a game on the graph with an additional edge(s) representing the zero-day vulnerability. In other words, considering a single zero-day vulnerability at a time, $G_2 = G_1 + \{e\}$, where $\{e\}$ is the new edge due to zero-day vulnerability.

Figure 1 denotes 7-node tree attack graph consists of one entry node(1), 4 intermediate nodes(2,3,4,6) and 2 target nodes(5,6). In this network, one available path for reaching every target nodes. However, with two zero-day vulnerabilities(2,3) and (3,5) increases the available attack path to every target node form attacker perspective.

3.1 Defender Model

The defender allocates one or more honeypots along the network edges as fake vulnerabilities to capture malicious traffic and illegitimate users. Let H denote the honeypot budget. The defender's action is to allocate up to H honeypots over the different edges. Therefore, the defender action space $\mathcal{A}_d = \{\mathbf{e} \in 2^{\mathcal{E}} \mid \mathbf{e}^T 1 \le H\}$. Where, $\mathbf{e}$ is a binary vector of length $|\mathcal{E}|$, such that the ith entry $\mathbf{e}(i) = 1$ indicates a honeypot is allocated along the ith edge, and is set to zero otherwise. The defender incurs a cost associated with each action that takes into account the number of allocated honeypots. Otherwise, the defender will always max out the number of allocated honeypots. Let C_d denote the cost per honeypot. Hence, the total cost is $C_d \times \|a_d\|_1$, where $\|a_d\|_1$ is the number of honeypots allocated by a_d. The defender tries to reduce the attacker reward via placing more honeypots at the edges of high potential that are attractive to attacker, while reducing the total deception cost.

3.2 Attacker Model

The attacker is assumed to launch a targeted attack. Therefore, she selects one of the possible attack paths to reach a target node to maximize his/her expected reward. Hence, the attacker's action space, $\mathcal{A}_a$, is the set of all the possible attack paths starting at an entry node $u \in E$ to a target node $v \in T$. The attacker pays an attack cost that depends on the selected attack path. We consider a cost due to traversing a node in the attack graph denoted by C_a. The attacker faces a tradeoff between traversing through important nodes while reducing his overall attack cost.

3.3   Reward Function

We define the reward function to capture the tradeoff that faces each player. For each action profile played by the defender and attacker $(a_d, a_a) \in \mathcal{A}_d \times \mathcal{A}_a$, the defender receives a reward $R_d(a_d, a_a)$ and the attacker reward is $R_a(a_d, a_a)$. The defender is interested in protecting specific nodes than others. Recall that each node $i \in \mathcal{N}$ is assigned a value $v(i)$ that reflect its importance for the attacker, the defender gains more by protecting high valued nodes. On the other hand, the attacker reward increases when attacking nodes of high values along the selected attack path.

The defender reward is expressed as:

$$R_d(a_d, a_a) = \sum_{i \in a_a} Cap \cdot v(i) \cdot \mathbf{1}_{\{i \in a_d\}} - Esc \cdot v(i) \cdot \mathbf{1}_{\{i \notin a_d\}}$$
$$- C_d \cdot \|a_d\|_1 + C_a(a_a) \tag{1}$$

where Cap denotes the capture reward received by the defender when the attacker hits a honeypot along the selected attack path a_a. Esc is the attacker gain upon successful attack from one node to another in the way toward the target node. Finally, C_d and $C_a(a_a)$ are the cost per honeypot, and attack cost, respectively. The attack cost is proportional to the length of the attack path as the attacker could become less stealthy due to numerous moves. We consider a zero-sum game where $R_a + R_d = 0$. Now we readily define a two-player zero-sum game $\Gamma(\mathcal{P}, \mathcal{A}, \mathcal{R})$, where $\mathcal{P}$ is the set of the two players (i.e., defender and attacker). The game action space $\mathcal{A} = \mathcal{A}_d \times \mathcal{A}_a$ as defined above, and the reward function $\mathcal{R} = (R_d, R_a)$.

Due to the combinatorial nature of the action spaces in terms of the network size, characterizing a Nash equilibrium (NE) in pure strategy is challenging. However, the finite game developed above, holds a NE in mixed strategies. Let $\mathbf{x}_1$ and $\mathbf{y}_1$ denote the mixed strategies of defender, and attacker, when the game is played on known-to-all graph, G_1. The defender expected reward of game 1 (i.e., game on G_1 with no zero-day vulnerabilities) is expressed as:

$$U_d(G_1) = \mathbf{x}_1^T R_d(G_1) \mathbf{y}_1 \tag{2}$$

where $R_d(G_1)$ is the matrix of the game played on G_1 and the attacker expected reward $U_a(G_1) = -U_d(G_1)$. Both defender and attacker can obtain their NE mixed strategies $\mathbf{x}_1^*$ and $\mathbf{y}_1^*$ via a linear program (LP) as follows,

$$\underset{\mathbf{x}}{\text{maximize}} \qquad\qquad\qquad U_d$$

$$\text{subject to} \quad \sum_{a_d \in \mathcal{A}_d} R_d(a_d, a_a) x_{a_d} \geq U_d, \qquad \forall a_a \in \mathcal{A}_a. \tag{3}$$

$$\sum_{a_d \in \mathcal{A}_d} x_{a_d} = 1, \quad x_{a_d} \geq 0,$$

where x_{a_d} is the probability of taking action $a_d \in \mathcal{A}_d$.

Similarly, the attacker's mixed strategy can be obtained through a minimizer LP under $\mathbf{y}$ of U_d.

4   Zero-Day Vulnerability Analysis

We conduct a zero-day vulnerability analysis by modifying the original graph G_1 via considering one vulnerability at a time. The goal of this analysis is to identify the most critical zero-day vulnerability in terms of the impact of each vulnerability to the attacker's reward against a base deception strategy. The base deception strategy is $\mathbf{x}_1$ that is obtained from the game played on G_1. In other words, the attacker expected reward is $U_a(G_1) = \mathbf{x}_1^T R_a(G_1) \mathbf{y}_1$, for any game 1 mixed strategies $\mathbf{x}_1$ and $\mathbf{y}_1$, and $U_a(G_2) = \mathbf{x}_2^T R_a(G_2) \mathbf{y}_2$ for the game played on G_2. The game played under G_1 is referred to as game 1, and the game played on G_2 is referred to as game 2. Where, $\mathbf{x}_2$ and $\mathbf{y}_2$ denote the mixed strategies of the game played on the G_2 graph (i.e., under zero-day vulnerability).

However, x_2 is infeasible in practice for the defender since the defender has no information about the zero-day vulnerability nor its location. However, the attacker's action space expands to contain additional attack paths induced by zero-day vulnerabilities. Each of these vulnerabilities may produce one or more new attack path leading to the target node.

Although the defender does not actually know that the network suffers a zero-day vulnerability at a specific location, he may have the knowledge that such vulnerability exists. Therefore, the attacker is not fully certain that this specific vulnerability is unknown to the defender. The attacker uncertainty regarding the defender knowledge leads to two possible game settings and hence two evaluation criteria as follows:

- The first criterion considers an attacker that uncertain whether his opponent knows about the zero-day vulnerability. In fact, the defender has no such information, yet the attacker accounts for some infeasible defender actions. We refer to this criterion as *'optimistic'*. Hence, the expected game value for the attacker, $U_a^{opt}(G_2) = \hat{\mathbf{x}}_1^T R_a(G_2) \mathbf{y}_2$, where $\hat{\mathbf{x}}_1$ is a mixed strategy adopted from $\mathbf{x}^1$ and padded with zeros to ensure proper matrix multiplication while it zero-enforce infeasible actions for the defender.
- Secondly, we consider a *'pessimistic'* criterion, where the attacker is certain that the defender does not know the zero-day vulnerability. Hence, the defender action space is exactly similar to game 1. The expected reward is $U_a^{pes}(G_2) = \mathbf{x}_1^T R_a(G_2) \mathbf{y}_2$. This pessimistic criterion is referred to as game 3.

Remark 1. Considering one zero-day vulnerability at a time allows the defender to study the impact of each vulnerability separately, reduces the game complexity, and enables parallel analysis by decoupling the dependencies between different vulnerabilities.

As explained above, we augment zeros to $\mathbf{x}_1$ to restrict the defender honeypot allocation strategy and make the defender strategy consistent with the $R_a(G_2)$ matrix.

Let, $\mathbf{x}^1 = [x_0, x_1, x_2, \cdots, x_r]$, and $\hat{\mathbf{x}}_1 = [x_0, x_1, x_2, \cdots, x_r, \cdots, x_n]$. Hence, $\hat{\mathbf{x}}_1 = [\mathbf{x}^1, \cdots, x_n]$, where $n \geq r$, and value of all strategies from x_{r+1} to x_n will be zero after sorting the corresponding actions in $\hat{\mathbf{x}}_1$. For the pessimistic case (i.e., game 3), the defender is forced to play the base deception strategy $\mathbf{x}_1$ in which he also deviates from the NE of game 3.

We solve one game corresponding to each zero-day vulnerability. Assume we have a set of possible zero-day vulnerabilities $\mathcal{E}_0$ such that $G_2(e) = G_1 + e$; $\forall e \in \mathcal{E}_0$. For each game we record the expected attack reward, hence we sort the vulnerabilities to find the most impactful that results in the highest increase of the attacker's reward.

Without loss of generality, assuming the new vulnerability introduced one new pure strategy a_e for the attacker (if $e \in \mathcal{E}_0$ induces more than one new attack path, we select a_e to be the path that has higher reward), then we can establish the following theorem.

Theorem 1. *For the game Γ defined in Sect. 3, given any base policy of the defender $\mathbf{x}$, for the new attacker pure strategy a_e:*

$\mathbf{y}_2[a_e] = 1$; *if* $U_a(\mathbf{x}, s_e) > U_a(\mathbf{x}, \neg a_e)$
$\mathbf{y}_2[a_e] = 0$; *if* $U_a(\mathbf{x}, a_e) < U_a(\mathbf{x}, a_a)$ $\forall a_a \in \text{supp}\{\mathbf{y}_1\}$ *and* $U_a(\mathbf{x}, a_e) < U_a(\mathbf{x}, \mathbf{y}_1)$.

Proof. The proof follows strong dominance definition [25].

In Theorem 1, we characterize two main conditions: (1) when the zero-day vulnerability generates a new attack path that strongly dominates every other existing attack path and (2) when it is being dominated by every path in terms of both pure and mixed strategy.

5   Zero-Day Mitigating Strategies

The defender takes additional actions to mitigate the possible zero-day vulnerability exploits. The performed game-theoretic analysis identifies the impact of each vulnerability, and the attacker's strategy for exploiting such vulnerability. The defender does not know which of the vulnerabilities will take place. However, to mitigate the zero-day attack, the defender allocates an additional honeypot. We consider four different strategies such as impact-based, capture-based, worst case mitigation, and critical point analysis to select the location of the new mitigating honeypot.

5.1 Impact-Based Mitigation (Alpha-Mitigation)

First, we allocate based on the impact of each zero-day vulnerability. The impact measures the increase of the attacker reward due to each introduced vulnerability, $e \in \mathcal{E}_0$, where $\mathcal{E}_0$ is the set of zero-day vulnerabilities. We allocate the new honeypot to combat the most impactful vulnerability such that, $U_a(G_2(e))$ is the highest. The defender may allocate more honeypots following the same order of impact of each $e \in \mathcal{E}_0$. In this mitigating strategy, we assume no information is available to the defender about which vulnerability is introduced. In the next subsection, we consider the probability of each of these vulnerabilities. In Sect. 6, we shed more light on the formation of the set of zero-day vulnerabilities $\mathcal{E}_0$ overcoming the possible explosion in its carnality and applying several rules to exclude dominated elements that are obviously useless or infeasible to the attacker.

5.2 Capture-Based Mitigation (LP-Mitigation)

In the previous strategy (i.e., Alpha-mitigation), the defender does not account for the probability that a zero-day vulnerability may occur. Let $P(e)$ denote the probability that a vulnerability located at edge $e \in \mathcal{E}_0$ exists. The impact of such vulnerability is denoted by $i(e)$, where the impact is the innovation in reward received by the attacker due to exploiting e on $G_1 + \{e\}$ compared to the attacker's reward on G_1. Let $J(x)$ denote the cost function for the defender as follows:

$$J(x) = \sum_{e \in \mathcal{E}_0} P(e) \cdot i(e) \cdot (1 - y(e) \cdot x(e)) \qquad (4)$$

where $y(e)$ is the probability that $e \in \mathcal{E}_0$ is exploited during an attack, and $x(e)$ is the unknown probability to assign honeypot at e.

The goal of the defender is to find $x \in [0,1]^{|\mathcal{E}_0|}$ that minimizes the cost function $J(x)$. This results in a linear program that can be solved efficiently. The outcome of this LP will pick the location e, of the highest impact and most likely to occur (i.e., $argmax_e P(e) \cdot i(e)$). However, since the defender may not know the probability of existence priorly, we consider a worst-case scenario. In other words, we assume that nature will play against the defender and try to minimize its reward. Hence, the defender mitigating strategy should be characterized in response to the selection of the nature that can be obtained by solving a max-min problem as discussed next.

Worst-Case Mitigation (Play Against Nature): After identifying the most impactful vulnerability location or set of vulnerabilities by doing graph analysis defender does not sure about which zero-day vulnerabilities the attacker is going to exploit. Therefore, we do game formulation to find defender mitigating strategies based on the available information of the high impactful locations.

The attacker chooses one vulnerability at a time to exploit and selects a possible attack path associated with that vulnerability. Hence, the attacker's action space, $\mathcal{A}_n$, is the set of all possible zero-day vulnerabilities, and defender action space, $\mathcal{A}_{md}$, is the set of all possible high impacted locations. This problem is formulated as an auxiliary game played between the defender and nature.

For each action profile played by both players $(a_{md}, a_n) \in \mathcal{A}_{md} \times \mathcal{A}_n$, the defender receives a reward $R_{md}(a_{md}, a_n)$ after zero-day attack mitigation and the attacker reward is $R_n(a_{md}, a_n)$. When the attacker selects vulnerability and the defender selected high impact location, does not match the defender's mitigating reward simply comes from the defender expected reward based on which criteria we are following. When they match we just follow Eq. (1) based on which attack path and honeypot allocation are selected by the attacker and defender respectively.

The defender reward is expressed as

$$R_d^{mitigate}(G_1) = \begin{cases} U_d(G_2) \ or \ U_d(G_3) & i \neq j \\ R_d^{mitigate}(a_d^{mitigate}, a_n) & i = j \end{cases}$$

We consider a zero-sum game. Let $\mathbf{x}_{mitigating}$ and $\mathbf{y}_{nature}$ denote the mitigating strategies of defender, and nature mixed strategies, when the game is played on known-to-all graph, G_1. The defender expected reward in worst case mitigation play against nature is expressed as:

$$U_d^{mitigate}(G_1) = \mathbf{x}_{mitigating}^T R_d^{mitigate}(G_1) \mathbf{y}_{nature}$$

where $R_d^{mitigate}(G_1)$ is the matrix of the game played on G_1 and the nature(attacker) expected reward $U_n(G_1) = -U_d^{mitigate}(G_1)$.

This game has played over high impact locations in graph and gives defender mitigating strategies which location to focus for mitigation and nature mixed strategies what location attacker may choose to exploit. After having defender mitigating strategies and nature mixed strategies of the attacker, any mitigation approaches can run and eventually evaluate over it.

5.3 Critical Point Mitigation

Previously, we specified a honeypot to combat zero-day attacks in addition to the honeypots used via the defender's base deception policy. Now aim at modifying the base deception policy itself to combat the zero-day attack given the outcome of our analysis of the impact associated with each zero-day vulnerability. An insightful observation is that the defender tends to greedily deploy honeypots in locations that are closer to the target nodes in the network. However, when the attacker chooses a different path to attack and reach the target node, this approach does not help. It is worth noting that, in defending against zero-day attacks, when the defender selects a location that protects high-degree nodes (this is captured in node values $v(i)$) that belong to multiple attack paths while being far from target nodes, the defender successfully captures the attacker more often. Interestingly, high-impact locations align with high-degree locations to be protected more often following Nash equilibrium deception strategies.

These observations led us to conduct critical point mitigation to find overlapping locations in the graph. In critical point mitigation, we choose one of the high impacted locations which is also an overlapping location where we deploy mitigation. After having critical points we increase the cost of accessing these points, consequently re-run the game on increased cost locations to find updated defender strategies and align optimistic and pessimistic defender strategies based on the updated defender strategies.

In our critical point mitigation, we modify the base policy of the defender, x_1, as we do not deploy additional honeypots. After identifying the most impactful vulnerability locations, we increase node values of the nodes most affected (i.e., neighbors) by such vulnerabilities. This shifts the defender's attention to these locations and in turn, results in a modified base policy (which we refer to as critical point mitigation) that considers the significance of these nodes. We show that critical point mitigation increased the capture rate of attackers when tested in different settings such as increased number of honeypots, different vulnerable entry nodes, and target nodes.

6   Numerical Results

In this section, we present our numerical results to validate the proposed game-theoretic model. We evaluate our analysis of zero-day vulnerability and the proposed mitigating strategies. First, we present game results to identify impact of possible zero-day vulnerabilities for the optimistic and pessimistic defender. Second, we show the results of the proposed deception and mitigation strategies. Finally, we discuss our findings, limitations, and future directions of our current research.

6.1   Experiment

The initial honeypot allocation strategy follows the Nash equilibrium of the game model (game 1). We formulate the problem as a zero-sum game, solve the game defined in Sect. 4 and find the Nash equilibrium in terms of the mixed strategies, x^* and y^*, for the defender and attacker strategies, respectively.

For the analysis of the potential impact of zero-day vulnerabilities, we consider a 20-node network topology with 22 edges shown in Fig. 2. The 20-node network topology shown in Fig. 2 represents an attack graph with multiple root node (i.e., the entry node $\mathcal{E} = \{0, 1, 2\}$). In this scenario we define the set of target nodes as three nodes, $T = \{18, 19, 20\}$.

To form the set of zero-day vulnerabilities $\mathcal{E}_0$, we analyze our 20 nodes network topology. If we consider all possible new edges in the network which is impractical as time complexity is n^2 for n nodes network. Since the vulnerability analysis is independent between different elements in $\mathcal{E}_0$, it can run in parallel computing nodes to reduce the run-time. Moreover, some locations are practically infeasible or useless to the attacker. We implemented a set of rules that excluded useless edges and edges that do not benefit our analysis. For instance, we excluded edges leading to dead-end nodes and edges from nodes that are unreachable from any attack path. Also, direct edges between targets and entry nodes are dominant edges without further analysis.

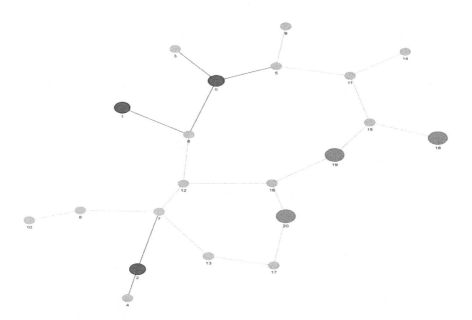

Fig. 2. Network topology of 20 nodes with blue red, and yellow color for entry, target and intermediate nodes respectively (Color figure online)

We compare the Nash equilibrium strategy for honeypot allocation with existing attack policies to illustrate the effectiveness of our proposed cyber deception approach. For that, we observe defender and attacker gain under different conditions. Figure 3 illustrates how defender reward change on several conditions including escape reward of honeypot and capture cost of the attacker.

Figure 3a shows the defender reward against different cost values for escaping a single honeypot in the network over different attack policies. We also compare the Nash equilibrium reward against the greedy and random attacker. A greedy attacker always selects nodes that have the highest values to attack regardless of their cost. A random attacker does not that informed about network that is unable to distinguish between possible attack paths and hence uniformly selects among available attack paths.

When the attacker deviates from equilibrium strategies $\mathbf{y}^*$, such as choosing greedy or random strategies, the defender reward tends to be higher or the same. For low Esc values, defender reward against greedy attacker higher compare to Nash equilibrium which less motivates an attacker to play rational strategies. On the other hand, high Esc values lure the attacker to take more risk in attacking valuable nodes, and as a consequence a gradual decrease in defender reward.

Figure 3b shows a linearly increase in defender reward for different attacker policies. For high cap values, defender reward increases if the attacker deviates from rational strategies.

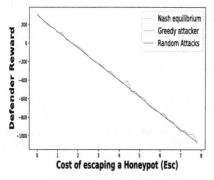 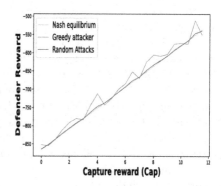

(a) Defender reward versus attacker cost of escaping a honeypot.

(b) Defender reward versus capture cost of attacker.

Fig. 3. Defender reward over different Cap and Esc values.

In addition, we also examine attacker's reward against different defender policies to deceive attacker and protect the network. Figure 4 shows how attacker gain decreases as the number of honeypots increases and its dependence on the entry nodes.

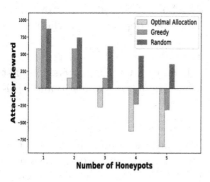 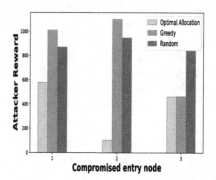

(a) Attacker reward versus the number of honeypots.

(b) Attacker reward versus compromised entry node.

Fig. 4. Attacker reward over different condition such as variation in honeypot number and compromised entry node.

In Fig. 4a we plot the average attack reward for different defender policies on honeypot budgets. We compare the performance of our optimal allocation with the greedy allocation that always allocates honeypots in the path of highest values nodes and random policies where defender uniformly select one node to protect rather than considering network topology analysis. The analysis of Fig. 4a illustrates that the optimal budget of honeypot in this network is three or more honeypots, as it dramatically reduces the effect of the attack. Also deploying 3 or more honeypots is very costly.

In our 20-node network, three entry nodes are compromised at the start of the attack, so the attacker can attack using all possible existing paths in the network starting from any of the compromised entry nodes. We also plot the attacker's reward for a different number of compromised nodes in the network as shown in Fig. 4b over different defender policies. Here greedy and optimal allocation produces the same magnitude result.

Both Fig. 3 and Fig. 4 illustrate that deviating from Nash equilibrium and selecting some naive policies would not be optimal. Developing optimal miti-gating strategies against a well-informed attacker critical for the defender to outperform naive deception policies such as random or greedy policies.

6.2   Impact of Zero-Days Vulnerability

In our analysis, we find out high impact locations (zero-day vulnerabilities) for the 20-node network. We measure the impact of zero-day vulnerability. We con-sider two scenarios, first, when the attacker is certain that the defender does not know zero-day vulnerability. Second, the attacker is not sure whether the defender is aware of these zero-day vulnerabilities.

We also observe some zero-day vulnerabilities increase attacker reward mas-sively and some remain the same compared to the naive defender. It is worth mentioning that some zero-day vulnerabilities also increase attacker reward in both cases, some increase only one scenario, not both depending on the reward function.

In Table 1 we present attacker reward for different high-impact locations against the naive, optimistic, and pessimistic defender. Attacker reward against naive defender is the benchmark, attacker reward against pessimistic and opti-mistic defender defines how impactful that zero-days is.

Attacker Reward Increases: Based on our study, we highlight several rea-sons why certain zero-day vulnerabilities cause high damage to the defender compared to others. First, if a zero-day vulnerability creates multiple attack paths to any or all target nodes, that challenges the defender base-deception policy with limited honeypots in place and hence, causes significant damage. Second, zero-day vulnerabilities that are very close to any target nodes on the attack graph empower the attacker through a shortcut and enhance her reward. Also, a combination of the first two features leads to a significant loss for the defender.

Table 1. Attacker reward against naive defender, optimistic defender, pessimistic defender for top 10 edges

Edge	Naive defender	Optimistic defender	Pessimistic defender
(6, 7)	153.43	401.03	398.70
(5, 7)	153.43	374.65	370.26
(3, 7)	153.43	344.39	345.20
(16, 17)	153.43	326.52	326.52
(12, 13)	153.43	325.54	325.55
(15, 17)	153.43	323.60	323.60
(11, 13)	153.43	322.42	322.42
(11, 17)	153.43	315.72	315.71
(14, 17)	153.43	313.99	313.99
(12, 17)	153.43	307.24	307.23

Attacker Reward Remain Same: Interestingly, not all potential zero-day vulnerabilities cause significant damage to defender in terms of increasing attacker reward. Such zero-day vulnerabilities do not add useful actions to attacker action spaces that benefits the defender, consequently, the defender does not need to take mitigating measures for these types of vulnerabilities. Therefore, these observations benefit the defender to develop proactive defense focusing on most critical vulnerability locations.

6.3 Mitigation

As detailed in Sect. 5, we proposed several approaches to develop mitigating strategies against zero-day attacks. In our approach, the defender goal is to thwart the attacker's progress in the network by observing network information. We present numerical results to show the effectiveness of our mitigating approaches such as measuring proportion under various settings.

In Fig. 5 we show the proportion of attacker capture both for the optimistic and pessimistic defender with impact and linear programming-based mitigation. Figure 5a presents the result of our impact-based mitigation. In our Alpha mitigation, we place honeypot based on the high-impact location whereas random strategies choose a location uniformly to place honeypot. Mitigation effectiveness denotes the percentage of zero-day vulnerabilities defender mitigation (Alpha) prevents among all vulnerabilities. And capture proportion denotes the percentage of time an attacker is captured when exploiting a particular vulnerability.

Figure 5a shows optimistic defender Alpha mitigation with one honeypot has higher mitigation effectiveness compared to random mitigation with one honeypot. On the other hand, the same strategies with 2 honeypots show a higher degree of deviation compared to the previous which denotes an increasing number of honeypots is useful but not a feasible solution.

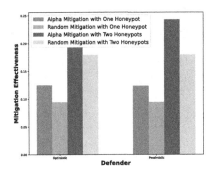

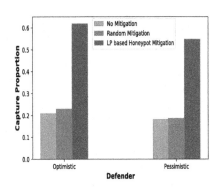

(a) Capture proportion of defender over zero-days vulnerabilities with single and multiple honeypot for both Alpha and random strategies.

(b) Capture proportion of defender with no, random, and LP-based honeypot mitigating strategies.

Fig. 5. Attacker capture proportion over different mitigating strategies of defender including Alpha or LP.

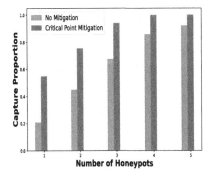

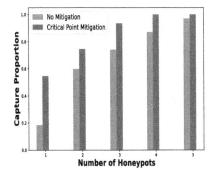

(a) Proportion of capture of attacker versus the number of honeypots by optimistic defender.

(b) Proportion of capture of attacker versus the number of honeypots by pessimistic defender.

Fig. 6. Attacker's capture proportion over different number of honeypots for defender on before and after critical node mitigation.

Figure 5b denotes attacker capture proportion over no, random, and LP-based honeypot mitigation both for the optimistic and pessimistic defender. No-mitigation and random mitigation are very close to each other meaning that randomly allocating honeypots will not bring any gain. After having the probability of allocating mitigating honeypot at different locations by solving a linear program explained in Sect. 5, we place honeypot on the corresponding location(s) and measure the proportion of capture the attacker increases.

In critical point mitigation, we modify the base policy without additional honeypot to take into account the criticality of the most impactful vulnerability.

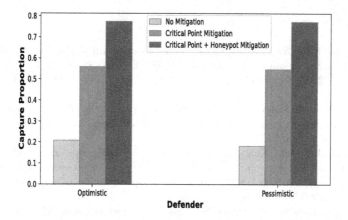

Fig. 7. Capture proportion on critical point based defender mitigation strategies

Figure 6 denotes the capture proportion over the increased number of honeypots for the defender.

Figure 6a shows capture rate increase for both no-mitigation and critical point mitigation strategies at different deception budgets (numbers of honeypots in the base policy). The difference between no and critical point mitigation reduces over the increased number of honeypots, which denotes that the number of honeypots more than three is not useful for mitigation. Figure 6b shows the same result compare to Fig. 6a.

Figure 7 demonstrates capture proportion on different defender mitigation strategies. Critical point mitigation and critical point mitigation with added honeypot outperform no mitigation. It is worth noting that adding one honeypot with critical point mitigation is useful as it increases the proportion of capturing the attacker.

7 Conclusion

In this paper, we proposed a security resource allocation problem for cyber deception against reconnaissance attacks. We proposed a novel framework to assess the effectiveness of cyber deception against zero-day attacks using an attack graph. We formulated this problem as a two-player game played on an attack graph with asymmetric information assuming that part of the attack graph is unknown to the defender. We identified the critical locations that may impact the defender payoff the most if specific nodes suffer a zero-day vulnerability. The proposed analysis is limited to considering a single vulnerability at a time, and focusing on the node location. Our future work will consider a set of vulnerabilities at a time which will follow the proposed analysis while significantly increasing the action space of the game model.

References

1. Yadav, T., Rao, A.M.: Technical aspects of cyber kill chain. In: Abawajy, J.H., Mukherjea, S., Thampi, S.M., Ruiz-Martínez, A. (eds.) SSCC 2015. CCIS, vol. 536, pp. 438–452. Springer, Cham (2015). https://doi.org/10.1007/978-3-319-22915-7_40

2. Schuster, R., Shmatikov, V., Tromer, E.: Beauty and the burst: remote identification of encrypted video streams. In: 26th USENIX Security Symposium (USENIX Security 2017), pp. 1357–1374 (2017)

3. Fu, X., Graham, B., Xuan, D., Bettati, R., Zhao, W.: Empirical and theoretical evaluation of active probing attacks and their countermeasures. In: Fridrich, J. (ed.) IH 2004. LNCS, vol. 3200, pp. 266–281. Springer, Heidelberg (2004). https://doi.org/10.1007/978-3-540-30114-1_19

4. Bansal, G., Kumar, N., Nandi, S., Biswas, S.: Detection of NDP based attacks using MLD. In: Proceedings of the Fifth International Conference on Security of Information and Networks, pp. 163–167 (2012)

5. Çeker, H., Zhuang, J., Upadhyaya, S., La, Q.D., Soong, B.-H.: Deception-based game theoretical approach to mitigate DoS attacks. In: Zhu, Q., Alpcan, T., Panaousis, E., Tambe, M., Casey, W. (eds.) GameSec 2016. LNCS, vol. 9996, pp. 18–38. Springer, Cham (2016). https://doi.org/10.1007/978-3-319-47413-7_2

6. Zhu, Q., Rass, S.: On multi-phase and multi-stage game-theoretic modeling of advanced persistent threats. IEEE Access **6**, 13958–13971 (2018)

7. Anwar, A.H., Kamhoua, C., Leslie, N.: A game-theoretic framework for dynamic cyber deception in Internet of Battlefield Things. In: Proceedings of the 16th EAI International Conference on Mobile and Ubiquitous Systems: Computing, Networking and Services, pp. 522–526 (2019)

8. Wang, C., Zhuo, L.: Cyber deception: overview and the road ahead. IEEE Secur. Priv. **16**(2), 80–85 (2018)

9. Mokube, I., Adams, M.: Honeypots: concepts, approaches, and challenges. In: Proceedings of the 45th Annual Southeast Regional Conference, pp. 321–326 (2007)

10. Lallie, H.S., Debattista, K., Bal, J.: A review of attack graph and attack tree visual syntax in cyber security. Comput. Sci. Rev. **35**, 100219 (2020)

11. Ou, X., Boyer, W.F., McQueen, M.A.: A scalable approach to attack graph generation. In: Proceedings of the 13th ACM Conference on Computer and Communications Security, pp. 336–345 (2006)

12. Bilge, L., Dumitraş, T.: Before we knew it: an empirical study of zero-day attacks in the real world. In: Proceedings of the 2012 ACM Conference on Computer and Communications Security, pp. 833–844 (2012)

13. Zhu, M., Anwar, A.H., Wan, Z., Cho, J.-H., Kamhoua, C.A., Singh, M.P.: A survey of defensive deception: approaches using game theory and machine learning. IEEE Commun. Surv. Tutor. **23**(4), 2460–2493 (2021)

14. Schlenker, A., Thakoor, O., Xu, H., Fang, F., Tambe, M., Vayanos, P.: Game theoretic cyber deception to foil adversarial network reconnaissance. In: Jajodia, S., Cybenko, G., Subrahmanian, V.S., Swarup, V., Wang, C., Wellman, M. (eds.) Adaptive Autonomous Secure Cyber Systems, pp. 183–204. Springer, Cham (2020). https://doi.org/10.1007/978-3-030-33432-1_9

15. Pawlick, J., Zhu, Q.: Deception by design: evidence-based signaling games for network defense. arXiv preprint arXiv:1503.05458 (2015)

16. Fraser, N.M., Hipel, K.W.: Conflict Analysis: Models and Resolutions. North-Holland (1984)

17. Vane, R., Lehner, P.E.: Using hypergames to select plans in adversarial environments. In: Proceedings of the 1st Workshop on Game Theoretic and Decision Theoretic Agents, pp. 103–111 (1999)
18. Ferguson-Walter, K., Fugate, S., Mauger, J., Major, M.: Game theory for adaptive defensive cyber deception. In: Proceedings of the 6th Annual Symposium on Hot Topics in the Science of Security, p. 4. ACM (2019)
19. Cho, J.-H., Zhu, M., Singh, M.: Modeling and analysis of deception games based on hypergame theory. In: Al-Shaer, E., Wei, J., Hamlen, K.W., Wang, C. (eds.) Autonomous Cyber Deception, pp. 49–74. Springer, Cham (2019). https://doi.org/10.1007/978-3-030-02110-8_4
20. Nguyen, T., Yang, R., Azaria, A., Kraus, S., Tambe, M.: Analyzing the effectiveness of adversary modeling in security games. In: Proceedings of the AAAI Conference on Artificial Intelligence, vol. 27, pp. 718–724 (2013)
21. Sinha, A., Fang, F., An, B., Kiekintveld, C., Tambe, M.: Stackelberg security games: looking beyond a decade of success. IJCAI (2018)
22. Eder-Neuhauser, P., Zseby, T., Fabini, J., Vormayr, G.: Cyber attack models for smart grid environments. Sustain. Energy Grids Netw. **12**, 10–29 (2017)
23. Al-Rushdan, H., Shurman, M., Alnabelsi, S.H., Althebyan, Q.: Zero-day attack detection and prevention in software-defined networks. In: 2019 International Arab Conference on Information Technology (ACIT), pp. 278–282. IEEE (2019)
24. Ammann, P., Wijesekera, D., Kaushik, S.: Scalable, graph-based network vulnerability analysis. In: Proceedings of the 9th ACM Conference on Computer and Communications Security, pp. 217–224 (2002)
25. Başar, T., Olsder, G.J.: Dynamic Noncooperative Game Theory, vol. 23. SIAM (1999)

Planning and Learning in Dynamic Environments

On Almost-Sure Intention Deception Planning that Exploits Imperfect Observers

Jie Fu[✉][ID]

University of Florida, Gainesville, FL 32611, USA
fujie@ufl.edu

Abstract. Intention deception involves computing a strategy which deceives the opponent into a wrong belief about the agent's intention or objective. This paper studies a class of probabilistic planning problems with intention deception and investigates how a defender's limited sensing modality can be exploited by an attacker to achieve its attack objective almost surely (with probability one) while hiding its intention. In particular, we model the attack planning in a stochastic system modeled as a Markov decision process (MDP). The attacker is to reach some target states while avoiding unsafe states in the system and knows that his behavior is monitored by a defender with partial observations. Given partial state observations for the defender, we develop qualitative intention deception planning algorithms that construct attack strategies to play against an action-visible defender and an action-invisible defender, respectively. The synthesized attack strategy not only ensures the attack objective is satisfied almost surely but also deceives the defender into believing that the observed behavior is generated by a normal/legitimate user and thus failing to detect the presence of an attack. We show the proposed algorithms are correct and complete and illustrate the deceptive planning methods with examples.

Keywords: Game theory · Deception · Formal methods · Opacity · Discrete event systems

1 Introduction

We study a class of intention deception where an attacker pretends to be a legitimate agent with a benign intention, in order to achieve an adversarial objective without being detected. Such deceptive behaviors are seen in many strategic interactions between players with conflicts. For example, in a cyber network, an attacker who carries out advanced persistent attacks can exploit the limitations of the network monitoring capability and operate in a "low-and-slow" fashion to

Research was sponsored by the Army Research Office and was accomplished under Grant Number W911NF-22-1-0034.

avoid detection [6]. Intention deception is the feature of a masquerade attack [18], in which an attacker uses a fake identity to achieve the attack objective without being detected. The success of the intention deception attacks may depend on three factors: First, the defender has incomplete knowledge about the presence and intention of the attacker; Second, the defender has imperfect information during an active attack and the lack of information imposes limitations to detect the attack; Third, the attacker can strategically hide his intention behind some behavior that is deemed normal/legitimate from the defender's viewpoint.

The synthesis of deception enables us to assess the vulnerabilities of a defense system against stealthy, intention deception attacks and will aid in developing effective detection methods. Motivated by this need, we develop a formal-methods approach to synthesize intention deception attack strategies. We model the interaction between the attacker and the targeted system as a Markov Decision Process (MDP), in which the attacker has a stealthy reach-avoid objective, i.e. , to reach a set of target states *with probability one* without being detected or running into any unsafe states. Meanwhile, the defender employs a detection mechanism based on the promise that any attack behavior will sufficiently deviate from a normal user's behavior and thus can be recognized prior to the success of the attack. Our technical approach is motivated by the following question, "when the defender has an imperfect sensing capability, does the attacker has a stealthy intention deception strategy to achieve the goal, *almost-surely(with probability one)*, while deceiving the defender into thinking his behavior is normal?"

Our main contribution is a class of non-revealing intention deception planning algorithms. Non-revealing deception means that the mark (deceivee) is unaware that deception is being used. Assuming that the state is partially observable to the defender, we study two cases, referred to as action visible and action invisible defenders, depending on whether the defender observes the actions of the agent (either a normal user or an attacker). The two cases differ in how the defender refines her belief based on her observations and also what she considers to be rational actions for a normal user. For each case, we develop an attack planning algorithm which constructs an augmented MDP that incorporates, into the planning state space, the attacker's information and higher-order information—what the attacker knows that the defender's information. We show that the synthesis of an almost-sure winning, non-revealing intention deception strategy reduces to the computation of an almost-sure winning strategy in the augmented MDP. We formally prove the correctness and completeness of the proposed algorithms and illustrate the proposed methods with both illustrative examples and adversarial motion planning examples.

Related Work. Intention deception in MDPs has been investigated by [10]. In their formulation, the optimal deceptive planning is to minimize the Kullback-Leibler (KL) divergence between the (observations of) agent's strategy and (that of) the reference strategy, provided by the supervisor. Comparing to their information-theoretic approaches, our formulation focuses on qualitative planning with intention deception which exploits the partial observations of the defender/supervisor and does not assume that the attacker/defender knows any specific reference strategy except for an intention of a legitimate user. Such a formulation is similar to the work in goal/plan obfuscation [16], in which an agent performs path planning in a deterministic environment while making an observer, equipped with goal recognition algorithms, unable to recognize its goal until the last moment. Recent works on goal obfuscation [3,11,12,19] study how a deceptive agent hides its true goal among finitely many possible decoy goals from an observer. In [16], the authors study deceptive path planning and define the dissimulation (hiding the real) to occur when the planner ensures the probability of reaching the true goal is smaller than the probability of reaching any other decoy goals. This dissimulation does not extend to almost-sure deceptive planning when the agent is to ensure that, the probability of satisfying the normal user's objective is one from the defender's partial observations, while also satisfying the attack objective with probability one. The authors [3] formulate an optimization-based approach for goal obfuscation given uncertainty in the observer's behaviors. Intention deception is also related to opacity-enforcing control for discrete event system [7,9,15,17], where the supervisor is to design a controller that enforces initial state opacity or its target language from an intruder with partial observations. However, the discrete-event system models the deterministic transition systems with controllable and uncontrollable actions, i.e. , two-player deterministic games, while our work considers planning in MDPs, i.e. , one-player stochastic games, monitored by a defender with imperfect observations.

Our problem formulations and solutions are different from existing work in several aspects: 1) we consider probabilistic planning given a partially observable defender, as opposed to deterministic planning in goal obfuscation and path planning. In deterministic planning problems, it does not matter whether the observer observes the agent's actions. This is not the case with probabilistic planning where the deceptive strategies computed against action-visible and action-invisible defenders require different algorithms; 2) The attacker aims to ensure, with probability one, one of the goals is reached and undetected. In addition, the attacker also needs to satisfy some safety constraints before reaching the goal. This objective is different from goal obfuscation where the agent only plans to reach a single goal, but hides its intention behind multiple decoys; 3) Intention deception is also different from opacity. Opacity in discrete event systems means that from the observer's perspective, the observer cannot infer whether a property is true or false, whileas intention deception is to ensure the observation of a strategy given the attack intention can be mistaken as an observation of a strategy given a benign intention.

The paper is structured as follows: In the next section, we introduce the problem formulation. Section 3 presents the main result for synthesizing almost-surely, non-revealing, intention deception attack strategies against two types of defenders (action visible/invisible and state partially invisible). Section 4 illustrates the attack planning algorithms with examples. Section 5 concludes.

2   Problem Formulation

Notations. Let Σ be a finite set of symbols, also known as the *alphabet*. A sequence of symbols $w = \sigma_0\sigma_1\ldots\sigma_n$ with $\sigma_i \in \Sigma$ for any $0 \le i \le n$, is called a *finite word*. The set Σ^* is the set of all finite words that can be generated with alphabet Σ. The length of a word is denoted by $|w|$. Given a finite and discrete set X, let $\mathcal{D}(X)$ be the set of all probability distributions over X. Given a distribution $d \in \mathcal{D}(X)$, let $\text{Supp}(d) = \{x \in X \mid d(x) > 0\}$ be the support of this distribution. The notation $[i..j]$ is an interval of integers between i and j (including i, j.)

We consider the interaction between an agent (pronoun he/him/his)) and a stochastic environment, monitored by a defender (pronoun she/her) with partial observations. There are two classes of agents: One is an attacker and another is a normal user. The stochastic dynamics of the interaction between the agent and his environment is captured by a Markov decision process (without the reward function but a reach-avoid objective).

Definition 1 (Markov decision process (MDP) with a reach-avoid objective). *An MDP with a reach-avoid objective is a tuple $M = \langle S, A, s_0, P, (U, F)\rangle$, where S and A are finite state and action sets, and $A(s)$ is the set of actions enabled at state s, s_0 is the initial state, $P : S \times A \to \mathcal{D}(S)$ is the probabilistic transition function such that $P(s' \mid s, a)$ is the probability of reaching $s' \in S$ given action $a \in A$ is chosen at state $s \in S$. The last component is a pair (U, F) that includes a set $U \subseteq S$ of unsafe states and a set $F \subseteq S\backslash U$ of target/goal states. The reach-avoid objective is defined as $\neg U \,\mathsf{U}\, F$, where U is a temporal operator for "until". It reads "Not U until F" and represents a set of runs $\{s_0 a_0 s_1 \ldots \in \mathsf{Plays}(M) \mid \exists k \ge 0 : s_k \in F \wedge \forall i < k : s_i \notin U \cup F\}$ in which a target state in F is visited at least once and prior to reach a state in F, a state in U is never visited.*

The consideration of reach-avoid objectives is motivated by the fact that for MDPs with more complex objectives described by a subclass of temporal logic formula [13], one can employ a product construction to reduce the planning into an MDP with a reach-avoid objective (see Chap. 10 of [1] and [14]). It is also noted that general goal-reaching objectives (also known as reachability objectives) are special cases of reach-avoid objectives when the unsafe set U is empty. Likewise, the safety objective in which the agent is tasked to avoid a set of states is also a special case of reach-avoid objectives with $F = \emptyset$[1].

A *history* $h = s_0 a_0 s_1 a_1 \ldots s_n$ is an alternating sequence of states and actions, which starts from an initial state and ends in a state and satisfies $P(s_{i+1} \mid s_i, a_i) > 0$ for each $0 < i < n$. Let $H \subseteq (S \times A)^* S$ be the set of finite histories generated from the MDP. A history at time t is a prefix $s_0 a_1 s_1 a_1 \ldots s_{t-1} a_{t-1} s_t$ of a history h. A *path* ρ is a projection of a history onto the state set S, i.e. , for history $h = s_0 a_0 s_1 \ldots s_n$, the path is $\rho = s_0 s_1 \ldots s_n$. The last state of a history

---

[1] In temporal logic, the reachability objective is expressed as $\mathsf{true}\,\mathsf{U}\,F$ and the safety objective is expressed as $\neg(\mathsf{true}\,\mathsf{U}\,U)$.

is denoted $\mathsf{Last}(h)$. The *state-occurrence* function $\mathsf{Occ} : H \to 2^S$ maps a history to a set of states visited by that history, i.e. , $\mathsf{Occ}(s_0 a_0 s_1 a_1 \ldots s_n) = \{s_i \mid i = 0, \ldots, n\}$.

A randomized, finite-memory strategy is a function $\pi : H \to \mathcal{D}(A)$ that maps a history into a distribution over actions. A randomized, Markov strategy is a function $\pi : S \to \mathcal{D}(A)$ that maps the current state to a distribution over actions. Let Π be the set of randomized finite-memory strategies and Π^M be the set of randomized, Markov strategies. We denote $M_\pi = (H, P_\pi, s_0)$ as the stochastic process induced by strategy $\pi \in \Pi$ from the MDP M, where $P_\pi(has' \mid h) = P(s' \mid s, a) \cdot \pi(h, a)$ where s is the last state in the history h.

An *event* E is a measurable set of histories. Given an MDP and a strategy π, the probability of events are uniquely defined. We denote by $\Pr(E; M_\pi)$ the probability of event E occurring in the stochastic process M_π. For a reach-avoid objective $\varphi := \neg U \cup F$, we denote by $\Pr_s(\varphi; M_\pi)$ the probability that φ is satisfied, starting from s given the stochastic process M_π.

Definition 2 (Almost-sure winning strategy and region). *Given an objective φ, a strategy $\pi : H \to \mathcal{D}(A)$ is almost-sure winning for state s if and only if $\Pr_s(\varphi; M_\pi) = 1$. A set of states from which there exists an almost-sure winning strategy is called the* almost-sure winning region, *denoted* ASW. *Formally,* $\mathsf{ASW}(\varphi) = \{s \in S \mid \exists \pi \in \Pi : \Pr_s(\varphi; M_\pi) = 1\}$.

It is known that for MDPs with reach-avoid objectives, Markov strategies can be sufficient for almost-sure winning. We provide an algorithm to compute the Almost-Sure Winning (ASW) Markov strategy in the Appendix.

For simplicity, we introduce a function called the "post", defined as follows: For a subset $X \subseteq S$ of states and an action $a \in A$, $\mathsf{Post}(X, a) = \{s \in S \mid \exists s' \in X, P(s \mid s', a) > 0\}$, which is the set of states that can be reached by action a with a positive probability from a state in the set X.

The Attacker's and User's Objectives. The attacker's reach-avoid objective is given by $\varphi_1 := \neg U_1 \cup F_1$ and the user's objective is given by $\varphi_0 := \neg U_0 \cup F_0$, where $U_i, F_i \subseteq S$, $i = 1, 2$.

We refer an attacker and a normal user as an *agent* and consider the setting when the agent's activities are monitored by a supervisor/defender, who has however imperfect observations. Specifically, the defender's observation is defined by his observations of states and actions of the agent:

Definition 3 (State-observation function). *The state-observation function of the defender is* $\mathsf{DObs}_S : S \to 2^S$ *that maps a state s to a set $\mathsf{DObs}_S(s)$ of states that are observation equivalent to s. For any $s' \in \mathsf{DObs}_S(s)$, it holds that $\mathsf{DObs}_S(s') = \mathsf{DObs}_S(s)$.*

The observation equivalence relation defined by DObs_S forms a partition over the state set S. For the observation function to be properly defined, it holds that $s \in \mathsf{DObs}(s)$ for any $s \in S$. The following standard assumption is made.

Assumption 1. *For any state $s' \in \mathsf{DObs}_S(s)$ that $s \neq s'$, the sets of enabled actions satisfy $A(s) = A(s')$.*

That is, if two states are observation equivalent, then the agent have the same set of actions enabled from these two states. Similarly, We define the action-observation function.

Definition 4 (Action-observation function). *The action-observation function of the defender* $\mathsf{DObs}_A : A \rightarrow 2^A$ *maps an action* a *to a set of actions observation equivalent to* a. *For any* $a' \in \mathsf{DObs}_A(a)$, *it holds that* $\mathsf{DObs}_A(a') = \mathsf{DObs}_A(a)$.

In the scope of this work, we restrict to two special cases with action observation: 1) The defender is *action invisible* if she cannot observe which action is taken by the agent. In this case, $\mathsf{DObs}_A(a) = A$—that is, all actions generate the same observation and are indistinguishable. 2) Otherwise, the defender is said to be *action visible* and $\mathsf{DObs}_A(a) = \{a\}$. These two classes of action observation functions are commonly considered in qualitative analysis of partially observable stochastic systems [4].

We combine the state observation and action observation functions into a single observation function $\mathsf{DObs} : A \times S \rightarrow 2^A \times 2^S$ such that $\mathsf{DObs}(a, s) = (\mathsf{DObs}_A(a), \mathsf{DObs}_S(s))$. The observation function extends to histories of the MDP recursively, that is, given a history $h = s_0 a_0 s_1 a_1 \ldots s_n$, the defender's observation history is $\mathsf{DObs}(h) = \mathsf{DObs}_S(s_0)\mathsf{DObs}_A(a_0) \ldots \mathsf{DObs}_S(s_n)$.

3   Main Results

We are interested in the following question: Given an attacker who aims to achieve an attack objective in the MDP, does he has a strategy to do so while the defender, who observes his behaviors, mistakes the attacker as a normal user? If the answer is affirmative, the strategy used by the attacker is called *non-revealing, intention deception strategy*. We investigate the problem for both action-invisible and action-visible defenders, with partial state observations.

3.1   Nonrevealing Intention Deception Attack Planning Against Action-Visible Defender

The following information structure is considered for the attacker, the normal user, and the defender.

Information Structure: An Action-Visible Defender Against an Attacker with Perfect Information. 1) Both the attacker and the defender know the user's objective φ_0. 2) The defender does not know the attacker's objective φ_1. 3) The defender has partial observations over states, defined by the state-observation function $\mathsf{DObs}_S : S \rightarrow 2^S$ and is *action visible*.

Definition 5 (Observation-equivalent histories and strategies). *Two histories* h, h' *are observation equivalent if and only if* $\mathsf{DObs}(h) = \mathsf{DObs}(h')$.

Two strategies π_0, π_1 are qualitatively observation-equivalent *if and only if the following condition holds:*

$$\forall h \in H, \Pr(h; M_{\pi_0}) > 0 \implies$$
$$\exists h' \in H, (\mathsf{DObs}(h') = \mathsf{DObs}(h)) \text{ and } \Pr(h'; M_{\pi_1}) > 0,$$

and vice versa.

Intuitively, for an attacker's strategy to be qualitatively observation equivalent to a user's strategy, it means that when the attacker carries out his attack strategy, for any history h with a nonzero probability to be generated, there is an observation-equivalent history h' that has a nonzero probability to be generated by the user's strategy.

The reason for us to define the observation equivalence in this manner is because for qualitative planning with the almost-sure winning objective, the planner only needs to reason about whether a history has a positive probability to be sampled but not the exact probability. This is due to the following property of almost-sure winning strategy.

Proposition 1. *Let π be an ASW strategy in the MDP $M = \langle S, A, s_0, P, (U, F) \rangle$ with reach-avoid objective, for any history h such that $\Pr(h, M_\pi) > 0$ and $\mathsf{Occ}(h) \cap F = \mathsf{Occ}(h) \cap U = \emptyset$, $\Pr(\exists h' \in (A \times S)^* : \mathsf{Occ}(hh') \cap F \neq \emptyset$ and $\mathsf{Occ}(hh') \cap U = \emptyset; M_\pi) = 1$.*

In words, any finite history with a positive probability to be sampled in M_π will have a suffix that visits a state in F while avoiding U. It directly follows from the definition of almost-sure winning strategy (see also [2]).

Based on Definition 5, we now define formally the attacker's non-revealing, intention-deception, ASW strategy.

Definition 6. *An attack strategy π_1^* is called* non-revealing intention deception, ASW strategy *if and only if it satisfies the following conditions: 1) π_1^* is qualitatively observation-equivalent to an ASW strategy π_0 of the user in the MDP M with the objective φ_0. 2) π_1^* is almost-sure winning in the MDP M with the objective φ_1.*

Note that the user may have multiple (potentially infinite, randomized) ASW strategies. Thus, instead of following a specific user's ASW strategy, the attacker would like to know what set of actions will be rational for the user in any ASW strategy. This brings us to define the set of permissible actions.

Definition 7 (Permissible Actions). *Given an MDP M with a reach-avoid objective $\varphi := \neg U \cup F$, for $s \in \mathsf{ASW}(\varphi)$, an action $a \in A(s)$ is permissible if there exists an ASW strategy $\pi : S \to \mathcal{D}(A)$ such that $\pi(s, a) > 0$.*

Lemma 1. *Given an MDP M with a reach-avoid objective $\varphi = \neg U \cup F$, for $s \in \mathsf{ASW}(\varphi)$, action $a \in A(s)$ is permissible only if $\mathsf{Post}(s, a) \subseteq \mathsf{ASW}(\varphi)$.*

In words, a permissible action ensures the agent stay within his almost-sure winning region.

Let Allowed : $S \to 2^A$ be a function defined by $\mathsf{Allowed}(s) = \{a \in A(s) \mid \mathsf{Post}(s, a) \subseteq \mathsf{ASW}(F)\}$.

Proposition 2. *Given MDP M with a reach-avoid objective $\varphi := \neg U \cup F$, a Markov strategy $\pi : \mathsf{ASW}(\varphi) \to \mathcal{D}(A)$ that satisfies $Supp(\pi(s)) = \mathsf{Allowed}(s), \forall s \in \mathsf{ASW}(\varphi)$, is almost-sure winning.*

The proof is in the Appendix. With this proposition, we will allow the attacker to "hide" his attack strategy behind a user's ASW strategy by calculating the permissible actions for the user. We denote by $\mathsf{Allowed}_0$ the function that maps a state to a set of user's permissible actions.

Next, we construct an MDP with augmented state space for synthesizing a non-revealing, intention deception, ASW strategy for the attacker.

Definition 8 (Attacker's deceptive planning against action-visible defender). *Given the MDP M and two objectives $\varphi_0 = \neg U_0 \cup F_0, \varphi_1 = \neg U_1 \cup F_1$ capturing the normal user and attacker's objectives, respectively. The following augmented MDP is constructed:*

$$\tilde{M} = \langle S \times 2^S, A, \tilde{P}, (s_0, \mathsf{DObs}_S(s_0)), (\tilde{U}_1, \tilde{F}_1) \rangle,$$

where

- *$S \times 2^S$ is a set of states. A state (s, B), where $B \subseteq S$, consists of a state s in the original MDP M and a belief $B \subseteq S$ of the defender about the state from past observations;*
- *The transition function $\tilde{P}$ is constructed as follows. For $(s, B) \in S \times 2^S$ and $B \neq \emptyset$, if there exists $s^o \in B$, $a \in \mathsf{Allowed}_0(s^o)$, then for each state $s'' \in \mathsf{Post}(s, a)$, let $\tilde{P}((s'', B')|(s, B), a) = P(s''|s, a)$ where*

$$B' = \bigcup_{s^o \in B: a \in \mathsf{Allowed}_0(s^o)} \{s' \mid s' \in \mathsf{Post}(s^o, a) \text{ and } \mathsf{DObs}_S(s') = \mathsf{DObs}_S(s'')\}.$$

(1)

For any $s \in S$, any $a \in A(s)$, let $\tilde{P}((s, \emptyset)|(s, \emptyset), a) = 1$.
- *$(s_0, \mathsf{DObs}_S(s_0))$ is the initial augmented state.*
- *$\tilde{U}_1 = \{(s, X) \mid s \in U_1, X \subseteq S, X \neq \emptyset\} \cup \{(s, \emptyset) \mid s \in S\}$ and $\tilde{F}_1 = F_1 \times (2^S \setminus \emptyset)$ are the set of unsafe states and the set of target states in the augmented MDP for the attacker, respectively. The attacker's objective is a reach-avoid objective $\neg \tilde{U}_1 \cup \tilde{F}_1$.*

The transition function in $\tilde{M}$ is well-defined because given the next state, the observation is determined and thus the new belief given the state and action observations is determined.

The second component of an augmented state represents the defender's belief given past observations. The probabilistic transition function is understood as follows: Consider the defender holds a belief B about the current state, and observes that action a is taken. Then, for each state $s^o \in B$, the defender considers if a is a permissible action at s^o. If the answer is yes, then the defender will compute the set of reachable states from s^o given a using $\mathsf{Post}(s^o, a)$ and removes a subset of reachable states that are not consistent with the observation generated by the actually reached state s''. In this process, the defender eliminates some states in B for which the action a is not permissible, under the rationality assumption for the normal user.

Finally, the objective is defined using an unsafe set $\tilde{U}_1$. By definition, if any state in $\tilde{U}_1$ is reached, then either 1) the attacker reaches an unsafe state $s \in U_1$ in the original MDP and thus violate the reach-avoid objective; or 2) the defender's belief given past observation becomes an empty set. This means the defender knows the observed behavior is not a normal user's behavior. Thus, $(s, \emptyset)$ is a sink state. Once a sink $(s, \emptyset)$ is reached, the attack is revealed.

Given the augmented MDP $\tilde{M}$ and the attack objective $\neg \tilde{U}_1 \cup \tilde{F}_1$, we can compute an ASW strategy $\tilde{\pi}_1 : S \times 2^S \to \mathcal{D}(A)$ such that for any state (s, B) where $\tilde{\pi}_1$ is defined, by following $\tilde{\pi}_1$, the attacker can ensure a state in $\tilde{F}$ is reached with probability one. It is observed that $\tilde{\pi}_1$ cannot be reduced to a Markov strategy in the original MDP because for the same state, say s, but different belief states $B \neq B'$, $\tilde{\pi}_1(s, B)$ may not equal $\tilde{\pi}_1(s, B')$. As the size of belief states is finite, the attack strategy $\tilde{\pi}_1$ can be viewed as a finite-memory strategy in the original MDP, with memory states as the defender's belief states. The finite-memory strategy induces a stochastic process $M_{\tilde{\pi}_1}$ from the original MDP.

Theorem 1. *An intention deception, non-revealing, almost-sure winning strategy for the attacker is the ASW strategy in the augmented MDP $\tilde{M}$ with reach-avoid objective $\neg \tilde{U}_1 \cup \tilde{F}_1$.*

Proof. We show that the ASW strategy $\tilde{\pi}_1 : S \times 2^S \to \mathcal{D}(A)$ obtained from the augmented MDP is qualitatively observation-equivalent to an ASW strategy for the user, as per Definition 6 and Definition 5.

Consider a history $h = s_0 a_0 s_1 a_1 \ldots s_n$ which is sampled from the stochastic process $M_{\tilde{\pi}_1}$ and satisfies $s_i \notin F_1 \cup U_1$ for $0 \le i < n$ and $s_n \in F_1$. The history is associated with a history in the augmented MDP,

$$\tilde{h} = (s_0, B_0)a_0(s_1, B_1)a_1 \ldots (s_n, B_n),$$

where $B_0 = \mathsf{DObs}_S(s_0)$ is the initial belief for the defender. Due to the construction of the augmented MDP, for all $0 \le i \le n - 1$, $B_i \neq \emptyset$. Otherwise if there exists $i = 1, \ldots, n - 1$, $B_i = \emptyset$, then $\tilde{F}_1$ will not be reached because state $(s, \emptyset)$ for any $s \in S$ is a sink state. By the definition of qualitatively observation-equivalence, we only need to show that there exists a history $h' = s'_0 a_0 s'_1 a_1 \ldots s'_n$ where $s'_i \in B_i, i = 0, \ldots, n$, such that $\Pr(h'; M_{\pi_0}) > 0$ where M_{π_0} is the Markov chain induced by a user's ASW strategy π_0 from the MDP M.

Suppose, for any state-action sequence $h' = s'_0 a_0 s'_1 a_1 \ldots s'_n$ where $s'_i \in B_i$ for $0 \le i \le n$, it holds that $\Pr(h'; M_{\pi_0}) = 0$. When $\Pr(h'; M_{\pi_0}) = 0$, there are two possible cases: First case: there exists some $i \ge 0$ such that for all $s \in B_i$,

$a_i \notin \mathsf{Allowed}_0(s)$; second case: for any $s \in B_i$ that $a_i \in \mathsf{Allowed}_0(s)$, there does not exist $s' \in B_{i+1}$ such that $P(s'|s, a_i) > 0$.

Clearly, the first case is not possible because in that case, no transition will be defined for action a_i given the belief B_i (See (1)) and thus $B_{i+1} = \emptyset$. It contradicts the fact that $B_{i+1} \neq \emptyset$. In the second case, it holds that $\mathsf{Post}(s, a_i) \cap B_{i+1} = \emptyset$ for any $s \in B_i$. However, by construction, we have $B_{i+1} = \bigcup_{s \in B_i, a_i \in \mathsf{Allowed}_0(s)} \mathsf{Post}(s, a_i) \cap \mathsf{DObs}_S(s_{i+1})$ and thus $B_{i+1} \subseteq \bigcup_{s \in B_i, a_i \in \mathsf{Allowed}_0(s)} \mathsf{Post}(s, a_i)$. If $\mathsf{Post}(s, a_i) \cap B_{i+1} = \emptyset$ for any $s \in B_i$, then it is only possible that $B_{i+1} = \emptyset$, which is again a contradiction.

Combining the analysis of these two cases, we show that there exists such a history h' such that $\mathsf{DObs}(h) = \mathsf{DObs}(h')$ and $\Pr(h'; M_{\pi_0}) > 0$. As the history h is chosen arbitrarily, it holds that for any history sampled from $M_{\tilde{\pi}_1}$, we can find an observation-equivalent history that has a non-zero probability to be generated in the Markov chain M_{π_0}.

3.2 Non-revealing Intention Deception Against Action-Invisible Defender

We anticipate that the attacker have more advantages in non-revealing intention deception if the defender is action-invisible. To this end, we construct the attacker's planning problem against an action-invisible defender. The information structure is similar to that for the action-visible defender, except the defender cannot observe the attacker/user's actions.

Definition 9 (Attacker's deceptive planning against action-invisible defender). *Given the MDP M and φ_0, φ_1 capturing the user's and attacker's objectives, respectively. Assuming that the defender is action invisible and partially observes the states, the attacker constructs the following augmented MDP:*

$$\widehat{M} = \langle S \times 2^S, A, \widehat{P}, (s_0, \mathsf{DObs}_S(s_0)), (\widehat{U}_1, \widehat{F}_1) \rangle,$$

where

- *$S \times 2^S$ is a set of states. A state (s, B), where $B \subseteq S$, consists of a state s in the original MDP M and a belief $B \subseteq S$ of the defender about the state from past observations;*
- *The transition function $\widehat{P}$ is constructed as follows. For $(s, B) \in S \times 2^S$, If $\bigcup_{s^o \in B} \mathsf{Allowed}_0(s^o) \neq \emptyset$, then for each action $a \in \left(\bigcup_{s^o \in B} \mathsf{Allowed}_0(s^o) \right) \cap A(s)$, let $\widehat{P}((s'', B')|(s, B), a) = P(s''|s, a)$ where the new belief B' is computed as*

$$B' = \bigcup_{s^o \in B} \{ s' \mid \exists a^o \in \mathsf{Allowed}_0(s^o).\ s' \in \mathsf{Post}(s^o, a^o)$$

$$\text{and } \mathsf{DObs}_S(s') = \mathsf{DObs}_S(s'') \}. \quad (2)$$

Note that action a^o does not necessarily equal action a.
If $\bigcup_{s^o \in B} \mathsf{Allowed}_0(s^o) = \emptyset$, $\widehat{P}((s, \emptyset)|(s, B), a) = 1$, and $\widehat{P}((s, \emptyset)|(s, \emptyset), a) = 1$ for any $a \in A(s)$.

- $(s_0, \mathsf{DObs}_S(s_0))$ *is the initial augmented state.*
- $\widehat{U}_1 = \{(s, X) \mid s \in U_1, X \subseteq S, X \neq \emptyset\} \cup \{(s, \emptyset) \mid s \in S\}$ *and* $\widehat{F}_1 = F_1 \times (2^S \setminus \emptyset)$ *is a set of unsafe states and target states in the augmented MDP for the attacker. The attacker's objective is a reach-avoid objective* $\neg \widehat{U}_1 \cup \widehat{F}_1$.

The main difference between the augmented MDP $\widetilde{M}$ and $\widehat{M}$ is in the definition of the transition function: For action-invisible defender, its belief update takes into account of all possible and permissible actions for a normal user, and the observation of that reached state. For action-visible defender, the belief update will be employ the action observation.

Theorem 2. *An intention deception, non-revealing, almost-sure winning strategy for the attacker is the ASW strategy in the augmented MDP* $\widehat{M}$ *with the reach-avoid objective* $\neg \widehat{U}_1 \cup \widehat{F}_1$.

The proof is similar to that of the action visible defender case and thus omitted. The reader can find the complete proof in the Appendix.

It is not difficult to see the following statement holds.

Lemma 2. *Any non-revealing intention-deception ASW attack strategy against an action-visible defender is a non-revealing intention-deception ASW attack strategy against an action-invisible defender.*

Proof (Sketch of the proof). If the defender cannot detect a deviation from the user's strategy given the observations of states and the actions, he cannot detect such a deviation when he has no action information.

Remark 1. It is noted that the qualitative objective for almost-sure winning does not consider the cost/time it takes for the attacker to achieve the objective. The ASW strategy is not unique (See Proposition 2). Therefore, additional planning objectives can be considered to compute an ASW strategy, such as, minimizing the expected number of steps or total cost to reach the target set while avoiding unsafe states.

3.3   Complexity Analysis

The time complexity of ASW strategy in an MDP is polynomial in the size of the MDP [2,8]. Therefore, the computation of nonrevealing intention deception ASW strategy for either action-visible or action-invisible defender is polynomial in the size of the augmented MDP and thereby exponential in the original MDP due to the subset belief construction. This is expected for qualitative analysis of partially observable stochastic games on graphs [4,5].

4   Examples

This section includes a number of illustrative examples and examples with real-world security applications to demonstrate the methods.

4.1 Illustrative Examples

We first use an illustrative example, shown in Fig. 1 to show the construction of deceptive policies. In this example, the attacker is to reach $F_1 = \{f_1\}$ and the user is to reach set $F_0 = \{f_0\}$, where the unsafe sets U_0 and U_1 are empty. The edges are labeled with actions that triggers a probabilistic transition. For example, if action a is taken at state 2, then the next state is either 2 or 3, with some positive probabilities. For clarity, we omitted the exact probabilities on these transitions in Fig. 1. States f_0, f_1 are sink states. First, we synthesize the user's ASW region (see Algorithm in the supplement) to compute the permissible actions for each state: $\mathsf{Allowed}_0(1) = \{a, b\}$, $\mathsf{Allowed}_0(2) = \{a, b\}$, $\mathsf{Allowed}_0(3) = \{a\}$, and $\mathsf{Allowed}_0(4) = \{a\}$. It can be shown that at each state, if the user takes an allowed action with a positive probability, he can reach f_0 with probability one. Clearly, if the attacker does not play intention detection, he will select action b from state 3 to reach f_1 directly, but also reveal himself to the defender, had the defender knows that the current state is 3 and is action-visible.

Deceiving an Action-Visible Defender. We construct the augmented MDP according to Definition 8 and solve the non-revealing deceptive attack policy. The transitions in the augmented MDP in Fig. 2 is understood as follows: Consider for example the state $(2, \{2\})$ which means the current state is 2 and the defender's belief is $\{2\}$. When the defender observes action a being taken, he can deduce that the next state can be either 2 or 3. The transitions $(2, \{2\}) \xrightarrow{a} (2, \{2, 3\})$ and $(2, \{2\}) \xrightarrow{a} (3, \{2, 3\})$ describe the probabilistic outcomes to reach states 2 and 3, and the defender's belief is updated to $\{2, 3\}$. At state $(3, \{2, 3\})$, if the action b is taken, then the only possible next state is f_1. However, because the defender does not know the exact state (3 in this case), she observes $\{4, f_1\}$ and thinks the behavior is still normal if the current state is 2. This is because state 4 is still in the ASW region for the user.

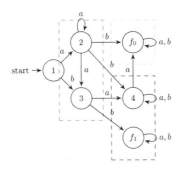

Fig. 1. An MDP without reward. Each box includes a set of observation-equivalent states.

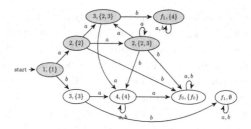

Fig. 2. The augmented MDP for attack planning against an action-visible defender. The red notes are the attacker's ASW region for nonrevealing intention deception. (Color figure online)

However, if action b is observed at the state $(3, \{3\})$, then with probability one, the next state is $(f_1, \emptyset)$, which is a sink state. The reason for the second component to be $\emptyset$ is because action b is not permissible from 3 for the user. Similarly, when action b is taken from $(3, \{2, 3\})$, the next state is $(f_1, \{4\})$ because $b \in \mathsf{Allowed}_0(2)$, $\mathsf{Post}(2, b) \cap \mathsf{DObs}_S(f_1) = \{f_0, 4\} \cap \{4, f_1\} = \{4\}$. This is an interesting case where the defender's belief no longer contains the true state. The reason for this to happen is that the defender assumes that only permissible actions will be taken by a user.

Next, we compute the ASW policy for the attacker in the augmented MDP given the goal to reach $(f_1, \{4\})$. The policy is the following: $\pi((3, \{2, 3\})) = b$, $\pi(2, \{2, 3\}) = \pi(2, \{2\}) = a$, and $\pi((1, \{1\})) = a$. The red nodes are the attacker's ASW region for intention deception. This policy ensures the state f_1 will be reached with probability one and from the defender's partial observation, the behavior is possible for a normal user. For example, a history h can be $1 \xrightarrow{a} 2 \xrightarrow{a} 2 \xrightarrow{b} 4$, which is consistent with the defender's observation and the user's policy. It is a prefix of a history $1 \xrightarrow{a} 2 \xrightarrow{a} 2 \xrightarrow{b} 4 \xrightarrow{a} f_0$ that reaches f_0. The true history h^* is $1 \xrightarrow{a} 2 \xrightarrow{a} 3 \xrightarrow{b} f_1$, which is observation equivalent to h.

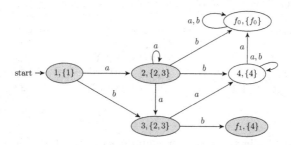

Fig. 3. The augmented MDP for attack planning against an action-invisible defender. The red nodes are the attacker's ASW region for intention deception. (Color figure online)

Deceiving an Action-Invisible Defender. We construct the augmented MDP according to Definition 9. The transition in the augmented MDP in Fig. 3 is understood as follows: Consider for example the state $(1, \{1\})$, $\widehat{P}((3, \{2,3\}) \mid (1, \{1\}), b) > 0$, where 2 is included in the belief is because the action a is allowed at 1 for user and with that action, 2 can be reached with a positive probability and $\mathsf{DObs}_S(2) = \mathsf{DObs}_S(3)$. Note that states $(2, \{2\})$ and $(3, \{3\})$ are not reachable in the action-invisible case because the defender cannot observe if action a or b is taken at the initial state. One of the attacker's ASW deceptive policy is $\hat{\pi}_1((1, \{1\})) = b$ and $\hat{\pi}_1((3, \{2,3\})) = b$. When the attacker commits to this policy, the observation obtained by the defender is $\{1\}, \{2,3\}, \{4\}$, for which the following history $1 \xrightarrow{b} 3 \xrightarrow{a} 4$ is possible and may be generated by an ASW user policy as from state 4, the user can still reach f_0 with probability one by taking action a. It is interesting to see that this non-revealing ASW policy for the attacker would be revealing if the defender is action-visible.

4.2 Intention Deception Planning Against a Security Monitoring System

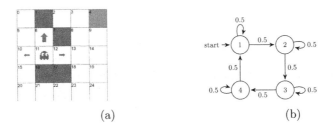

Fig. 4. (a) A stochastic gridworld. (b) The probabilistic sensor scheduler.

State	Coverage	State	Coverage	State	Coverage
1	$\{0,1,2,3,4\}$	1	$\{5,6,7,8,9\}$	1	$\{0,1,2,5,6,7\}$
2	$\{3,8,13,18,23\}$	2	$\{3,8,13,18,23\}$	2	$\{22,23,24\}$
3	$\{15,16,17,18,19\}$	3	$\{5,6,7,8,9\}$	3	$\{0,1,2,5,6,7\}$
4	$\{1,6,11,16,21\}$	4	$\{3,8,13,18,23\}$	4	$\{22,23,24\}$
(a)		(b)		(c)	

Fig. 5. Sensor configurations (a), (b), (c).

We now use another example to demonstrate the applications of the methods in security applications. Consider a stochastic gridworld environment shown in Fig. 4a in which an agent (a user or an attacker, shown as the red ghost) is to achieve some reach-avoid objective. The agent has four actions: "up", "down", "left", "right". For each cell $s \in S$, after taking an action, the robot transits to the *correct* cell with probability p and slips to unintended cells with probability $1 - p$. As illustrated in the figure: When the agent decides to go "up", with probability p, it reaches the intended cell 6, and with $\frac{1-p}{2}$ probability to reach 10 and 12, respectively. Red cells are obstacles. If the agent runs into an obstacle, it gets stuck. The environment is surrounded by bouncing walls. If the agent takes an action and hits a wall, then the agent stays in the original cell.

The environment is monitored by a sensor network with a randomized schedule shown in Fig. 4b. The monitoring system runs a finite-memory probabilistic scheduler with four states: $Q = \{1, 2, 3, 4\}$ with the probabilistic transition dynamics shown in Fig. 4b. At every time step, the scheduler has a 50% chance of staying in the same state for next time step and 50% chance of switching to a different state. At each state $q \in Q$, the sensor coverage is given by $\gamma(q)$. We consider two types of sensors: 1) type (B) is a Boolean sensor that returns true if the agent's state is in the coverage. For example, if $\gamma(1) = \{5, 6, 7, 8, 9\}$, then under the sensor state 1, if the agent is in one of the cells in $\gamma(1)$, the sensor returns true. Otherwise, the sensor returns false. 2) Type (P) is a precise range sensor that returns the exact agent's state if the agent's state is in the coverage. For example, if $\gamma(1) = \{5, 6, 7\}$ and the agent is in state 5 and the sensor is in state 1, then the sensor returns $\{5\}$. Different sensor types and coverages as well as different finite memory schedulers will generate numerous sensor configurations for the defender to obtain the state information of the agent. We consider three sensor configurations (different coverages but the same scheduler) in Table 5a, 5b, and 5c. The configurations $(b), (c)$ have essentially two sensors that are switched on and off probabilistically. We assume that the defender knows the agent's state at the beginning of the game.

User's and Attacker's Intentions: The user's objective is to avoid obstacles and state 4 until the goal 0 is reached, i.e. , $\varphi_0 := \neg U_0 \cup F_0$ where $U_0 = \{1, 7, 16, 17, 4\}$ and $F_0 = \{0\}$. The attacker's objective is to avoid obstacle until the goal $\{4\}$ is reached, i.e. , $\varphi_1 := \neg U_1 \cup F_1$ where $U_1 = \{1, 7, 16, 17\}$ and $F_1 = \{4\}$. Given that the two objectives conflict with each other, $\varphi_0 \wedge \varphi_1 = $ false, if the defender has complete observations over the state space, regardless action visible or not, the defender should be able to detect the attacker.

To illustrate the exploitability of such a sensor network, we sample a number of sensor configurations and investigate when the attacker has an intention deception strategy in each of the configurations. The result is concluded in Table 1[2]. The sensor configuration id is shown as (x)-Y-Z where $x \in \{a, b, c\}$ represents to the sensor coverage configurations in Fig. 5, $Y \in \{B, P\}$ represents if the sensor type is Boolean (B) or precise (P), and $Z \in \{I, V\}$ represents if action is invisible (I) or visible (V). We show the sets of initial states from which the attacker has an ASW deception strategy, regardless of the sensor states. These states

---

[2] The computation is performed in a MacBook Pro with 16 GB memory and Apple M1 Pro chip. The computation time is the total time taken to compute the attacker's intention deception ASW region in the augmented MDP.

are referred to as the winning initial states. Comparing (a)-B-I with (b)-B-I, it shows that (b)-B-I includes more initial states that are deceptively winning for the attacker, as well as a larger ratio of states in the augmented MDP belonging to the almost-sure winning region. In this example, when the defender is action visible, the winning initial state sets for both configuration $(a), (b)$ are empty.

In the case of sensor configuration (c), when the defender is action invisible, the attacker has a non-revealing, intention deception, ASW strategy for a set of initial states for both Boolean and precise sensor types. The set of winning initial states is smaller when the sensors are precise. However, when we have both action visible and precise sensor type, the winning initial state set is empty for (c)-P-V. The non-empty ASW region in the case of (c)-P-V includes these states in the augmented MDP at which the defender's belief is not a singleton.

Note that the attack strategy outputs a set of actions to be taken at each augmented state. An ASW strategy only needs to take each action with a nonzero probability to ensure the objective is satisfied with probability one. It is possible to compute a non-revealing, intention deception ASW strategy that minimizes the number of time steps for the attacker to reach the goal. This is solved using a stochastic shortest path algorithms in the augmented MDP where the attacker's actions are restricted to actions allowed by the deception ASW strategy. Next, we exercise the optimal attack strategy in the game with different sensor configurations to obtain sampled winning runs for the attacker. In Fig. 6, the blue lines describes the size of the defender's belief over time and the red crosses represents if the current state is in the belief of the defender (1 for yes and 0 for no). Comparing (a)-B-I to (b)-B-I, it is observed that the defender can reduce the uncertainty in his belief more frequently in the case of (a)-B-I and the attacker has to spend a longer time in order to satisfy the attack objective with deceptive strategy. In the case of (b)-B-I, the defender is uncertain of the attacker's state for a majority of time steps. When it comes to the sensor configuration (c)-B-I, (c)-P-I, we observe that the attacker achieves the objective in a much shorter time comparing to the previous cases. From the experiment, we observed that under the sensor configuration (c)-B-I, the attacker can quickly reach a state 22 at which the defender's belief no longer contains the true state. After reaching that state, the attacker can take a stochastic shortest path policy to reach the attack goal state while the defender is misled into believing the agent's state remains in the right two columns in the gridworld[3].

Given this analysis, the synthesized intention deception attack strategy can be used to effectively evaluate the blind spots of a security monitoring system. It is also possible to use that attack strategy as a counterexample for counterexample guided security system design.

---

[3] Videos of the sampled runs for case (c)-B-I, (c)-P-I can be found at https://bit.ly/3BiPRb9 where the light green cells are states in the defender's belief.

Table 1. Experiment results with different sensor configurations.

Sensor config.	Win initial states	Computation time	Size of augmented MDP	|ASW|
(a)-B-I	[20..24]	0.233	1091	374
(b)-B-I	5, 10, 15, [20..24]	0.4086	1339	682
(c)-B-I	5, 10, 15, [20..24]	0.0569	497	340
(c)-P-I	[20..24]	0.0415	359	170
(c)-P-V	∅	0.0562	519	20

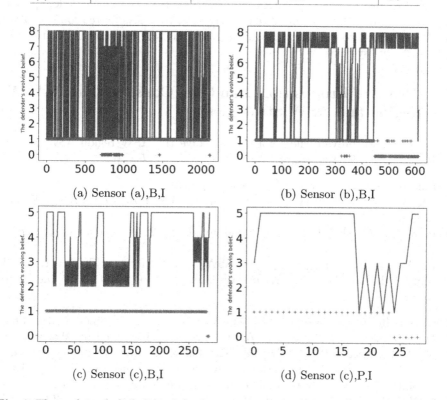

(a) Sensor (a),B,I

(b) Sensor (b),B,I

(c) Sensor (c),B,I

(d) Sensor (c),P,I

Fig. 6. The evolving belief of the defender over time in a single run under the attacker's ASW deception strategy for different sensor configurations.

5   Conclusion and Future Work

We develop a formal-method approach to synthesize an almost-sure winning strategy with intention deception in stochastic systems. Such a strategy exploits the defender's partial observations over state-action space. With the proposed methods, it is possible to assess whether a defender's monitoring capability is vulnerable to such intention deception attacks. This work has several future extensions: First, the insight from synthesizing intention deception can lead to possible counter-deception. For example, the defender can design her observation function/sensing modality to eliminate the existence of such deceptive attack strategies; Second, the paper investigates an attacker to hide his identity as one normal user. If there are multiple normal user behaviors, we hypothesize that the attacker can have more advantages by exploiting the defender's uncertainty about the type of normal user whose behavior is being observed. Third, the relation between qualitative intention deception and quantitative intention deception using information-theoretic approaches [10] may be established. Instead of finding the almost-sure nonrevealing intention deception strategy, it may be practical to also compute an intention deception strategy that has a low probability of revealing the true intention. Lastly, the synthesis of intention deception can be extended to general observation functions for practical applications in cyber-physical systems.

A   Proof of Proposition 2 and the Construction of ASW Region and ASW Strategies

Proof. First, we provide the algorithm to solve the ASW region $\mathsf{ASW}(\varphi)$ and ASW strategy π for the task $\varphi := \neg U \mathsf{U} F$ where $U \cap F = \emptyset$.

1. Initiate $X_0 = F$ and $Y_0 = S \backslash U$. Let $i = j = 1$.
2. Let $X_{i+1} = \{X_i\} \cup \{s \in Y_j \backslash X_i \mid \exists a \in A(s), \mathsf{Post}(s,a) \cap X_i \neq \emptyset$ and $\mathsf{Post}(s,a) \subseteq Y_j\}$
3. If $X_{i+1} \neq X_i$, then let $i = i + 1$ and go to step 2; else, let $n = i$ and go to step 4.
4. Let $Y_{j+1} = X_i$. If $Y_{j+1} = Y_j$, then $\mathsf{ASW}(\varphi) = Y_j$. Return $\{X_i, i = 1, \ldots, n\}$ computed from the last iteration. Else, let $j = j + 1$ and $i = 0$ and go to step 2.

The algorithm returns a set of level sets $X_i, i = 0, \ldots, n$ for some $n \geq 0$ and the ASW region $\mathsf{ASW}(\varphi)$. Recall that $\mathsf{Allowed} : S \rightarrow 2^A$ is defined by $\mathsf{Allowed}(s) = \{a \in A(s) \mid \mathsf{Post}(s,a) \subseteq \mathsf{ASW}(\varphi)\}$. The following property holds: For each $s \in X_i \backslash X_{i-1}$, there exists an action $a \in \mathsf{Allowed}(s)$ that ensures, with a positive probability, the next state is in X_{i-1} and with probability one, the next state is in $\mathsf{ASW}(\varphi)$. The strategy $\pi : \mathsf{ASW}(\varphi) \rightarrow \mathcal{D}(A)$ is almost-sure winning if for every state $s \in \mathsf{ASW}(\varphi)$, $\mathsf{Supp}(\pi(s)) = \mathsf{Allowed}(s)$. That is, for every permissible action a at state $s \in \mathsf{ASW}(\varphi)$, $\pi(s)$ selects that action with a non-zero probability. The ASW strategy may not be unique.

Let's define a function $\mathsf{Prog} : \mathsf{ASW}(\varphi) \rightarrow 2^A$ such that for each $s \in X_i \backslash X_{i-1}$, $\mathsf{Prog}(s) = \{a \in \mathsf{Allowed}(s) \mid \mathsf{Post}(s,a) \cap X_{i-1} \neq \emptyset\}$. Intuitively, the set $\mathsf{Prog}(s)$ is a set of actions, each of which ensures that a progress (to a lower level set) can be made with a positive probability.

Therefore, by following a policy π that selects any action in $\mathsf{Allowed}(s)$ with probability > 0, the probability of starting from a state $s \in X_i \backslash X_{i-1}$ and not reaching a state in $X_0 = F$ in i steps is less than $(1 - p)^i$ where $p = \min_{0 < i \leq n, s \in S, a \in \mathsf{Prog}(s)} \pi(s,a) P(s' \mid s, a)$ and is nonzero. If in the i-th step, the set X_0 is not reached, the agent will reach a state $s' \in \mathsf{ASW}(\varphi)$ from which an action in $\mathsf{Prog}(s')$ will be selected with a nonzero probability. Thus, the probability of never reaching a state in F is $\lim_{k \to \infty}(1-p)^k = 0$. In other words, the policy π ensure F is eventually reached with probability one. At the same time, because the set $Y_j \cap U = \emptyset$ for all $j > 0$ during iterations, $\mathsf{ASW}(\varphi) \cap U = \emptyset$ and thus the probability of reaching a state in U is zero by following the policy π.

B   Proof of Theorem 2

Proof. We show that the ASW policy $\widehat{\pi}_1 : S \times 2^S \to \mathcal{D}(A)$ obtained from the augmented MDP is qualitatively observation-equivalent to an ASW policy for the user.

Consider a history $h = s_0 a_0 s_1 a_1 \ldots s_n$ which is sampled from the stochastic process $M_{\widehat{\pi}_1}$ and satisfies $s_i \notin F_1 \cup U_1$ for $0 \leq i < n$ and $s_n \in F_1$. The history is associated with a history in the augmented MDP, $\widehat{h} = (s_0, B_0) a_0 (s_1, B_1) a_1 \ldots (s_n, B_n)$ where $B_0 = \mathsf{DObs}_S(s_0)$ is the initial belief for the defender. Due to the construction of the augmented MDP, for all $0 \leq i \leq n$, $B_i \neq \emptyset$.

By the definition of qualitatively observation-equivalence, we only need to show that there exists $h' = s_0' a_0' s_1' a_1' \ldots s_n'$ where $s_i' \in B_i$, for all $i = 0, \ldots, n$, such that $\Pr(h', M_{\pi_0}) > 0$ where M_{π_0} is the Markov chain induced by a user's ASW policy π_0 from the MDP M. It is observed that a_i and a_i' may not be the same. By way of contradiction, suppose, for any state-action sequence $h' = s_0' a_0' s_1' a_1' \ldots s_n'$ where $s_i' \in B_i$ and $a_i' \in A(s_i')$ for $0 \leq i \leq n$, it holds that $\Pr(h', M_{\pi_0}) = 0$. When $\Pr(h', M_{\pi_0}) = 0$, there are two possible cases: First case: there exists some $i \geq 0$ such that for all $s \in B_i$, $\mathsf{Allowed}(s) = \emptyset$; second case: there does not exists an action a enabled from the belief B_i and a state $s' \in B_{i+1}$ such that $P(s'|s, a) > 0$.

The first case is not possible because when for all $s \in B_i$, $\mathsf{Allowed}(s) = \emptyset$, then the next state reached will be $(s_i, \emptyset)$ which is a sink state, contradicting the fact that $\widehat{h}$ satisfies the reach-avoid objective. In the second case, if for any state $s \in B_i$, for any action a enabled from s, $\mathsf{Post}(s, a) \cap B_{i+1} = \emptyset$, then $B_{i+1} = \emptyset$, this again contracts that $\widehat{h}$ visits a state in $\widehat{F}$.

Thus, it holds that there exists h' such that $\mathsf{DObs}_S(h) = \mathsf{DObs}_S(h')$ and $\Pr(h', M_{\pi_0}) > 0$.

References

1. Baier, C., Katoen, J.P.: Principles of Model Checking. MIT Press, Cambridge (2008)
2. Baier, C., Katoen, J.P.: Principles of Model Checking (Representation and Mind Series). The MIT Press, Cambridge (2008)
3. Bernardini, S., Fagnani, F., Franco, S.: An optimization approach to robust goal obfuscation. In: Proceedings of the Seventeenth International Conference on Principles of Knowledge Representation and Reasoning, pp. 119–129. International Joint Conferences on Artificial Intelligence Organization, Rhodes (2020)

4. Chatterjee, K., Doyen, L.: Partial-observation stochastic games: how to win when belief fails. CoRR (2011)

5. Chatterjee, K., Doyen, L., Henzinger, T.A.: Qualitative analysis of partially-observable Markov decision processes. In: Hliněný, P., Kučera, A. (eds.) MFCS 2010. LNCS, vol. 6281, pp. 258–269. Springer, Heidelberg (2010). https://doi.org/10.1007/978-3-642-15155-2_24

6. Chen, P., Desmet, L., Huygens, C.: A study on advanced persistent threats. In: De Decker, B., Zúquete, A. (eds.) CMS 2014. LNCS, vol. 8735, pp. 63–72. Springer, Heidelberg (2014). https://doi.org/10.1007/978-3-662-44885-4_5

7. Dubreil, J., Darondeau, P., Marchand, H.: Supervisory control for opacity. IEEE Trans. Autom. Control **55**(5), 1089–1100 (2010)

8. Gimbert, H., Oualhadj, Y., Paul, S.: Computing optimal strategies for Markov decision processes with parity and positive-average conditions (2011). https://hal.archives-ouvertes.fr/hal-00559173

9. Jacob, R., Lesage, J.J., Faure, J.M.: Overview of discrete event systems opacity: models, validation, and quantification. Annu. Rev. Control. **41**, 135–146 (2016)

10. Karabag, M.O., Ornik, M., Topcu, U.: Deception in supervisory control. IEEE Trans. Autom. Control 1 (2021)

11. Kulkarni, A., Srivastava, S., Kambhampati, S.: A unified framework for planning in adversarial and cooperative environments. In: Proceedings of the AAAI Conference on Artificial Intelligence, vol. 33, no. 01, pp. 2479–2487 (2019)

12. Kulkarni, A., Srivastava, S., Kambhampati, S.: Signaling friends and head-faking enemies simultaneously: balancing goal obfuscation and goal legibility. In: Proceedings of the 19th International Conference on Autonomous Agents and MultiAgent Systems, AAMAS 2020, pp. 1889–1891. International Foundation for Autonomous Agents and Multiagent Systems, Richland (2020)

13. Kupferman, O., Vardi, M.Y.: Model checking of safety properties. Formal Methods Syst. Design **19**(3), 291–314 (2001)

14. Kwiatkowska, M., Norman, G., Parker, D.: PRISM 4.0: verification of probabilistic real-time systems. In: Gopalakrishnan, G., Qadeer, S. (eds.) CAV 2011. LNCS, vol. 6806, pp. 585–591. Springer, Heidelberg (2011). https://doi.org/10.1007/978-3-642-22110-1_47

15. Lin, F.: Opacity of discrete event systems and its applications. Automatica **47**(3), 496–503 (2011). https://doi.org/10.1016/j.automatica.2011.01.002

16. Masters, P., Sardina, S.: Deceptive path-planning. In: Proceedings of the Twenty-Sixth International Joint Conference on Artificial Intelligence, pp. 4368–4375. International Joint Conferences on Artificial Intelligence Organization, Melbourne (2017). https://doi.org/10.24963/ijcai.2017/610, https://www.ijcai.org/proceedings/2017/610

17. Saboori, A., Hadjicostis, C.N.: Opacity-enforcing supervisory strategies via state estimator constructions. IEEE Trans. Autom. Control **57**(5), 1155–1165 (2012). https://doi.org/10.1109/TAC.2011.2170453

18. Salem, M.B., Hershkop, S., Stolfo, S.J.: A survey of insider attack detection research. In: Stolfo, S.J., Bellovin, S.M., Keromytis, A.D., Hershkop, S., Smith, S.W., Sinclair, S. (eds.) Insider Attack and Cyber Security: Beyond the Hacker. Advances in Information Security, vol. 39, pp. 69–90. Springer, Boston (2008). https://doi.org/10.1007/978-0-387-77322-3_5

19. Zhang, Y., Shell, D.A.: Plans that remain private, even in hindsight. In: The AAAI Workshop on Privacy-Preserving Artificial Intelligence (AAAI-PPAI), p. 5 (2020)

Using Deception in Markov Game to Understand Adversarial Behaviors Through a Capture-The-Flag Environment

Siddhant Bhambri[1]([⊠]), Purv Chauhan[1], Frederico Araujo[2], Adam Doupé[1], and Subbarao Kambhampati[1]

[1] Arizona State University, Tempe, AZ, USA
{sbhambr1,prchauha,doupe,rao}@asu.edu
[2] IBM Research, Yorktown Heights, NY, USA
frederico.araujo@ibm.com

Abstract. Identifying the actual adversarial threat against a system vulnerability has been a long-standing challenge for cybersecurity research. To determine an optimal strategy for the defender, game-theoretic based decision models have been widely used to simulate the real-world attacker-defender scenarios while taking the defender's constraints into consideration. In this work, we focus on understanding human attacker behaviors in order to optimize the defender's strategy. To achieve this goal, we model attacker-defender engagements as Markov Games and search for their Bayesian Stackelberg Equilibrium. We validate our modeling approach and report our empirical findings using a Capture-The-Flag (CTF) setup, and we conduct user studies on adversaries with varying skill-levels. Our studies show that application-level deceptions are an optimal mitigation strategy against targeted attacks—outperforming classic cyber-defensive maneuvers, such as patching or blocking network requests. We use this result to further hypothesize over the attacker's behaviors when trapped in an embedded honeypot environment and present a detailed analysis of the same.

Keywords: Adversarial behavior · Markov Games · Capture-The-Flag

1 Introduction

Cybersecurity research, particularly that focused on finding optimal decision strategies for a system defender, when faced by an adversarial threat, has almost always involved a strong dependence on the assumptions made over the adversary's capabilities and the associated threat posed on the system vulnerabilities. Assuming a rational adversary, who will always choose the action or strategy that rewards highest returns, does not typically map to real-world situations [1]. However, this assumption has been a part of a common staple of approaches

---

S. Bhambri and P. Chauhan—These authors contributed equally to this work.

© The Author(s), under exclusive license to Springer Nature Switzerland AG 2023
F. Fang et al. (Eds.): GameSec 2022, LNCS 13727, pp. 87–106, 2023.
https://doi.org/10.1007/978-3-031-26369-9_5

that model attacker-defender interactions to compute an *optimal* strategy for the defender, motivated by its practical performance [2].

Such adversarial interactions become more interesting and complex when defenders use cyber-deceptive techniques to respond to and thwart attacks. Deception strategies in cybersecurity frameworks, such as installing honeypot configurations to misdirect attackers, have been shown to be effective tools to disrupt attack kill chains and perform attacker reconnaissance [3–7]. Understanding an adversary's behavior can aid cybersecurity defenders to optimally use the available resources to deploy deceptions and mitigate potential threats, while optimizing over the system constraints. Such knowledge can substantially aid a decision-making model, reducing the magnitude of the assumptions a defender must provide about the adversary to make the model operational.

In this paper, we build on the insight that an embedded honeypot [8]—a decoy environment that is inlined with genuine service functionality—can be configured in a way that is invisible to attackers while providing the defender with essential knowledge about the attacker's techniques in real operational settings. Moreover, we show that the expected payoffs for the defender may vary when compared to the real-world scenario where the attacker's behaviors may not meet the defender's expectations or prior beliefs.

Our contributions are summarized as follows:

- To ground this problem, we created a real-world Capture-The-Flag (CTF) environment hosting three system vulnerabilities, and we conduct studies using human subjects with varying system and attack skill levels who try to capture the corresponding (real) flags. Each of these vulnerabilities are protected by different real and practical mitigation strategies, one of which is a deception-based honey-patch [4], which misdirects an adversary to an embedded honeypot configuration that yields the attacker a fake, or as we refer to it in this work, a *honeypot flag*.
- In parallel to these studies, we model this attacker-defender system interaction as a Markov Game and find its Bayesian Stackelberg Equilibrium. We start with the assumption of inputs to this Markov Game being set by a system expert.
- Later, by varying these inputs, especially for cases when the attacker may be trapped in a honeypot configuration, we leverage the statistical results received from the conducted user studies, which further allows us to understand the differences between the obtained equilibria and the empirical setting.

The paper is structured as follows: we begin in Sect. 2 by providing a background on the CTF environment, Markov Games, and the system vulnerabilities with the corresponding mitigations used in this work. We present our hypotheses over the adversary behaviors and explain our user study setup along with the Markov Game modeling in Sect. 3. Experimental details and results, particularly involving a case-by-case evaluation and discussion on the observations is presented in Sect. 4. We then talk about related work in Sect. 5, with the conclusion discussing future directions for this work in Sect. 6.

2 Background

In this section, we first present a brief overview of the Capture-The-Flag style setup that we employed to host our user studies. Then, we introduce the real-world vulnerabilities that we used to design the user study test-bed and game-theoretic model evaluations, followed by the defense mechanisms deployed as mitigation strategies. We also describe the Markov Game formalism used for finding an optimal strategy for the defender.

2.1 Capture-The-Flag Setup

The primary goal of conducting the user studies is to gather realistic data on attacker behaviors using CTF environments, rather than artificially generating the data based on commonly accepted assumption over adversaries [9]. One way to achieve this is through creating prototype components to run CTF style experiments. We further integrate them into an existing open-source framework known as *the iCTF framework* [10,11][1]. This infrastructure allowed experiments to be run with a sizable number of human subjects to gather enough data for our desired analysis.

The *iCTF framework* is the core framework used for conducting user studies. It is primarily used to host attack-and-defense style CTF competitions every year[2]. For the purpose of collecting data for this study, we made several modifications to the existing implementation of the framework. Most of these modifications include deploying defense mechanisms and data collection tools. Since our goal is to simulate real-life scenarios, we choose three vulnerabilities (which are still prominent in current software applications) and develop three corresponding vulnerable applications for this purpose. The vulnerabilities are selected and deployed in a manner that it is possible to exploit them in a reasonable amount of time (which we verified through pilot studies), therefore faithfully representing typical large-scale cyber-attacks. The vulnerabilities selected include command injection and buffer overflow. The vulnerable applications are written in C and dockerized to isolate them from the host machine. Also, all modern security mitigations, including Position Independent Executable (PIE), Data Execution Prevention (DEP), and Address Space Layer Randomization (ASLR) are disabled.

2.2 Vulnerabilities and Exploits

We developed three different vulnerable applications. *backup* is the first application which allows users to store and retrieve data that is stored as files on the host system. One of the functions in this application concatenates a string with the user input and passes that string to the C function `system()`, and the user's input is not sanitized, thus resulting in a command injection vulnerability.

---

[1] https://github.com/shellphish/ictf-framework.
[2] https://shellphish.net/ictf/.

The second application, *sampleak*, allows users to store and retrieve notes which are also stored as files, but unlike the *backup* application, a password is stored in the files, so that the user is required to provide a password when creating a note and needs to enter the correct password when retrieving them. The user input is stored in the application's memory using buffers, but the function `read()` unintentionally reads in more bytes than the buffer can hold, thus resulting in a buffer overflow vulnerability.

The third vulnerable application is *exploit-market*, which allows users to store, retrieve, and list payloads, which are stored in the memory of the program. The vulnerability in this application is due to buffers being initialized with different sizes in separate functions, so when the function `strcpy()` is called to copy the contents of the buffer, a carefully crafted payload can result into a buffer overflow vulnerability. Another intentional bug is also placed in the form of a memory disclosure which leaks heap addresses of the string buffers.

2.3 Defense Strategies and Analysis Tools

The defense mitigations are selected for protecting the vulnerable applications. The mitigations include deploying *Snort*, an intrusion detection system on a router machine acting as a gateway between the attacker machine and the defender machine. *Snort* uses a rule-based configuration file for setup, and this rule filter has a list of commonly used *shellcodes* for exploiting various applications running on multiple architectures. We also extended a live-patching framework [12] to enable cyber-deceptive attack countermeasures.

To collect valuable attacker and defender information, we further deploy tools on our host machines that include: *tcpdump*, which is a network packet analyzer to capture network traffic for further analysis, and *SysFlow* [13,14], an open-source system-call monitoring framework that encodes the representation of system activities into a compact entity-relational format that captures the interactions of processes with system resources, including file and network activity. This provides a richer context for post-exploitation analysis [15].

2.4 Attack Graph

Attack graphs (AGs) have been established as useful structures to represent exploit possibilities and derive attack behaviors for an adversary [16,17]. An attack graph is represented as $\mathcal{G}(\mathcal{V}, \mathcal{E})$, where $v \in \mathcal{V}$ denotes vertices or nodes representing the different states the adversary can be in, and $e \in \mathcal{E}$ denotes the edges between these nodes that represent the actions the adversary can take to move one from one state of the exploit to another.

Figure 1 is an example of an attack graph for an attacker trying to exploit the vulnerabilities present in the environment with the possibility of one or more of them being honey-patched, i.e., deceiving and misdirecting the attacker into a honeypot configuration where the system defender can extract useful insights about attacker behavior.

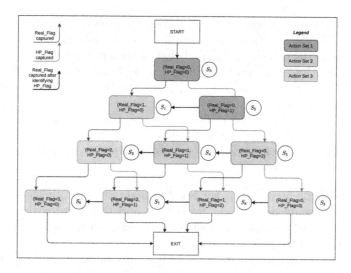

Fig. 1. A complete representation of the attacker's possible attack graphs in the current game setup. (Color figure online)

As noted in [18], an attack graph can be represented as the tuple $\mathcal{G} = (S, \tau, S_0, S_S, L, EX)$, where:

- S is the finite set of states or nodes, in our case a total of 10, on one of which the attacker will be present during the exploit,
- $\tau \subseteq S \times S$ represents the transition function which defines the probabilities of the attacker taking an available action in a state and reaching another state,
- $S_0 \subseteq S$ represents the set of initial states, and in our case, it is the state where the attacker has captured 0 real or honeypot flags,
- $S_S \subseteq S$ represents the set of final states (success or failure) for the attacker, and in our case, states where the attacker has tried exploiting each of the three vulnerabilities and has either captured the real flag or the honeypot flag,
- L represents the atomic propositions used for labeling these states or nodes, which in our case correspond to the number of real flags and honeypot flags captured by the attacker,
- and, finally, EX represents a finite set of actions, such as shown by different colored nodes representing different sets of actions available to the attacker in our attack graph. We talk about the different action sets corresponding to each of the states separately in Sect. 3.3.

2.5 Markov Game

We define a Markov Game, and the associated notations, between the attacker ($\mathcal{A}$) and defender ($\mathcal{D}$) as:

- a set of states S representing the collection of states,
- action set $A : (A_A \times A_D)$ which comprises of the cross-product between the action sets of the attacker (A_A) and that of the defender (A_D),
- T represents the transition probability matrix from a state $s_i \in S$ to $s_j \in S$ when the attacker takes an action $a_A \in A_A$ and the defender takes an action $a_D \in A_D$,
- $U(s \in S, a \in A)$ denotes the utility or the rewards received by the player (A or D) in state s when action a is taken, and
- to take discounted future rewards into consideration, we define $\gamma : [0, 1)$ for both the players A and D.

Basak et al. [19] highlight that it is not straightforward to make the assumption that the γ would be the same for both A and D. Following the limitations or the absence of a formal study as shown in [9], we take a similar approach and assume for the time being that $\gamma = \gamma_A = \gamma_D$.

For the zero-sum game that we assume in this work, an optimal policy for the defender's strategy can be computed [20], and can be updated to induce a min-max strategy for the two players [9], by calculating the Q-value or the expected return for an actor (A or D) in state $s \in S$ and taking action a_i for $i \in (A, D)$ as:

$$Q(s, a_D, a_A) = U(s, a_D, a_A) + \gamma \sum_{s'} T(s, a_D, a_A, s') V(s') \tag{1}$$

where the defender takes action a_D against the attacker's action a_A and reaches another state s'. The value-function for the defender's mixed policy $\pi(s)$ for the probability π_{a_D} of choosing action a_D is defined as:

$$V(s) = \max_{\pi(s)} \min_{a_A} \sum_{a_D} Q(s, a_D, a_A) \pi_{a_D} \tag{2}$$

We use this to compute the optimal mixed strategy for our defender for the different experimental settings, as explained in more detail in Sect. 4. Given the components of our Markov Game for a fixed set of utilities, which are dependent on the exploitable vulnerabilities and available mitigations used, the transition probability matrix $T(s, a_D, a_A, s')$ may vary based on the threat level posed by an adversary. This motivates us to test our Markov Game modeling by varying these input parameters, and we discuss these variations further in detail in Sect. 3.3.

3   Methodology

In the current setup, we assumed that the system contains 3 vulnerabilities, $exploit_i$ for $i \in [1, 3]$. One or more of these vulnerabilities may be honey-patched by the system defender. Honey-patches [4] are software security patches that are modified to avoid alerting adversaries when their exploit attempts fail. Instead of blocking the attempted exploit, the honey-patch transparently redirects the attacker session to an isolated honeypot environment. Adversaries attempting to exploit a honey-patched vulnerability observe software responses that resemble unpatched software, even though the vulnerability is actually patched. This allows defenders to observe attack actions until the deception is uncovered.

Figure 1 shows a scenario where all three vulnerabilities are honey-patched. Note that the attack graph for a case where one or more vulnerabilities are not honey-patched will be a special case of the attack graph shown in the figure, with those particular vulnerabilities leading to a real flag, and not to a honeypot flag.

In the beginning of the game, the attacker has the option to exploit one of the vulnerabilities, denoted by starting state $(real\_flag = 0, hp\_flag = 0)$. To illustrate how the game advances, assuming that the initial target is the honey-patched vulnerability $exploit_1$, the resulting attacker state would be $(real\_flag = 0, hp\_flag = 1)$, denotation the state where the attacker is trapped into a decoy and fails to capture the real flag. The attacker then progresses through the game and eventually reaches a terminal state $(real\_flag = i, hp\_flag = j)$, where $i \in [0, 3]$ & $j \in [0, 3]$ and $i + j \leq 3$, since an attacker can obtain at most either of the two flags for each exploit, or none at all. Section 3.1 details our hypotheses about the dynamics of the game.

3.1 Hypotheses

We design our study to test two different sets of strategies that can be adopted by an attacker once trapped into a honeypot configuration. We also state here the assumptions behind each hypothesis that we test.

H1. Once trapped in a honeypot environment, the attacker chooses to *continue* with the existing strategy to exploit the remaining vulnerabilities.

H2. Once trapped in a honeypot environment, the attacker chooses to *change* the current strategy to exploit the remaining vulnerabilities.

Hypothesis 1 assumes that the attacker did not discover the deception, i.e., a state where a honeypot flag was obtained. Hence, the attacker chooses to to continue with the existing strategy without worrying about subsequent traps.

Hypothesis 2, on the other hand, assumes that the attacker becomes aware of the new state, i.e., a state where a honeypot flag is discovered. Hence, the attacker chooses to change the current strategy (i.e., attempts to escape the honeypot environment). This would allow the attacker to retry exploiting the honey-patched vulnerability while avoiding getting trapped in the honeypot. In case the attempt to escape the particular honeypot configuration is unsuccessful, the attacker awareness of the deception will influence the attack strategy to be more cautious and observant of subsequent honey-patches.

Next, we discuss the user study that allows us to track the varying attack behaviors generated by each of the adversaries, followed by our Markov Game modeling used for running the experiments.

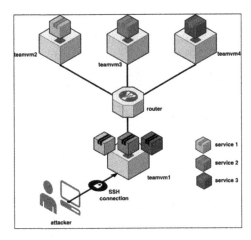

Fig. 2. iCTF infrastructure setup for running experiments.

3.2   User Study

The *ictf framework* is intended to be used for hosting multi-team (over 100 have been accomplished) attack-defense style CTFs. In our user studies, the goal is to have a human participant assuming the role of an attacker and several security defense mechanisms assuming the role of defenders. The attacker's machine has identical copies of the vulnerable applications to enable attackers to analyze the application, identify vulnerabilities, and develop working exploits. On the defender's machines, the vulnerable applications are deployed with either one of the security mitigations or no mitigation.

A pre-generated string called the *flag* is placed inside the root directory of the docker containers running the vulnerable applications. The goal of the attacker is to successfully exploit the vulnerabilities and read the flag, which is only accomplished by successfully exploiting the vulnerable application.

Figure 2 shows the infrastructure setup. The router serves as a gateway between all of the team virtual machines (VMs). The attacker participant is granted SSH access to the team-VM1 machine. They can only interact with the vulnerable services through the team-VM1 machine. All team-VMs run the same environment (Ubuntu 18.04) and have copies of docker images for all vulnerable applications, which will be referred to as services. As a result, the attacker has access to copies of all the services used in the experiment in order to analyze and develop exploits for them.

Once the infrastructure is created, a random setup of services and defenses is selected. The service-defense relationship is one-to-one. Figure 3 shows one randomly selected setup wherein *backup* has no defense mitigation, *sampleak* has *honey-patching* as a mitigation and *exploit-market* has a *Snort* filter as a mitigation. One participant at a time assumes the role of an attacker and we describe that their goal is to identify vulnerabilities in the vulnerable service and write an exploit for the vulnerability that reads the flag. The participant is

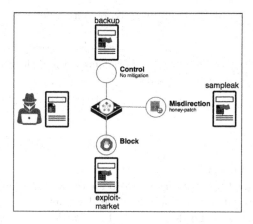

Fig. 3. The experimental setup used for conducting the iCTF user studies.

given sufficient time to work on each service. Whether they successfully exploit it or run out of time, they try to exploit one service at a time, in the consistent order of: *backup, sampleak, exploit-market*. Once the experiment concludes, the data is collected and stored for further analysis.

3.3 Markov Game Modeling

The different stages of the attack graph in Fig. 1 represent the diverse scenarios that an attacker might be in, when trying to exploit the different vulnerabilities present on the defender's system. In each of these unique stages, the attacker has a set of actions available to execute on the system. Intuitively, as the game progresses, the number of possible actions for both the attacker and the defender decreases, which limits their control over the game. Hence, we formulate the model which can recommend the action probabilities for the defender at each of these stages. We further analyze what varying costs the defender incurs when taking each of these actions and how the future expectations of the defender's actions can influence the adopted mitigation strategies.

State Space. S for the Markov Game $\mathcal{M}$ is defined by the nodes of the attack graph. The attacker enters the system to begin exploits without any real or honeypot flags, represented by state S_0. Similarly, after attempting exploits on each of the three vulnerabilities, the attacker may end up with a set of real and honeypot flags and be end in one of the terminal states from S_6 to S_9, after which the attacker exits the system. The blue, orange, and yellow colors in these nodes represent the action sets available to the agent in each of these states, and we explain these action states in more detail next.

Action Space. A for the Markov Game $\mathcal{M}$ comprises of the action sets $A_\mathcal{A} \times A_\mathcal{D}$, i.e., of both the players. Intuitively, as the game progresses and the number of

Table 1. Utility matrix for Action Set 1

		Defender's actions ($A_\mathcal{D}$)			
		no_mon	hp_1	hp_2	hp_3
Attacker's actions ($A_\mathcal{A}$)	no_op	0	−3	−3	−3
	exp_1	−5.9	2.9	−8.9	−8.9
	exp_2	−5.9	−8.9	2.9	−8.9
	exp_3	−5.9	−8.9	−8.9	2.9

vulnerabilities remaining to exploit for the attacker reduce, the possible action set also minimizes for the attacker, and also for the defender given the naturally assumed resource constraints. Note that the defender takes actions before the game begins and assigns the desired set of mitigations on one or more of the existing system vulnerabilities.

In the example attack graph shown in Fig. 1, Action Set 1 comprises of four actions for the attacker: *do nothing, exploit vulnerability 1, exploit vulnerability 2* or *exploit vulnerability 3*. For the defender, the four actions available are: *no mitigation, honey-patch vulnerability 1, honey-patch vulnerability 2* or *honey-patch vulnerability 3*.

Further in the game for Action Set 2, the attacker has three actions remaining as the attacker cannot return to exploiting the first vulnerability. Similarly, the defender has all the actions available except deploying honey-patch for the first vulnerability for which an exploit was attempted.

Lastly, for Action Set 3, the attacker has two actions remaining: *do nothing*, and *exploit vulnerability 3*. Similarly, the defender has two actions remaining: *no mitigation*, and *honey-patch vulnerability 3*.

Utility Matrices: A_1 for states S_0 and S_2 comprises of the actions, along with the corresponding utilities shown in Table 1. Similarly, Table 2 and Table 3 represent the actions for both the attacker and the defender for states S_1, S_4, and S_5, and, states S_3, S_6–S_9 respectively. By running some initial experimental studies comparing the payoffs received, we conclude that honey-patching offers the highest returns to the defender against any vulnerability exploit, as compared to deploying no mitigation or using *Snort*. We further analyze the cases where the defender has an option of honey-patching one or more vulnerabilities present in the system. Hence, Tables 1, 2 and 3 only comprise of the honey-patching actions for the defender, and the scores for which have been computed using the scoring system of CVSS v3.1[3]. These CVSS scores determine the exploitability and severity of the three exploits used in this study.

Transition Matrices vary based on the modeling of the game. We model three different scenarios to evaluate the results from our user studies. We begin with the assumption that the system defender either does not have any prior knowledge on the threat level posed by the adversary, in which case the transition

---

[3] https://www.first.org/cvss/v3.1/specification-document.

Table 2. Utility matrix for Action Set 2

		Defender's actions ($A_\mathcal{D}$)		
		no_mon	hp_2	hp_3
Attacker's actions($A_\mathcal{A}$)	no_op	0	−3	−3
	exp_2	−5.9	2.9	−8.9
	exp_3	−5.9	−8.9	2.9

Table 3. Utility matrix for Action Set 3

		Defender's actions ($A_\mathcal{D}$)	
		no_mon	hp_3
Attacker's actions ($A_\mathcal{A}$)	no_op	0	−3
	exp_3	−5.9	2.9

probabilities can either be set randomly with non-zero probabilities assigned to all feasible state transitions, or, as an expert with the knowledge of the state transitions for any attacker interacting with the environment. The transition matrix for the **Naive Model** thus comprises of preset probabilities to the different possible transitions. This model can also assume that the defender incurs an equal cost of deploying a honey-patch for each of the three vulnerabilities. Later, we also relax this assumption and assign relatively higher costs to mitigations which are more difficult to deploy by the defender on the system. We randomly generate probabilities for all feasible transitions for the former case, and for the latter, the different probabilities associated with the model are shown in Table 4.

Note, that the probability of not capturing any flag for any vulnerability is 0.2 in the case where honeypot is present, and 0.25 when it is not deployed.

For the third model which is the **Updated Model with Tuned Parameters** using the data collected through the successful iCTF user studies and observations drawn from the attacker participants' behavior, we update the transition matrix for the model to better emulate the real-life scenario. The different probability inputs associated with this model are shown in Table 5.

Table 4. Transition probabilities set by system expert for the Naive Model.

Observation	Probability
Real flag captured if no honeypot	0.75
Real flag captured if honeypot present	0.4
Trapped in honeypot	0.4

Table 5. Transition probabilities derived from iCTF user studies' statistics.

Observation	Vulnerable application	Probability
Real flag captured if no honeypot	*backup*	1.0
	sampleak	0.43
	exploit-market	0.4
Trapped in honeypot	*backup*	1.0
	sampleak	0.5
	exploit-market	0.6

We also remove the assumption that the defender incurs equal cost of deploying the honeypot configuration as a mitigation, since configuring a honeypot is harder for a stronger suite of vulnerabilities that may be targeted by a system adversary. For all the above-mentioned modeling scenarios, we vary the costs of honey-patching these vulnerabilities accordingly and thus have a uniform and a non-uniform mitigation cost scenario for all three the models. In the non-uniform variants, the minimum cost of 1 is associated with honey-patching *backup* and the maximum cost of 3 is associated with honey-patching *exploit-market*. On the other hand, for the uniform cost variants, a cost of 3 is associated with deploying a honey-patch against each of the three vulnerabilities.

4   Experimental Evaluation and Results

4.1   iCTF User Studies

After running six pilot studies, and making necessary infrastructure changes to gather data on the adversary's behavior, we conducted 18 user studies. Participants were recruited from a pool of people known to have prerequisite skill-set (vulnerability analysis and software exploitation) and were rewarded $50 USD for their participation. Prior to this, we obtained an IRB approval from our institution for conducting the user studies.

Table 6 shows the summary of these user studies. The first column represents each service used in the experiments. The second column represents the total number of experiments conducted, and the third column represents the number of times the participant timed out without being able exploit a particular service. The last column is broken down by the defense mechanism deployed, the numerator represents successful exploitation of the service, and the denominator represents the total number of times the service is deployed with the particular defense.

4.2   Markov Game Strategy Evaluation

We first discuss the performance of our zero-sum Markov Game model against Uniform Random Strategy (URS), which has been shown to be effective in similar attacker-defender settings [21–23], and Min-Max Pure (MMP) Strategy. The

Table 6. Summary of iCTF Experiments.

| | | | Flag captured w/defense mechanism | | | |
| | | | None | Snort | Honeypatch | |
Challenge	Total experiments	Timed out	Real flag	Real flag	Honeypot flag
backup	18	0	6/6	6/6	0/6	6/6
sampleak	18	9	4/6	2/5	0/7	3/7
exploit-market	15	6	3/5	3/5	0/5	3/5

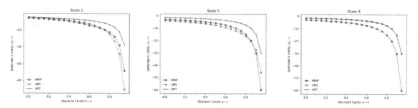

(a) Returns for state S_2. (b) Returns for state S_5. (c) Returns for state S_8.

Fig. 4. Defender's payoffs for Naive Model - randomly set transition probabilities and uniform mitigation deployment costs.

utility payoffs in our results correspond to the payoffs of the defender. As it has been previously shown [9], Optimal Mixed Strategy outperforms the other two algorithms with respect to returns gained by the system defender. By testing the three algorithms for the **Naive Model** with both randomly set and expertly assumed set of transition probabilities with uniform costs of deploying honeypots, we establish a baseline that would later help us understand how additional knowledge of the attacker that the system defender gained, can improve upon the decision making model.

With reference to the state space represented in Fig. 1, we show the results for state S_2 where the attacker is trapped in the first honeypot, state S_5 (similar to S_4) where the attacker is trapped in the second honeypot, and finally state S_8 (similar to state S_7 and state S_9) where the attacker is trapped in the honeypot set for the third vulnerability. We are more interested to analyze these states where deception is successful for the defender, and thus we would want to compare the usefulness gained by the user-studies later, particularly for these states.

Figures 4 and 5 show that Optimal Mixed Strategy (OPT) outperforms MMP and URS for states seen early (Figs. 4a, 5a) and in the middle (Figs. 4b, 5b) of the game, and returns payoffs for the defender equal to URS in the later stages (Figs. 4c, 5c) of the game where both URS and OPT output the same distribution over the remaining two actions for the defender.

We further apply the Optimal Mixed Strategy to the updated model scenario that we discussed in Sect. 3. We only focus on the Optimal Mixed Strategy to compare the Stackelberg equilibrium obtained under the following case studies. We divide each case study using the discount factor $\gamma \in [0, 1)$ to understand the variation in the model's decision making as the weightage for future exploit

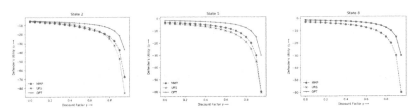

(a) Returns for state S_2. (b) Returns for state S_5. (c) Returns for state S_8.

Fig. 5. Defender's payoffs for Naive Model - system expert set transition probabilities and uniform mitigation deployment costs.

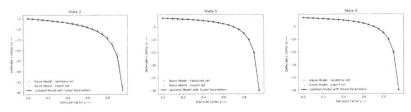

(a) Returns for state S_2. (b) Returns for state S_5. (c) Returns for state S_8.

Fig. 6. Defender's payoffs compared for the three models using uniform mitigation deployment costs.

mitigations varies for the system defender, and particularly discuss the two corner cases of $\gamma = 0$ and $\gamma = 0.95$. We compare the equilibria obtained among the three model variations under uniform costs of deploying mitigations, i.e., **Naive Model** with randomly set transition probabilities, **Naive Model** with expertly assumed transition probabilities, and **Updated Model with Tuned Parameters**. We carry out a similar comparison among the three models for non-uniform costs later.

Case Study 1. The first case focuses on the first honey-patch mitigation deployed in the game where both the attacker and the defender can take any possible

Table 7. Comparing the three modeling scenarios for Case Study 1

Case study 1	γ	Probability of honey-patching		
		backup	*sampleak*	*exploit-market*
Naive model (randomly set)	0	0.33	0.33	0.33
	0.95	0.45	0.09	0.09
Naive model (expert set)	0	0.33	0.33	0.33
	0.95	0.46	0.08	0.08
Updated model with tuned parameters	0	0.33	0.33	0.33
	0.95	0.5	0.1	0.05

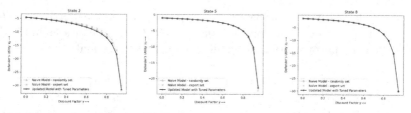

(a) Returns for state S_2. (b) Returns for state S_5. (c) Returns for state S_8.

Fig. 7. Defender's payoffs compared for the three models using non-uniform mitigation deployment costs.

actions, i.e., the attacker may choose to exploit any vulnerability or none at all, and the defender may choose to honey-patch any one or more vulnerabilities or choose to deploy no mitigation at all. As shown in Fig. 1, we are dealing with the case when Action Set 1 is available (Table 7).

For the minimum weightage given to future actions and their corresponding expected payoffs using $\gamma = 0$, each of the three models provide an equal probability to honey-patch each of the three vulnerabilities with the respective probabilities being 0.33 each. This is expected as independent of the transition probabilities, all three models share the same utility gains for honey-patching all three vulnerabilities, and the Q-value or the expected return does not depend on the transition matrix for $\gamma = 0$, as shown in Eq. 1.

For the maximum weightage given to future actions and their corresponding expected payoffs using $\gamma = 0.95$,

- The randomly set Naive model provides a probability of 0.45 to honey-patch *backup*, and an equal probability of 0.09 to *sampleak* and *exploit-market*.
- The expert set Naive model follows a similar trend and provides 0.46 to honey-patch *backup* and 0.08 to the other two.
- The Updated Model with Tuned Parameters provides the highest probability of 0.5 to honey-patch *backup*, a much smaller probability of 0.1 to *sampleak*, and 0.05 to *exploit-market*.

Figures 6a and 7a show that the expected payoffs (Naive Model setups) are marginally higher than the actual payoffs received when the true knowledge about the attacker was used by the Updated Model with Tuned Parameters. Hence, we conclude that the defender's payoffs may not be as high as we may estimate them to be when modeling the attacker's behavior from the defender's perspective.

Case Study 2. The second case is when the attacker has captured either the real-flag or the honeypot flag for *backup*, and the defender can choose to honey-patch either the second or the third vulnerability or choose to deploy no mitigation at all. Thus, this scenario represents the case when Action Set 2 is available.

For the minimum and the maximum weightage given to future actions and their corresponding expected payoffs using $\gamma = 0$ and $\gamma = 0.95$, respectively, all the three models give a 0.5 probability on deploying a honey-patch for *sampleak* and 0 probability for deploying one on *exploit-market*. This can be seen in Figs. 6b and 7b when the payoffs returned by all three models are equal.

Case Study 3. For each of the later states when the defender has the option either to honey-patch *exploit-market* or use no mitigation at all, these states are cases when either the attacker captured 2 real-flags, 2 honeypot flags, or 1 of each kind for the first two vulnerabilities. Thus, this scenario represents the case when Action Set 3 is available.

For the minimum and maximum weightage given to future actions and their corresponding expected payoffs using $\gamma = 0$ and $\gamma = 0.95$, respectively, all the three models provide a 0.5 probability to honey-patch *exploit-market*. Figures 6c and 7c show equal payoffs for the defender in all three models. Note that in each of the case studies, the remaining probabilities (as the distribution over actions totals to 1.0) have been provided to the *no mitigation* action for the defender.

4.3 Discussion

When using uniform and non-uniform costs for the defender to deploy mitigation strategies, we note that the three models show slight variations only for the first three states of the game, particularly for the case when a high weightage is given to future gains or payoffs. Recall that these three states correspond to the following scenarios:

– State S_0: when the attacker is at the starting state of the game and has acquired no flags so far.
– State S_1: when the attacker tried exploiting the first vulnerability and successfully obtained a real flag.
– State S_2: when the attacker tried exploiting the first vulnerability and was successfully trapped into the honeypot, thereby incurring a fake flag.

For all the other states, i.e., from state S_3 to state S_9, we note that all three models give the exact same utility returns. Also, irrespective of the state the defender is at the start when attempting the first vulnerability exploit, the three models provide a similar probability of ≈ 0.5 to deploy a honey-patch to mitigate the next possible exploit. Hence, we hypothesize that *the earlier the adversary is trapped in a honeypot, the better it is for the defender.*

The difference in the utility returns is the most prominent for state S_2, as shown in Figs. 6a and 7a, where the attacker was trapped in the first honeypot of the game while exploiting the first vulnerability. The initial model with transition probabilities set by the expert dominates the other initializations and gives the highest return, followed by the initial model with probabilities set randomly, and the least returns are obtained through the model initialized using data. The most important observation here is that *model parameters set randomly or by expert may not imitate the true model representative of the real-world attack scenario.* Hence, in the most important stages of the game, when the model results differ, defensive strategies tend to overestimate the returns from the randomly set or expert set model initializations as compared to the model we obtained from the real-world user studies.

Evaluating the Hypotheses. In the first hypothesis, we assumed that the attacker, once trapped in a honeypot, may continue with the existing strategy without worrying about future honeypots. The results from the user studies show that none of the attackers received the observation, until informed explicitly about the honeypot flag, that they failed to get the real flag, thus verifying our expectation behind this hypothesis. From the equilibria comparison shown in Figs. 6 and 7, we note that the payoffs for the defender are primarily equal to the payoffs obtained by the Naive Models, both with randomly set and expert set transition probabilities, thereby confirming that the adversary's behaviors did not deviate much from the system defender's expectations in this case.

In the second hypothesis, we assumed that the attacker, once trapped in a honeypot and knowing about the current state, will change the existing strategy to get out of the honeypot and exploit the future vulnerabilities with caution. Only in one instance, an attacker is able to escape the honeypot for *sampleak* after the user study ends and the attacker is informed about the honeypot flag. In this case, factors such as attacker's experience and expertise level, ease of exploiting the vulnerability and the effectiveness of the deployed honey-patch (e.g., an incomplete patch), all play an influential role. Due to these reasons, it is not easy to validate this hypothesis with 100% confidence, and hence, we see this as one open direction for future research to investigate in detail.

5   Related Work

Learning attack behaviors for a cybersecurity system has been a problem of relevant interest, particularly when designing decision making model frameworks for the defender. In an Internet of Things setting, Galinkin et al. [24] classify attackers as risk-averse and risk-seeking to understand the suite of scenarios preferred by such adversaries. Assessing the different modalities that influence an attacker's decision making in real-world scenarios has proven to be a challenging task, and necessitates the requirement of better models that can capture such behavioral patterns more closely [19]. One of the recent attempts on learning attacker's behavior have been based on approximating the preferences and capabilities of the attacker based on previously collected data over network packets, to learn about the preferences, choices or capabilities of a potential adversary [25]. However, understanding and collecting such data for adversaries, particularly when faced with decoy mitigation strategy, has not been analysed so far.

Do et al. [26] survey existing game-theoretic techniques on cyber security and privacy challenges, and highlights the advantages and limitations from the design to implementation of defense systems. Such evaluations strongly encourage the need to utilize such effective modeling frameworks to fully comprehend the evolving security and privacy problems in cyberspace and to find viable solutions. On the other hand, cybersecurity exercises have also been popularly used as a platform to teach cyber security concepts, and also to conduct experiments to study, analyze and solve issues related to cybersecurity [27–35].

The study setup presented in [35] explores the use of cyber security exercises and competitions to obtain vital data on measuring the impact of mitigations against exploits and their corresponding success. In this work, our primary focus stayed on the deception-based mitigation of honey-patching vulnerabilities and how the adversary interacted when faced with such a scenario.

6   Conclusion and Future Work

Cybersecurity exercises enable the collection of data on the interactions between attackers and a system defender, to gain insightful knowledge about the attacker's *state*, which can be used to further to improve the strategy adopted by a defender when faced by a potential threat. In this work, we take on the challenge of analyzing closely these interactions in deception-based experimental setups where the adversary is faced by three different types of decoy traps. We started with a baseline game-theoretic framework where we manually set the probability distribution over the attacker's strategy, and update this model with the results collected using the cybersecurity exercise carried over a real-world CTF platform. We observe that the interactions between the defender and the adversary in the initial stages of the game makes a more significant difference in the total expected utility gain for the defender, than in the later stages of the interaction. Moreover, models initialized randomly or using subject-expert knowledge may also lead to the problem of overestimation for the defender's payoffs in certain scenarios. Since we have a constrained control over the different modalities influencing the adversarial behavior noted in these studies, we believe that gaining further knowledge on the attack behavior when faced with deception-based mitigation strategies holds promise for improving the defender's decision-making model.

Acknowledgements. This work was supported in part by U.S. ACC-APG/DARPA award W912CG-19-C-0003 and the U.S. Army Research Laboratory under Cooperative Agreement Number W911NF-13-2-0045. Any opinions, recommendations, or conclusions expressed are those of the authors and should not be interpreted as representing the official views or policies of the Department of Defense or the U.S. Government. Approved for Public Release, Distribution Unlimited. We would also like to thank Sailik Sengupta for his useful insights, helpful discussions and feedback on this work.

References

1. Abbasi, Y., et al.: Know your adversary: insights for a better adversarial behavioral model. In: CogSci (2016)
2. Conitzer, V., Sandholm, T.: Computing the optimal strategy to commit to. In: Proceedings of the 7th ACM Conference on Electronic Commerce, pp. 82–90 (2006)

3. Heckman, K.E., Stech, F.J., Thomas, R.K., Schmoker, B., Tsow, A.W.: Cyber denial, deception and counter deception: a framework for supporting active cyber defense. Adv. Inf. Secur. **64** (2015)

4. Araujo, F., Hamlen, K.W., Biedermann, S., Katzenbeisser, S.: From patches to honey-patches: lightweight attacker misdirection, deception, and disinformation. In: Proceedings of the 2014 ACM SIGSAC Conference on Computer and Communications Security, pp. 942–953 (2014)

5. Araujo, F., Sengupta, S., Jang, J., Doupé, A., Hamlen, K.W., Kambhampati, S.: Software deception steering through version emulation. In: HICSS, pp. 1–10 (2021)

6. Han, X., Kheir, N., Balzarotti, D.: Deception techniques in computer security: a research perspective. ACM Comput. Surv. **51**(4), 1–36 (2018)

7. Almeshekah, M.H., Spafford, E.H.: Planning and integrating deception into computer security defenses. In: Proceedings of the New Security Paradigms Workshop, pp. 127–138 (2014)

8. Araujo, F., Hamlen, K.W.: Embedded honeypotting. In: Jajodia, S., Subrahmanian, V.S.S., Swarup, V., Wang, C. (eds.) Cyber Deception, pp. 203–233. Springer, Cham (2016). https://doi.org/10.1007/978-3-319-32699-3_9

9. Sengupta, S., Chowdhary, A., Huang, D., Kambhampati, S.: General sum Markov games for strategic detection of advanced persistent threats using moving target defense in cloud networks. In: Alpcan, T., Vorobeychik, Y., Baras, J.S., Dán, G. (eds.) GameSec 2019. LNCS, vol. 11836, pp. 492–512. Springer, Cham (2019). https://doi.org/10.1007/978-3-030-32430-8_29

10. Trickel, E., et al.: Shell we play a game? CTF-as-a-service for security education. In: 2017 USENIX Workshop on Advances in Security Education (ASE 17), Vancouver, BC (2017)

11. Vigna, G., et al.: Ten years of iCTF: the good, the bad, and the ugly. In: 2014 USENIX Summit on Gaming, Games, and Gamification in Security Education, 3GSE 2014 (2014)

12. Araujo, F., Taylor, T.: Improving cybersecurity hygiene through JIT patching. In: Proceedings of the 28th ACM Joint Meeting on European Software Engineering Conference and Symposium on the Foundations of Software Engineering, pp. 1421–1432 (2020)

13. Taylor, T., Araujo, F., Shu, X.: Towards an open format for scalable system telemetry. In: 2020 IEEE International Conference on Big Data (Big Data), pp. 1031–1040 (2020)

14. SysFlow. Cloud-native system telemetry pipeline (2022). https://github.com/sysflow-telemetry

15. Araujo, F., Taylor, T.: A pluggable edge-processing pipeline for SysFlow. In FloCon (2021)

16. Durkota, K., Lisý, V., Bošanský, B., Kiekintveld, C.: Optimal network security hardening using attack graph games. In: Twenty-Fourth International Joint Conference on Artificial Intelligence (2015)d

17. Letchford, J., Vorobeychik, Y.: Optimal interdiction of attack plans. In: AAMAS, pp. 199–206. Citeseer (2013)

18. Lallie, H.S., Debattista, K., Bal, J.: A review of attack graph and attack tree visual syntax in cyber security. Comput. Sci. Rev. **35**, 100219 (2020)

19. Basak, A., et al.: An initial study of targeted personality models in the FlipIt game. In: Bushnell, L., Poovendran, R., Başar, T. (eds.) GameSec 2018. LNCS, vol. 11199, pp. 623–636. Springer, Cham (2018). https://doi.org/10.1007/978-3-030-01554-1_36

20. Littman, M.L.: Markov games as a framework for multi-agent reinforcement learning. In: Machine Learning Proceedings 1994, pp. 157–163. Elsevier (1994)
21. Zhuang, R., Deloach, S., Ou, X.: Towards a theory of moving target defense. In: 2014 Proceedings of the ACM Conference on Computer and Communications Security, pp. 31–40 (2014)
22. Taguinod, M., Doupé, A., Zhao, Z., Ahn, G.-J.: Toward a moving target defense for web applications. In: 2015 IEEE International Conference on Information Reuse and Integration, pp. 510–517 (2015)
23. Winterrose, M.L., Carter, K.M., Wagner, N., Streilein, W.W.: Adaptive attacker strategy development against moving target cyber defenses. In: Shandilya, S.K., Wagner, N., Nagar, A.K. (eds.) Advances in Cyber Security Analytics and Decision Systems. EICC, pp. 1–14. Springer, Cham (2020). https://doi.org/10.1007/978-3-030-19353-9_1
24. Galinkin, E., Carter, J., Mancoridis, S.: Evaluating attacker risk behavior in an internet of things ecosystem. In: Bošanský, B., Gonzalez, C., Rass, S., Sinha, A. (eds.) GameSec 2021. LNCS, vol. 13061, pp. 354–364. Springer, Cham (2021). https://doi.org/10.1007/978-3-030-90370-1_19
25. Zychowski, A., Mandziuk, J.: Learning attacker's bounded rationality model in security games. CoRR, abs/2109.13036 (2021)
26. Do, C.T., et al.: Game theory for cyber security and privacy. ACM Comput. Surv. **50**(2), 1–37 (2017)
27. Stransky, C., et al.: Lessons learned from using an online platform to conduct {Large-Scale}, online controlled security experiments with software developers. In: 10th USENIX Workshop on Cyber Security Experimentation and Test (CSET 2017) (2017)
28. Schwab, S., Kline, E.: Cybersecurity experimentation at program scale: guidelines and principles for future testbeds. In: 2019 IEEE European Symposium on Security and Privacy Workshops (EuroS&PW), pp. 94–102. IEEE (2019)
29. Salem, M.B., Stolfo, S.J.: On the design and execution of {Cyber-Security} user studies: methodology, challenges, and lessons learned. In: 4th Workshop on Cyber Security Experimentation and Test (CSET 2011) (2011)
30. Salah, K., Hammoud, M., Zeadally, S.: Teaching cybersecurity using the cloud. IEEE Trans. Learn. Technol. **8**(4), 383–392 (2015)
31. Mirkovic, J., Benzel, T.: Teaching cybersecurity with DeterLab. IEEE Secur. Priv. **10**(1), 73–76 (2012)
32. Mäses, S., Kikerpill, K., Jüristo, K., Maennel, O.: Mixed methods research approach and experimental procedure for measuring human factors in cybersecurity using phishing simulations. In: 18th European Conference on Research Methodology for Business and Management Studies, p. 218 (2019)
33. Kavak, H., Padilla, J.J., Vernon-Bido, D., Gore, R., Diallo, S.: A characterization of cybersecurity simulation scenarios. In: SpringSim (CNS) (2016)
34. Aljohani, A., Jones, J.: Conducting malicious cybersecurity experiments on crowdsourcing platforms. In: The 2021 3rd International Conference on Big Data Engineering, pp. 150–161 (2021)
35. Sommestad, T., Hallberg, J.: Cyber security exercises and competitions as a platform for cyber security experiments. In: Jøsang, A., Carlsson, B. (eds.) NordSec 2012. LNCS, vol. 7617, pp. 47–60. Springer, Heidelberg (2012). https://doi.org/10.1007/978-3-642-34210-3_4

Robust Moving Target Defense Against Unknown Attacks: A Meta-reinforcement Learning Approach

Henger Li[✉] and Zizhan Zheng

Tulane University, New Orleans, LA 70118, USA
{hli30,zzheng3}@tulane.edu

Abstract. Moving target defense (MTD) provides a systematic framework to achieving proactive defense in the presence of advanced and stealthy attacks. To obtain robust MTD in the face of unknown attack strategies, a promising approach is to model the sequential attacker-defender interactions as a two-player Markov game, and formulate the defender's problem as finding the Stackelberg equilibrium (or a variant of it) with the defender and the leader and the attacker as the follower. To solve the game, however, existing approaches typically assume that the attacker type (including its physical, cognitive, and computational abilities and constraints) is known or is sampled from a known distribution. The former rarely holds in practice as the initial guess about the attacker type is often inaccurate, while the latter leads to suboptimal solutions even when there is no distribution shift between when the MTD policy is trained and when it is applied. On the other hand, it is often infeasible to collect enough samples covering various attack scenarios on the fly in security-sensitive domains. To address this dilemma, we propose a two-stage meta-reinforcement learning based MTD framework in this work. At the training stage, a meta-MTD policy is learned using experiences sampled from a set of possible attacks. At the test stage, the meta-policy is quickly adapted against a real attack using a small number of samples. We show that our two-stage MTD defense obtains superb performance in the face of uncertain/unknown attacker type and attack behavior.

1 Introduction

The relatively static nature of the current IT and infrastructure systems provides adaptive and stealthy cyber-attackers enough time to explore and then exploit a well-designed attack in a "low-and-slow" way [6]. Even worse, the increasingly more complex software technologies make the completely secure defense nearly impossible against an advanced adversary [21]. To reduce or even inverse the attacker's asymmetric information advantage, a promising approach is moving target defense (MTD), where the defender proactively updates the system configuration to increase the uncertainty and complexity for potential attackers. MTD has been successfully applied to many technology domains, including web

F. Fang et al. (Eds.): GameSec 2022, LNCS 13727, pp. 107–126, 2023.
https://doi.org/10.1007/978-3-031-26369-9_6

applications [38], cloud computing [30], operating systems [40], and Internet of things [32].

In order to capture the trade-off between security and efficiency in MTD, a game-theoretic approach is often adopted. In particular, early works have modeled the sequential attacker-defender interactions in MTD as a symmetric two-player Markov game [11] or a repeated Bayesian Stackelberg game (BSG) [34]. To achieve robust MTD in the face of uncertain attack behavior, a promising direction is to consider an asymmetric Markov game [22] where the defender (as the leader) first commits to an MTD policy assuming that the attacker (as the follower) will respond to it optimally. Several recent works have followed this direction by formulating the defender's problem as finding the Stackelberg equilibrium (or some variant of it) of the Markov MTD game, using either model-based [23] or model-free [33] reinforcement learning algorithms. The main advantage of this approach is that it provides a guaranteed level of protection by considering the worst-case attack behavior. However, the solution thus obtained can be conservative when the real attack is "weaker" than the worst-case scenario.

Although existing approaches have (partially) addressed the problem of uncertain attack behavior by using a game-theoretic solution concept, they typically assume that the attacker type (including its physical, cognitive, and computational abilities and constraints) is known or sampled from a known distribution. The former rarely holds in practice as the initial guess about the attacker type is often inaccurate, while the latter can lead to overly conservative solutions even when there is no distribution shift (on the attacker type) between when the MTD policy is trained and when it is applied. One possible solution is to consider a fully online approach where the defender assumes zero prior knowledge of the attacker and continuously adapts its policy using feedback obtained during its interactions with the attacker. However, this approach requires collecting a large number of samples covering various attack scenarios, which is typically infeasible in security-sensitive domains.

In this work, we take a first step towards solving the above dilemma, by proposing a two-stage meta-reinforcement learning (meta-RL) based MTD framework. At the training stage, a meta-MTD policy is learned by solving multiple Stackelberg Markov games using experiences sampled from a set of possible attacks. When facing a real attacker with initially uncertain/unknown type and behavior at the test stage, the meta-policy is quickly adapted using a small number of samples collected on the fly. Note that our approach assumes that the defender has a rough estimate of possible attacks, which is weaker than assuming a pre-defined attacker type distribution as in [33]. Further, the meta-defense is still effective even when the real attack at test time is not in the training set, thanks to the generalization property of meta-learning [12]. We show that our new MTD defense obtains superb performance in the practical setting where the defender has very limited prior knowledge of the attacker's type and behavior.

The main contributions of the paper are summarized below.

- We propose a two-stage meta-RL based defense framework for achieving robust moving target defense in the face of uncertain/unknown attack type and behavior.
- We show that the meta-RL defense framework can be efficiently implemented by proving that in our two-player MTD game, the problem of finding the strong Stackelberg equilibrium (SSE) can be reduced to solving a single-agent Markov decision process for the defender.
- Using data collected from the National Vulnerability Database (NVD), we show that our two-stage defense obtains superb performance by quickly adapting the pre-trained meta-defense policy to real attacks. Code is available at https://github.com/HengerLi/meta-RL.

2   The MTD Game Model

In this section, we first describe our system and attack models in detail. We then formulate the attack-defender interactions as a two-player Markov game. Finally, we provide an overview of the proposed two-stage MTD defense framework.

2.1   System Model

We consider a time-slotted system where in each time step, the system can be in any one of the n possible configurations. Let s^t denote the configuration of the system in time t. Each configuration consists of multiple adjustable parameters across different layers of the system called adaptation aspects [8]. Typical examples of adaptation aspects include port numbers [25], IP addresses [1,20,35], virtual machines [46], operating systems [40], and software programs [19]. We define the system configuration space as $S = [n]$, where n is the number of possible configurations.

At the beginning of each time t, the defender chooses the next system configuration s^t according to a migration policy π_D^t (to be defined). The system stays in the current configuration if $s^t = s^{t-1}$. To increase the attacker's uncertainty, the defense policy should be randomized. Further, the optimal defense policy is in general time-varying and can depend on the system state and the defender's knowledge of the attacker. We assume that a migration happens instantaneously subject to a cost $m_{ij} \geq 0$ when the system moves from configuration i to configuration j. Although not required in our model, we typically have $m_{ii} = 0$. Let $M = \{m_{ij}\}_{n \times n}$ denote the migration cost matrix.

In addition to the migration cost, the defender incurs a loss $l_{s_t} \geq 0$ at the end of time slot t if the system is compromised at t. The value of l_{s_t} varies over the system configuration and the attack type as we discuss below. In this work, we assume that the defender discovers whether the system is compromised or not at the end of each time step t and recovers the system if it is compromised. Therefore, l_{s_t} includes the cost to recover the system from potential damages. This also implies that the system is always protected at the beginning of any time step.

Although we consider the simplified setting where the defender receives immediate feedback on potential attacks in this work, our approach can be generalized to the setting when the feedback is delayed or imperfect.

With the above assumptions, it is natural to consider a randomized stationary policy $\pi_\mathcal{D} : S \to \triangle(S)$ where $\triangle(S)$ denotes the space of probability distributions over S. Equivalently, $\pi_\mathcal{D} = \{\mathbf{p}_i\}_{i\in[n]}$ where p_{ij} gives the probability of moving to configuration j when the system is in configuration i in the previous time step. That is, the defense policy in time t is determined by the system configuration s^{t-1} only. The defender's goal is to minimize its expected total loss including the loss from attacks and the migration cost.

2.2   Threat Model

We consider a persistent adversary that continuously attacks the system according to a chosen policy. At the beginning of each time step t, the attacker chooses a system configuration $\tilde{s}^t$ to attack. The attack fails if the attacker chooses the wrong target, that is, $\tilde{s}^t \neq s^t$. Otherwise, the attack succeeds with a probability μ_{s^t} and fails with a probability $1 - \mu_{s^t}$. If the attack succeeds, it leads to a loss of l_{s^t} to the defender (including the recovery cost as discussed above). That is, we model the attacker's *type* using a tuple $(\mu, \mathbf{l})$, where $\mu = \{\mu_j\}_n$ are the attack success rates over the set of configurations and $\mathbf{l} = \{l_j\}_n$ are the unit time system losses for all configurations. The attacker type captures its capability and effectiveness to compromise a set of configurations. Different types of attacks may target the same vulnerability of a configuration but may result in different loss to the system. In practice, these values can be derived from real measurements or publicly available databases such as the National Vulnerability Database (NVD) [5] (see the experiment section for the details).

We assume that the attacker always learns the system configuration s^t at the end of time step t whether the system is compromised at t or not (a worst-case scenario from the defender's perspective). Then it is without loss of generality to consider a randomized stationary policy for the attacker $\pi_\mathcal{A} : S \to \triangle(S)$, which can equivalently be defined by $\{\mathbf{q}_i\}_{i\in[n]}$ where q_{ij} denotes the probability of attacking configuration j if the system is in configuration i in the previous time step.

We define an attack as $\xi = (\mu, \mathbf{l}, \pi_A)$ to include its type and policy. In general, the true attack encountered at any time is initially unknown to the defender. However, the defender may have a rough estimate of the possible attacks.

2.3   The Markov Game Model for MTD

With the definitions and assumptions given above, we can model the sequential interactions between the defender and the attacker of a given type as a two-player general-sum Markov game (MG), denoted by $G = (S, A, \mathcal{P}, r, \gamma)$, where

- S is the state space. In this work, we model the system state s^t at any time t as its configuration. Note that both the defender and the attacker know the true system configuration s^{t-1} at the beginning of time t. Thus, they share the same state space.

- $A = A_\mathcal{D} \times A_\mathcal{A}$ is the joint action space, where $A_\mathcal{D}$ and $A_\mathcal{A}$ are the defender's action space and the attacker's action space, respectively. In this work, we have $A_\mathcal{D} = A_\mathcal{A} = S$. At the beginning of each time step, the defender pick the next configuration s^t to switch to while the attacker picks a target configuration $\tilde{s}^t$ to attack simultaneously according to their policies to fight for control of the system. Let $a^t = (s^t, \tilde{s}^t)$ denote the joint action.

- $\mathcal{P} : S \times A \to \triangle(S)$ is the state transition function that represents the probability of reaching a state $s' \in S$ given the current state $s \in S$ and the joint action $a \in A$. In our setting, the system transition is deterministic as the next state is completely determined by the defender's action.

- $r = \{r_\mathcal{D}, r_\mathcal{A}\}$ where $r_\mathcal{D} : S \times A \to \mathbb{R}_{\leq 0}$ and $r_\mathcal{A} : S \times A \to \mathbb{R}_{\geq 0}$ are the reward functions for the defender and the attacker, respectively. Precisely, given the previous system configuration s^{t-1}, the defender's action s^t, and the attacker's action $\tilde{s}^t$, the defender obtains a reward $r_\mathcal{D}^t = r_\mathcal{D}(s^{t-1}, (s^t, \tilde{s}^t)) = -\mathbf{1}_{s^t = \tilde{s}^t}\mu_{s^t}l_{s^t} - m_{s^{t-1}s^t}$ and the attack obtains a reward $r_\mathcal{A}^t = r_\mathcal{A}(s^{t-1}, (s^t, \tilde{s}^t)) = \mathbf{1}_{s^t = \tilde{s}^t}\mu_{s^t}l_{s^t}$ where $\mathbf{1}_{(.)}$ is the indicator function.

- $\gamma \in (0, 1]$ is the discount factor.

Given the initial state s^0 and a pair of policies $\pi_\mathcal{D}$ and $\pi_\mathcal{A}$ for the defender and the attacker, respectively, let $V_i^{\pi_\mathcal{D}, \pi_\mathcal{A}}(s^0) = \mathbb{E}_{\pi_\mathcal{D}, \pi_\mathcal{A}}[\sum_{t=0}^{\infty} \gamma^t r_i(s^{t-1}, (s^t, \tilde{s}^t)|s^0)]$ denote the total expected return for the player i, where $i \in \{\mathcal{D}, \mathcal{A}\}$. The goal of each player is to maximize its total expected return. Similar to normal-form games, various solution concepts have been considered for Markov games, including Nash equilibrium [17], correlated equilibrium [45], and Stackelberg equilibrium [22]. In this work, we consider the Stackelberg equilibrium as the solution concept. Given the asymmetric information structure commonly seen in cybersecurity and to derive a robust defense, it is typical to consider the Stackelberg equilibrium (or a variant of it) with the defender as the leader and the attacker as the follower. In particular, the defender first commits to a policy π_D, and the attacker as the follower observes π_D (e.g., by stealthily collecting enough samples of defense actions before attacking) and then picks π_A optimally. This approach has been extensively studied for one-shot security games including models such as Stackelberg security games (SSG) and Bayesian Stackelberg games (BSG) [28,36]. Recently, it has been applied for defending against persistent attacks using techniques such as MTD [23,33,34]. Note that when π_D is random as is typical in security domains, knowing π_D does not let the attacker learn the defender's true action in each time step.

When the attacker has multiple best responses to the defender's policy, a common assumption in security games is that the attacker always chooses the one in favor of the defender. This gives the concept of the Strong Stackelberg equilibrium (SSE) formally defined below, which is the solution concept we use in this work.

Definition 1 (SSE). *For each defense policy $\pi_{\mathcal{D}}$, let $B(\pi_{\mathcal{D}})$ denote the set of attack policies that maximize $V_{\mathcal{D}}^{\pi_{\mathcal{D}},'}(s^0)$ for any s^0, i.e.,*

$$B(\pi_{\mathcal{D}}) := \{\pi_{\mathcal{A}} : V_{\mathcal{A}}^{\pi_{\mathcal{D}},\pi_{\mathcal{A}}}(s^0) = \max_{\pi'_{\mathcal{A}}} V_{\mathcal{A}}^{\pi_{\mathcal{D}},\pi'_{\mathcal{A}}}(s^0), \forall s^0 \in S\} \tag{1}$$

A pair of stationary policies $(\pi_{\mathcal{D}}^*, \pi_{\mathcal{A}}^*)$ forms a strong Stackelberg equilibrium if for any $s^0 \in S$, we have

$$V_{\mathcal{D}}^{\pi_{\mathcal{D}}^*,\pi_{\mathcal{A}}^*}(s^0) = \max_{\pi_{\mathcal{D}},\pi_{\mathcal{A}} \in B(\pi_{\mathcal{D}})} V_{\mathcal{D}}^{\pi_{\mathcal{D}},\pi_{\mathcal{A}}}(s^0) \tag{2}$$

Since the Markov game defined above has finite state and action spaces and the transition is deterministic, an SSE (when the leader is restricted to randomized stationary policies) is guaranteed to exist and provides a unique game value to the defender [3,37,41]. Further, an SSE can be found using either an exact solution [41] or an approximation solution such as Stackelberg Q-learning [22,33] and Stackelberg policy gradient [18,42] for large games. The following simple observation justifies the use of SSE as the solution concept in our MTD framework. In particular, it shows that by following the defense policy given by an SSE, the defender's loss in the face of an arbitrary attacker is upper bounded by the loss specified by the SSE.

Lemma 1. *Let $(\pi_{\mathcal{D}}^*, \pi_{\mathcal{A}}^*)$ be a strong Stackelberg equilibrium. For an arbitrary attack policy $\pi_{\mathcal{A}}$, we have $V_{\mathcal{D}}^{\pi_{\mathcal{D}}^*,\pi_{\mathcal{A}}}(s^0) \geq V_{\mathcal{D}}^{\pi_{\mathcal{D}}^*,\pi_{\mathcal{A}}^*}(s^0)$ for any s^0.*

Proof. For any pair of policies $(\pi_{\mathcal{D}}, \pi_{\mathcal{A}})$ and initial state s^0, we can write $V_{\mathcal{D}}^{\pi_{\mathcal{D}},\pi_{\mathcal{A}}}(s^0) = -L(\pi_{\mathcal{D}}, \pi_{\mathcal{A}}) - \mathcal{M}(\pi_{\mathcal{D}})$, where the first term captures the total expected attack loss, and the second term specifies the total expected migration cost. The result then follows by observing that $V_{\mathcal{D}}^{\pi_{\mathcal{D}}^*,\pi_{\mathcal{A}}}(s^0) = -L(\pi_{\mathcal{D}}^*, \pi_{\mathcal{A}}) - \mathcal{M}(\pi_{\mathcal{D}}^*) \geq -L(\pi_{\mathcal{D}}^*, \pi_{\mathcal{A}}^*) - \mathcal{M}(\pi_{\mathcal{D}}^*) = V_{\mathcal{D}}^{\pi_{\mathcal{D}}^*,\pi_{\mathcal{A}}^*}(s^0)$, where the inequality is due to the fact that $\pi_{\mathcal{A}}^*$ is the attacker's best response to $\pi_{\mathcal{D}}^*$ and the migration cost is independent of the attack policy.

Note that Lemma 1 does not hold for general non-zero-sum Markov games. It holds in our setting because the defender's total attack loss $L(\pi_{\mathcal{D}}, \pi_{\mathcal{A}})$ is exactly the attacker's total gain and the migration cost $\mathcal{M}(\pi_{\mathcal{D}})$ is independent of the attacker's policy.

2.4   Two-Stage Defense Overview

The asymmetric Markov game presented above provides a reasonable solution to robust MTD by considering the worst-case attack behavior. However, the solution thus obtained can be overly conservative in the face of a "weaker" attacker (e.g., a dumb attacker that does not respond to the defense strategically). Moreover, to solve the game, the defender needs to know the exact attacker type, which can lead to a poor solution when the true attacker type deviates from

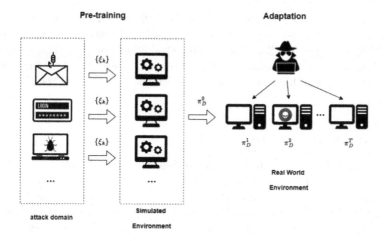

Fig. 1. Two-stage defense overview.

the guessed one as shown in our experiments. One possible solution is to consider a distribution of possible attacker types and optimize the defense policy for either the worst case using distributionally robust optimization [9] or the average case using a Bayesian approach [16,33]. However, these approaches miss the opportunity of online adaption and can lead to suboptimal defense.

To effectively thwart a potentially unknown attacker, we propose a meta-learning based two-stage defense framework (see Fig. 1) to pre-train a meta-policy on a variety of attacks in an simulated environment, such that it can be quickly adapted to a new attack using only a small number of real samples.

The training stage is implemented in a simulated environment, which allows sufficient training using trajectories generated from a pool of potential attacks. The possible set of attack types can be generated using existing databases, such as the National Vulnerability Database (NVD) [5] or penetration testing tools like Kali Linux [2]. On the other hand, to generate diverse attack behavior, we consider both the worst-case scenario specified by the SSE, where the attacker responds to the defense policy optimally, as well as "weaker" attacks, e.g., a random attack that is agnostic of the defense policy. At the test stage, the learned meta-policy π_D^0 is applied and updated using feedback (i.e., rewards) received in the face of real attacks that are not necessarily in the training set (in terms of both attack type and attack behavior).

3   Meta-RL Based MTD Solution Framework

In this section, we discuss the details of our meta-reinforcement learning based MTD solution. We first present an important observation that from the defender's perspective, the problem of finding its optimal MTD policy can be reformulated as a single-agent Markov decision process (MDP). This result holds both when the attacker follows a fixed stationary policy that is known to the defender as well as when it first observes the defense policy and then responds to it optimally (as in the case of solving the SSE of the Markov game presented above). This observation allows us to reduce the bilevel optimization problem to a single level optimization problem. Based on this observation, we then present our two-stage defense that adapts model-agnostic meta-learning (MAML) [14,27] to MTD.

3.1   Reducing the MG to an MDP

Before starting the main results in this section, we first generalize the definition of SSE by allowing the attacker to respond to the defense policy in a suboptimal way, which allows us to incorporate diverse attack behavior into meta-learning. In particular, we will assume that after the defender commits to a stationary policy π_D, the attacker chooses a policy $\mathbf{q}_s \in R(s, \pi_D)$ for any s, where $R(\cdot, \pi_D)$ denotes a set of response policies [22]. Note that this includes the cases when the attacker responds in an optimal way (as in the case of SSE), when it responds in a suboptimal way, as well as the case when the attack policy is fixed and independent of the defense. We define a pair of policies (π_D, π_A) to be a *generalized SSE* if π_D minimizes the defender's loss assuming the attack responds according to its response set R and in favor of the defender when there is a tie.

We first show that the defender's problem can be viewed as a single agent MDP whenever the following assumptions hold.

Assumption 1. *For any state $s \in S$, the attacker's response set is either a singleton or all the responses are equally good to the defender.*

Assumption 2. *For any state $s \in S$, the attacker's policy $\mathbf{q}_s$ in state s only depends on s and $\mathbf{p}_s$, i.e., the defender's policy at state s, and is independent of the defender's policy in other states. That is, given π_D, we can write $\mathbf{q}_s \triangleq R(s, \mathbf{p}_s)$ for any $s \in S$.*

In particular, Assumption 1 allows the defender to infer the attack policy under each state, while Assumption 2 ensures that the defender's reward at any time depends on the current state and defense action only but not the future states (see the proof of Lemma 2).

Lemma 2. *When Assumptions 1 and 2 hold, the optimal defense policy in the sense of a generalized SSE can be found by solving a single-agent Markov decision process with continuous actions for the defender.*

Proof. Consider the following MDP for the defender $M = (S, A', T', r', \gamma)$, which is derived from the Markov game in Sect. 2.3, where

- S is the state space, which is defined as the set of configurations.
- $A' = \triangle(S)$ is the action space of the defender, where we redefine the defender's action in configuration s as the probability vector $\mathbf{p}_s$, which is critical for converting the Markov game into an MDP.

- $\mathcal{P}' : S \times A' \to \triangle(S)$ is the state transition function. Given the previous system configuration s and the defender's action $\mathbf{p}_s$, the probability of reaching a configuration s' in the current time step is $\mathcal{P}'(s'|s, \mathbf{p}_s) = p_{ss'}$. Note that the state transition is stochastic rather than deterministic as in the Markov game.
- $r' : S \times A' \to \mathbb{R}_{\leq 0}$ is the reward function for the defender. Given the previous configuration s^{t-1}, the defender's action $\mathbf{p}_{s^{t-1}}$, the attacker's policy can be represented as $\mathbf{q}_{s^{t-1}} = R(s^{t-1}, \mathbf{p}_{s^{t-1}})$ according to Assumptions 1 and 2 (with ties broken arbitrarily when $R(s^{t-1}, \mathbf{p}_{s^{t-1}})$ is not a singleton). The defender's reward is defined as $r'(s^{t-1}, \mathbf{p}_{s^{t-1}}) = \sum_{s^t, \tilde{s}^t} p_{s^{t-1}s^t} q_{s^{t-1}\tilde{s}^t} r_D(s^{t-1}, (s^t, \tilde{s}^t))$.
- $\gamma \in (0, 1)$ is the discount factor, which is the same as the discount factor in the Markov game.

It is crucial to note that while the defender's reward function r_D in the Markov game depends on the joint action of both the attacker and the defender, r' only depends on the defender's action and is therefore well defined. This is achieved by redefining the defection's action in any configuration as the corresponding migration probability vector and using the two assumptions. Given the MDP above, it is easy to check that the problem of finding the best defense policy can be reduced to finding a deterministic policy $\pi : S \to A'$ that maximizes the total expected return $\mathbb{E}_\pi[\sum_{t=0}^{\infty} \gamma^t r'(s^{t-1}, \mathbf{p}_{s^{t-1}}|s^0)]$ in the MDP.

Note that both assumptions automatically hold when the attacker is agnostic to the defense policy, and Assumption 1 holds for an SSE. Below we show that for any stationary defense policy, there is a best-response attack that satisfies Assumption 2.

Lemma 3. *For any stationary defense policy $\mathbf{p}$, any deterministic policy $\mathbf{q}$ of the following form is in the attacker's best response set: for any $i \in S$, there is $j \in S$ such that $q_{ij} = 1$, $q_{ik} = 0$ for $k \neq j$, and $j \in \arg\max_j p_{ij}\mu_j l_j$.*

Proof. Given a stationary defense policy $\mathbf{p}$ and initial state s^0, the attacker's goal is to maximize its expected total reward, that is

$$
\max_{\mathbf{q}} V_{\mathcal{A}}^{\mathbf{p,q}}(s^0) = \max_{\mathbf{q}} \mathbb{E}_{\mathbf{p,q}} \left(\sum_{t=0}^{\infty} \gamma^t r_{\mathcal{A}}(s^{t-1}, (s^t, \tilde{s}^t)) \right)
$$

$$
\overset{a}{=} \max_{\mathbf{q}(s^0)} \sum_{s^1, \tilde{s}^1} p_{s^0 s^1} q_{s^0 \tilde{s}^1} r_{\mathcal{A}}(s^0, (s^1, \tilde{s}^1)) + \gamma \max_{\mathbf{q}} V_{\mathcal{A}}^{\mathbf{p,q}}(s^1)
$$

$$
= \max_{s^1} p_{s^0 s^1} r_{\mathcal{A}}(s^0, (s^1, s^1)) + \gamma \max_{\mathbf{q}} V_{\mathcal{A}}^{\mathbf{p,q}}(s^1)
$$

$$
\overset{b}{=} \max_{s^1} p_{s^0 s^1} \mu_{s^1} l_{s^1} + \gamma \max_{\mathbf{q}} V_{\mathcal{A}}^{\mathbf{p,q}}(s^1)
$$

where (a) is due to the fact that the transition probabilities only depend on the current state and the defender's action, and (b) follows from the definition of $r_{\mathcal{A}}$. The result then follows by induction.

The following result follows directly from Lemma 2 and Lemma 3.

Proposition 1. *An SSE defense policy can be found by solving a single-agent Markov decision process with continuous actions for the defender.*

From the above proposition, the defender can identify a near-optimal defense by solving the MDP above whenever the attack type is known and the attack behavior follows a known response set. This can be done using either dynamic programming or a model-free reinforcement learning algorithm with samples generated from a simulator of the MDP, the latter is more suitable for MTDs with a large configuration space. In both cases, the defense policy can be derived in a simulated environment without interacting with the true attacks.

3.2 Robust Defense via Meta-RL

In order to cope with real attacks with uncertain or unknown types and behaviors, we propose a meta reinforcement learning based two-stage defense framework. The core idea is to pre-train a meta-policy over a distribution of defender's MDPs, where each MDP corresponds to interactions with a particular attack. At test time, the pre-trained meta defense policy is quickly adapted to the true attack encountered using a small number of samples.

Meta-learning (or learning-to-learn) is a principled approach for developing algorithms that can adapt experiences collected from training tasks to solving unseen tasks quickly and efficiently, which has been successfully applied to various learning domains including reinforcement learning. In this work, we adopt a first-order model-agnostic meta-learning algorithm, Reptile [27] to MTD by viewing the defender's problem of solving its MDP against a particular attack $\xi^k = (\mu_k, l_k, R_k)$ as a task (see Algorithm 1). Here R_k is the response function defined in Sect. 3.1 that completely captures the attack behavior. The input to the algorithm includes a distribution of attacks $\mathcal{P}(\xi)$, which can be estimated from public datasets or through experiments, and two step sizes.

We consider the defender's policy to be represented by a parametrized function (e.g., a neural network) $\pi_{\mathcal{D}}(\theta)$ with parameters θ. The algorithm starts with an initial model θ^0, and updates it over T iterations. In each iteration, the algorithm first samples a batch of K attacks from $\mathcal{P}(\xi)$. For each attack, a trajectory of length H is generated, which is used to compute the meta-policy θ_k^t for the k-th attack by performing gradient descent for m steps with step size α. Given an initial state s_0, we define the loss function for a particular attack over H time steps as

$$\mathcal{L}_{\xi^k}(\pi_{\mathcal{D}}(\theta)) = -\mathbb{E}_{\pi_{\mathcal{D}}(\theta)}\left[\sum_{t=1}^{H} r'(s^{t-1}, \mathbf{p}_{s^{t-1}})\right] \tag{3}$$

We consider a fixed horizon setting (with $\gamma = 1$) such that the defender is allowed to query a limited number of samples for updating its policy. Let H denote the length of an episode. The policy gradient method is performed on the loss $\mathcal{L}_{\xi^k}$ starting with initial parameters $\theta_k^t = \theta^{t-1}$ and returns the final

---

Algorithm 1. Reptile Meta-Reinforcement Learning for Robust MTD

Input: a distribution over attacks $\mathcal{P}(\xi)$, step size parameters α, β
Output: θ^T
randomly initialize θ^0
for iteration $= 1$ to T **do**
    Sample K attacks ξ^k from $\mathcal{P}(\xi)$
    for all ξ^k **do**
        Sample a trajectory $\mathcal{H}$ of length H using $\pi_\mathcal{D}(\theta^{t-1})$ and attack ξ^k
        $\theta_k^t \leftarrow \theta^{t-1}$
        for $l = 1$ to m **do**
            Evaluate $\nabla_\theta \mathcal{L}_{\xi^k}(\pi_\mathcal{D}(\theta_k^t))$ using $\mathcal{H}$ and $\mathcal{L}_{\xi^k}$ in Eq. (3)
            $\theta_k^t \leftarrow \theta_k^t - \alpha \nabla_\theta \mathcal{L}_{\xi^k}(\pi_\mathcal{D}(\theta_k^t))$
        end for
    end for
    Update $\theta^t \leftarrow \theta^{t-1} - \beta \sum_{k=1}^K (\theta^{t-1} - \theta_k^t)$
end for

---

parameters. With model parameters collected from all the tasks in the batch, θ^t is then updated towards these new parameters. Note that the single-task gradient is defined as $(\theta - \theta_k)/\alpha$, where α is the step size used by the gradient decent operation. According to [27], we assume that policy $\pi_\mathcal{D}(\theta_k)$ achieves the best performance for task ξ^k when θ_k lays on the surface of the manifold of optimal network configuration. We want to find the closest point on the optimal task manifold. This cannot be computed exactly, but Reptile approximates it using $\mathcal{L}_{\xi^k}$. The trained meta-defense policy is then adapted at test time with a few more samples from interactions with the real attacks.

Remark 1. In more complicated scenarios where the defender's SSE policy cannot be formulated as an MDP, we may still adopt the above meta-learning framework by solving the Markov game defined in Sect. 2.3 to identify the SSE defense at both the meta-training stage and the testing stage. Extension of the meta-RL algorithm to this more general setting (e.g., delayed/noisy feedback from both attacker's and defender's perspectives) is left to future work.

4 Experiment Results

In this section, we validate our MTD framework using the data from the National Vulnerability Database (NVD) [5]. We aim to understand if the SSE defense can provide a robust solution in the face of uncertain/unknown attacks and how meta-learning can help further improve the security of the system.

4.1 Experiment Setup and Baselines

System Configurations. We consider a web system with four configuration $S = \{(Python, SQL), (Python, secureSQL), (PHP, SQL), (PHP, secureSQL)\}$

	Python, SQL	Python, secureSQL	PHP, SQL	PHP, secureSQL
Python, SQL	0	1	2	3
Python, secureSQL	2	0	1	2
PHP, SQL	2	3	0	1
PHP, secureSQL	3	2	1	0

	Python, SQL	Python, secureSQL	PHP, SQL	PHP, secureSQL
Mainstream Hacker (MH) attack success rate	0.2	0.1	0.7	0.5
Database Hacker (DH) attack success rate	0.2	0	0.7	0
Mainstream Hacker (MH) unit system loss	40	50	10	25
Database Hacker (DH) unit system loss	80	0	60	0

Fig. 2. Defender's and attacker's parameters. The upper table gives the migration cost for the MTD system. Each row represents a source configuration and each column represents a destination configuration. The lower table shows the attack parameters including the attack success rate and the unit time system loss (see Sect. 2.2 for details), for the Mainstream Hacker (MH) and the Database Hacker (DH), respectively.

across two layers, similar to [23,34]. The first layer specifies the programming language used for web applications including Python and PHP. The second layer specifies the database technology used, where SQL stands for the case when the database layer naively uses the structured query language without protection, while secureSQL indicates the case when the database layer is protected using methods including but not limited to isolating the database server, regulating SQL traffic, and restricting the ability users to perform unauthorized tasks [29,39]. By doing so, we create some 'safe' configurations for certain types of attacks (e.g., configurations using secureSQL is immune to the Database Hacker defined below). The migration cost matrix is given in Fig. 2, which is designed with the following considerations in mind: (1) switching between configurations across different layers incurs a higher cost than switching within the same layer; (2) the migration cost between two configurations could be asymmetric; (3) the migration cost should be significantly lower than the loss caused by a successful attack.

Attack Types. Inspired by [23,34], we derive the key attack parameters (i.e., the attack success rate and the unit time system loss) from the Common Vulnerabilities Exposure (CVE) scores given by the Common Vulnerability Scoring System (CVSS) [26] in NVD. In particular, for a given vulnerability, an attack with an Impact Score (IS) $\in [0,10]$ and an Exploitability Scores (ES) $\in [0,10]$ will generate $10 \times$IS unit time loss, and will have a $0.1 \times$ ES attack success rate. We consider two attack types, the Mainstream Hacker (MH) and the Database Hacker (DH) as in [34]. An MH attack can exploit a large set of vulnerabilities, but causes less loss when the attack succeeds. In contrast, the DH targets only a few database specific vulnerabilities, but causes critical loss when it succeeds. We collect CVEs in NVD ranging from 2019 to 2021 according to CVSS v3.0, targeting keywords Python, PHP, and SQL, then calculate their rounded average scores. The attack parameters obtained for MH and DH are shown in Fig. 2. We use them to simulate attack types at test time while considering a broader class of attack types at training time (see Sect. 4.3).

Baseline Defense and Attack Strategies. We consider the following defense strategies in the experiments.

- Uniform Random Strategy (URS) [36]: In a URS defense, the defender uniformly samples a configuration from S to switch to in each time step.
- Reinforcement Learning Strategy (RL): In an RL defense, the defender identifies its optimal defense by solving a single-agent MDP using reinforcement learning. This requires the defender (as the leader) to guess the attacker's response as discussed in Sect. 3.1. This includes the SSE defense as a special case when the attacker is assumed to respond optimally.

We consider the following attack strategies in the experiments.

- Uniform Random Strategy (URS) [36]: In a URS attack, the attacker uniformly samples a configuration from S to attack in each time step.
- Reinforcement Learning Strategy (RL): When the defender adopts a stationary policy, the attacker (as the follower) can learn the defense policy and then identify its optimal attack policy by solving a single-agent MDP using reinforcement learning. We call such an attack RL attack.
- Best Response Strategy (BS): Instead of using the RL attack, the attacker can also identify its best response by solving a simple optimizing problem in each time step as proved in Lemma 3. We call this attack BS attack.
- Worst Response Strategy (WS): We further consider the opposite of the best-response attack where the attacker takes the worst-response (WS) action in each time step, that is, $q_{ij} = 1$ for some $j \in \arg\min_j p_{ij}\mu_j l_j$ and $q_{ik} = 0$ for $k \neq j$ (see Lemma 3).

Meta-RL Settings. We implement our MTD environment using Pytorch and OpenAI gym [7]. We use Twin Delayed DDPG (TD3) [15] implemented by OpenAI Stable Baseline3 [31] as the policy updating algorithm in both the pre-training and adaptation stages. The initial state is uniformly sampled from the configuration space. At the training stage, we set the number of iterations $T = 100$. In each iteration, we uniformly sample $K = 20$ attacks from the attack domain (see Sect. 4.3 for details). For each attack, we generate a trajectory of length $H = 100$ and update the corresponding meta-policy for 10 steps using TD3 (i.e., $m = 10$). At the test stage, the meta-policy is adapted for 100 steps using TD3 with $T = 10$, $H = 10$, and $m = 1$. Other parameters are described as follows: single task step size $\alpha = 0.001$, meta-optimization step size $\beta = 1$, adaptation step size $= 0.01$, the policy model is *MlpPolicy*, batch size $= 100$ and $\gamma = 1$ for updating the target networks. All the experiments are conducted

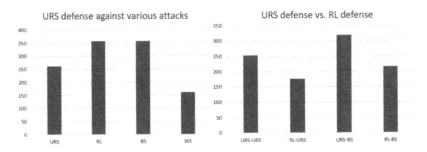

Fig. 3. Left: a comparison of defender's total loss for 100 time steps under the URS defense against different attacks (i.e., URS, RL, BS, and WS). Right: a comparison of defender's total loss for 100 time steps under URS defense and RL defense against URS attack and BS attack, respectively. Here the RL defense is trained against URS attack. All parameters are described in Sect. 4.1.

on the same 2.30 GHz Linux machine with 16 GB NVIDIA Tesla P100 GPU. We run all the tests for 1,000 times and report the mean value. Since the standard deviations are below 0.04, we omit the error bar for better visualization.

4.2   Results for a Single Attack Type

Before presenting the results for our meta-RL based MTD framework, we first verify our observations made in previous sections regarding the best-response attack and SSE by considering a single attack type (the Mainstream Hacker (MH)) where the defender knows the attack parameters (μ and l) but not necessarily the attack policy.

Optimal Attack vs. Random Attack. Figure 3(left) compares the performance of URS defense under different attacks. Among them, RL attack and BS attack incur the highest total loss ($\sim$356) in 100 steps, indicating that reinforcement learning can also be used to identify the best response attack although it is more time-consuming to train. Both URS and BS attacks perform better than WS as expected. Figure 3(right) shows the performance of URS defense and RL defense (trained against the URS attack) in the face of URS attack and BS attack, respectively. RL against URS (RL-URS) achieves the lowest cost, indicating that the RL defense is effective when the defender knows both the attack type and attack policy. In contrast, RL-BS incurs a higher cost indicating the impact when the defender's guess on the attack policy is wrong. However, RL defense outperforms URS defense in both cases.

The Robustness of SSE Defense. We show in Lemma 3 that when the defender adopts the SSE defense, it can obtain a guaranteed (albeit conservative) level of protection even when the attacker deviates from the best response behavior. We verify this observation in Fig. 4 where under the SSE defense, the total loss incurred by the BS attack is always higher than the URS attack over all the training lengths. We further observe that longer training improves

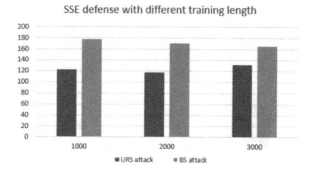

Fig. 4. A comparison of defender's total loss over 100 time steps under the SSE defense (with different training length) against URS and BS attacks.

the defense performance against the BS attack (the attack used in training the defense policy), but is not always helpful to defend against other attacks (due to overfitting).

4.3 The Effectiveness and Efficiency of Meta-RL Defense

To demonstrate the advantage of our meta-RL defense, we consider two attacks at the test stage, the Mainstream Hacker (MH) and the Database Hacker (DH), both using the BS strategy as the attack policy. We further consider two meta-training settings. In the white-box setting, all attacks for training are sampled from the four combinations of the two attack types (e.g., MH and DH) and the two attack policies (e.g., URS and BS). In the black-box setting, the attack domain includes infinite number of attack types, where each has an uniformly random IS $\in [0, 10]$ and an uniformly random ES $\in [0, 10]$ for every configuration, with the attack policies uniformly sampled from URS and BS. Thus, the white-box setting captures the scenario when the test-stage attack is uncertain to the defender while the black-box setting captures the scenario when the test-stage attack type is essentially unseen to the defender. In both cases, we use the SSE defense trained against the MH attack as the baseline.

Figure 5 shows the defender's test-stage loss over 1,000 time steps, where the meta-policy is adapted for 100 steps at the beginning of the test stage. Note that the RL policy trained against the MH attack is optimal in the face of the same MH attack at test time, which is expected. We observe that both the white-box and the black-box meta-RL defenses perform close to the optimal defense policy. For the DH attack, the RL defense performs poorly due to the mismatch between the training stage and testing stage attack types, while both meta-RL defenses significantly reduce the defender's cost, indicating the benefit of meta-learning. Specifically, the white-box meta-RL defense quickly adapts to the optimal policy, i.e., staying at configuration ($Python, secureSQL$) or configuration ($PHP, secureSQL$) since DH has zero impact on these states.

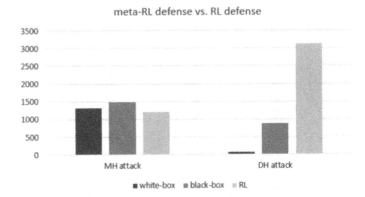

Fig. 5. A comparison of defender's total loss over 1,000 testing time steps for white-box and black-box meta-RL defenses and RL defense (trained against MH attack), against MH attack and DH attack, respectively. The meta-RL polices are adapted for 100 steps at the beginning of the test stage. All attacks adopt the BS strategy at the test stage.

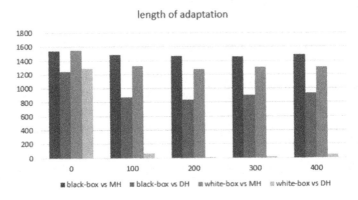

Fig. 6. The defender's total loss over 1,000 testing time steps under different adaptation length for black-box and white-box meta-RL defenses against MH and DH attacks, respectively. We only show the results for policies obtained at step 0, 100, 200, 300 and 400, respectively. All attacks adopt the BS strategy at the test stage.

Figure 6 shows how the defender's test-stage loss over 1,000 time steps varies across different adaptation duration, where we only plot the results for policies obtained at time step 0, 100, 200, 300, and 400, respectively. As expected, the white-box meta-RL adapts faster since the both attacks considered at testing time are included in the training stage attack domain. Note that the adaptation for the MH attack is less significant since the meta-policy without adaptation is already close to optimal with respect to the MH attack. Although not shown in the figure, we observe that it is much more effective to adapt a well-trained meta-policy (around 10 times faster) than training a new RL policy from scratch (e.g., starting from a random initial policy) to obtain a similar level of protection.

5   Related Work

Stackelberg Games for MTD. Stackelberg games [4] have been widely used to derive robust defense against strategic attacks. In particular, one-shot Stackelberg games such as the classic Stackelberg security games (SSG) have been extensively studied for various physical security and cybersecurity domains [36]. In the vanilla SSG, the defender commits to a mixed strategy while the attack observes the strategy and chooses a best response accordingly. Various extensions of SSG have been considered including Bayesian Stackelberg games (BSG) [28], where a Bayesian approach is adopted to model the defender's uncertainty about attack types. A repeated BSG has been applied to MTD in [34] where the defense policy is independent of the current system configuration. More recently, asymmetric Markov game models have been proposed for MTD [13,23,24], which allow state-dependent defense but assume a fixed attack type. In [33], a Bayesian Stackelberg Markov game (BSMG) is proposed where the attack type can vary over time according to a pre-defined distribution.

Meta-reinforcement Learning. The purpose of meta-RL is to generalize the experience learned from training tasks to new tasks that can be never encountered during training. The adaptation stage in meta-learning is required to have limited exposure to the new tasks, which is crucial for security or safety sensitive domains as it can be expensive or even dangerous to collect samples in real settings. Various approaches have been proposed for meta-learning including metrics-based, model-based, and optimization-based methods [44]. In [43] and [10], the meta-learning algorithm is encoded in the weights of a recurrent neural network, hence gradient descent is not performed at test time. In [14], a model-agnostic meta-learning (MAML) framework is proposed, which does not require a recurrent model, but instead learns the parameters of any standard model via solving a second-order meta-objective optimization. Reptile [27] is a first-order meta-learning optimization algorithm, which is similar to MAML in many ways, given that both relying on meta-optimization through gradient descent and both are model-agnostic.

6   Conclusion

In this paper, we propose a meta-reinforcement learning based moving target defense framework. The key observation of our work is that existing security game models built upon the strong Stackelberg equilibrium (SSE) solution concept (and its Bayesian variant) can lead to suboptimal defense due to the distribution shift between the attacks used for training the defense policy and the true attacks encountered in reality. To this end, we first formulate the MTD problem as an asymmetric Markov game with the defender as the leader and the attacker as the follower. We show that the best-response attack at each state can be determined by the current state of the system and the defender's mix strategy in the current state. This allows us to formulate the problem of finding the SSE defense as a single agent Markov decision process (MDP). We then show that by pre-training the defense policy across a pool of attacks (defined as different MDPs) using model-agnostic meta-learning, the meta-defense policy can quickly adapt to the true attacks at test time. Our two-stage defense approach improves upon the SSE defense in the presence of uncertain/unknown attack type and attack behavior.

Acknowledgement. This work has been funded in part by NSF grant CNS-1816495. We thank the anonymous reviewers for their valuable and constructive comments.

References

1. Al-Shaer, E., Duan, Q., Jafarian, J.H.: Random host mutation for moving target defense. In: Keromytis, A.D., Di Pietro, R. (eds.) SecureComm 2012. LNICST, vol. 106, pp. 310–327. Springer, Heidelberg (2013). https://doi.org/10.1007/978-3-642-36883-7_19
2. Allen, L., Heriyanto, T., Ali, S.: Kali Linux-Assuring Security by Penetration Testing. Packt Publishing Ltd. (2014)
3. Basar, T.: Lecture notes on non-cooperative game theory (2010). https://www.hamilton.ie/ollie/Downloads/Game.pdf
4. Başar, T., Olsder, G.J.: Dynamic Noncooperative Game Theory. SIAM (1998)
5. Booth, H., Rike, D., Witte, G.A., et al.: The national vulnerability database (NVD): overview (2013)
6. Bowers, K.D., Dijk, M.E.V., Juels, A., Oprea, A.M., Rivest, R.L., Triandopoulos, N.: Graph-based approach to deterring persistent security threats. US Patent 8813234 (2014)
7. Brockman, G., et al.: OpenAI gym. ArXiv abs/1606.01540 (2016)
8. Cho, J.H., et al.: Toward proactive, adaptive defense: a survey on moving target defense. IEEE Commun. Surv. Tutor. **22**(1), 709–745 (2020)
9. Derman, E., Mannor, S.: Distributional robustness and regularization in reinforcement learning. In: The Theoretical Foundations of Reinforcement Learning Workshop at ICML 2020 (2020)
10. Duan, Y., Schulman, J., Chen, X., Bartlett, P.L., Sutskever, I., Abbeel, P.: RL^2: fast reinforcement learning via slow reinforcement learning. arXiv preprint arXiv:1611.02779 (2016)
11. Eldosouky, A., Saad, W., Niyato, D.: Single controller stochastic games for optimized moving target defense. In: IEEE International Conference on Communications (ICC) (2016)
12. Fallah, A., Mokhtari, A., Ozdaglar, A.: Generalization of model-agnostic meta-learning algorithms: recurring and unseen tasks. In: NeurIPS (2021)
13. Feng, X., Zheng, Z., Mohapatra, P., Cansever, D.: A Stackelberg game and Markov modeling of moving target defense. In: Rass, S., An, B., Kiekintveld, C., Fang, F., Schauer, S. (eds.) GameSec 2017. LNCS, vol. 10575, pp. 315–335. Springer, Cham (2017). https://doi.org/10.1007/978-3-319-68711-7_17
14. Finn, C., Abbeel, P., Levine, S.: Model-agnostic meta-learning for fast adaptation of deep networks. In: International Conference on Machine Learning (ICML), pp. 1126–1135 (2017)
15. Fujimoto, S., Hoof, H., Meger, D.: Addressing function approximation error in actor-critic methods. In: International Conference on Machine Learning (ICML), pp. 1587–1596 (2018)

16. Ghavamzadeh, M., Mannor, S., Pineau, J., Tamar, A.: Bayesian reinforcement learning: a survey. Found. Trends Mach. Learn. **8**(5–6), 359–492 (2015)
17. Hu, J., Wellman, M.P.: Nash Q-learning for general-sum stochastic games. J. Mach. Learn. Res. **4**, 1039–1069 (2003)
18. Huang, P., Xu, M., Fang, F., Zhao, D.: Robust reinforcement learning as a Stackelberg game via adaptively-regularized adversarial training. arXiv preprint arXiv:2202.09514 (2022)
19. Jackson, T., et al.: Compiler-generated software diversity. In: Jajodia, S., Ghosh, A., Swarup, V., Wang, C., Wang, X. (eds.) Moving Target Defense. Advances in Information Security, vol. 54, pp. 77–98. Springer, New York (2011). https://doi.org/10.1007/978-1-4614-0977-9_4
20. Jafarian, J.H., Al-Shaer, E., Duan, Q.: OpenFlow random host mutation: transparent moving target defense using software defined networking. In: Proceedings of the First Workshop on Hot Topics in Software Defined Networks (HotSDN), pp. 127–132 (2012)
21. Jajodia, S., Ghosh, A.K., Swarup, V., Wang, C., Wang, X.S.: Moving Target Defense: Creating Asymmetric Uncertainty for Cyber Threats, vol. 54. Springer, Heidelberg (2011). https://doi.org/10.1007/978-1-4614-0977-9
22. Könönen, V.: Asymmetric multiagent reinforcement learning. Web Intell. Agent Syst. Int. J. (WIAS) **2**(2), 105–121 (2004)
23. Li, H., Shen, W., Zheng, Z.: Spatial-temporal moving target defense: a Markov Stackelberg game model. In: International Conference on Autonomous Agents and Multi-Agent Systems (AAMAS) (2020)
24. Li, H., Zheng, Z.: Optimal timing of moving target defense: a Stackelberg game model. In: IEEE Military Communications Conference (MILCOM). IEEE (2019)
25. Luo, Y.B., Wang, B.S., Wang, X.F., Hu, X.F., Cai, G.L., Sun, H.: RPAH: random port and address hopping for thwarting internal and external adversaries. In: 2015 IEEE Trustcom/BigDataSE/ISPA, vol. 1, pp. 263–270. IEEE (2015)
26. Mell, P., Scarfone, K., Romanosky, S.: Common vulnerability scoring system. IEEE Secur. Priv. **4**(6), 85–89 (2006)
27. Nichol, A., Achiam, J., Schulman, J.: On first-order meta-learning algorithms. arXiv preprint arXiv:1803.02999 (2018)
28. Paruchuri, P., Pearce, J.P., Marecki, J., Tambe, M., Ordonez, F., Kraus, S.: Playing games for security: an efficient exact algorithm for solving Bayesian Stackelberg games. In: Proceedings of the 7th International Joint Conference on Autonomous Agents and Multiagent Systems (AAMAS), pp. 895–902 (2008)
29. Paulin, A.: Secure SQL server-enabling secure access to remote relational data. arXiv preprint arXiv:1201.1081 (2012)
30. Peng, W., Li, F., Huang, C.T., Zou, X.: A moving-target defense strategy for cloud-based services with heterogeneous and dynamic attack surfaces. In: International Conference on Communications (ICC), pp. 804–809. IEEE (2014)
31. Raffin, A., Hill, A., Gleave, A., Kanervisto, A., Ernestus, M., Dormann, N.: Stable-baselines3: Reliable reinforcement learning implementations. J. Mach. Learn. Res. (2021)
32. Saputro, N., Tonyali, S., Aydeger, A., Akkaya, K., Rahman, M.A., Uluagac, S.: A review of moving target defense mechanisms for internet of things applications. Model. Design Secure Internet Things 563–614 (2020)
33. Sengupta, S., Kambhampati, S.: Multi-agent reinforcement learning in bayesian Stackelberg Markov games for adaptive moving target defense. arXiv preprint arXiv:2007.10457 (2020)

34. Sengupta, S., et al.: A game theoretic approach to strategy generation for moving target defense in web applications. In: International Conference on Autonomous Agents and Multi-Agent Systems (AAMAS), pp. 178–186 (2017)

35. Sharma, D.P., Kim, D.S., Yoon, S., Lim, H., Cho, J.H., Moore, T.J.: FRVM: flexible random virtual IP multiplexing in software-defined networks. In: IEEE International Conference on Trust, Security and Privacy in Computing and Communications (TrustCom), pp. 579–587. IEEE (2018)

36. Sinha, A., Nguyen, T.H., Kar, D., Brown, M., Tambe, M., Jiang, A.X.: From physical security to cybersecurity. J. Cybersecur. **1**(1), 19–35 (2015)

37. von Stengel, B., Zamir, S.: Leadership with commitment to mixed strategies. CDAM Research Report LSE-CDAM-2004-01 (2004)

38. Taguinod, M., Doupé, A., Zhao, Z., Ahn, G.J.: Toward a moving target defense for web applications. In: 2015 IEEE International Conference on Information Reuse and Integration, pp. 510–517. IEEE (2015)

39. Thomas, S., Williams, L.: Using automated fix generation to secure SQL statements. In: International Workshop on Software Engineering for Secure Systems (SESS). IEEE (2007)

40. Thompson, M., Evans, N., Kisekka, V.: Multiple OS rotational environment an implemented moving target defense. In: The 7th International Symposium on Resilient Control Systems (ISRCS), pp. 1–6. IEEE (2014)

41. Vorobeychik, Y., Singh, S.: Computing Stackelberg equilibria in discounted stochastic games (corrected version). In: Twenty-Sixth Conference on Artificial Intelligence (AAAI) (2012)

42. Vu, Q.L., et al.: Stackelberg policy gradient: evaluating the performance of leaders and followers. In: ICLR 2022 Workshop on Gamification and Multiagent Solutions (2022)

43. Wang, J.X., et al.: Learning to reinforcement learn. arXiv preprint arXiv:1611.05763 (2016)

44. Weng, L.: Meta-learning: learning to learn fast. lilianweng.github.io (2018). https://lilianweng.github.io/posts/2018-11-30-meta-learning/

45. Xie, Q., Chen, Y., Wang, Z., Yang, Z.: Learning zero-sum simultaneous-move Markov games using function approximation and correlated equilibrium. In: COLT (2020)

46. Zhang, Y., Li, M., Bai, K., Yu, M., Zang, W.: Incentive compatible moving target defense against VM-colocation attacks in clouds. In: Gritzalis, D., Furnell, S., Theoharidou, M. (eds.) SEC 2012. IAICT, vol. 376, pp. 388–399. Springer, Heidelberg (2012). https://doi.org/10.1007/978-3-642-30436-1_32

Security Games

Synchronization in Security Games

Stefan Rass[1,3](✉)[ID] and Sandra König[2][ID]

[1] Johannes Kepler University, LIT Secure and Correct Systems Lab,
Altenbergerstraße 69, 4040 Linz, Austria
`stefan.rass@jku.at`
[2] Austrian Institute of Technology, Center for Digital Safety and Security,
Giefinggasse 4, 1210 Vienna, Austria
`sandra.koenig@ait.ac.at`
[3] Universität Klagenfurt, Institute for Artificial Intelligence and Cybersecurity,
Universitätsstrasse 65-67, 9020 Klagenfurt, Austria

Abstract. Security games often assume a fixed pattern in which players become active, like leader-follower alternation in Stackelberg games or simultaneous moves in Nash games. Stackelberg games are of particular popularity as models for security since they well describe adversaries that adapt to the defender's actions. Games in extensive or normal form herein induce a fixed sequence of when players become active. But why would a player in a security game wait for the opponent's move and not just take further actions to cause more damage or gain more? This work studies generalized interaction patterns motivated from the security context, in which each player can take actions as often as it likes, and receives a payoff from the game upon every activity. The practical scenario motivating this study is an adversary who does not wait for the defender to take action, but rather makes the most of the periods during which the defender is idle. This can mean to learn as possible about the victim system while the defender is not present, or to cause as much damage as possible before the defender can strike back.

We show how to convert the situation of arbitrary, in particular non-synchronized, activity schedules back into the classical setting of games in which players take actions in fixed orders. To this end, we introduce conditions under which Nash- and Stackelberg equilibria are invariant to different speeds of playing, and introduce the separate concept of a synchronized equilibrium, in which each player adapts its activity level optimally to those of its opponents, based on an underlying (Nash) equilibrium. We give constructive results about the existence and computation of a synchronized equilibrium, up to its reachability by online learning.

Keywords: Synchronization · Defense policy · Advanced persistent threats · Security game

1 Introduction

In most game theoretic models, the players make their moves in a fixed order. This is inspired by and suitable for many kinds of board games, where players follow a fixed schedule and rule set. Actions are either taken simultaneously and independently, as in a Nash model, or sequentially in direct response to the other player's action, such as in Stackelberg leader-follower models. The latter is popular model for security, since it covers the case of an adversary adapting to the defender's action (adversary following the defender), but also covers reactive defense policies where the defender becomes active upon noticing adversarial activity (defender following the attacker, for example, in an intrusion detection setting). In both situations (simultaneous or leader-follower), there is some synchronicity between the players as they take actions in fixed turns and orders. Figure 1 illustrates the actions of players in both games as solid-line arrows on a timeline. However, *why should players stick to such a fixed schedule?* Especially in security, wouldn't it be plausible or rational for a player to try taking as much as possible from the other player (zero-sum models) or from the game itself (nonzero-sum model) instead of politely waiting for the opponent to make the next move? Conventional models seem to rarely cover this possibility.

Contemporary attacks like Advanced Persistent Threats (APTs) are composed of alternating phases of passively learning and actively attacking. The learning phase is about gaining as much knowledge as possible, but not necessarily damaging the victim (a nonzero-sum situation, since one player unilaterally gains knowledge). In later stages, based on what has been learned, the game may enter a zero-sum-like phase, where the attacker is penetrating and causing damage, perhaps unbeknownst to the defender.

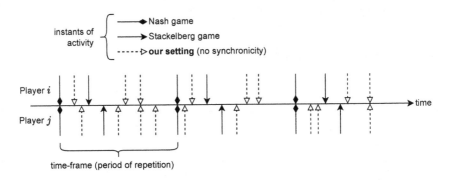

Fig. 1. The considered setting in comparison with Nash and Stackelberg games

The two phases are inherently different in terms of how players take actions: while the learning phase to prepare for the next move is about taking as many actions as possible (to maximize the learning outcome), the defender may be idle during this period. Thus there is no natural synchronicity between the actors. When it comes to the penetration, the defender may become active and follow the attacker's action, and a certain synchronicity pattern between the players kicks in.

It is common to account for this alternation in extensive form or dynamic games: The players can define each stage individually and according to the sub-goals (learning, penetrating, or others). However, most game theoretic models nonetheless assume a fixed order in which players become active, not least due to the historical development of game theory itself.

Our research question is if such models with a 'fixed schedule', whether implicit or not, are applicable in a setting where we allow both players to become active *independently* of one another and *at any time*. This scenario is illustrated with dashed arrows in Fig. 1, in relation to the standard setting (solid lines): Nash games let players take moves simultaneously, Stackelberg games let one player adapt to the other player's actions. Our version lets both players act whenever they like and not necessarily wait for each other. This view considers the game as a mere utility re-distribution mechanism, with (Nash- or Stackelberg) equilibria being there to get the most utility whenever the game is played (a simple example of such a repeated utility-reassignment is the FlipIt game).

The frequency of a players' move, however, is not determined nor characterizable as part of or yet another classical equilibrium, as we will show in Sect. 2.2. This is due to the underlying Nash- or Stackelberg equilibrium to be invariant to changes of the playing speed (Sect. 2.1), and hence we need another method of optimizing the speeds of playing, *based on* an already *pre-determined* equilibrium in the underlying security game.

The defender has an incentive to keep up with the attacker's activities, but to avoid wasting its limited resources on security gains that are negligible or not noticeable. Thus, the frequency of changing passwords, patching systems, running malware checks, or similar, is a matter of finding a cost-benefit balance.

We believe this situation to be realistic in security settings in general and for APTs in particular. We consider two kinds of APTs: if the attack is about killing the victim, the adversary will hit as often as possible and take as much from the victim as it can. In a parasitic type APT, which is about stealing resources but preserving the victim system as a 'battery', the adversary has an incentive to slow down actions to avoid being discovered or keep the victim alive (games like FlipIt are about such continuous resource takeover, for example). The action frequency is not only a strategic choice for the attacker but also for the defender.

This paper is organized as follows. In the remainder of this section we describe our contribution and present assumptions, setup and notation employed throughout. Section 2 collects some preliminary results that help compiling the main results presented and illustrated in Sect. 3. Section 4 discusses whether players will eventually synchronize. Section 5 gives on overview on related work and Sect. 6 provides conclusion and outlook.

1.1   Our Contribution

This work analyzes the strategic choice of how often to become active in a game, to optimize one's own rewards if additional revenue can be earned by increasing the activity level. Our finding, as derived and proven in the remainder, is that with the number of repetitions being an optimized strategic choice, we can convert the situation of players moving freely in time into a standard game model with a fixed schedule. This conversion is performed by computing an optimal number of moves and accordingly scaling the utility functions for all the players.

The optimal number determined will be called a *synchronized equilibrium*, and is an auxiliary and independent concept to the game's (Nash- or Stackelberg) equilibrium.

Our findings imply that, although game-theoretic models usually impose some synchronicity pattern between players, we can let the players nonetheless move freely in time, and reduce the resulting generalized situation to a game in which the players act in a fixed Nash or Stackelberg pattern. Thus, we extend the validity of the usual modeling to such generalized settings without natural synchronicity.

1.2   Assumptions and Setup

We let $\Gamma = (N = \{1, 2, \ldots, n\}, \mathcal{S}, H)$ denote an arbitrary n-person game, with action spaces $\mathcal{S} = \{AS_i \mid |AS_i| < \infty, i = 1, 2, \ldots, n\}$ and utility functions $H = \{u_i : S_i \times S_{-i} \to \mathbb{R} \mid i = 1, 2, \ldots, n\}$ where $S_i := \triangle(AS_i)$ denotes the simplex over the set AS_i, corresponding to the set of mixed (randomized) choices over the action space AS_i. We assume all action spaces AS_i as compact or finite. For a finite set $X = \{x_1, x_2, \ldots, x_k\}$ this yields $\triangle(X) = \{\mathbf{p} \in [0, 1]^k \mid \mathbf{p}^\top \cdot \mathbf{1} = 1\}$, where $\mathbf{1}$ is the vector of all ones. The notation S_{-i} denotes the Cartesian product of all sets $S_1, \ldots, S_n$, excluding the set S_i. It is the joint action of player i's opponents. For simplicity, we will write $\mathbf{x} \in S_1 \times \ldots \times S_n$ to mean the actions of all players. Optimized quantities are annotated with an asterisk, like $\mathbf{x}^*$. So far, this is nothing but the general specification of a game. We leave the specific security game Γ intentionally unspecified, since our interest is studying the difference made if players can move freely in continuous time. Essentially, the answer will be that:

– equilibrium actions (if they exist) will be the same as in Γ,
– equilibrium payoffs from Γ will scale, and
– there is a strategic optimum for how many moves should be taken per time unit to mutually optimize revenues. In other words, there is also an 'equilibrium speed of gameplay'. This will be the newly introduced synchronized equilibrium.

For a rigorous justification of these anticipated results, we need a few more specific assumptions:

A1: The game is static, i.e., it is repeatable, and the payoff structure does not change over time. Thus, we include extensive form games, but not stochastic games with discounted payoffs.

A2: The time axis is continuous, but partitioned into periods during which players can run the game Γ repeatedly. That is, we introduce an infinite partition of $[0, \infty) = T_1 \cup T_2 \cup T_3 \cup \ldots$, with pairwise disjoint intervals $T_i = [t_i, t_i + T)$ for a sequence of time instants $t_1 = 0 < t_2 < t_3 < \ldots$, whose constant difference T is understood as a *time unit*. Inside each interval, all players can take a random number of actions, each triggering another payoff event to all players. This duration T is assumed sufficiently long to complete the game Γ at least once.

A3: Every action of every player takes some positive but finite time to be completed. For the i-th player taking action $a \in AS_i$, we write $d(a) > 0$ for the duration of completing action a. From the bounded duration T, it follows that the i-th player can take no more than $\ell_i := \lfloor T / \sup_{a_i \in AS_i} d(a_i) \rfloor$ moves per repetition of the game. In combination with Assumption **A2**, we have $\ell_i > 0$, so that a player can take at least one round of Γ. This assumption prevents players from becoming active at infinite frequency, and hence discretizes the choices of speed to a finite set in each time-frame T_j. However, the points in time when a player can take the action remains continuous over T_j.

A4: If player i takes action at time t, we write $x_i(t)$, to make this time-dependence explicit. At any time, if another player $j \neq i$ takes action $x_j(t')$ at a later time $t' > t$, the game rewards all players with their utilities determined by the action that all players have taken most recently. For player i having been active last time at t and player j having been active at time t', the two players receive revenues at both time instants t and t': letting $t'' < t$ be the last time when player j was active before player i took action, the rewards for times $t'' < t < t'$ are

at time t: player i gets $u_i(\ldots, x_i(t), \ldots, x_j(t''), \ldots)$
             player j gets $u_j(\ldots, x_i(t), \ldots, x_j(t''), \ldots)$
at time t':   player i gets $u_i(\ldots, x_i(t), \ldots, x_j(t'), \ldots)$
             player j gets $u_j(\ldots, x_i(t), \ldots, x_j(t'), \ldots)$

At the beginning of time $t = 0$, we assume some default action (even if none) to determine the payoffs to the player who first became active.

A5: Upon every new period $T_j = [t_j, t_j + T)$ each player i will at time t_j sample a random number $\lambda_i \in \Lambda_i := \{1, 2, \ldots, \ell_i\}$ of moves to make within the current unit of time (this is the count of moves per time unit, whose long-run average over all time units would be the action "rate"). This choice will be made *strategically*, but is *independent* of the actual actions[1] being taken during the time-frame T_j.

A6: The utilities of all players are accumulated within a unit of time, and the game's optimization is about the long-run average of utility per unit of time. This is for consistency with the usual definition of equilibria as maximizing the expected revenue over (an infinitude of) repetitions of the game Γ.

A7: We assume each function u_i to be continuously differentiable w.r.t. all variables that it depends on, including strategies of other players *and* parameters to define the utilities.

2   Preliminary Results

We divide our analysis into several sections, collecting observations incrementally, and compiling them into a recipe on how to treat the case of free moves in

---

[1] We remark that the inclusion of speed is always possible by letting *every* action be played with *every* possible speed $\lambda \in \Lambda$. In our setting, allowing a player to take a different action in each of the $\lambda \in \Lambda$ repetitions, this would expand the action count from $|AS|$ to $|AS|^{|\Lambda|}$. We want to avoid this combinatorial blow-up.

time, within the framework of the given game model Γ. First, note that assumption **A7** implies the existence of a Nash- or Stackelberg equilibrium in the game Γ, which we denote as $\mathbf{x}^*$. Our first observation will be that this equilibrium goes unaffected if players choose to take more or fewer actions over time, such as depicted in Fig. 1.

Since an equilibrium is generally a best response to the moves of other players, we introduce the best response correspondence for the i-th player, depending on the mixed strategies $\mathbf{x}_{-i}$ of player i's opponents as

$$\mathrm{BR}_{u_i}(\mathbf{x}_{-i}) = \underset{\mathbf{x} \in \triangle(AS_i)}{\mathrm{argmax}} \ \mathrm{E}_{\mathbf{y} \sim \mathbf{x}_{-i}}\big[u_i(\mathbf{x}, \mathbf{y})\big].$$

If this set is a singleton, we can let $\mathrm{BR}_{u_i}(\mathbf{x})$ appear in formulas to denote a best response strategy. If this best response is ambiguous, i.e., BR is a set with more than one element, we will let BR mean an *arbitrary* element from the set. For an equilibrium strategy $(\mathbf{x}_i^*, \mathbf{x}_{-i}^*)$ we let $v_i^* = u_i(\mathbf{x}_i^*, \mathbf{x}_{-i}^*)$ denote the *equilibrium payoff* to the i-th player. This value can be individually different between equilibria (if multiple ones exist) in general games, hence the particular value v_i is always linked to a specific equilibrium that will be made clear in the respective context.

A simple technical but later important observation is that this set is invariant to scaling of the utilities by positive constants: for every $\lambda > 0$, we have

$$\mathrm{BR}_{\lambda \cdot u_i}(\mathbf{x}_{-i}) = \mathrm{BR}_{u_i}(\mathbf{x}_{-i}) \tag{1}$$

2.1   Equilibria are Invariant to Changes of Playing Speed

At the beginning of the time-frame $T_j = [t_j, t_j + T)$, we let the i-th player anticipate $\lambda_{i,T_j} = \lambda_i(t_j) \in \Lambda_i$ actions on its own, enumerated as $a_i^{(1)}, a_i^{(2)}, \ldots, a_i^{(\lambda_{T_j})} \in AS_i$, independently of the random choices of the actions themselves (see Assumption **A5**). The other players in the game can likewise make their decisions about how often to move within the time frame T_j, and the game rewards all players if any of them becomes active (see Assumption **A4**), giving, for the time-frame T_j, a total number of $\lambda_{T_j} \leq \sum_{i \in N} \lambda_i(t_j)$ payments.

The i-th player thus receives a series of random utilities $U_i^{(k)} := u_i(a_i^{(k)}, \mathbf{a}_{-i})$ for $k = 1, \ldots, \lambda_{T_j}$, where $\mathbf{a}_{-i}$ is determined according to Assumption **A4**. By Assumption **A6**, the payoff to player i accumulates to

$$U_i^{(1)} + U_i^{(2)} + \ldots + U_i^{(\lambda_{T_j})}. \tag{2}$$

Since λ_{T_j} depends only on variables $\lambda_i(t_j)$ of all players $i \in N$ that are stochastically independent of U_i for all $i \in N$, λ_{T_j} is itself independent of U_i, and we can apply Wald's identity to find the expectation of (2) as

$$\mathrm{E}(\lambda_{T_j}) \cdot \mathrm{E}(U_i), \tag{3}$$

where the expectations are w.r.t. the distributions that the player needs to optimize (individually) in each unit of time. Upon entering period $[t_j, t_j + T)$, we thus let a player make two choices from fixed distributions: first, the number of moves to take (λ_{T_j}), and second, the series of actions, sampled from (some) equilibrium distribution. Both distributions do not change between time-frames and remain constant.

The point here is the (stochastic) independence in the choice of $\lambda_i(t_j)$ from the actions (Assumption **A5**), and since the game's reward mechanism is static (Assumption **A1**), a player can optimize the two expectations in (3) *separately*:

1. For the term $E(U_i)$, the optimization is the normal computation of equilibria, as implied by the game Γ. Whether this is a Stackelberg-, Nash- or other equilibrium does not matter here.
2. For the term $E(\lambda_{T_j})$, the optimization of the i-th players contribution to this number is a strategic choice of main interest in this work, and subject to a deeper look in the next Sect. 3.

We let each player adopt, for all time-frames, the *same* optimized choice rule $\boldsymbol{\lambda}_i \in \triangle(\Lambda_i)$, to sample the number of moves $\lambda_{T_j} = \lambda_i(t_j) \sim \boldsymbol{\lambda}_i$ at time-frame $T_j = [t_j, t_j + T)$, giving a constant average $\overline{\lambda}_i = \lim_{n\to\infty} \frac{1}{n} \sum_{j=1}^{n} \lambda_{T_j}$, over the whole time line. This value is positive and finite, since each $0 < \lambda_i(t) \leq \ell_i$ at all times t by Assumption **A3**. Thus, the expected equilibrium reward $E(U_i)$ from Γ in (3) will (only) scale by the factor $0 < \overline{\lambda} \leq \sum_{i\in N} \overline{\lambda}_i$, leaving the best-response correspondence that leads to it unchanged by (1). This applies to Nash as well as Stackelberg equilibria, since either are expressible in terms of best-response correspondences:

Nash Models: Let $i \in \{1, \ldots, N\}$ denote an arbitrary player, determining its best action as $\mathbf{x}_i^* \in \mathrm{BR}_{u_i}(\mathbf{x}_{-i}^*) = \mathrm{BR}_{\lambda \cdot u_i}(\mathbf{x}_{-i}^*)$, for all $\lambda > 0$, i.e., the equilibrium remains the same if one player moves faster than the other players.

Stackelberg Models: Consider a two player game and let, w.l.o.g., player 1 be leading and player 2 be following. The general problem for player 1 is to find a best response to whatever anticipated action of the other player. This is invariant to utility scaling by $\lambda > 0$, since by (1),

$$\mathbf{x}_1^* \in \mathrm{BR}_{u_1}(\mathbf{x}_1^*, \mathrm{BR}_{u_2}(\mathbf{x}_1^*))$$
$$= \mathrm{BR}_{\lambda \cdot u_1}(\mathbf{x}_1^*, \mathrm{BR}_{u_2}(\mathbf{x}_1^*)) = \mathrm{BR}_{u_1}(\mathbf{x}_1^*, \mathrm{BR}_{\lambda \cdot u_2}(\mathbf{x}_1^*)), \qquad (4)$$

so the equilibrium does not change either.

Summarizing the findings, we arrive at the claim that gave this section its title. Specifically, if a player moves $\lambda = \lambda_i(t_j)$ times within time-frame T_j, i.e., plays faster than the opponents, the modified game has the same equilibria as a game where all players move simultaneously, yet the revenue for the fast moving player scales linearly by a factor of λ. The same holds if the number of moves is made at random, in which the utilities scale up by the according average $E(\lambda_{i,T_j}) = \overline{\lambda}_i$.

In both cases, we have not made any assumption about zero- or nonzero sum games, making the results hold in either class, as experiments confirmed (see Sect. 3.4).

2.2   Optimizing Speeds by Equilibrium Analysis

It is natural to consider conventional equilibrium analysis as a method to optimize the speeds of playing. However, it turns out that this delivers only trivial
and hence uninteresting results. To see this, consider the two-player case, in
which player 1 has a negative saddle point payoff $v < 0$. If player 1 takes $\lambda > 0$
moves per time-unit, it will effectively lose $\lambda \cdot v$ and hence would act best by
dropping out of the game at all (not surprisingly, since $v < 0$ means that the
game is unfair). Similarly, if $v > 0$, then player 1 would be best advised to take
as many moves as possible, to maximize its reward $\lambda \cdot v > 0$. In both cases, the
optimum is at the ends of the interval $0 \leq \lambda_i \leq \ell_i$, where ℓ_i is the maximum
number of actions possible for the i-th player (see Assumption **A3**). This likewise
remains true for games with more than two players, since any (of possibly many)
players should either (i) drop out if it can, if its equilibrium payoff is $v_i < 0$, or
(ii) play as fast as possible, if it can expect $v_i > 0$ as reward.

   This analysis, however, misses cases in which a player suffers a loss from the
interaction with one opponent, and later decides to recover from this by increased
interaction with another player. Continuing this thinking raises the question of
there being a circular flow of utility that overall can be 'stable'. Hence, we will
turn to graph theoretic circulations as our method to find nontrivial solutions
in the optimization problem of the playing speeds.

3   Optimizing the Speeds by Flow Circulations

Following Sect. 2.1, let $\mathbf{x}^*$ hereafter be an arbitrary but fixed equilibrium in Γ.

   To capture the nature of the game in the sense of how rewards to one player
affect the payoffs to other players, let us first look at the zero-sum games: the
zero-sum condition $u_1 + u_2 + \ldots + u_n = 0$ lets us express $u_i = -u_1 - u_2 -$
$\ldots - u_{i-1} - u_{i+1} - \ldots - u_n$. The change of revenue to u_1 upon a change to
u_2 is the derivative $\frac{\partial u_i}{\partial u_j} = -1$ for all players i, j, assuming the variables as
mutually independent. This makes sense, since it only says that player i's gain
is player j's loss (for all opponents $j \neq i$). However, this reasoning becomes void
for a nonzero sum game, as a simple bimatrix game with payoff matrices $\mathbf{A}, \mathbf{B}$
shows: we could likewise put $u_1(\mathbf{x}_1, \mathbf{x}_2) + u_2(\mathbf{x}_1, \mathbf{x}_2) = f(\mathbf{x}_1, \mathbf{x}_2) \neq 0$, such that
$u_1 = f - u_2$. Differentiating this w.r.t. u_2 and at a fixed strategy $(\mathbf{x}_1, \mathbf{x}_2)$ gives
the constant -1, but the reduction of rewards is, in the nonzero sum case, not
necessarily independent of which strategy is chosen. Definition 1 thus introduces
a refined measure of 'mutual payment':

Definition 1. *Let a game* $\Gamma = (N, \mathcal{S}, H)$ *satisfy assumptions **A1**, ..., **A7**,
and in addition, assume w.l.o.g. that the payoff at the equilibrium* $\mathbf{x}^*$ *is* $v_i^* = E_{\mathbf{x}^*}(u_i) > 0$ *for all* $i \in N$, *and that all players are utility maximizers.*

   Under this setting, we define the quantity

$$\rho_{ij} := E_{\mathbf{x}^*}\left(\frac{\partial u_i}{\partial u_j}\right) \cdot v_j^*, \tag{5}$$

where the partial derivative takes all variables u_j *for* $j \neq i$ *as constants.*

The partial derivatives are to be taken from the relation between the utilities, which are *constant* relative to one another, since the players all adhere to the equilibrium $\mathbf{x}^*$. That is, there is no implicit dependency of u_j on u_i through the intermediate action profile $\mathbf{x}^*$ that governs both of the payoffs.

The value ρ_{ij} captures how much player j 'takes away' from player i upon increasing its own revenue: one unit of additional payoff to player j (acting as a maximizer) will then increase or decrease the rewards of player i proportionally, depending on the monotonicity of u_i w.r.t. u_j. Locally, we linearize at the equilibrium point $\mathbf{x}^*$, with the sign of the change being determined only by the derivative, since we assumed $v_j^* > 0$. Moreover, note that assumption **A7** desired the differentiability w.r.t. all parameters that u_i may depend on, which includes u_2 in particular, if it appears in the definition of the utility. A trivial example where this happens is a zero-sum game, but we will let a more general example follow below.

We stress that (5) should *not* be understood, nor interpreted, as a measure of correlation! In fact, the derivative term accounts for a functional relationship (causality) of how the payoff to one player affects the rewards to another player.

Example 1. *Consider a 2-player zero-sum matrix game with payoff functions u_1, u_2, related as $u_1 = -u_2$. Then $\frac{\partial u_1}{\partial u_2} = -1$. For the equilibrium values paid to both players, the game would give $v^* > 0$ to player 1, and $-v^*$ to player 2. To meet the assumption of Definition 1, we can let player 2 be maximizing player 1's regret function $\|u_1\|_\infty - u_1$, where $\|u_1\|_\infty$ is finite due to the underlying assumption on the game (continuity of payoffs and compactness of strategy spaces).*

It is fair to remark that player 2 can equivalently also maximize any shifted version of player 1's regret, e.g., we could equally well have put $u_2 = -u_1 + 3v^*$ to make the equilibrium payoff to player 2 equal to $2v^* > 0$. Then, ρ_{12} would tell that player 2 takes away twice as much from player 1 as vice versa.

The lesson from Example 1 is that ρ_{ij} can be different for strategically equivalent games, since it depends on the particular saddle point value. This dependence will, however, only affect the numeric computation, but not the existence of the equilibrium notion to capture the optimal playing speeds for all players. Hence, as far as it concerns the existence of an optimal playing speed, the assumption that all players have a strictly positive equilibrium payoff from the game is made without loss of generality (we prove this as Theorem 1).

Example 2. *Now, let us look at a bimatrix game as an instance of a nonzero sum model. The payoff functions are $u_1(\mathbf{x}_1, \mathbf{x}_2) = \mathbf{x}_1^\top \mathbf{A} \mathbf{x}_2$ and $u_2(\mathbf{x}_1, \mathbf{x}_2) = \mathbf{x}_1^\top \mathbf{B} \mathbf{x}_2$ with constant payoff matrices $\mathbf{A}, \mathbf{B}$. Here, there is no explicit relationship between u_1 and u_2, and for a fixed equilibrium $\mathbf{x}^*$, u_1 is constant as a function of u_2 and vice versa. Hence, $\frac{\partial u_1}{\partial u_2} = \frac{\partial u_2}{\partial u_1} = 0$, since neither variable appears in the definition of the other. Hence $\rho_{ij} = 0$. We will discuss the implications of this in Sect. 3.3.*

3.1 Synchronized Equilibria

We now turn to the question of how to find the optimal activity frequency for all players, given the mutual pairwise revenue flows ρ_{ij}, as if the game were played at a Nash or Stackelberg equilibrium, and hence under *hypothetical synchronicity*. Let $\lambda_i \in \mathbb{R}^+$ be the average number of moves per time unit taken by the i-th player for all $i \in N$. If a player is unhappy with the current revenues, then two options are available:

- play a *different strategy* to perhaps gain more: this would not work, since it means an unilateral deviation, which can only decrease the revenues, since we are already at the equilibrium (giving the best possible response).
- or *play faster* to gain more per unit of time. This means to increase the playing speed λ_i accordingly, but this will make the other players react to this, depending on how this affects their own payoffs. These effects are captured by the quantity ρ_{ij} for the j-th opponent.

This reveals a possibly unpleasant dynamics if the payoff 'flows' between the players are 'unbalanced' in the sense that one player could have its resources drained empty if other players decide to just take more. The dynamics will hence become more and more aggressive, until the players run at their maximum possible speeds or drop out of the game upon being void of any more resources. This makes the overall situation unstable and convergent towards a terminal 'death state'. If the goal, however, is not to kill the victim (lethal-type APT) but rather to keep it alive as a battery to get resources from (parasitic-type APT), then a stable situation can be desirable. We call this stable situation a *synchronized equilibrium*:

Definition 2 (Synchronized Equilibrium). *Let Γ be an n-person game that satisfies assumptions $\mathbf{A1}, \ldots, \mathbf{A7}$ and with all players being utility-maximizers. In this game, fix an equilibrium $\mathbf{x}^*$, and let $v_i^* > 0$ be an equilibrium payoff to the i-th player under strategy $\mathbf{x}^*$. With ρ_{ij} as in Definition 1, measuring the amount of expected payment made from player i to player j in one round of the game (not unit of time), we can set up a directed graph $G = (N, E)$, with $E = \{(i, j) \in N \times N \mid \rho_{ij} \neq 0\}$.*

Introducing the value $\lambda_i \geq 0$ as the average number of moves that player i takes during a unit of time, we can describe G by a generalized incidence matrix $\mathbf{L}(\boldsymbol{\lambda}) = (m_{ij}) \in \mathbb{R}^{n \times |E|}$ that depends on the vector $\boldsymbol{\lambda} = (\lambda_1, \ldots, \lambda_n)$ as

$$m_{ij} = \begin{cases} -\lambda_i \rho_{ij} & \text{if } i \text{ is the tail of } e_j \text{ (i.e., player } i \text{ pays to player } j) \\ +\lambda_i \rho_{ij} & \text{if } i \text{ is the head of } e_j \text{ (i.e., player } i \text{ receives from player } j) \\ 0 & \text{otherwise.} \end{cases}$$

A synchronized equilibrium is any vector $\boldsymbol{\lambda} \in (0, \infty)^n$ for which $\mathbf{L}(\boldsymbol{\lambda}) \cdot \mathbf{1} = \mathbf{0}$, if one exists.

We stress that a synchronized equilibrium is, by definition, not the same as a Nash-equilibrium nor part of it (as also follows from the discussion in Sect. 2.2). The graph representation that Definition 2 introduces relates our work to the concept of *separable network games* [6, 9, 11], which studies graphs whose edges represent two-player games. The solution concept there is the Nash equilibrium again, but our setting is different here in the lack of separability. More precisely, our players all engage in the same (large) game, while in a separable network, a player engages in a distinct game with each of its neighbor in the graph. The graph structure, in our case, comes from the secondary condition on how the utility flow is described between players, which is explicit in zero-sum games, but not necessarily expressed in nonzero sum games. A goal of this work is pointing out the importance of this modeling detail.

Existence of Synchronized Equilibria: The computation of an synchronized equilibrium comes to the solution of a linear equation system expressing a flow preservation condition: the total of what player i takes from a set of opponents on incoming edges, is paid towards other players along outgoing edges of node i in the graph G. This is nothing else than a graph-theoretic *circulation* or flow preservation condition, and assures that no player has a trend towards infinite gains or losses if players are not bound to any synchronicity. A trivial solution to $\mathbf{L}(\boldsymbol{\lambda}) \cdot \mathbf{1} = \mathbf{0}$ is $\boldsymbol{\lambda} = \mathbf{0}$, but this means that no player would take any action (and is hence excluded by Definition 2). Nonetheless, directly solving $\mathbf{L}(\boldsymbol{\lambda}) \cdot \mathbf{1} = \mathbf{0}$ for $\boldsymbol{\lambda}$ without constraints may deliver $\lambda_i = 0$ for some players. This indicates that a player either can receive or lose infinitely much from/to other players. In that case, the game mechanism in the sense of player's interaction structure could be reconsidered in the security setting, since there will be an all-winning or all-losing player in the game.

Example 3 (2-player game, not necessarily zero-sum). *Consider a simple 2-player game, with $\rho_{12} = 2$ and $\rho_{21} = 1$, as Fig. 2a illustrates. In this game, player 1 pays 2 units of revenue to player 2, while player 2 pays only 1 unit back to player 1. Then, if both players turn to their maximum speeds, player 2 will end up receiving infinitely much from player 2, since the total flow is $+2$ from $1 \to 2$ and $+1$ from $2 \to 1$ (equivalently -1 from $1 \to 2$).*

For a stable situation, player 1 can thus become more active to annihilate this imbalance, and the exact factor of acceleration is determined from a synchronized equilibrium. Player 1 has "income" $\lambda_1 \rho_{21} = \lambda_1$ and "expenses" $\lambda_2 \rho_{12} = 2\lambda_2$. In equilibrium, the two should be equal, i.e., the first equation to solve is $2\lambda_2 = \lambda_1$. The equation is obtained for the second player, which gives a continuum

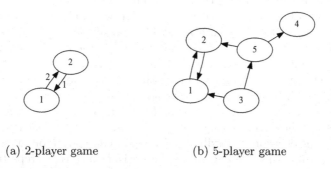

(a) 2-player game   (b) 5-player game

Fig. 2. Utility flows in different games (examples)

of synchronized equilibria as $(2\lambda, \lambda)$ for any $\lambda > 0$. This, consistent with our intuition, advises player 1 to act twice as often as player 2 for stability.

Example 4 (5-player game). *The situation becomes more interesting if there are more players involved, so let their interaction pattern be as the directed graph in Fig. 2b shows.*

It is already visible from this structure that player 3 only pays but never receives from any of the other players (except it gets revenue from an infinite background budget), and player 4 can just receive but never loses anything to other players. This already shows that an synchronized equilibrium cannot exist. The incidence matrix as in Definition 2 is found as

$$\mathbf{L}(\boldsymbol{\lambda}) = \begin{matrix} & \overset{2 \to 1}{} & \overset{1 \to 2}{} & \overset{3 \to 1}{} & \overset{3 \to 5}{} & \overset{5 \to 4}{} & \overset{5 \to 2}{} \\ 1 \\ 2 \\ 3 \\ 4 \\ 5 \end{matrix} \begin{pmatrix} \lambda_2\rho_{21} & -\lambda_1\rho_{12} & \lambda_3\rho_{31} & 0 & 0 & 0 \\ -\lambda_2\rho_{21} & \lambda_1\rho_{12} & 0 & 0 & 0 & \lambda_5\rho_{52} \\ 0 & 0 & -\lambda_3\rho_{31} & -\lambda_3\rho_{35} & 0 & 0 \\ 0 & 0 & 0 & 0 & \lambda_5\rho_{54} & 0 \\ 0 & 0 & 0 & \lambda_3\rho_{35} & -\lambda_5\rho_{54} & -\lambda_5\rho_{52} \end{pmatrix}$$

The flow preservation is observed in the column sums to be all zero. Imposing an "$= 0$" condition on the sum per row and solving the equation system gives $\lambda_2 = \lambda_1 \cdot \frac{\rho_{12}}{\rho_{21}}, \lambda_3 = \lambda_5 = 0$ for arbitrary $\lambda_1 > 0$ and arbitrary $\lambda_4 > 0$. The last variable does not appear here, because player 4 makes no payments to any other player, so, in equilibrium, it can act at any speed. However, the solution advise players 3 and 5 to drop out of the game, and hence no synchronized equilibrium exists. For players 3 and 5, this means that they can (and likely will) eventually suffer unbounded losses, and will not receive saddle point revenue that the (Nash) equilibrium would predict. Thus, dropping out of the game is rational for these (and only these) players, if they can (drop out).

For a synchronized equilibrium to exist, it is necessary but not sufficient to have an equilibrium in the underlying game $\Gamma = (N, \mathcal{S}, H)$. The existence of a solution to $\mathbf{L}(\boldsymbol{\lambda}) \cdot \mathbf{1} = \mathbf{0}$ is easy to decide and compute by Gaussian elimination, and does *not* require the prior computation of an n-person equilibrium, as Example 4 already demonstrated. We can, without loss of generality, assume that $v_i^* = 1$ for all players $i \in N$ in some strategically equivalent game. This assumption leaves the Gaussian elimination unaffected: suppose that player i has the unknown saddle point payoff $v_i^* \neq 1$. Then, we can scale its utility function by the factor $\mu_i > 0$ and an additive shift to make the saddle point payoff $= 1$ for this player. This constant factor then changes the original ρ_{ij} into $\mu_i \cdot \rho_{ij}$ (the additive shift cancels out when taking the derivative), and in the equation system, we get the term $\lambda_i \cdot \mu_i \cdot \rho_{ij}$ under this modification. Then, changing variables into $\lambda_i' := \lambda_i \cdot \mu_i$, we get $\lambda_i \neq 0$ if and only if $\lambda_i' \neq 0$. Thus, the existence of a synchronized equilibrium is *decidable* under the assumption $v_i^* = 1$ for all $i \in N$, even without computing the equilibrium payoffs to each player before. Given that this decision is possible by Gaussian elimination on an equation system with n unknowns, we can make the decision in $O(n^3)$ steps (even faster, using optimized algorithms). Thus, we have proven:

Theorem 1 (Existence of synchronized equilibria). *Let an n-player game* $\Gamma = (N, \mathcal{S}, H)$ *be given as in Definition 2. Then, whether a synchronized equilibrium exists or not is decidable in polynomial time (at most $O(n^3)$) without computing an equilibrium in Γ, and only requires ρ_{ij}, putting $v_i^* := 1$ for all $i \in N$.*

We emphasize that the actual synchronized equilibrium will, through the dependence of the ρ_{ij} on the (chosen) $\mathbf{x}^*$, have a dependence on the game's equilibrium. Let us briefly revisit the generic cases of zero-sum and nonzero sum games, since both enjoy widespread use to compute defense policies.

3.2 Synchronized Equilibria in Zero-Sum Games

We compute a synchronized equilibrium for the two-player zero-sum case of Example 1 using Theorem 1. From the zero-sum condition $u_1 = -u_2$, we find $\rho_{12} = \rho_{21} = 1$, and we assume $v > 0$. The graph is the same as in Fig. 2a but without weights, and has the incidence matrix $\mathbf{L}(\lambda_1, \lambda_2) = \begin{pmatrix} -\lambda_1 \cdot v & \lambda_2 \cdot v \\ \lambda_1 \cdot v & -\lambda_2 \cdot v \end{pmatrix}$, which leads to the equation system

$$\left. \begin{array}{l} 0 = \lambda_1 \cdot v - \lambda_2 \cdot v \\ 0 = \lambda_2 \cdot v - \lambda_1 \cdot v \end{array} \right\} \tag{6}$$

whose set of synchronized equilibria is $\{\lambda_1 = \lambda_2 = \lambda \mid$ for any λ in the range permissible for both players$\}$.

   This solutions is, however, unstable in the strong sense that it *only holds if all players adhere to a fixed speed*. If one player relies on the others to play at the current constant speed, it does have an incentive to accelerate to increase its own revenues. This, in turn, will give the opponents a reason to keep up (to avoid their payoffs diminishing), thus leading to a dynamics in which all players act at their maximal speeds. The critical point of all equal speeds is, in a sense, *repelling*. It becomes attracting, if we add another incentive to slow down to avoid making the opponents more aggressive. We will study this variation in Sect. 4 where we look at learning the equilibrium online, and conclude our intermediate finding:

Theorem 2. *Take a zero-sum game $\Gamma = (N, \mathcal{S}, H)$ that satisfies assumptions $A1 \ldots A7$. Let its saddle point payoff be v_i for each player $i \in N$, let all players have additional strategic choices to play $1 \leq \lambda_i \leq \ell_i$ (with ℓ_i being a constant) actions per time unit (i.e., before the game restarts at a later time instant).*

   An unstable situation is given if all players take moves in a synchronized way, i.e., at the same speeds $\lambda_i = \lambda_j$ for all $i, j \in N$. In this case, each player will receive the payoff $\lambda_i \cdot v_i$. This situation is a repelling fixed point of the modified game's payoff correspondence, in which all utility functions u_i are replaced by their scaled versions $\lambda_i \cdot u_i$. This payoff correspondence also has an attracting fixed point at which all players take moves at their maximal speeds. The result remains true if the speeds are chosen at random, but with pairwise equal, resp. individually maximal averages $\mathrm{E}(\lambda_i)$. The revenues then scale proportionally by a factor of $\mathrm{E}(\lambda_i)$ for the i-th player.

3.3   Synchronized Equilibrium in a Non-zero-sum Game

For a general nonzero sum case we use Example 1 as our template: now, let $u_1(x_1, x_2) = \mathbf{x}_1^\top \mathbf{A} \mathbf{x}_2$ and $u_2(x_1, x_2) = \mathbf{x}_1^\top \mathbf{B} \mathbf{x}_2$. In that case, the derivative $\frac{\partial u_i}{\partial u_j} = 0$, since u_1 has no dependence on u_2 (the payoff structure $\mathbf{B}$ is different and unrelated to $\mathbf{A}$). Thus, $\rho_1 = \rho_2 = 0$, and both players end up optimizing their speeds by just maximizing their activity towards $\lambda_1 = \ell_1$ and $\lambda_2 = \ell_2$. As a consequence, we obtain:

Theorem 3. *Let a nonzero sum game Γ satisfying Assumptions $\textbf{A1} \ldots \textbf{A7}$ be specified with utilities that have an explicit dependence on the players actions, but no explicit functional dependence on each other's utilities (that is, $\rho_{ij} = 0$ for all $i, j \in N$). Then, a stable synchronized equilibrium is all players acting at their maximum possible speeds.*

It may be questionable if the situation predicted by Theorem 3 is realistic or not, and the nontrivial interesting practical cases are sure where $\rho_{ij} \neq 0$ for many pairs ij. If the mutual payments are all independent, then we may reconsider the specification of utilities as having been implausible. As an example, let a game be specified, for instance in extensive form, and assume that at the leafs of the game tree, some player receives revenue $a \in \mathbb{R}$, while the other player receives revenue $b \in \mathbb{R}$. Such a specification is quite common in many security game models, as for example, [4,5,17], to name only a few. The point is that there is no functional relationship between the values a and b, since the modeling suggests that these are paid from some resource that is itself unlimited. In turn, each player, drawing from this infinite budget in the background, can maximize its own gains by playing as fast as possible, and independent of the others. Even more, if the actions of one player reduce the rewards to the other, then this second player can recover from this loss not only by choosing different actions, but alternatively also by just becoming active more often.

This reveals a perhaps unwanted dynamics in real life, if the payoff values are specified without a causal relationship among them. Zero-sum games do have such an explicit relationship via the side-condition $\sum_{i \in N} u_i = 0$. Nonzero sum games are popular for being more general and less restrictive here, but, in light of Theorem 3, should not go unreflectingly without any functional or causal relation between the payoffs to each player. This is an indication to reconsider the game model specification, as we will demonstrate in the next section's example. Even if the zero-sum condition is overly strong in a given context, a weaker form of dependence may be in order. Computing the values ρ_{ij} as defined by (5) is a simple indicator of such a potential modeling issue. If this value comes to constant zero, Theorem 3 will predict the dynamics to be expected. If this dynamics is implausible, it may be necessary to reconsider the modeling.

3.4   Experimental Verification

We simulated the process of players acting differently often (i.e., at different speeds) by implementing a fictitious play (FP) online learning process in Octave

[8], similar to [15]. In our first experiment, we used a pair of (2×2)-bimatrix Nash game, such that the convergence of FP is assured if the matrices are non-degenerate [12], if players take their actions simultaneously or alternatingly. For a verification of Theorem 3, we modified the FP process by letting the second player take a fixed *additional* number of $\lambda - 1 > 0$ moves after player 1 took action. Although this modification renders the usual convergence conditions of FP void, the fact that *if* FP converges, then the limit is an equilibrium, remains intact [10, Prop.2.2]. Indeed, the simulations all converged (over several runs with randomly chosen payoff matrices), and confirmed the equilibrium to remain unchanged (cf. Sect. 2.1) with only the payoffs to the second player scaling up, exactly as foretold by Theorem 3.

We also let another implementation of FP run on bimatrix Nash games of a larger dimension, also observing convergence of FP in all (random) test-cases, and the stability of the equilibrium up to the scaling of the payoff proportional to the lot of additional moves. Likewise, for a verification of the random speed case of Theorem 2, we repeated the experiment with a fresh Poisson distributed random number of additional moves in each iteration of the FP process. Using a random average value $E(\Lambda)$ chosen at the beginning, we repeated the FP experiment and averaged the resulting factors by which the rewards were scaled, numerically confirming that the revenues scale proportionally as Theorem 2 tells.

Similarly, to validate Theorem 2 for Nash games, we implemented the (same) FP process on a zero-sum competition, but also with the second player moving faster than player 1. As in the previous case, Theorem 2 was experimentally confirmed over a large number of trials with random matrices chosen afresh each time, and letting each player take its own revenue "away" from the opponents.

For a verification of Theorem 2 on Stackelberg games, we modified the FP process to let player 1 try out all its options $i \in AS_1$, anticipating that the follower (attacker) would first update its estimate of the leader's behavior by observing strategy a, and then best-responding to it, according to (4). Among all $a \in AS_1$, the leader picks the strategy that gives the maximum revenue if the follower replies optimally in its own interest. We let the follower play $\lambda > 0$ best such replies in a row, letting the leader be idle during this period. Again, we observed convergence of FP in that case, confirming the statement of Theorem 2, and also its claim about randomly chosen speeds, letting the follower move fast by a Poissonian number of steps.

4   Online Learning

A natural question is whether the players, even if they start off with different speeds, will eventually, perhaps implicitly, synchronize their actions. In other words, will the game along an online learning process ultimately reach a synchronized equilibrium? In light of the dynamics to be towards maximum speeds in games where the aim is to exhaust the opponent, we will hereafter focus on the parasitic type of attacks, i.e., APTs about stealing resources over a long time. In that case, both the defender and the attacker may have incentives to accelerate or slow down accordingly:

Defender's Perspective: If the defender notices that the attacker moves faster than itself, it will need to increase his own playing speed to keep up. Conversely, if the defender notices that the attacker was less active, then playing fast will have no direct effect and mostly comes to a friction loss. So, the defender may choose to slow down, since there is apparently no ongoing attack to counteract.

Attacker's Perspective: If the attacker moves faster than the defender, it takes the risk of the defender noticing this and hence becoming more aggressive in the defense, thus lowering the attacker's chances to drain resources from the defender. Consequently, the attacker has an incentive to slow down, to avoid taking all of the defender's resources (remember that this kind of APT is not about killing the victim). Similarly, if the attacker notices that the defender is more active than itself, it will need to increase its speed to keep up, for otherwise, it will eventually drop out of the game, if this is a possibility.

For both (attacker and defender), the utility functions should be designed to reflect the gain and loss flows between the players accordingly, to compute optimal speeds. Since these will depend on the equilibrium, the problem of equilibrium selection comes in as relevant here. We leave this question open for the time being, and continue the discussion of Sect. 3.2, letting both players adapt their playing speeds towards getting, more importantly preserving, their individual optimum v_1, v_2 from the game.

We let $k \in \mathbb{N}$ denote the k-th time-frame in which the game repeats, and write $\lambda_1(k), \lambda_2(k)$ for average number of moves in period k as Fig. 1 depicts. Moreover, we have a zero-sum game, so that both players will act towards the equilibrium payoff $v = v_1 = -v_2$, and $\rho_{12} = \rho_{21} = -1$.

In period k, if player 2 takes an average of $\lambda_2(k)$ moves, player 1 will receive its own revenue $\lambda_1(k) \cdot v$, reduced by what player 2 will acquire. Hence, player 1 is, after period k, left with the residual revenue $\Delta u_1 = \lambda_1(k) \cdot v - \lambda_2(k) \cdot v$. If player 2 moves fast, then $\Delta u_1 < 0$, and player 1 will try to recover this loss by playing faster in the next time-frame. Knowing the expected payoff, the player can estimate how many moves the opponent has taken, which is $\approx \frac{\Delta u_1}{v}$. Hence, both players will adapt their accordingly as

$$\Delta\lambda_1(k+1) = \lambda_1(k+1) - \lambda_1(k) = -\frac{\Delta u_1}{v} = \lambda_2(k) - \lambda_1(k) \qquad (7)$$

$$\Delta\lambda_2(k+1) = \lambda_2(k+1) - \lambda_2(k) = -\frac{\Delta u_2}{-v} = \lambda_1(k) - \lambda_2(k) \qquad (8)$$

Observe that we have just arrived at (6) again albeit from a different incentive assumption: namely, we let players slow down to avoid making the opponent more aggressive, rather than just seeking to maximize the own gains by playing fast(er). Consequently, the question is whether the coupled dynamic system defined by (7) and (8) will synchronize in the sense that $|\lambda_1(k) - \lambda_2(k)| \to 0$ as $k \to \infty$. If so, we would reach the equality of speeds as an attractive situation, a synchronized equilibrium.

A quick implementation in Octave to simulate the dynamics using matrix games shows that the two systems in general *do not* synchronize. So, the heuristic by which both players will attempt to fully recover their losses from the last round in the next round will generally not lead to a stable situation. However, the learning can be adapted by introducing a 'damping factor' $0 < \alpha < 1$ that slightly reduces the recovery per time unit, and thereby makes the coupled system converge (by simple calculations and Theorem 3.15 in [19]):

$$\left.\begin{aligned} \lambda_1(k+1) - \lambda_1(k) &= \alpha \cdot (\lambda_2(k) - \lambda_1(k)), \\ \lambda_2(k+1) - \lambda_2(k) &= \alpha \cdot (\lambda_1(k) - \lambda_2(k)). \end{aligned}\right\} \tag{9}$$

For this system, we have $\lambda_1(k) \to \lambda_2(k)$ (resp. vice versa) as $k \to \infty$, which is readily confirmed by simulations for $0 < \alpha < 1$ (synchronicity is not attained if we put $\alpha = 1$, as the simulation also shows).

5   Related Work

The concept of asynchronicity in games is most commonly reflected by either a player's move being precluded by a previous opponent's blocking action, or by dividing the players into leader and follower. Both are a conceptual part of the game, expressible in extensive form or by definition of the players' sequence. However, security is naturally without much coordination between the players, and hence cannot rely safely on such assumptions. The work on games that allow asynchronicity is not overly abundant, but some notable contributions shall receive attention.

Games with asynchronous moving pattern have been studied before, e.g., in [18], with the aim of putting them into the realm of folk theorems, discussing how strategic interaction may change in the long run, compared to a single shot. Our work extends this view by adding a security perspective to it, which has not been explicitly in the center of attention so far. Like the folk theorem, we also have a kind of discounting here, if the players seek to cover their full losses, this will result in a dynamics of mutually increasing 'aggressiveness' that destabilizes the overall dynamics. We stress that this is not the exact counterpart of discounting as in the context of the folk theorem, but conceptually related. A similar situation, with non-simultaneous but nonetheless 'phase-locked' moves is considered by [7], where payments are made one phase ahead. Again, this has a relation to security (although this reference does not refer to it), if the defender takes action to anticipate some gain for the next phase (and not the current round). For security and with long-running APTs as a matter of fact, such short-sighted views appear insufficient and hence call for a more general treatment. The work of [1,2] considers the same temporal payoff and action pattern as we sketched in Fig. 1, yet let the game be dynamic. They discovered a much more complex landscape of possible equilibria. However, this prior research provides no answer to the security-specific converse question of this work, about how to convert a security game model that assumes synchronicity of moves to apply in a situation that has no such natural synchronicity. Our goal is thus not about new characterizations, but rather to extend the validity of (many) existing security models to situations of asynchronous movement.

Using a different formalization, [20] models the setting in which, among multiple players, not every player takes action in each round, and the set of 'movers' can change over time and in dependence of past moves. This is interesting as it includes both, dynamic games, and also (to some extent) switching costs [16] that may inhibit players from taking action in the next round. Specifying the moving pattern under this so extended model is a matter of describing the random distribution of subsets of the player set that take moves in each round. Another treatment of asynchronicity is that of [13,21], where the former is focused on the prisoner's dilemma, while the latter treats the interesting aspect of complexity in the computation of equilibria. The work of [3,14] provides similar charactizations of optimal timing, but do so on Markov decision processes, while our approach is generic and not tailored to a specific underlying game model.

6   Conclusion and Outlook

Lessons for APT Defense: Coming back to the two types of APT, and with both involving phases of learning (nonzero sum) and attacking (zero-sum), we can derive the following advice:

- Lethal type APT: since the goal is killing the victim, the attacker will seek to move (i) faster than the defender, (ii) but without getting notice by becoming overly active. Likewise, it is rational for the defender to go as fast as possible, based on the results of Sect. 3, as resource bounds permit. If the defender takes action at speed λ_1, the lethal APT will succeed for the attacker, if it manages to take $\lambda_2 > \lambda_1$ actions per time unit, so that $u_1 \to -\infty$ as time goes by, unless the defender notices the attacker's activity early enough to take permanent actions against the attack.
- Parasitic type APT: Here, the player's interaction may lead to synchronicity, since the attacker's goal is draining resources in a long term, without killing the victim as its source.

In both cases, however, Theorem 2 and Theorem 3 can give indications to reconsider the modeling towards perhaps introducing functional relationships between the presumed payoffs to the players, if the dynamics predicted by the two results appear implausible or unwanted. The significance of the two theorems is thus being aids for the modeling, rather than providing numeric results.

Extensions: A natural extension of the route so far is towards dynamic games. We may not expect as simple results as before, in light of related findings, such as those of [1]. However, dynamic game models are important in the context of modeling APTs, defense in depth and many other security scenarios. An open issue besides the dynamic nature and potential friction loss when speeding up (proportional increase of switching cost) is the speed of synchronization. Lyapunov functions may help quantifying the speed, and the experimental findings suggest that synchronization kicks in rather soon. However, the real question is not about absolute convergence speed, but whether the synchronicity occurs fast enough for the defender to not suffer critical losses (assuming that it can only take a limited total amount of leeching). Another important generalization refers to dropping assumption **A5**, to cover cases of strategic planning ahead, e.g., if the attacker anticipates to take some actions very frequently, and others only sporadically. This would introduce a (stochastic) dependence of actions and frequencies, not assumed in this work. Finally, it will be interesting to extend the model by strategic factors to actively seek or avoid synchronicity, e.g., based on strategic choices, information or other inputs.

Assuming Nash- or Stackelberg Synchronicity is Justifiable. The main finding of this work is that the possibly unrealistic assumption of player's synchronicity in security games is not making the models less useful, since the case of players acting in continuous time is reducible to the case of players moving in a fixed pattern, only up to a proper scaling of their payoff functions. The precise scaling factors are given by a synchronized equilibrium, if one exists, and this decision is efficient even in games with many players, without having to compute their individual saddle point payoffs. If no synchronized equilibrium exists, we can conclude about the model rewarding one player up to infinity, or other players losing an infinitude in the long run. In either case, the game dynamics may not carry towards a Nash or Stackelberg equilibrium, because no synchronized equilibrium exists.

Overall, arguments against a game theoretic security model because of an implausible assumption of players following certain patterns (simultaneous moves or one waiting for/following the other) can be invalidated. In positive words: the assumption that players take synchronized moves, either in a Nash or Stackelberg model, is generally valid, even though the interaction mechanisms in reality may not directly enforce or support such assumptions.

Acknowledgment. We thank the anonymous reviewers for invaluable comments on the manuscript, which helped to improve content and readability in our view. This publication resulted from research supported by the Karl-Popper Doctoral Kolleg "Responsible Safe and Secure Robotic Systems Engineering (SEEROSE)", which is funded and supported by the Alpen-Adria-Universität Klagenfurt.

References

1. Ambrus, A.: Continuous-time games with asynchronous moves: theory and applications (2011). https://grantome.com/grant/NSF/SES-1123759
2. Ambrus, A., Ishii, Y.: Asynchronous choice in battle of the sexes games: unique equilibrium selection for intermediate levels of patience (2011). https://public.econ.duke.edu/~aa231/Bos_6.pdf
3. Ambrus, A., Ishii, Y.: On asynchronicity of moves and coordination (2015). https://doi.org/10.2139/ssrn.2584631
4. Avenhaus, R., von Stengel, B., Zamir, S.: Inspection games: 51. In: Aumann, R.J., Hart, S. (eds.) Handbook of Game Theory with Economic Applications, Handbook of Game Theory with Economic Applications, vol. 3, pp. 1947–1987. Elsevier (2002)

5. Boumkheld, N., Panda, S., Rass, S., Panaousis, E.: Honeypot type selection games for smart grid networks. In: Alpcan, T., Vorobeychik, Y., Baras, J.S., Dán, G. (eds.) GameSec 2019. LNCS, vol. 11836, pp. 85–96. Springer, Cham (2019). https://doi.org/10.1007/978-3-030-32430-8_6

6. Cai, Y., Daskalakis, C.: On minmax theorems for multiplayer games. In: Proceedings of the the 22nd Annual ACM-SIAM Symposium on Discrete Algorithms, pp. 217–234. SIAM (2011). https://doi.org/10.1137/1.9781611973082.20

7. Dutta, P.K., Siconolfi, P.: Asynchronous games with transfers: uniqueness and optimality. J. of Econ. Theory **183**, 46–75 (2019). https://doi.org/10.1016/j.jet.2019.05.005

8. Eaton, J.W., Bateman, D., Hauberg, S., Wehbring, R.: GNU Octave version 6.1.0 manual: a high-level interactive language for numerical computations (2020). https://www.gnu.org/software/octave/doc/v6.1.0/

9. Ewerhart, C., Valkanova, K.: Fictitious play in networks. Games Econom. Behav. **123**, 182–206 (2020). https://doi.org/10.1016/j.geb.2020.06.006

10. Fudenberg, D., Levine, D.K.: The Theory of Learning in Games. MIT Press, Cambridge (1998)

11. Kroupa, T., Vannucci, S., Votroubek, T.: Separable network games with compact strategy sets. In: Bošanský, B., Gonzalez, C., Rass, S., Sinha, A. (eds.) GameSec 2021. LNCS, vol. 13061, pp. 37–56. Springer, Cham (2021). https://doi.org/10.1007/978-3-030-90370-1_3

12. Monderer, D., Shapley, L.S.: Potential games. Games Econom. Behav. **14**(1), 124–143 (1996). https://doi.org/10.1006/game.1996.0044

13. Nisan, N., Schapira, M., Zohar, A.: Asynchronous best-reply dynamics. In: Papadimitriou, C., Zhang, S. (eds.) WINE 2008. LNCS, vol. 5385, pp. 531–538. Springer, Heidelberg (2008). https://doi.org/10.1007/978-3-540-92185-1_59

14. Pawlick, J., Nguyen, T.T.H., Colbert, E., Zhu, Q.: Optimal timing in dynamic and robust attacker engagement during advanced persistent threats. In: 2019 17th International Symposium on Modeling and Optimization in Mobile, Ad Hoc, and Wireless Networks (WiOpt), pp. 1–6. IEEE (2019)

15. Pedroso, J.P.: Numerical solution of Nash and Stackelberg equilibria: an evolutionary approach (2008). https://www.dcc.fc.up.pt/~jpp/publications/PDF/nash-es.pdf

16. Rass, S., König, S., Schauer, S.: On the cost of game playing: how to control the expenses in mixed strategies. In: Rass, S., An, B., Kiekintveld, C., Fang, F., Schauer, S. (eds.) GameSec 2017. LNCS, pp. 494–505. Springer, Cham (2017). https://doi.org/10.1007/978-3-319-68711-7_26

17. Zhu, Q., Alpcan, T., Panaousis, E., Tambe, M., Casey, W. (eds.): GameSec 2016. LNCS, vol. 9996. Springer, Cham (2016). https://doi.org/10.1007/978-3-319-47413-7

18. Wen, Q.: Repeated games with asynchronous moves. undefined (2002). https://paper/Repeated-Games-with-Asynchronous-Moves-Wen/10f0f9c55f4f0b0024000b9709b9ad60cd3a346b

19. Wu, C.W.: Synchronization in complex networks of nonlinear dynamical systems. World Scientific, New Jersey (2007). oCLC: ocn170923077

20. Yoon, K.: The effective minimax value of asynchronously repeated games. Int. J. Game Theory **32**(4), 431–442 (2004). https://doi.org/10.1007/s001820300161, https://link.springer.com/10.1007/s001820300161

21. Young, R.D.: Press-dyson analysis of asynchronous, sequential prisoner's dilemma. arXiv:1712.05048 [physics] (2017). https://arxiv.org/abs/1712.05048, arXiv: 1712.05048

Multiple Oracle Algorithm to Solve Continuous Games

Tomáš Kroupa[✉][iD] and Tomáš Votroubek[iD]

Artificial Intelligence Center, Department of Computer Science, Faculty of Electrical Engineering, Czech Technical University in Prague, Prague, Czech Republic
{tomas.kroupa,votroto1}@fel.cvut.cz
https://aic.fel.cvut.cz/

Abstract. Continuous games are multiplayer games in which strategy sets are compact and utility functions are continuous. These games typically have a highly complicated structure of Nash equilibria, and numerical methods for the equilibrium computation are known only for particular classes of continuous games, such as two-player polynomial games or games in which pure equilibria are guaranteed to exist. This contribution focuses on the computation and approximation of a mixed strategy equilibrium for the whole class of multiplayer general-sum continuous games. We vastly extend the scope of applicability of the double oracle algorithm, initially designed and proved to converge only for two-player zero-sum games. Specifically, we propose an iterative strategy generation technique, which splits the original problem into the master problem with only a finite subset of strategies being considered, and the subproblem in which an oracle finds the best response of each player. This simple method is guaranteed to recover an approximate equilibrium in finitely many iterations. Further, we argue that the Wasserstein distance (the earth mover's distance) is the right metric for the space of mixed strategies for our purposes. Our main result is the convergence of this algorithm in the Wasserstein distance to an equilibrium of the original continuous game. The numerical experiments show the performance of our method on several classes of games including randomly generated examples.

Keywords: Non-cooperative game · Continuous game · Polynomial game · Nash equilibrium

1 Introduction

A strategic n-player game is called continuous if the action space of each player is a compact subset of Euclidean space and all utility functions are continuous. Many application domains have a continuum of actions expressing the amount of time, resources, location in space [20], or parameters of classifiers [40]. This involves also several games modeling the cybersecurity scenaria; see [30,35,40].

The authors acknowledge the support by the project *Research Center for Informatics* (CZ.02.1.01/0.0/0.0/16_019/0000765).

F. Fang et al. (Eds.): GameSec 2022, LNCS 13727, pp. 149–167, 2023.
https://doi.org/10.1007/978-3-031-26369-9_8

Continuous games have equilibria in mixed strategies by Glicksberg's generalization of the Nash's theorem [14], but those equilibria are usually very hard to characterize and compute. We point out the main difficulties in the development of algorithms and numerical methods for continuous games.

- The equilibrium can be any tuple of mixed strategies with infinite supports [21] or almost any tuple of finitely-supported mixed strategies [34].
- Bounds on the size of supports of equilibrium strategies are known only for particular classes of continuous games [36].
- Some important games have only mixed equilibria; for example, certain variants of Colonel Blotto games [15].
- Finding a mixed strategy equilibrium involves locating its support, which lies inside a continuum of points.

To the best of our knowledge, algorithms or numerical methods exist only for very special classes of continuous games. In particular, two-player zero-sum polynomial games can be solved by the sum-of-squares optimization based on the sequence of semidefinite relaxations of the original problem [23,32]. The book [2] contains a detailed analysis of equilibria for some families of games with a particular shape of utility functions (games of timing, bell-shaped kernels, etc.) Fictitious play, one of the principal learning methods for finite games, was recently extended to continuous action spaces and applied to Blotto games [12]. The dynamics of fictitious play were analyzed only under further restrictive assumptions in the continuous setting [19]. No-regret learning studied in [29] can be applied to finding pure equilibria or to mixed strategy learning in finite games. Convergence guaranteess for algorithms in the distributed environment solving convex-concave games and some generalizations thereof are developed in [28]. In a similar setting, [7] provide convergence guarantees to a neighborhood of a stable Nash equilibrium for gradient-based learning algorithms.

The double oracle algorithm [27] was extended from finite games and proved to converge for all two-player zero-sum continuous games [1]. The algorithm is relatively straightforward. It is based on the iterative solution of finite subgames and the subsequent extension of the current strategy sets with best response strategies. Despite its simplicity, this method was successfully adapted to large extensive-form games [5], Bayesian games [25], and security domains with complex policy spaces [39].

In this contribution, we extend the double oracle algorithm beyond two-player zero-sum continuous games [1]. This is a significant extension since we had to design a new convergence criterion to track the behavior of the algorithm. On top of that, there are relatively few methods for computing or approximating equilibria of continuous games, which narrows down the continuous games for which the exact solution can be found and used as a benchmark in our experiments. Our main result guarantees that the new method converges in the Wasserstein distance to an equilibrium for any general-sum n-player continuous game. Interestingly enough, it turns out that the Wasserstein distance represents a very natural metric on the space of mixed strategies. We demonstrate the computational performance of our method on selected examples of games appearing in the literature and on randomly generated games.

2 Basic Notions

The player set is $N = \{1, \ldots, n\}$. Each player $i \in N$ selects a pure strategy x_i from a nonempty compact set $X_i \subseteq \mathbb{R}^{d_i}$, where d_i is a positive integer. Put

$$\mathbf{X} = X_1 \times \cdots \times X_n.$$

A pure strategy profile is an n-tuple $\mathbf{x} = (x_1, \ldots, x_n) \in \mathbf{X}$. We assume that each utility function $u_i \colon \mathbf{X} \to \mathbb{R}$ is continuous. A *continuous game* is the tuple

$$\mathcal{G} = \langle N, (X_i)_{i \in N}, (u_i)_{i \in N} \rangle.$$

We say that $\mathcal{G}$ is *finite* if each strategy set X_i is finite.

Consider nonempty compact subsets $Y_i \subseteq X_i$ for $i \in N$. When each u_i is restricted to $Y_1 \times \cdots \times Y_n$, the continuous game $\langle N, (Y_i)_{i \in N}, (u_i)_{i \in N} \rangle$ is called the *subgame* of $\mathcal{G}$.

A *mixed strategy* of player i is a Borel probability measure p over X_i. The *support* of p is the compact set defined by

$$\operatorname{spt} p = \bigcap \{ K \subseteq X \mid K \text{ compact}, p(K) = 1 \}.$$

In the paper, we construct only the mixed strategies with finite supports. The support of Dirac measure δ_x is the singleton $\operatorname{spt} \delta_x = \{x\}$, where $x \in X_i$. In general, when the support $\operatorname{spt} p$ of a mixed strategy p is finite, it means that $p(x) > 0$ for all $x \in \operatorname{spt} p$ and $\sum_{x \in \operatorname{spt} p} p(x) = 1$. For clarity, we emphasize that a finitely-supported mixed strategy p of player i should be interpreted as the function $p \colon X_i \to [0,1]$ vanishing outside $\operatorname{spt} p$, and not as a vector of probabilities with a fixed dimension. This is because only the former viewpoint enables us to consider the distance between *any* pair of pure strategies in X_i, which makes it possible to compute a distance between mixed strategies with *arbitrary* supports.

The set of all mixed strategies of player i is M_i. Define

$$\mathbf{M} = M_1 \times \cdots \times M_n.$$

For a mixed strategy profile $\mathbf{p} = (p_1, \ldots, p_n) \in \mathbf{M}$, the expected utility of player $i \in N$ is

$$U_i(\mathbf{p}) = \int_{\mathbf{X}} u_i \, d(p_1 \times \cdots \times p_n),$$

where $p_1 \times \cdots \times p_n$ is the product probability measure. This definition yields a function $U_i \colon \mathbf{M} \to \mathbb{R}$, which can be effectively evaluated only in special cases (for example, when each $\operatorname{spt} p_i$ is finite). For each $i \in N$, let

$$\mathbf{M}_{-i} = \underset{\substack{k \in N \\ k \neq i}}{\bigtimes} M_k.$$

A generic profile of mixed strategies from $\mathbf{M}_{-i}$ is denoted by

$$\mathbf{p}_{-i} = (p_1, \ldots, p_{i-1}, p_{i+1}, \ldots, p_n).$$

If player i uses a pure strategy $x \in X_i$ and the rest of the players play $\mathbf{p}_{-i} \in \mathbf{M}_{-i}$, we write simply $U_k(x, \mathbf{p}_{-i})$ in place of $U_k(\delta_x, \mathbf{p}_{-i})$ to denote the expected utility of player k.

A mixed strategy profile $\mathbf{p}^* = (p_1^*, \ldots, p_n^*) \in \mathbf{M}$ is a *(Nash) equilibrium* in a continuous game $\mathcal{G}$ if

$$U_i(p_i, \mathbf{p}_{-i}^*) \leq U_i(\mathbf{p}^*), \qquad \text{for every } i \in N \text{ and all } p_i \in M_i.$$

Glicksberg's theorem [14] says that any continuous game $\mathcal{G}$ has an equilibrium. The following useful characterization is a consequence of Proposition 2: A profile $\mathbf{p}^*$ is an equilibrium if, and only if,

$$U_i(x_i, \mathbf{p}_{-i}^*) \leq U_i(\mathbf{p}^*), \qquad \text{for every } i \in N \text{ and all } x_i \in X_i.$$

Let $\epsilon \geq 0$. An *ϵ-equilibrium* is a mixed strategy profile $\mathbf{p}^* \in \mathbf{M}$ such that

$$U_i(x_i, \mathbf{p}_{-i}^*) - U_i(\mathbf{p}^*) \leq \epsilon, \qquad \text{for every } i \in N \text{ and } x_i \in X_i.$$

This implies that, for every $p_i \in M_i$, the inequality $U_i(p_i, \mathbf{p}_{-i}^*) - U_i(\mathbf{p}^*) \leq \epsilon$ holds, too. Let

$$\mathbf{U}(\mathbf{p}) = (U_1(\mathbf{p}), \ldots, U_n(\mathbf{p})).$$

Define

$$\mathbf{U}(\mathbf{x}, \mathbf{p}) = (U_1(x_1, \mathbf{p}_{-1}), \ldots, U_n(x_n, \mathbf{p}_{-n})),$$

where $\mathbf{x} \in \mathbf{X}$ and $\mathbf{p} \in \mathbf{M}$. Let $\boldsymbol{\epsilon} = (\epsilon, \ldots, \epsilon)$. Using the above introduced vectorial notation, a mixed strategy profile $\mathbf{p}^* \in \mathbf{M}$ is an ϵ-equilibrium if, and only if,

$$\mathbf{U}(\mathbf{x}, \mathbf{p}^*) - \mathbf{U}(\mathbf{p}^*) \leq \boldsymbol{\epsilon}, \qquad \text{for all } \mathbf{x} \in \mathbf{X}.$$

3   Convergence of Mixed Strategies

We consider an arbitrary metric ρ_i on the compact strategy space $X_i \subseteq \mathbb{R}^{m_i}$ of each player $i \in N$. This enables us to quantify a distance between pure strategies $x, y \in X_i$ by the number $\rho_i(x, y) \geq 0$. Consequently, we can define the Wasserstein distance d_W on M_i, which is compatible with the metric of the underlying strategy space X_i in the sense that

$$d_W(\delta_x, \delta_y) = \rho_i(x, y), \qquad \text{for all } x, y \in X_i.$$

The preservation of distance from X_i to M_i is a very natural property, since the space of pure strategies X_i is embedded in M_i via the correspondence $x \mapsto \delta_x$ mapping the pure strategy x to the Dirac measure δ_x.

The Wasserstein distance originated from optimal transport theory. It is nowadays highly instrumental in solving many problems of computer science. Specifically, the *Wasserstein distance* of mixed strategies $p, q \in M_i$ is

$$d_W(p, q) = \inf_{\mu} \int_{X_i^2} \rho_i(x, y) \, \mathrm{d}\mu(x, y),$$

where the infimum is over all Borel probability measures μ on X_i^2 whose one-dimensional marginals are p and q:

$$\mu(A \times X_i) = p(A),$$
$$\mu(X_i \times A) = q(A), \qquad \text{for all Borel subsets } A \subseteq X_i.$$

The dependence of d_W on the metric ρ_i is understood. The function d_W is a metric on M_i. Since X_i is compact, it has necessarily bounded diameter. This implies that the convergence in (M_i, d_W) coincides with the weak convergence [31, Corollary 2.2.2]. Specifically, the following two assertions are equivalent for any sequence (p^j) in M_i:

1. (p^j) converges to p in (M_i, d_W).
2. (p^j) *weakly converges* to p, which means by the definition that

$$\lim_{j} \int_{X_i} f \, \mathrm{d}p^j = \int_{X_i} f \, \mathrm{d}p, \qquad \text{for every continuous function } f \colon X_i \to \mathbb{R}.$$

The metric space (M_i, d_W) is compact by [31, Proposition 2.2.3]. Consequently, the joint strategy space $\mathbf{M}$ is compact in a product metric as well, and any sequence $(\mathbf{p}^j)$ in $\mathbf{M}$ has an accumulation point. Equivalently, the previous assertion can be formulated as follows.

Proposition 1. *Any sequence of mixed strategy profiles $(\mathbf{p}^j)$ in $\mathbf{M}$ contains a weakly convergent subsequence.*

The function U_i is continuous on $\mathbf{M}$ by the definition of weak convergence. This implies that if $(\mathbf{p}^j)$ weakly converges to $\mathbf{p}$ in $\mathbf{M}$, then the corresponding values of expected utility goes to $U_i(\mathbf{p})$, that is, $\lim_j U_i(\mathbf{p}^j) = U_i(\mathbf{p})$. By compactness of M_i and continuity of U_i, all maxima and maximizers appearing in the paper exist. This implies that the optimal value of utility function in response to the mixed strategies of other players is attained for some pure strategy. Proposition 2 is the precise formulation of this useful fact.

Proposition 2. *For each player $i \in N$ and any mixed strategy profile $\mathbf{p}_{-i} \in \mathbf{M}_{-i}$, there exists a pure strategy $x_i \in X_i$ such that*

$$\max_{p \in M_i} U_i(p, \mathbf{p}_{-i}) = \max_{x \in X_i} U_i(x, \mathbf{p}_{-i}) = U_i(x_i, \mathbf{p}_i).$$

In the rest of this section, we will discuss the problem of computing and approximating the Wasserstein distance $d_W(p, q)$ of any pair of mixed strategies

$p, q \in M_i$ for player i. In general, this is a difficult infinite-dimensional optimization problem. The existing numerical methods for this problem are reviewed in
[33]. In our setting it suffices to evaluate $d_W(p, q)$ only for mixed strategies with
finite supports. In particular, it follows immediatelly from the definition of d_W
that

$$d_W(p, \delta_y) = \sum_{x \in \text{spt } p} \rho_i(x, y) p(x),$$

for every finitely-supported mixed strategy $p \in M_i$ and any $y \in X_i$. If mixed
strategies p and q have finite supports, then computing $d_W(p, q)$ becomes the
linear programming problem with variables $\mu(x, y)$ indexed by $(x, y) \in \text{spt } p \times$
$\text{spt } q$. Specifically, the objective function to be minimized is

$$\sum_{x \in \text{spt } p} \sum_{y \in \text{spt } q} \rho_i(x, y) \mu(x, y), \tag{1}$$

and the constraints are

$$\mu(x, y) \geq 0, \quad \forall (x, y) \in \text{spt } p \times \text{spt } q,$$

$$\sum_{x \in \text{spt } p} \sum_{y \in \text{spt } q} \mu(x, y) = 1,$$

$$\sum_{y \in \text{spt } q} \mu(x, y) = p(x), \quad \forall x \in \text{spt } p$$

$$\sum_{x \in \text{spt } p} \mu(x, y) = q(y), \quad \forall y \in \text{spt } q.$$

We will briefly mention one of the frequently used alternatives to the Wasserstein distance. The *total variation distance* between mixed strategies $p, q \in M_i$
of player i is

$$d_{TV}(p, q) = \sup_A |p(A) - q(A)|,$$

where the supremum is over all Borel subsets $A \subseteq X_i$. When both mixed strate-
gies p and q have finite supports, we have $d_{TV}(p, q) = \frac{1}{2} \sum_x |p(x) - q(x)|$, where
the sum is over $\text{spt } p \cup \text{spt } q$. In this case, d_W and d_{TV} satisfy the following
inequalities (see [13]):

$$d_{min} \cdot d_{TV}(p, q) \leq d_W(p, q) \leq d_{max} \cdot d_{TV}(p, q), \tag{2}$$

where

$$d_{min} = \min\{\rho_i(x, y) \mid x, y \in \text{spt } p \cup \text{spt } q, x \neq y\},$$
$$d_{max} = \max\{\rho_i(x, y) \mid x, y \in \text{spt } p \cup \text{spt } q\}.$$

If (p^j) converges to p in the total variation distance, then (p^j) converges
weakly, but the converse fails. For example, if a sequence (x^j) converges to
$x \in X_i$ and $x^j \neq x$ for all j, then the corresponding sequence of Dirac measures
converges weakly in M_i, as $d_W(\delta_{x^j}, \delta_x) = \rho_i(x^j, x) \to 0$. By contrast, it fails to
converge in the total variation distance, since $d_{TV}(\delta_{x^j}, \delta_x) = 1$ for all j.

Algorithm 1

Input: Continuous game $\mathcal{G} = \langle N, (X_i)_{i \in N}, (u_i)_{i \in N} \rangle$, nonempty finite subsets of initial strategies $X_1^1 \subseteq X_1, \ldots, X_n^1 \subseteq X_n$, and $\epsilon \geq 0$
Output: ϵ-equilibrium $\mathbf{p}^j$ of game $\mathcal{G}$.

1: $j = 0$
2: **repeat**
3:    $j = j + 1$
4:    Find an equilibrium $\mathbf{p}^j$ of $\langle N, (X_i^j)_{i \in N}, (u_i)_{i \in N} \rangle$
5:    **for** $i \in N$ **do**
6:      Find some $x_i^{j+1} \in \beta_i(\mathbf{p}_{-i}^j)$
7:      $X_i^{j+1} = X_i^j \cup \{x_i^{j+1}\}$
8:    **end for**
9: **until** $\mathbf{U}(\mathbf{x}^{j+1}, \mathbf{p}^j) - \mathbf{U}(\mathbf{p}^j) \leq \epsilon$

Remark 1. We refrained from the detailed discussion of numerous metrics on the space of mixed strategies [13]. However, we point out the concepts of limit games and equilibria introduced in [11] to study the asymptotic (topological) behavior of equilibria for subgames embedded in a given game. It turns out that the weak topology used in this paper is finer than the inherent product topology introduced in [11].

4 Main Results

We propose Algorithm 1 as an iterative strategy-generation technique for (approximately) solving any continuous game $\mathcal{G} = \langle N, (X_i)_{i \in N}, (u_i)_{i \in N} \rangle$. We recall that the *best response set* of player $i \in N$ with respect to a mixed strategy profile $\mathbf{p}_{-i} \in \mathbf{P}_{-i}$ is

$$\beta_i(\mathbf{p}_{-i}) = \operatorname*{argmax}_{x \in X_i} U_i(x, \mathbf{p}_{-i}).$$

The set $\beta_i(\mathbf{p}_{-i})$ is always nonempty by Proposition 2. We assume that every player uses an oracle to recover at least one best response strategy, which means that the player is able to solve the corresponding optimization problem to global optimality. In Sect. 5 we will see the instances of games for which this is possible.

Algorithm 1 proceeds as follows. In every iteration j, finite strategy sets X_i^j are constructed for each player $i \in N$ and the corresponding finite subgame of $\mathcal{G}$ is solved. Let $\mathbf{p}^j$ be its equilibrium. Then, an arbitrary best response strategy x_i^{j+1} with respect to $\mathbf{p}_{-i}^j$ is added to each strategy set X_i^j. Those steps are repeated until

$$U_i(x_i^{j+1}, \mathbf{p}_{-i}^j) - U_i(\mathbf{p}^j) \leq \epsilon \qquad \text{for each } i \in N. \tag{3}$$

First we discuss basic properties of the algorithm. At each step j, we have the inequality

$$\mathbf{U}(\mathbf{x}^{j+1}, \mathbf{p}^j) \geq \mathbf{U}(\mathbf{p}^j). \tag{4}$$

Indeed, for each player $i \in N$, we get

$$U_i(x_i^{j+1}, \mathbf{p}_{-i}^j) = \max_{x \in X_i} U_i(x, \mathbf{p}_{-i}^j) \geq \max_{x \in X_i^j} U_i(x, \mathbf{p}_{-i}^j) = U_i(\mathbf{p}^j).$$

We note that the stopping condition of the double oracle algorithm for two-player zero-sum continuous games [1] is necessarily different from (3). Namely the former condition, which is tailored to the zero-sum games, is

$$U_1(x_1^{j+1}, p_2^j) - U_1(x_2^{j+1}, p_1^j) \leq \epsilon. \qquad (5)$$

When $\mathcal{G}$ is a two-player zero-sum continuous game, it follows immediately from (4) that (5) implies (3).

We prove correctness of Algorithm 1—the eventual output $\mathbf{p}^j$ is an ϵ-equilibrium of the original game $\mathcal{G}$.

Lemma 1. *The strategy profile* $\mathbf{p}^j$ *is an* ϵ-*equilibrium of* $\mathcal{G}$, *whenever Algorithm 1 terminates at step* j.

Proof. Let $\mathbf{x} \in \mathbf{X}$. We get

$$\mathbf{U}(\mathbf{x}, \mathbf{p}^j) - \mathbf{U}(\mathbf{p}^j) = \mathbf{U}(\mathbf{x}, \mathbf{p}^j) - \mathbf{U}(\mathbf{x}^{j+1}, \mathbf{p}^j) + \mathbf{U}(\mathbf{x}^{j+1}, \mathbf{p}^j) - \mathbf{U}(\mathbf{p}^j).$$

Then $\mathbf{U}(\mathbf{x}, \mathbf{p}^j) - \mathbf{U}(\mathbf{x}^{j+1}, \mathbf{p}^j) \leq \mathbf{0}$, since $\mathbf{x}^{j+1}$ is the profile of best response strategies. Consequently, we obtain

$$\mathbf{U}(\mathbf{x}, \mathbf{p}^j) - \mathbf{U}(\mathbf{p}^j) \leq \mathbf{U}(\mathbf{x}^{j+1}, \mathbf{p}^j) - \mathbf{U}(\mathbf{p}^j) \leq \epsilon,$$

where the last inequality is just the terminating condition (3). Therefore, $\mathbf{p}^j$ is an ϵ-equilibrium of $\mathcal{G}$. $\qquad \square$

If the set $\mathbf{X}^j = X_1^j \times \cdots \times X_n^j$ cannot be further inflated, Algorithm 1 terminates.

Lemma 2. *Assume that* $\mathbf{X}^j = \mathbf{X}^{j+1}$ *at step* j *of Algorithm 1. Then*

$$\mathbf{U}(\mathbf{x}^{j+1}, \mathbf{p}^j) = \mathbf{U}(\mathbf{p}^j).$$

Proof. The condition $\mathbf{X}^j = \mathbf{X}^{j+1}$ implies $\mathbf{x}^{j+1} \in \mathbf{X}^j$. For each player $i \in N$,

$$U_i(x_i^{j+1}, \mathbf{p}_{-i}^j) = \max_{x \in X_i^j} U_i(x, \mathbf{p}_{-i}^j) = U_i(\mathbf{p}^j).$$

$\qquad \square$

The original double oracle algorithm for two-player zero-sum finite games [27] makes it possible to find exact equilibria. The following proposition generalizes this result to the setting of multiplayer general-sum finite games.

Proposition 3. *If* $\mathcal{G}$ *is a finite game and* $\epsilon = 0$, *then Algorithm 1 recovers an equilibrium of* $\mathcal{G}$ *in finitely-many steps.*

Proof. Let $\mathcal{G}$ be finite and $\epsilon = 0$. Since each X_i is finite, there exists an iteration j in which $\mathbf{X}^{j+1} = \mathbf{X}^j$. Then the terminating condition of Algorithm 1 is satisfied with $\epsilon = 0$ (Lemma 2) and $\mathbf{p}^j$ is an equilibrium of $\mathcal{G}$ (Lemma 1).   □

Theorem 1 is our main result, which is a significant extension of the convergence theorem from [1]. We emphasize that Theorem 1 holds without additional assumptions about a continuous game $\mathcal{G}$ or its equilibria. It is worth mentioning that Theorem 1(1) provides an alternative proof of Glicksberg's theorem [14] about existence of equilibria in continuous games. Indeed, the sequence $\mathbf{p}^1, \mathbf{p}^2, \ldots$ has at least one accumulation point by Proposition 1. Further, the consequence of Theorem 1(2) is that a finitely-supported ϵ-equilibrium of $\mathcal{G}$ can always be found in finitely-many steps, although game $\mathcal{G}$ may have no finitely-supported equilibria.

Theorem 1. *Let $\mathcal{G}$ be a continuous game.*

1. *Let $\epsilon = 0$. If Algorithm 1 stops at step j, then $\mathbf{p}^j$ is an equilibrium of $\mathcal{G}$. Otherwise, any accumulation point of $\mathbf{p}^1, \mathbf{p}^2, \ldots$ is an equilibrium of $\mathcal{G}$.*
2. *Let $\epsilon > 0$. Then Algorithm 1 terminates at some step j and $\mathbf{p}^j$ is an ϵ-equilibrium of $\mathcal{G}$.*

Proof. Item 1. Let $\epsilon = 0$. If Algorithm 1 terminates at step j, then Lemma 1 implies that $\mathbf{p}^j$ is an equilibrium of $\mathcal{G}$. In the opposite case, the algorithm generates a sequence of mixed strategy profiles $\mathbf{p}^1, \mathbf{p}^2, \ldots$ Consider any weakly convergent subsequence of this sequence—at least one such subsequence exists by Proposition 1. Without loss of generality, such a subsequence will be denoted by the same indices as the original sequence. Therefore, for each player $i \in N$, there exists some $p_i^* \in M_i$, such that the sequence $p_i^1, p_i^2, \ldots$ weakly converges to p_i^*. We need to show that $\mathbf{p}^* = (p_1^*, \ldots, p_n^*) \in \mathbf{M}$ is an equilibrium of $\mathcal{G}$.

Let $i \in N$. Define

$$Y_i = \bigcup_{j=1}^{\infty} X_i^j.$$

First, assume that $x \in Y_i$. Then there exists j_0 with $x \in X_i^j$ for each $j \geq j_0$. Hence the inequality $U_i(\mathbf{p}^j) \geq U_i(x, \mathbf{p}_{-i}^j)$, for each $j \geq j_0$, since $\mathbf{p}^j$ is an equilibrium of the corresponding finite subgame. Therefore,

$$U_i(\mathbf{p}^*) = \lim_j U_i(\mathbf{p}^j) \geq \lim_j U_i(x, \mathbf{p}_{-i}^j) = U_i(x, \mathbf{p}_{-i}^*).$$

Further, by continuity of U_i,

$$U_i(\mathbf{p}^*) \geq U_i(x, \mathbf{p}_{-i}^*) \quad \text{for all } x \in \text{cl}(Y_i). \tag{6}$$

Now, consider an arbitrary $x \in X_i \setminus \text{cl}(Y_i)$. The definition of x_i^{j+1} yields $U_i(x_i^{j+1}, \mathbf{p}_{-i}^j) \geq U_i(x, \mathbf{p}_{-i}^j)$ for each j. This implies, by continuity,

$$\lim_j U_i(x_i^{j+1}, \mathbf{p}_{-i}^*) \geq \lim_j U_i(x, \mathbf{p}_{-i}^j) = U_i(x, \mathbf{p}_{-i}^*). \tag{7}$$

Since $x_i^{j+1} \in X_i^{j+1}$, compactness of X_i provides a convergent subsequence (denoted by the same indices) such that $x' = \lim_j x_i^j \in \mathrm{cl}(Y_i)$. Then (6) gives

$$U_i(\mathbf{p}^*) \geq U_i(x', \mathbf{p}^*_{-i}) = \lim_j U_i(x_i^{j+1}, \mathbf{p}^*_{-i}). \tag{8}$$

Combining (7) and (8) shows that $U_i(\mathbf{p}^*) \geq U_i(x, \mathbf{p}^*_{-i})$.

Item 2. Let $\epsilon > 0$. If Algorithm 1 terminates at step j, then Lemma 1 implies that $\mathbf{p}^j$ is an ϵ-equilibrium of $\mathcal{G}$. Otherwise Algorithm 1 produces a sequence $\mathbf{p}^1, \mathbf{p}^2, \ldots$ and we can repeat the analysis as in Item 1 for convergent subsequences of $(\mathbf{p}^j)$ and $(\mathbf{x}^j)$, which are denoted by the same indices. Define $x' = \lim_j x_i^j$. Then

$$U_i(\mathbf{p}^*) \geq U_i(x', \mathbf{p}^*_{-i}) = \lim_j U_i(x_i^{j+1}, \mathbf{p}^j_{-i}). \tag{9}$$

At every step j we have $U_i(x_i^{j+1}, \mathbf{p}^j_{-i}) \geq U_i(\mathbf{p}^j)$ for each $i \in N$ by (4). Hence $\lim_j U_i(x_i^{j+1}, \mathbf{p}^j_{-i}) \geq U_i(\mathbf{p}^*)$. Putting together the last inequality with (9), we get

$$\lim_j (U_i(x_i^{j+1}, \mathbf{p}^j_{-i}) - U_i(\mathbf{p}^j)) = 0 \tag{10}$$

for each $i \in N$. This equality means that Algorithm 1 stops at some step j and $\mathbf{p}^j$ is an ϵ-equilibrium by Lemma 1. $\square$

Algorithm 1 generates the sequence of equilibria $\mathbf{p}^1, \mathbf{p}^2, \ldots$ in increasingly larger subgames of $\mathcal{G}$. The sequence itself may fail to converge weakly in $\mathbf{M}$ even for a two-player zero-sum continuous game; see Example 1 from [1]. In fact, Theorem 1 guarantees only convergence to an accumulation point. We recall that this is a typical feature of some globally convergent methods not only in infinite-dimensional spaces [18, Theorem 2.2], but also in Euclidean spaces. For example, a gradient method generates the sequence such that only its accumulation points are guaranteed to be stationary points; see [4, Proposition 1.2.1] for details. One necessary condition for the weak convergence of $\mathbf{p}^1, \mathbf{p}^2, \ldots$ is easy to formulate using the stopping condition of Algorithm 1.

Proposition 4. *If the sequence $\mathbf{p}^1, \mathbf{p}^2, \ldots$ generated by Algorithm 1 converges weakly to an equilibrium $\mathbf{p}$, then $\lim_j (U_i(x_i^{j+1}, \mathbf{p}^j_{-i}) - U_i(\mathbf{p}^j)) = 0$, for each $i \in N$.*

Proof. Using (4) and the triangle inequality,

$$U_i(x_i^{j+1}, \mathbf{p}^j_{-i}) - U_i(\mathbf{p}^j) = |U_i(x_i^{j+1}, \mathbf{p}^j_{-i}) - U_i(\mathbf{p}^j)|$$
$$\leq |U_i(x_i^{j+1}, \mathbf{p}^j_{-i}) - U_i(\mathbf{p})| + |U_i(\mathbf{p}) - U_i(\mathbf{p}^j)|.$$

As $j \to \infty$, the first summand goes to zero by (10) and the second by the assumption. Hence the conclusion. $\square$

In our numerical experiments (see Sect. 5), we compute the difference

$$U_i(x_i^{j+1}, \mathbf{p}^j_{-i}) - U_i(\mathbf{p}^j) \tag{11}$$

at each step j and check if such differences are diminishing with j increasing. This provides a simple heuristics to detect the quality of approximation and convergence. Another option is to calculate the Wasserstein distance

$$d_W(\mathbf{p}^j, \mathbf{p}^{j+1}), \tag{12}$$

which can be done with a linear program (1) or approximately using the bounds (2). If the sequence $\mathbf{p}^1, \mathbf{p}^2, \ldots$ converges weakly, then $d_W(\mathbf{p}^j, \mathbf{p}^{j+1}) \to 0$. We include the values (12) in the results of some numerical experiments and observe that they are decreasing to zero quickly. It can be shown that neither (11) nor (12) are monotone sequences. The lack of monotonicity is apparent from the graphs of our experiments; see Fig. 1, for example.

Algorithm 1 is a meta-algorithm, which is parameterized by

1. the algorithm for computing equilibria of subgames (the *master problem*) and
2. the optimization method for computing the best response (the *sub-problem*).

We detail this setup for each example in the next section. The choice of computational methods should reflect the properties of a continuous game, since the efficiency of methods for solving the master problem and subproblem is the decisive factor for the overall performance and precision of Algorithm 1. For example, polymatrix games are solvable in polynomial time [6], whereas finding even an approximate Nash equilibrium of a finite general-sum game is a very hard problem [8]. As for the solution of the subproblem, the best response computation can be based on global solvers for special classes of utility functions.

5   Numerical Experiments

We demonstrate the versatility of our method by solving (i) various games appearing in current papers and (ii) randomly generated games. In some cases we show the progress of the convergence-criterion value (11) called "instability" over the course of 10 iterations, and we also plot the Wasserstein distance (12) between mixed strategies in consecutive iterations. Each experiment was initialized with a randomly chosen pure strategy. In games with polynomial utility functions, the best response oracles employ methods of global polynomial optimization [24]. In games where the best response optimization was intractable we use local solvers, which perform sufficiently well, nevertheless.

We used a laptop running Linux 5.13 on an Intel Core i5-7200U CPU with 8 GiB of system memory to perform our experiments. Our implementation uses Julia 1.6, JuMP [9], Mosek, and Ipopt [37]. The Julia source codes will be attached to this paper. Examples 1–3 took between 0.1 and 0.2 s to compute and Example 4 took 1 s.

Example 1 (Zero-sum polynomial game [32]). Consider a two-player zero-sum game with strategy sets $[-1, 1]$ and with the utility function of the first player $u(x, y) = 2xy^2 - x^2 - y$ on $[-1, 1]^2$. As the generated subgames are all finite two-player zero-sum games, we can use linear programming to find their equilibria.

The global method for optimizing polynomials described in [32] is an appropriate best response oracle in this case. After 10 iterations, our method finds pure strategies $x \approx 0.4$ and $y \approx 0.63$, resulting in payoffs $(-0.47, 0.47)$. An oracle based on a hierarchy of semidefinite relaxations (as implemented in SumOfSquares [38]) can be used instead to handle games with semialgebraic strategy sets.

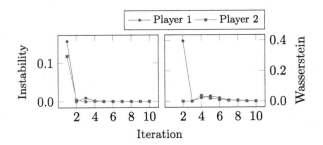

Fig. 1. Convergence in Example 1

Example 2 (General-sum polynomial game [36]). The strategy set of each player is $[-1, 1]$ and utility functions are

$$u_1(x, y) = -3x^2y^2 - 2x^3 + 3y^3 + 2xy - x,$$
$$u_2(x, y) = 2x^2y^2 + x^2y - 4y^3 - x^2 + 4y.$$

Our method finds mixed strategies

$$x \approx \begin{cases} 0.11 & 44.19, \% \\ -1.0 & 55.81, \% \end{cases} \quad y \approx 0.72,$$

resulting in payoffs $(1.13, 1.81)$. We use the PATH solver [10] for linear complementarity problems to find equilibria in the generated subgames (Fig. 2).

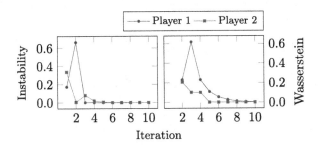

Fig. 2. Convergence in Example 2

Example 3 (Torus game [7]). Each strategy set is the unit circle $S^1 = [-\pi, \pi]$ and the utility functions are

$$u_1(\theta_1, \theta_2) = \alpha_1 \cos(\theta_1 - \phi_1) - \cos(\theta_1 - \theta_2),$$
$$u_2(\theta_1, \theta_2) = \alpha_2 \cos(\theta_2 - \phi_2) - \cos(\theta_2 - \theta_1).$$

where $\phi = (0, \pi/8)$ and $\alpha = (1, 1.5)$. Using Ipopt as the best response oracle, we obtain pure strategies $\theta_1 \approx 1.41$, $\theta_2 \approx -0.33$ resulting in payoffs $(0.32, 1.29)$ (Fig. 3).

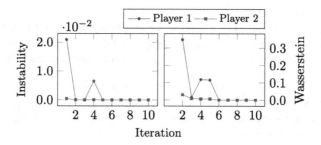

Fig. 3. Convergence in Example 3

Example 4 (General Blotto [15]). Each strategy set in this two-player zero-sum game is the standard 4-dimensional simplex in $\mathbb{R}^5$ and the utility function of the first player is $u(\mathbf{x}, \mathbf{y}) = \sum_{j=1}^{5} f(x_j - y_j)$, where $f(x) = \text{sgn}(x) \cdot x^2$. Using linear programming to solve the master problem and Ipopt for the approximation of best response, we recovered pure strategies $\mathbf{x} \approx (0, 0, 0, 1, 0)$ and $\mathbf{y} \approx (0, 1, 0, 0, 0)$ resulting in payoffs $(0, 0)$. This is an equilibrium by [15, Proposition 4] (Fig. 4).

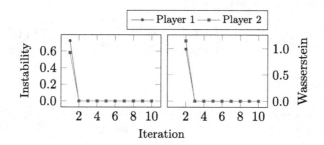

Fig. 4. Convergence in Example 4

We note that some well-known classes of games with compact actions spaces cannot be used in our experiments. The typical case in point are Colonel Blotto games [3] since their utility function is discontinuous. By contrast, certain General Blotto games [15] are continuous games (see Example 4).

5.1   Experiments with Separable Network Games

Separable network games (polymatrix games) with finitely many strategies of each player can be solved in polynomial time [6] by linear programming. We use Algorithm 1 to compute equilibria of five-player polymatrix games defined by 20 by 20 matrices. Specifically, we generated a random matrix for each edge in the network and then transposed and subtracted the matrix of utility functions to make the game globally zero sum. We remark that zero-sum polymatrix games are payoff-equivalent to the general polymatrix games by [6, Theorem 7]. In a test of 100 games, our algorithm found an ϵ-equilibrium with $\epsilon = 0.01$ after 17.69 iterations in a mean time of 0.29 s.

Further, we considered a continuous generalization of separable network games with strategy sets $[-1, 1]$ and polynomial utility functions. This class of games was analyzed with the tools of polynomial optimization in [22].

Example 5 (Three-player zero-sum polynomial game). There are 3 players. All pairs of players are involved in bilateral general-sum games and each player uses the same strategy across all such games. The sum of all utility functions is zero. The pairwise utility functions on $[-1, 1]^2$ are

$$u_{1,2}(x_1, x_2) = -2x_1x_2^2 + 5x_1x_2 - x_2$$
$$u_{1,3}(x_1, x_3) = -2x_1^2 - 4x_1x_3 - 2x_3$$
$$u_{2,1}(x_2, x_1) = 2x_1x_2^2 - 2x_1^2 - 5x_1x_2 + x_2$$
$$u_{2,3}(x_2, x_3) = -2x_2x_3^2 - 2x_2^2 + 5x_2x_3$$
$$u_{3,1}(x_3, x_1) = 4x_1^2 + 4x_1x_3 + 2x_3$$
$$u_{3,2}(x_3, x_2) = 2x_2x_3^2 + 2x_2^2 - 5x_2x_3$$

The polynomial (sum-of-squares) optimization serves as the best response oracle. Our method finds the mixed strategies

$$x_1 \approx -0.06, \quad x_2 \approx \begin{cases} 0.35 & 70.8\% \\ 0.36 & 29.2\% \end{cases}, \quad x_3 \approx \begin{cases} 1.0 & 72.11\% \\ -1.0 & 27.89\% \end{cases}$$

with the corresponding payoffs $(-1.23, 0.26, 0.97)$.

In the final round of experiments, we solved randomly generated network games of five players whose utility functions are quartic polynomials over the product of $[-1, 1]$ to show that this approach can also solve more complex games. In particular, we generated the network games by adding three random monomials of degree four or less to each pairwise game, then subtracted the transpose to satisfy the global zero-sum property. While the sum-of-squares approach scales poorly as the polynomial degree and the number of variables grows, its use as a best response oracle means that we only have to consider the variables of one player at a time. In a test of 100 games, our algorithm found an ϵ-equilibrium with $\epsilon = 0.01$ after 5.06 iterations in 0.78 s on average (Fig. 5).

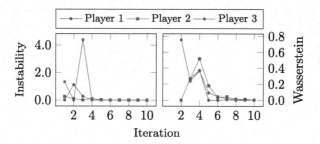

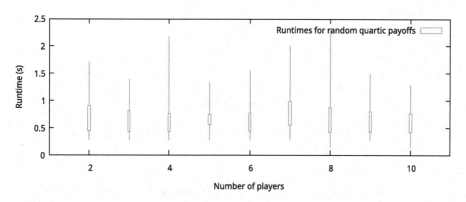

Fig. 5. Convergence in Example 5

5.2 Experiments with Random General-Sum Polynomial Games

In this experiment, we used the multiple oracle algorithm to find ϵ-equilibria ($\epsilon = 0.001$) in continuous multiplayer games with randomly generated quartic polynomial payoffs and $[0,1]$ strategy sets. The time to find equilibria does not appear strongly correlated with the number of players due to the small support of the equilibria—see Fig. 6. Similarly, the degrees of the payoff polynomials have only a small effect on the runtime.

Fig. 6. Plot showing the time required to find equilibria of multiplayer polynomial games depending on the number of players. For each player count, the plot shows 100 samples of quartic polynomials with normally distributed random coefficients.

We also conducted the simulation experiment with 100 samples of polynomial games where each strategy space is the cube $[0,1]^2$. Figure 7 and Fig. 8 show the runtimes needed to reach any 10^{-3}-equilibrium for multiplayer polynomial games with degrees less than 4 and up to 5 players.

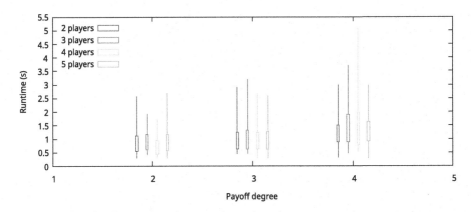

Fig. 7. This graph shows the dependence of runtime on the degree of polynomials for games up to 5 players.

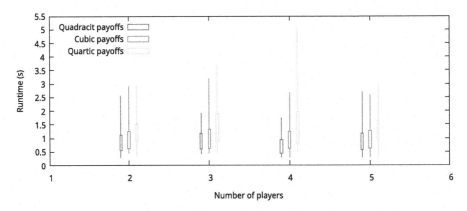

Fig. 8. This graph shows the dependence of runtime on the number of players for polynomial games up to degree 4.

5.3   Using the Multiple Oracle Algorithm to Accelerate Existing Solvers for Finite Games

Adding the multiple oracle algorithm on top of solvers such as those implemented in the Gambit library [26] can improve the solution time of large finite general-sum games. Unfortunately, the solvers implemented in Gambit occasionally fail to produce an output or will loop indefinitely. Nevertheless, our preliminary results suggest that the multiple oracle algorithm has the potential to accelerate existing solvers.

We used the global Newton method [16] to find equilibria using `pygambit` as an interface to Gambit, and when the method failed, we used the iterated polymatrix approximation [17] instead. Due to the significant overhead of this approach, our recorded runtimes are much higher than what is theoretically achievable with the multiple oracle algorithm (Fig. 9).

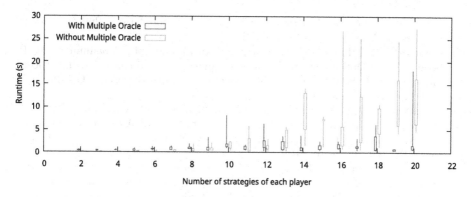

Fig. 9. Plot comparing the time required to find equilibria of three-player general-sum finite games with randomly generated payoffs when using algorithms of Gambit with/without the multiple oracle algorithm.

6   Conclusions and Future Research

The idea of multiple oracle algorithm is to construct a sequence of finite subgames whose equilibria approximate the equilibrium of a given continuous game in the Wasserstein metric. We have demonstrated performance of the algorithm on selected games appearing in current research papers and randomly generated games. Note that the multiple oracle algorithm makes it possible to approximate the equilibrium of *any* continuous games in the sense of Theorem 1, with the caveat that an individual sequence of equilibria may fail to converge. Although possible in theory (see [1]), this behavior has never been observed in the sample games. Another feature of the algorithm is that the choice of best response oracle and the method for solving finite subgames should be fine-tuned for every particular class of games. A good case in point is the class of polynomial games, which allows for globally optimal solvers for the sub-problem (the best response computation).

Several examples from the literature show that our method converges fast when the dimensions of strategy spaces are small and the generated subgames are not large. We plan to enlarge the scope of our experiments to include games with many-dimensional strategy spaces. Moreover, the results from Sect. 5.2 indicate that more appropriate methods for generating challenging polynomial games should be used to assess the scalability of the multiple oracle algorithm for solving multiplayer polynomial games.

References

1. Adam, L., Horčík, R., Kasl, T., Kroupa, T.: Double oracle algorithm for computing equilibria in continuous games. In: Proceedings of the AAAI Conference on Artificial Intelligence, pp. 5070–5077 (2021)

2. Başar, T., Olsder, G.: Dynamic Noncooperative Game Theory, 2nd edn. Society for Industrial and Applied Mathematics, Philadelphia (1999)
3. Behnezhad, S., Blum, A., Derakhshan, M., Hajiaghayi, M., Papadimitriou, C.H., Seddighin, S.: Optimal strategies of blotto games: beyond convexity. In: Proceedings of the 2019 ACM Conference on Economics and Computation, EC 2019, ACM, New York, pp. 597–616 (2019)
4. Bertsekas, D.: Nonlinear Programming. Athena Scientific, Nashua (2016)
5. Bošanský, B., Kiekintveld, C., Lisý, V., Pěchouček, M.: An exact double-oracle algorithm for zero-sum extensive-form games with imperfect information. J. Artif. Intell. Res. **51**, 829–866 (2014)
6. Cai, Y., Candogan, O., Daskalakis, C., Papadimitriou, C.: Zero-sum polymatrix games: a generalization of minmax. Math. Oper. Res. **41**(2), 648–655 (2016)
7. Chasnov, B., Ratliff, L., Mazumdar, E., Burden, S.: Convergence analysis of gradient-based learning in continuous games. In: Uncertainty in Artificial Intelligence, pp. 935–944. PMLR (2020)
8. Daskalakis, C., Goldberg, P.W., Papadimitriou, C.H.: The complexity of computing a Nash equilibrium. SIAM J. Comput. **39**(1), 195–259 (2009)
9. Dunning, I., Huchette, J., Lubin, M.: JuMP: a modeling language for mathematical optimization. SIAM Rev. **59**(2), 295–320 (2017). https://doi.org/10.1137/15M1020575
10. Ferris, M.C., Munson, T.S.: Complementarity problems in GAMS and the PATH solver. J. Econ. Dyn. Control **24**(2), 165–188 (2000)
11. Fudenberg, D., Levine, D.: Limit games and limit equilibria. J. Econ. Theor. **38**(2), 261–279 (1986)
12. Ganzfried, S.: Algorithm for computing approximate Nash equilibrium in continuous games with application to continuous Blotto. Games **12**(2), 47 (2021)
13. Gibbs, A.L., Su, F.E.: On choosing and bounding probability metrics. Int. Stat. Rev. **70**(3), 419–435 (2002)
14. Glicksberg, I.L.: A further generalization of the Kakutani fixed point theorem, with application to Nash equilibrium points. Proc. Am. Math. Soc. **3**, 170–174 (1952)
15. Golman, R., Page, S.E.: General blotto: games of allocative strategic mismatch. Public Choice **138**(3–4), 279–299 (2009)
16. Govindan, S., Wilson, R.: A global Newton method to compute Nash equilibria. J. Econ. Theor. **110**(1), 65–86 (2003)
17. Govindan, S., Wilson, R.: Computing Nash equilibria by iterated polymatrix approximation. J. Econ. Dyn. Control **28**(7), 1229–1241 (2004)
18. Hinze, M., Pinnau, R., Ulbrich, M., Ulbrich, S.: Optimization with PDE Constraints, vol. 23. Springer, Cham (2008)
19. Hofbauer, J., Sorin, S.: Best response dynamics for continuous zero-sum games. Discrete Continuous Dyn. Syst.-Ser. B **6**(1), 215 (2006)
20. Kamra, N., Gupta, U., Fang, F., Liu, Y., Tambe, M.: Policy learning for continuous space security games using neural networks. In: Thirty-Second AAAI Conference on Artificial Intelligence, pp. 1103–1112 (2018)
21. Karlin, S.: Mathematical Methods and Theory in Games, Programming and Economics, Vol. 2: The Theory of Infinite Games. Addison-Wesley Publishing Company, Boston (1959)
22. Kroupa, T., Vannucci, S., Votroubek, T.: Separable network games with compact strategy sets. In: Bošanský, B., Gonzalez, C., Rass, S., Sinha, A. (eds.) Decision and Game Theory for Security, pp. 37–56. Springer International Publishing, Cham (2021)

23. Laraki, R., Lasserre, J.B.: Semidefinite programming for min-max problems and games. Math. Program. **131**(1–2), 305–332 (2012)
24. Lasserre, J.B.: An Introduction To Polynomial And Semi-Algebraic Optimization, vol. 52. Cambridge University Press, Cambridge (2015)
25. Li, Z., Wellman, M.P.: Evolution strategies for approximate solution of Bayesian games. In: Proceedings of the AAAI Conference on Artificial Intelligence, vol. 35, pp. 5531–5540 (2021)
26. McKelvey, R.D., McLennan, A.M., Turocy, T.L.: Gambit: Software tools for game theory. Version 16.0.1 (2016)
27. McMahan, H.B., Gordon, G.J., Blum, A.: Planning in the presence of cost functions controlled by an adversary. In: Proceedings of the 20th International Conference on Machine Learning (ICML-03), pp. 536–543 (2003)
28. Mertikopoulos, P., Lecouat, B., Zenati, H., Foo, C.S., Chandrasekhar, V., Piliouras, G.: Optimistic mirror descent in saddle-point problems: Going the extra (gradient) mile (2018)
29. Mertikopoulos, P., Zhou, Z.: Learning in games with continuous action sets and unknown payoff functions. Math. Program. **173**(1), 465–507 (2019)
30. Niu, L., Sahabandu, D., Clark, A., Poovendran, R.: A game-theoretic framework for controlled islanding in the presence of adversaries. In: Bošanský, B., Gonzalez, C., Rass, S., Sinha, A. (eds.) GameSec 2021. LNCS, vol. 13061, pp. 231–250. Springer, Cham (2021). https://doi.org/10.1007/978-3-030-90370-1_13
31. Panaretos, V.M., Zemel, Y.: An Invitation To Statistics In Wasserstein Space. Springer Nature, Cham (2020)
32. Parrilo, P.: Polynomial games and sum of squares optimization. In: 2006 45th IEEE Conference on Decision and Control, pp. 2855–2860 (2006)
33. Peyré, G., Cuturi, M.: Computational optimal transport: with applications to data science. Found. Trends Mach. Learn. **11**(5–6), 355–607 (2019)
34. Rehbeck, J.: Note on unique Nash equilibrium in continuous games. Games Econ. Behav. **110**, 216–225 (2018)
35. Roussillon, B., Loiseau, P.: Scalable optimal classifiers for adversarial settings under uncertainty. In: Bošanský, B., Gonzalez, C., Rass, S., Sinha, A. (eds.) GameSec 2021. LNCS, vol. 13061, pp. 80–97. Springer, Cham (2021). https://doi.org/10.1007/978-3-030-90370-1_5
36. Stein, N.D., Ozdaglar, A., Parrilo, P.A.: Separable and low-rank continuous games. Int. J. Game Theor. **37**(4), 475–504 (2008)
37. Wächter, A., Biegler, L.T.: On the implementation of an interior-point filter line-search algorithm for large-scale nonlinear programming. Math. Program. **106**(1), 25–57 (2006). https://doi.org/10.1007/s10107-004-0559-y. https://doi.org/10.1007/s10107-004-0559-y
38. Weisser, T., Legat, B., Coey, C., Kapelevich, L., Vielma, J.P.: Polynomial and moment optimization in Julia and JuMP. In: JuliaCon (2019). https://pretalx.com/juliacon2019/talk/QZBKAU/
39. Xu, L., Perrault, A., Fang, F., Chen, H., Tambe, M.: Robust reinforcement learning under minimax regret for green security. In: Uncertainty in Artificial Intelligence, pp. 257–267. PMLR (2021)
40. Yasodharan, S., Loiseau, P.: Nonzero-sum adversarial hypothesis testing games. In: Advances in Neural Information Processing Systems, pp. 7310–7320 (2019)

Optimal Pursuit of Surveilling Agents
Near a High Value Target

Shivam Bajaj$^{(\boxtimes)}$ (ID) and Shaunak D. Bopardikar (ID)

Michigan State University, East Lansing, MI 48824, USA
{bajajshi,shaunak}@msu.edu

Abstract. We introduce a tracking evasion game comprising a single mobile pursuer, two mobile trackers and one static high value target. The trackers rely on individual measurements of the location of the target using, for instance, their individual distance to the target and are assumed to be slower than the pursuer. The pursuer seeks to minimize the square of the instantaneous distance to one of the trackers, while the trackers aim to jointly maximize a weighted combination of the determinant of the Fisher Information Matrix and the square of the distance between the pursuer and the tracker being pursued. This formulation models the objective of the trackers which is to maximize the information gathered about the target, while delaying capture. We show that the optimization problem for the trackers can be transformed into a Quadratically Constrained Quadratic Program. We then establish that the game admits a Nash equilibrium in the space of pure strategies and provide several numerical insights into the trajectories and the payoff of the mobile agents. Finally, we outline how this work can be generalized to the case of multiple trackers and multiple targets.

Keywords: Pursuit evasion · Game theory · Target tracking

1 Introduction

The decreasing cost and increasing capabilities of Unmanned Aerial Vehicles (UAVs) have led to their widespread use in many applications such as environmental monitoring, surveillance and defense [3,19]. However, ease of access to UAV technology has found adversarial use [23]. A commonly reported adversarial application is deploying multiple adversarial UAVs (or intruders) to breach a perimeter [2,27]. In most of the works on perimeter defense, it is assumed that the location of the perimeter is known to the adversary, which may not be true in all applications. For instance, the location of a high value defense/research facility (target/perimeter) is not precisely known to the adversary. In such scenarios, prior to deploying intruders to breach the perimeter, the adversary will typically obtain the estimates of the location of the facility by deploying adversarial

This work was supported by NSF Award ECCS-2030556.

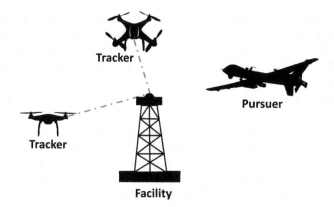

Fig. 1. Problem description. Adversarial UAVs (trackers) move to maximize the information gathered using the distance measurements to the facility (target) while simultaneously evading from the pursuer.

UAVs (or trackers) equipped with some low cost range sensor [5]. To counter these UAVs, the defense system can release mobile pursuers (cf. Fig. 1) that have the ability to intercept and disable the UAVs or to corrupt the information gathered by obstructing the line-of-sight. These scenarios raise an important question which has not yet been fully explored in the literature – *how does the motion strategy of adversarial trackers change in the presence of one or many pursuers?*

This work is a first step towards formulating an adversarial information gathering problem in presence of a mobile pursuer. Specifically, we introduce a *tracking pursuit* game in a planar environment comprising one single static high value target, a single mobile pursuer and two mobile trackers (adversarial UAVs). We assume that the trackers are slower than the pursuer and can only measure their individual distances from the target. The trackers jointly seek to maximize the tracking performance while simultaneously evading the pursuer at every time instant. On the other hand, the pursuer seeks to capture one of the trackers to hinder the tracking objective of the trackers. Although we consider a planar environment and range-only measurements, we also show how this work can be extended to other sensing models such as bearing measurements.

1.1 Related Works

General target tracking problems involve a static/moving target whose state (e.g., the position and velocity) needs to be estimated by trackers using measurements based on the distance or bearing or both [4,8,17,20]. A generic approach in these works is to optimize a measure (e.g., trace or determinant) of the estimation error covariance matrix obtained from an Extended Kalman Filter (EKF) used to estimate the state. We refer to [7] and the references therein for the application of state estimation to various target tracking scenarios. Since the relative geometry of the target and the trackers plays an important role in the tracking process, many works [4, 16, 24, 30, 31] have focused on identifying such geometries and motion strategies that optimize the tracking performance such as the determinant of the Fisher Information Matrix (FIM) or the trace of the estimation error covariance of the EKF. Tracking based on metrics of observability have also been considered [9, 21, 22].

All of the above mentioned works only focus on determining optimal trajectories for the trackers to optimize a certain tracking performance, but do not consider the presence of a pursuer. Authors in [14] design strategies for the pursuers to optimize the tracking performance while maintaining a desired formation. In [25], an adaptive sampling approach is considered to track mobile targets and maintain them in the field of view. Authors in [1] propose an algorithm based on rapidly exploring random trees for pursuers to detect and track a target.

Pursuit of mobile agents (or evaders) in the presence of a target has been extensively studied as a differential game known as Target-Attacker-Defender (TAD) games [10–12, 29]. In these works, the attacker tries to capture a target while simultaneously evading a defender. The objective in these works is to determine optimal cooperative strategies for the target and the defender to delay the time taken to capture or evade the attacker. This paper differs from the aforementioned TAD games as the trackers do not seek to capture the target. Instead, through the measurements obtained, the trackers aim to maximize the information gathered about the target while, evading the pursuer. Another variant of pursuit evasion games is pursuit tracking [18, 26, 32] where the objective of the pursuer is to track the evader by maintaining a fixed distance or Line of Sight to it. In contrast, in this work, the pursuer seeks to capture the trackers which are tracking a static target.

1.2 Preliminaries and Contributions

Recall that one of the objectives of the trackers is to maximize the information obtained from the set of range measurements to the target. This motivates the use of Fisher Information Matrix (FIM). The FIM is a symmetric, positive definite matrix that characterizes the amount of information provided by the measurements for the position of the target that is to be estimated. In other words, by moving to locations that provide the highest information, the trackers aim to improve the outcome of the estimation process. Maximizing the FIM can be achieved by maximizing a real-valued scalar function (or a metric) of the FIM. The most commonly used metrics are the trace, determinant and the eigenvalues of the FIM, also known as the A-optimality, D-optimality and E-optimality criteria, respectively [28]. Although the trace of the FIM is easy to compute, we consider the determinant as a metric to be maximized by the trackers. This is because the trace of FIM may be non zero even when the FIM is singular, implying that optimizing the trace of the FIM can result in singular configurations.

In this paper, we seek to understand the role of a pursuer in tracking problems. Equivalently, we aim to understand how the cost of evasion combined with the tracking cost affects the trajectories, and consequently, the payoff of the trackers. In particular, we consider an instantaneous two player zero sum game between the pursuer and the trackers wherein the pursuer seeks to minimize the (square of) distance to one of the trackers at every time instant whereas the trackers aim to jointly maximize a weighted combination of the determinant of the FIM at every time instant and the distance from the pursuer. Our main contributions are as follows:

1. **Tracking-Pursuit Game with a target:** We introduce a tracking-pursuit problem, modelled as a zero sum game, in a planar environment which consists of a single mobile pursuer, two mobile trackers and a single static target. For ease of presentation, we assume that the tracking agents can only measure the distance to the target and are assumed to be slower than the pursuer. At every time instant, the pursuer aims to minimize the square of the distance to a tracker, whereas the trackers aim to jointly maximize a weighted combination of the determinant of the FIM and the square of the distance to the pursuer from the nearest tracker. The game terminates when the pursuer captures a tracker.
2. **Computing Nash Equilibrium Strategies:** We first establish the optimal strategy for the pursuer. Although the payoff for the trackers is a non-convex function, we show that the optimization problem can be converted to a Quadratically Constrained Quadratic Program (QCQP). We further establish that the optimal strategies obtained for the pursuer and the trackers form a Nash equilibrium of this game.
3. **Numerical Insights:** We provide several numerical examples highlighting the trajectories of the mobile agents and the affect on the instantaneous payoff. In particular, we show that due to the presence of pursuer the determinant of the FIM achieves a lower value. We also show, through one of the examples, that the pursuer can capture a tracker even when the tracker is faster than the pursuer.
4. **Extension to multiple trackers and targets:** Finally, we thoroughly describe how this work extends to the scenarios when there are multiple trackers or multiple targets.

This paper is organized as follows. Section 2 comprises the formal problem definition. In Sect. 3, we derive optimal strategies for the pursuer and the trackers, Sect. 4 provides several numerical insights into the problem and Sect. 5 describes the extension of this work to the case of multiple targets and trackers. Finally, Sect. 6 summarizes this work and outlines future directions for this work.

2 Problem Description

We consider a *tracking evasion* problem in a planar environment which consists of a single static target, a single mobile pursuer and two mobile trackers. We denote the two trackers as E_1 and E_2, respectively (cf. Fig. 2). Each mobile agent is modelled as a single order integrator with bounded maximum speed.

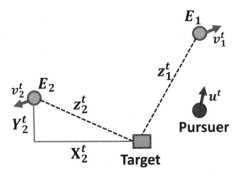

Fig. 2. Problem description with $\alpha = 1$. The trackers and the pursuer is denoted by the blue and the red circles, respectively. The (static) high value target is denoted by a green square. (Color figure online)

The pursuer is assumed to be faster than the trackers and can move with a maximum speed normalized to unity. At every time instant t, each tracker i, where $i \in \{1, 2\}$, has access to the range measurements, z_i^t, to the target located at $s \triangleq [s_x \ s_y]' \in \mathbb{R}^2$, where r' denotes the transpose of some vector r. Let $e_i^t \triangleq [e_{x,i}^t \ e_{y,i}^t]' \in \mathbb{R}^2$ (resp., $p^t \triangleq [p_x^t \ p_y^t]' \in \mathbb{R}^2$) denote the position of the ith tracker (resp. the pursuer) and let v_i^t (resp. u^t) denote the ith tracker's (pursuer's) control. Then, the motion model and the measurements are given by

$$
\begin{aligned}
e_i^{t+1} &= e_i^t + v_i^t + w_i^t, & \|v_i^t\| &\leq \mu_i < 1, \ \forall i \in \{1, 2\}, \\
p^{t+1} &= p^t + u^t + w_p^t, & \|u^t\| &\leq 1, \\
z_i^t &= \|s - e_i^t\| + \nu_i^t, & \forall i &\in \{1, 2\},
\end{aligned}
\tag{1}
$$

where, $\nu_i^t \sim \mathcal{N}(0, \sigma_\nu^2), \forall i \in \{1, 2\}$ denotes the measurement noise, assumed to be mutually independent, $w_i^t \sim \mathcal{N}(0, \sigma_{w_e})$ as well as $w_p^t \sim \mathcal{N}(0, \sigma_{w_p})$ denotes the process noise.

A tracker is said to be *captured* by the pursuer at time instant t, if its location is within a unit distance from the pursuer at time t. Note that since the pursuer is faster than both trackers, the pursuer can always capture both trackers successively. However, we will see that the game ends when the pursuer captures any one of the trackers. A strategy for the pursuer is defined as $u^t : \mathbb{R}^2 \times \mathbb{R}^2 \to \mathbb{R}^2$. Similarly, a strategy for an ith tracker is defined as $v_i^t : \mathbb{R}^2 \times \mathbb{R}^2 \times \mathbb{R}^2 \to \mathbb{R}^2, \forall i \in \{1, 2\}$.

We now determine the expression for the determinant of the FIM. Let $h(s, e_1^t, e_2^t) \triangleq [\|s - e_1^t\| \ \|s - e_2^t\|]'$ denote the measurement vector at time instant t and $\nabla_s \triangleq [\frac{\partial}{\partial s_x} \ \frac{\partial}{\partial s_y}]'$. Then, for a given model (1) and a measurement vector $h(s, e_1^t, e_2^t)$, the FIM at time instant $t + 1$ is [16]

$$f(s, e_1^t, e_2^t, v_1^t, v_2^t) = \frac{1}{\sigma_\nu^2} (\nabla_s h(s, e_1^t, e_2^t))'(\nabla_s h(s, e_1^t, e_2^t)),$$

$$= \frac{1}{\sigma_\nu^2} \sum_{i=1}^2 \frac{1}{S_i^2} \begin{bmatrix} (X_i^t - v_{x,i}^t)^2 & (X_i^t - v_{x,i}^t)(Y_i^t - v_{y,i}^t) \\ (X_i^t - v_{x,i}^t)(Y_i^t - v_{y,i}^t) & (Y_i^t - v_{y,i}^t)^2 \end{bmatrix},$$

where $X_i^t = s_x - e_{x,i}^t$ (resp. $Y_i^t = s_y - e_{y,i}^t$) denotes the difference in the x (resp. y)-coordinate of the target and the ith tracker (cf. Fig. 2) and $S_i = \sqrt{(X_i^t - v_{x,i}^t)^2 + (Y_i^t - v_{y,i}^t)^2}$. Since the trackers do not know the location of the target, we replace s by its estimate $\hat{s}$ which is obtained from a centralized EKF. Thus, we obtain the determinant of the FIM as

$$\det(f(\hat{s}, e_1^t, e_2^t, v_1^t, v_2^t)) = \frac{1}{\sigma_\nu^2} \Big[\sum_{i=1}^2 \frac{1}{\hat{S}_i^2} (\hat{X}_i^t - v_{x,i}^t)^2 \sum_{i=1}^2 \frac{1}{\hat{S}_i^2} (\hat{Y}_i^t - v_{y,i}^t)^2$$

$$- \Big(\sum_{i=1}^2 \frac{1}{\hat{S}_i^2} (\hat{X}_i^t - v_{x,i}^t)(\hat{Y}_i^t - v_{y,i}^t) \Big)^2 \Big]$$

$$= \frac{1}{\sigma_\nu^2 \hat{S}_1^2 \hat{S}_2^2} ((\hat{X}_1^t - v_{x,1}^t)(\hat{Y}_2^t - v_{y,2}^t) - (\hat{Y}_1^t - v_{y,1}^t)(\hat{X}_2^t - v_{x,2}^t))^2, \quad (2)$$

where $\hat{X}_i^t = \hat{s}_x - e_{x,i}^t$ and $\hat{Y}_i^t = \hat{s}_y - e_{y,i}^t$ for all $i \in \{1,2\}$. Note that the determinant of the FIM for a single tracker is equal to zero implying that the configuration is always singular in the case of one tracker.

At the first time instant ($t = 1$), the pursuer selects the tracker which is closest to the pursuer. This selection is characterized by $\alpha \in \{0, 1\}$. Specifically, if tracker E_1 is closest to the pursuer, then $\alpha = 1$. Otherwise, $\alpha = 0$. The pursuer, then selects its control, u^t, such that the square of the distance to the selected tracker is minimized at every time instant $t \geq 1$. On the other hand, the trackers jointly select their control at every time instant $t \geq 1$ to maximize a weighted combination of the determinant of the FIM and the square of the distance between the selected tracker and the pursuer. We assume that the trackers have information of the location of the pursuer and thus, the choice of α is known to the trackers. Since the two trackers jointly maximize the payoff, we model the interaction between the trackers and the pursuer as a two player zero sum game with the payoff, at time instant $t + 1$, defined as

$$J(v_1^t, v_2^t, u^t) = \det(f(\hat{s}, e_1^t, e_2^t, v_1^t, v_2^t)) + \delta(\alpha \| e_1^t + v_1^t - p^t - u^t \|^2$$
$$+ (1 - \alpha) \| e_2^t + v_2^t - p^t - u^t \|^2), \tag{3}$$

where $\delta \in \mathbb{R}$ is a fixed weight associated with the evasion cost (distance between the pursuer and the selected tracker) and is assumed to be known by all agents. The game terminates when the pursuer captures the selected tracker since the determinant of the FIM is always zero for one tracker. We use t_f to denote the time instant when the game terminates.

We now provide two definitions that will be helpful in establishing our main result in Sect. 3.

Definition 1 (Best Response). *For a two player zero sum game with the payoff defined as $J(\gamma, \sigma)$, the strategy $\gamma^* \in \Gamma_1$ for player 1 (minimizer) is called the best response to player 2's (maximizer) strategy $\sigma \in \Gamma_2$ if the following holds*

$$J(\gamma^*, \sigma^*) \leq J(\gamma, \sigma^*), \ \forall \gamma \in \Gamma_1.$$

Note that the best response for the maximizer can be analogously defined.

Definition 2 (Nash Equilibrium). *Given a strategy $\gamma \in \Gamma_1$ for player 1 and a strategy $\sigma \in \Gamma_2$ for player 2 in a two player zero sum game with the payoff $J(\gamma, \sigma)$, the pair of strategies (γ^*, σ^*) is said to be a saddle-point equilibrium strategy if the following holds.*

$$J(\gamma^*, \sigma) \leq J(\gamma^*, \sigma^*) \leq J(\gamma, \sigma^*), \ \forall \gamma \in \Gamma_1, \ \sigma \in \Gamma_2. \tag{4}$$

Observe that Eq. (4) in Definition 2 can be rewritten as [13]

$$J(\gamma^*, \sigma^*) = \min_{\gamma \in \Gamma_1} J(\gamma, \sigma^*), \text{ and } J(\gamma^*, \sigma^*) = \max_{\sigma \in \Gamma_2} J(\gamma^*, \sigma),$$

implying that the pair of strategies (γ^*, σ^*) form a Nash equilibrium if γ^* (resp. σ^*) is the best response to σ^* (resp. γ^*).

We now formally state our objective for the above model.

Problem 1. The aim of this work is to determine saddle-point strategies $u^{t^*} \in \mathbb{R}^2$ and $\{v_1^{t^*}, v_2^{t^*}\} \in \mathbb{R}^2 \times \mathbb{R}^2$ at every time instant $t < t_f$ such that

$$\max_{v_1^t, v_2^t} \min_{u^t} \ J(v_1^t, v_2^t, u^t) = \min_{u^t} \max_{v_1^t, v_2^t} \ J(v_1^t, v_2^t, u^t)$$

holds subject to the individual agents maximum speed constraints, i.e.,

$$\|u^t\| \leq 1, \ \|v_1^t\| \leq \mu_1 < 1, \ \|v_2^t\| \leq \mu_2 < 1.$$

For the problem to be well-posed, we make the following assumption.

Assumption 1 (EKF Convergence). *There exists a time instant $t_e < t_f$ at which the estimates obtained by the trackers are equal to the true location of the target, i.e., $\|\hat{s} - s\| = 0, \forall t \geq t_e$.*

3   Optimal Strategies

In this section, we determine the optimal strategies for the pursuer and the trackers. We start with the optimal strategy of the pursuer followed by that of the trackers.

3.1 Optimal Strategy of the Pursuer

Without loss of generality, let $\alpha = 1$ at the first time instant and suppose that v_1^t was known to the pursuer. Then, the pursuer solves the following optimization problem.

$$\min_{u^t} \ \delta(\|e_1^t + v_1^t - p^t - u^t\|)^2,$$

$$\text{subject to } \|u^t\| \leq 1 \tag{5}$$

where we used the fact that the term $\det(f(\hat{s}, e_1^t, e_2^t, v_1^t, v_2^t))$ is not a function of the pursuer's control u^t. It follows directly that the solution to the optimization problem (5) is

$$u^{t^*}(v_1^t) = \frac{e_1^t + v_1^t - p^t}{\|e_1^t + v_1^t - p^t\|},$$

meaning that the pursuer moves directly towards the first tracker, E_1, with unit speed as long as the tracker's position at time instant $t+1$, i.e., $e_1^t + v_1^t$, is not within a unit distance from the current position of the pursuer. Otherwise, the optimal pursuer strategy is $e_1^t + v_1^t - p^t$, implying that the tracker is guaranteed to be captured (evasion cost is zero) at time instant $t + 1 = t_f$. This further implies that the trackers will move only to maximize the determinant of FIM at time instant $t = t_f - 1$ as tracker E_1 is guaranteed to be captured at time $t+1$.

Thus, the optimal strategy for the pursuer at every time instant $t < t_f - 1$ is

$$u^{t^*}(v_1^t, v_2^t) = \begin{cases} \frac{e_1^t + v_1^t - p^t}{\|e_1^t + v_1^t - p^t\|}, \text{if } \alpha = 1, \\ \frac{e_2^t + v_2^t - p^t}{\|e_2^t + v_2^t - p^t\|}, \text{ otherwise.} \end{cases} \tag{6}$$

Further, the optimal strategy for the pursuer at time instant $t = t_f - 1$ is

$$u^{t^*}(v_1^t, v_2^t) = \begin{cases} e_1^t + v_1^t - p^t, \text{if } \alpha = 1, \\ e_2^t + v_2^t - p^t, \text{ otherwise} \end{cases} \tag{7}$$

if $\|e_1^t + v_1^t - p^t\| < 1$ (resp. $\|e_2^t + v_2^t - p^t\| < 1$) for $\alpha = 1$ (resp. $\alpha = 0$). Otherwise, the optimal strategy for the pursuer at time instant $t_f - 1$ is given by Eq. (6). Note that although we assumed that $v_i^t, \forall i \in \{1, 2\}$ was known to the pursuer, in reality, the pursuer does not have this information. This means that the optimal strategy defined in (6) is an *anticipatory* strategy of the pursuer based on the belief of the trackers' strategy. As will be clear from the next subsection, we use the optimal strategy, $u^{t^*}(v_1^t, v_2^t)$, of the pursuer to determine the optimal state-feedback strategies of the trackers $v_1^{t^*}$ and $v_2^{t^*}$. Substituting $v_1^{t^*}$ and $v_2^{t^*}$ into (6) implies that u^{t^*} is a state-feedback strategy.

In the next section, we determine the optimal strategies of the trackers. Since maximizing only the determinant of the FIM has been extensively studied [16], we only focus on the case that the position of the tracker being pursued at time instant $t_f - 1$ is more than a unit distance from the current position of the pursuer. In other words, the pursuer's optimal strategy is given by Eq. (6) at time $t_f - 1$. Note that the optimal strategy of the pursuer for any time instant $t < t_f - 1$ is given by Eq. (6). Further, for ease of presentation, we drop the dependency on time from the notations in the next subsection.

3.2   Optimal Strategies of the Trackers

For a given value of α, the trackers jointly solve the following optimization problem.

$$\max_{v_1, v_2}\ \det(f(\hat{s}, e_1, e_2, v_1, v_2)) + \delta(\|e_1 + v_1 - p - u\|)^2$$
$$\text{subject to } \|v_1\| \leq \mu_1, \|v_2\| \leq \mu_2,$$

where, without loss of generality, we assumed that $\alpha = 1$. Substituting $u^*(v_1, v_2)$ from Eq. 6 as well as the expression of the determinant yields

$$\max_{v_1, v_2}\ \frac{1}{\sigma_\nu^2 \hat{S}_1^2 \hat{S}_2^2}\left((\hat{X}_1 - v_{x,1})(\hat{Y}_2 - v_{y,2}) - (\hat{Y}_1 - v_{y,1})(\hat{X}_2 - v_{x,2})\right)^2$$
$$+ \delta(\|e_1 + v_1 - p\| - 1)^2, \tag{8}$$
$$\text{subject to } \|v_1\| \leq \mu_1,\ \|v_2\| \leq \mu_2.$$

Although the constraints are convex, the objective is a non-convex function of $v_i, \forall i \in \{1, 2\}$ and thus, computing a global maximizer is difficult. In what follows, we show that this optimization problem is equivalent to solving a quadratically constrained quadratic program (QCQP) [6].

For ease of presentation, we use the following notation in the next result. Let $V = \begin{bmatrix} v_{x,1} & v_{y,1} & v_{x,2} & v_{y,2} & v_{x,1}v_{y,2} & v_{x,2}v_{y,1} \end{bmatrix}' \in \mathbb{R}^6$ and let

$$z^2 = \frac{1}{\hat{S}_1^2 \hat{S}_2^2}\left((\hat{X}_1 - v_{x,1})(\hat{Y}_2 - v_{y,2}) - (\hat{Y}_1 - v_{y,1})(\hat{X}_2 - v_{x,2})\right)^2.$$

Lemma 1. *Suppose $\alpha = 1$ and let $m = \|e_1 + v_1 - p\|$. Then, the optimization problem defined in (8) is equivalent to solving a QCQP given by*

$$\max_{\tilde{V}} \tilde{V}'P\tilde{V}$$

$$\text{subject to}$$
$$\tilde{V}'Q_j\tilde{V} \leq 0, \forall j \in \{1, 2\}$$
$$\tilde{V}'F\tilde{V} = 0, \tag{9}$$
$$\tilde{V}'M_1\tilde{V} = 0,$$
$$\tilde{V}'L_g\tilde{V} = 0, \forall g \in \{1, \ldots, 10\}$$
$$\tilde{V}_8 = 1,$$

where $\tilde{V} \triangleq \begin{bmatrix} V' & m & 1 & zV' & zv_{x,1}v_{x,2} & zv_{y,1}v_{y,2} & z \end{bmatrix}' \in \mathbb{R}^{17}$, $\tilde{V}_k$ denotes the kth entry of vector $\tilde{V}$ and the matrices $P, M_1, Q_j, \forall j \in \{1, 2\}$ and $L_g, \forall g \in \{1, \ldots, 10\}$ are as defined in the Appendix.

Proof. By replacing $\|e_1 + v_1 - p\|$ by m, the optimization problem defined in (8) can be rewritten as

$$\max_{v_1, v_2, m, z} \frac{1}{\sigma_\nu^2} z^2 + \delta(m-1)^2$$

$$\text{subject to } \|v_1\| \le \mu_1, \ \|v_2\| \le \mu_2, \ m^2 = \|e_1 + v_1 - p\|^2,$$

$$\left((\hat{X}_1 - v_{x,1})(\hat{Y}_2 - v_{y,2}) - (\hat{Y}_1 - v_{y,1})(\hat{X}_2 - v_{x,2}) \right)^2 - z^2 \hat{S}_1^2 \hat{S}_2^2 = 0.$$

Observe that the optimization problem is now a polynomial in the original optimization variables and the additional variables z and m. By adding some extra variables corresponding to the terms that are polynomial in the optimization variables $v_{x,i}$ and $v_{y,i}, \forall i \in \{1, 2\}$, we now convert the aforementioned optimization problem into a QCQP.

Let $V = \begin{bmatrix} v_{x,1} & v_{y,1} & v_{x,2} & v_{y,2} & v_{x,1}v_{y,2} & v_{x,2}v_{y,1} \end{bmatrix}' \in \mathbb{R}^6$. Then, we define a vector of optimization variables $\tilde{V} \in \mathbb{R}^{17}$ as

$$\tilde{V} = \begin{bmatrix} V' & m & 1 & zV' & zv_{x,1}v_{x,2} & zv_{y,1}v_{y,2} & z \end{bmatrix}'.$$

Taking the square on both sides of the norm constraints, the above optimization problem yields the QCQP form as defined in (9). Note that the constraint $\tilde{V}' M_1 \tilde{V} \equiv \equiv \|e_1 + v_1 - p\|^2 - m^2$. Further, the set of constraints $\tilde{V}' L_g \tilde{V} = 0, \forall g \in \{1, \ldots, 10\}$ characterize the relationship between the elements of $\tilde{V}$. As described in [15], the equality constraints in optimization problem (9) can be replaced with two inequality constraints, thus, reducing the optimization problem in the standard QCQP form. This concludes the proof. □

Following similar steps, an analogous optimization problem when $\alpha = 0$ is

$$\max_{\tilde{V}} \tilde{V}' P \tilde{V}$$

$$\text{subject to}$$

$$\tilde{V}' Q_j \tilde{V} \le 0, \forall j \in \{1, 2\}$$

$$\tilde{V}' M_0 \tilde{V} = 0, \tag{10}$$

$$\tilde{V}' F \tilde{V} = 0,$$

$$\tilde{V}' L_g \tilde{V} = 0, \forall g \in \{1, \ldots, 10\}$$

$$\tilde{V}_8 = 1,$$

where matrix M_0 is as defined in the Appendix. Note that all of the matrices $Q_j, \forall j \in \{1, 2\}, P, M_0, M_1, F$ and $L_g, \forall g \in \{1, \ldots, 10\}$ are sparse matrices.

We now establish the main result of this paper, i.e., that the pair of strategies $(u^{t^*}, \{v_1^{t^*}, v_2^{t^*}\})$ form a pair of Nash equilibrium. Note that if the optimal strategies of the trackers and the pursuer form a pair of Nash equilibrium, there is no incentive for the trackers to deviate from their optimal strategy (see Definition 2). This means that the pursuer has the correct belief of the trackers strategy and can determine its state-feedback strategy, u^{t^*} by first solving the QCQP to determine $v_1^{t^*}$ and $v_2^{t^*}$ and then substituting these into (6). However, to determine the strategy of the trackers, the pursuer needs the information of the estimates that the trackers have of the target's location. Since the pursuer does not have this information, we propose that the pursuer uses the true value of the target's location to solve the QCQP and consequently determine u^{t^*}.

Theorem 1. *At every instant* $t_e \leq t < t_f$, *the pair of strategies* $(u^{t^*}, \{v_1^{t^*}, v_2^{t^*}\})$ *defined in* (6) *and obtained by solving the optimization problem* (8), *form a pair of Nash equilibrium strategies for the payoff function* $J(\hat{s}, e_i^t, p^t, v_i^t, u^t)$ *as defined in* (3).

Proof. Observe that once the estimates about the location of the target converges to the true value, all of the mobile agents use the same value of the target's location to solve the QCQP. Further, at every time instant $t_e \leq t < t_f$, the optimal strategy of the pursuer defined in Eq. (6) is the best-response of the pursuer to the trackers strategy. Similarly, the optimal strategy of the trackers obtained by solving the optimization problem defined (9) (if $\alpha = 1$) and (10) (otherwise) is the best response of the trackers to an optimal pursuer strategy. The result then follows directly from Definition 2. This concludes the proof. $\square$

We now briefly describe how the game is solved. At every time instant, depending on the value of α, the pursuer solves the optimization problem 9 or 10 using the true location of the target (s) to obtain $v_1^{t^*}$ and $v_2^{t^*}$. The pursuer then moves to the location by determining its control via Eq. 6. On the other hand, the trackers jointly solve the same optimization problem using the estimates of the target $(\hat{s})$ and move to the next location using $v_1^{t^*}$ and $v_2^{t^*}$.

Remark 1 (Bearing Measurements). If the trackers use a sensor that measures the bearing (angle) of the target relative to their positions instead of range measurements, then the determinant of the FIM is given by [20]

$$f(\hat{s}, e_1^t, e_2^t, v_1^t, v_2^t) = \frac{1}{\sigma_\nu^2 \hat{S}_1^4 \hat{S}_2^4} \left((\hat{X}_1^t - v_{x,1}^t)(\hat{Y}_2^t - v_{y,2}^t) - (\hat{Y}_1^t - v_{y,1}^t)(\hat{X}_2^t - v_{x,2}^t) \right)^2.$$

As the pursuer's optimal strategy does not change, by following similar steps as in Sect. 3.2, the optimization problem for the trackers can similarly be expressed as a QCQP and thus, this work easily extends to scenarios when trackers have access to bearing measurements.

4   Numerical Observations

We now present numerical simulations of the optimal strategies defined in Sect. 3 and highlight the trajectories of the mobile agents. In all of our simulations, the

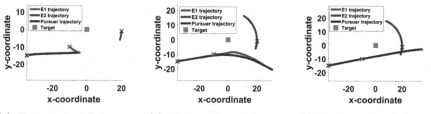

(a) Trajectories of the mo- (b) Trajectories of the mo- (c) Trajectories of the mo-
bile agents for $\delta = 0$. $t_f =$ bile agents for $\delta = 0.2$. $t_f =$ bile agents for $\delta = 5$. $t_f =$
44.   68.   71.

Fig. 3. Trajectories of the pursuer and the trackers for different values of δ. The cross represents the starting locations of the mobile agents. The target is denoted by the green square. (Color figure online)

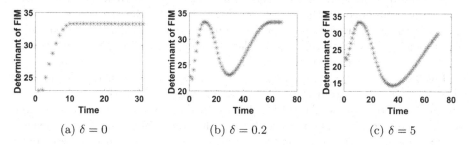

(a) $\delta = 0$ (b) $\delta = 0.2$ (c) $\delta = 5$

Fig. 4. Determinant of FIM vs Time plots for different values of δ.

parameter σ_ν^2 was kept fixed to 0.03 and the target's location was chosen to be $(0, 0)$. Due to the number and size of the sparse matrices in the proposed QCQP optimization problem (9), generating the trajectories was time consuming. Thus, we use fmincon function in MATLAB to determine the optimal strategies of the trackers which was verified to be consistent with the strategies obtained by solving optimization problem in (9).

4.1 Example 1 ($\alpha = 1$)

Our first numerical simulation (cf. Fig. 3) focuses on the trajectories of the mobile agents when the pursuer moves to capture the first tracker, E_1. Specifically, we select the initial locations such that $\alpha = 1$. To highlight the role of evasion by the trackers, we provide a numerical plot with $\delta = 0$ in Fig. 3, i.e., the evaders move to maximize only the determinant of the FIM. Note that the time taken by the pursuer to capture E_1 is mentioned in the description of each sub-figure in Fig. 3. The initial locations for all of the simulations presented in Fig. 3 were kept the same and selected to be $(-10, -10)$, $(20, -1)$ and $(-35, -15)$ for E_1, E_2 and the pursuer, respectively. Further, the parameters μ_1 and μ_2 were set to be 0.65 and 0.5, respectively.

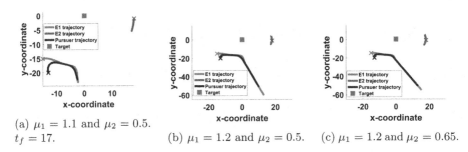

(a) $\mu_1 = 1.1$ and $\mu_2 = 0.5$. $t_f = 17$.

(b) $\mu_1 = 1.2$ and $\mu_2 = 0.5$.   (c) $\mu_1 = 1.2$ and $\mu_2 = 0.65$.

Fig. 5. Trajectories of the pursuer and the trackers for $\delta = 0.14$ and different values of $\mu_i, \forall i \in \{1, 2\}$.

Observe that in Fig. 3a, the trackers move to position themselves such that the angle subtended at the target by the position of the trackers is $\frac{\pi}{2}$. This is consistent with trajectories that maximize only the FIM as reported in [4]. Upon reaching that position, the trackers remain at that position until tracker E_1 is captured by the pursuer. Based on the value of δ in Fig. 3b as well as in Fig. 3c, observe that the tracker E_1 first moves away from the pursuer and then it moves away from the target, maximizing both the time to capture as well as the determinant of the FIM. Figure 3b shows the cooperative behaviour of E_2. In particular, although the pursuer does not move towards E_2, tracker E_2 first moves downwards and then changes its direction in order maximize the determinant of the FIM by moving to a location such that the position of the trackers subtend an angle of $\frac{\pi}{2}$ at the target. Once the angle between the position of the trackers is $\frac{\pi}{2}$, tracker E_2 remains stationary at its location while E_1 evades.

Finally, in Fig. 4, observe that the determinant of the FIM monotonically increases in Fig. 4a and then converges to 33.33. Although in Fig. 4b the determinant of FIM reaches the value 33.3, the value then decreases as the trackers cannot stay at that position due to the evasion cost. Note that at time $t = 60$, the cost converges to 33.3 highlighting the fact that the angle subtended by the position of the trackers to the target is now at $\frac{\pi}{2}$, and thus, tracker E_2 remains at its position whereas tracker E_1 moves in a straight line maintaining the same angle. Similar trend is observed in Fig. 4c. However, tracker E_1 is captured before the angle subtended by the trackers to the target is $\frac{\pi}{2}$. This is due to the higher value of δ as compared to that in Fig. 4b because of which tracker E_1 moves directly away from the pursuer. Thus, the trackers require more time to reach the positions from which the angle subtended to the target is $\frac{\pi}{2}$.

4.2   Example 2 (Faster Trackers)

This numerical simulation considers a scenario that at one tracker is faster than the pursuer. The initial locations of the trackers and the pursuer was set to $(18, -1)$, $(-15, -15)$ and $(-13, -20)$, respectively. Finally the parameter δ was kept fixed to 0.14 and from the initial locations, $\alpha = 1$.

In Fig. 5a, although tracker E_1 is faster ($\mu_1 = 1.1$ and $\mu_2 = 0.5$) than the pursuer, the pursuer is able to capture tracker E_1. However, for the same initial locations of all of the mobile agents, the pursuer is unable to capture tracker E_1 when $\mu_1 = 1.2$ and $\mu_2 = 0.5$ (cf. Fig. 5b), implying that for faster trackers, there may exist *winning regions* for the pursuer as well as the trackers. Specifically, it may be possible to partition the environment into a winning region (Ω_P) for the pursuer, i.e., the pursuer can always capture a tracker if the initial locations of all of the mobile agents lie inside Ω_P. Similarly, it may be possible to characterize the winning region (Ω_T) for the trackers, i.e., the trackers can always evade the pursuer if the initial locations of all of the mobile agents lie inside Ω_T. Finally, observe that for the same initial locations and $\mu_1 = 1.1$ (cf. Fig. 5c), the pursuer cannot capture tracker E_1 if the speed of the tracker E_2 is increased from 0.5 (Fig. 5a) to 0.65.

We now describe how this work extends to two different scenarios. We start with a scenario with multiple targets followed by a scenario with multiple trackers.

5 Extensions

In this section, we describe how our analysis extends to the case of multiple targets and multiple trackers. We also show that in both scenarios the pursuer's optimal strategy remains the same as established in Sect. 3. We further establish that the optimization problem for the trackers can be converted to a QCQP.

5.1 Multiple Targets

In this scenario, we consider that there are $N > 1$ targets, two mobile trackers and a single mobile pursuer. Each tracker has access only to range measurements from each of the N targets. Thus, in this case, the measurement vector is $h(s_1, \ldots, s_N, e_1^t, e_2^t) = \left[\|s_1 - e_1^t\| \ \|s_1 - e_2^t\| \ \ldots \ \|s_N - e_1^t\| \ \|s_N - e_2^t\| \right]'$, where $s_1, \ldots, s_N$ denote the fixed locations of the N targets. By taking the partial derivatives with respect to the locations of the targets and replacing $s_j \forall j \in \{1, \ldots, N\}$ with its estimate $\hat{s}_j$, the FIM at time instant $t+1$ becomes a block diagonal matrix given by

$$F(\hat{s}_1, \ldots, \hat{s}_N, e_i^t, v_i^t) = \begin{bmatrix} f(\hat{s}_1, e_i^t, v_i^t) & \mathbf{0}_{2\times 2} & \cdots & \mathbf{0}_{2\times 2} \\ \mathbf{0}_{2\times 2} & f(\hat{s}_2, e_i^t, v_i^t) & \cdots & \mathbf{0}_{2\times 2} \\ \vdots & \vdots & \ddots & \vdots \\ \mathbf{0}_{2\times 2} & \cdots & \cdots & f(\hat{s}_N, e_i^t, v_i^t) \end{bmatrix}$$

where $f(\hat{s}_j, e_i^t, v_i^t), \forall 1 \le j \le N$ is the FIM defined analogously as $f(\hat{s}_1, e_i^t, v_i^t)$ (see Sect. 2). Using the fact that determinant of a block diagonal matrix is the product of the determinant of its blocks yields

$$\det(F(\hat{s}_1, \ldots, \hat{s}_N, e_i^t, v_i^t)) = \prod_{j=1}^{N} \det(f(\hat{s}_j, e_i^t, v_i^t)).$$

Thus, the expression for the payoff is given by

$$J(\hat{s}_1, \ldots, \hat{s}_N, e_i^t, p^t, v_i^t, u^t) = \det(F(\hat{s}_1, \ldots, \hat{s}_N, e_i^t, v_i^t)) +$$
$$\delta(\alpha \|e_1^t + v_1^t - p^t - u^t\|^2 + (1-\alpha)\|e_2^t + v_2^t - p^t - u^t\|^2).$$

Since the determinant of the FIM is not a function of the pursuer's control, it follows that the pursuer's strategy remains the same as defined in (6). Observe that $\det(F(\hat{s}_1, \ldots, \hat{s}_N, e_i^t, v_i^t))$ is a polynomial function of $v_{x,i}^t$ and $v_{y,i}^t$ for all $i \in \{1,2\}$. Therefore, following similar steps as in Sect. 3 and from the fact that any polynomial can be expressed into the standard QCQP form [15], it follows that the optimization problem obtained for the trackers after substituting $u^{t^*}(v_1^t, v_2^t)$ can also be converted into a QCQP of the same form as defined in Lemma 1. Finally, given that the pair of strategies $(u^{t^*}, \{v_1^{t^*}, v_2^{t^*}\})$ are best responses to each other, it follows that the pair of strategies forms a Nash equilibrium.

5.2   Multiple Trackers

We now consider the scenario with a single target, $M > 2$ trackers and a single mobile pursuer.

Let at time instant $t < t_f$, $\alpha \triangleq [\alpha_1 \ldots \alpha_M]' \in \mathbb{R}^M$ such that $\sum_{j=1}^M \alpha_j = 1$ and $\alpha_j \in \{0,1\}, \forall j \in \{1, \ldots, M\}$. Let $\mathbf{D} \in \mathbb{R}^M$ denote a vector consisting of the distance between the pursuer and the trackers, i.e., $[\|p^t - e_1^t\| \ldots \|p - e_M^t\|]'$. Then, the payoff is given by

$$J(\hat{s}, e_1^t, \ldots, e_M^t, v_1^t, \ldots, v_M^t, p^t) = \det(f(\hat{s}, e_1^t, \ldots, e_M^t, v_1^t, \ldots, v_M^t)) + \delta\alpha_t'\mathbf{D},$$

where

$$\det(f(\hat{s}, e_1^t, \ldots, e_M^t, v_1^t, \ldots, v_M^t)) = \frac{1}{\sigma_\nu^2} \sum_{j=1}^M \sum_{l=j+1}^M \frac{1}{\hat{S}_j^2 \hat{S}_l^2} \Big((\hat{X}_j^t - v_{x,j}^t)(\hat{Y}_l^t - v_{y,l}^t)$$
$$- (\hat{Y}_j^t - v_{y,j}^t)(\hat{X}_l^t - v_{x,l}^t) \Big)^2.$$

For a given vector α at the first time instant, the strategy of the pursuer is the same as defined in Sect. 3 and thus, following similar steps, the payoff for the trackers can be expressed as a polynomial function in the optimization variables $v_{x,i}^t$ and $v_{y,i}^t$ for all $i \in \{1, \ldots, M\}$. Hence, following similar steps as in Sect. 3 and given the fact that any polynomial can be expressed into the standard QCQP form [15], it follows that the optimization problem obtained for the trackers after substituting $u^{t^*}(v_1^t, v_2^t)$ can also be converted into a QCQP of the same form as defined in Lemma 1.

Finally, given that the pair of strategies $(u^{t^*}, \{v_1^{t^*}, \ldots, v_M^{t^*}\})$ are best responses to each other, it follows that the pair of strategies forms a Nash equilibrium.

6   Conclusion and Future Directions

This paper introduced a tracking-evasion game consisting of a single pursuer, two trackers and a single target. The pursuer seeks to deter the tracking performance of the trackers by minimizing the square of the distance to the closest tracker, whereas, the trackers aim to jointly maximize a weighted combination of the determinant of the Fisher Information Matrix and the square of the distance between the pursuer to the tracker being pursued. We determined optimal strategies of the pursuer and showed that the optimal strategies of the trackers can be obtained by solving a Quadratically Constrained Quadratic Program. We then established that the pair of strategies form a Nash equilibrium and provided several numerical observations highlighting the trajectories and the payoff. Finally, we discussed the extension of this work to multiple trackers and multiple targets.

Apart from leveraging the sparse-structure of the matrices for the optimization problem, a key future direction includes a generalized setup with multiple pursuers and trackers with motion and energy constraints. Further, we conjecture that by relaxing Assumption 1, an $\bar{\epsilon}$-Nash Equilibrium may exist. This conjecture will also be explored in the subsequent works.

Acknowledgements. We thank Dr. Xiaobo Tan at Michigan State University for his valuable comments and feedback.

7   Appendix

In this section, we provide the expression for the matrices P, Q_j, M and L, respectively. For ease of notation, denote $a_i = \hat{X}_i^t$, $b_i = \hat{Y}_i^t$. Further, let $\mathbf{I}_{n \times p}$ (resp. $\mathbf{0}_{n \times p}$) denote the identity (resp. zero) matrix of dimension $n \times p$. Then,

$$
P = \frac{1}{\sigma_\nu^2} \times \begin{bmatrix}
\mathbf{0}_{6\times6} & \mathbf{0}_{6\times1} & \mathbf{0}_{6\times1} & \mathbf{0}_{6\times8} & \mathbf{0}_{6\times1} \\
\mathbf{0}_{1\times6} & \delta\sigma_\nu^2 & -\delta\sigma_\nu^2 & \mathbf{0}_{1\times8} & 0 \\
\mathbf{0}_{1\times6} & -\delta\sigma_\nu^2 & \delta\sigma_\nu^2 & \mathbf{0}_{1\times8} & 0 \\
\mathbf{0}_{8\times6} & \mathbf{0}_{8\times1} & \mathbf{0}_{8\times1} & \mathbf{0}_{8\times8} & \mathbf{0}_{8\times1} \\
\mathbf{0}_{1\times6} & 0 & 0 & \mathbf{0}_{1\times8} & 1
\end{bmatrix}, F = \begin{bmatrix} F_1 & \mathbf{0}_{8\times9} \\ \mathbf{0}_{9\times8} & F_2 \end{bmatrix},
$$

where $F_1 =$

$$
\begin{bmatrix}
b_2^2 & -a_2 b_2 & -b_1 b_2 & 2a_1 b_2 - a_2 b_1 & -b_2 & b_2 & 0 & a_2 b_1 b_2 - a_1 b_2^2 \\
-a_2 b_2 & a_2^2 & 2a_2 b_1 - a_1 b_2 & -a_1 a_2 & a_2 & -a_2 & 0 & a_1 a_2 b_2 - b_1 a_2^2 \\
-b_1 b_2 & 2a_2 b_1 - a_1 b_2 & b_1^2 & -a_1 b_1 & b_1 & -b_1 & 0 & a_1 b_1 b_2 - a_2 b_1^2 \\
2a_1 b_2 - a_2 b_1 & -a_1 a_2 & -a_1 b_1 & a_1^2 & -a_1 & a_1 & 0 & a_1 a_2 b_1 - b_2 a_1^2 \\
-b_2 & a_2 & b_1 & -a_1 & 1 & -1 & 0 & 0 \\
b_2 & -a_2 & -b_1 & a_1 & -1 & 1 & 0 & 0 \\
0 & 0 & 0 & 0 & 0 & 0 & 0 & 0 \\
a_2 b_1 b_2 - a_1 b_2^2 & a_1 a_2 b_2 - b_1 a_2^2 & a_1 b_1 b_2 - a_2 b_1^2 & a_1 a_2 b_1 - b_2 a_1^2 & 0 & 0 & 0 & (a_1 b_2 - a_2 b_1)^2
\end{bmatrix}
$$

and $F_2 =$

$$\begin{bmatrix}
-(a_2^2+b_2^2) & 0 & -2a_1a_2 & -2a_1b_2 & b_2 & 0 & a_2 & 0 & a_1(a_2^2+b_2^2) \\
0 & -(a_2^2+b_2^2) & -2a_2b_1 & -2b_1b_2 & 0 & a_2 & 0 & b_2 & b_1(a_2^2+b_2^2) \\
-2a_1a_2 & -2a_2b_1 & -(a_1^2+b_1^2) & 0 & 0 & b_1 & a_1 & 0 & a_2(a_1^2+b_1^2) \\
-2a_1b_2 & -2b_1b_2 & 0 & -(a_1^2+b_1^2) & a_1 & 0 & 0 & b_1 & b_2(a_1^2+b_1^2) \\
b_2 & 0 & 0 & a_1 & 1 & 0 & 0 & 0 & 0 \\
0 & a_2 & b_1 & 0 & 0 & 1 & 0 & 0 & 0 \\
a_2 & 0 & a_1 & 0 & 0 & 0 & 1 & 0 & 0 \\
0 & b_2 & 0 & b_1 & 0 & 0 & 0 & 1 & 0 \\
a_1(a_2^2+b_2^2) & b_1(a_2^2+b_2^2) & a_2(a_1^2+b_1^2) & b_2(a_1^2+b_1^2) & 0 & 0 & 0 & 0 & -(a_1^2+b_1^2)(a_2^2+b_2^2)
\end{bmatrix}.$$

Moreover,

$$Q_1 = \begin{bmatrix}
\mathbf{I}_{2\times2} & \mathbf{0}_{2\times6} & \mathbf{0}_{2\times9} \\
\mathbf{0}_{5\times4} & \mathbf{0}_{5\times4} & \mathbf{0}_{5\times9} \\
\mathbf{0}_{1\times7} & -\mu_1^2 & \mathbf{0}_{1\times9} \\
\mathbf{0}_{9\times4} & \mathbf{0}_{9\times4} & \mathbf{0}_{9\times9}
\end{bmatrix}, Q_2 = \begin{bmatrix}
\mathbf{0}_{2\times2} & \mathbf{0}_{2\times2} & \mathbf{0}_{2\times4} & \mathbf{0}_{2\times9} \\
\mathbf{0}_{2\times2} & \mathbf{I}_{2\times2} & \mathbf{0}_{2\times4} & \mathbf{0}_{2\times9} \\
\mathbf{0}_{3\times2} & \mathbf{0}_{3\times2} & \mathbf{0}_{3\times4} & \mathbf{0}_{3\times9} \\
\mathbf{0}_{1\times2} & \mathbf{0}_{1\times5} & -\mu_2^2 & \mathbf{0}_{1\times9} \\
\mathbf{0}_{9\times2} & \mathbf{0}_{9\times5} & \mathbf{0}_{9\times1} & \mathbf{0}_{9\times9}
\end{bmatrix},$$

$$M_1 = \begin{bmatrix}
\mathbf{I}_{2\times2} & \mathbf{0}_{2\times5} & [e_1^t - p^t] & \mathbf{0}_{2\times9} \\
\mathbf{0}_{4\times2} & \mathbf{0}_{4\times4} & \mathbf{0}_{4\times2} & \mathbf{0}_{4\times9} \\
\mathbf{0}_{1\times6} & -1 & 0 & \mathbf{0}_{1\times9} \\
[e_1^t - p^t]' & \mathbf{0}_{1\times5} & \|e_1^t - p^t\|^2 & \mathbf{0}_{1\times9} \\
\mathbf{0}_{9\times2} & \mathbf{0}_{9\times2} & \mathbf{0}_{9\times2} & \mathbf{0}_{9\times11}
\end{bmatrix},$$

$$M_0 = \begin{bmatrix}
\mathbf{0}_{2\times2} & \mathbf{0}_{2\times2} & \mathbf{0}_{2\times2} & \mathbf{0}_{2\times2} & \mathbf{0}_{2\times9} \\
\mathbf{0}_{2\times2} & \mathbf{I}_{2\times2} & \mathbf{0}_{2\times3} & [e_2^t - p^t] & \mathbf{0}_{2\times9} \\
\mathbf{0}_{2\times2} & \mathbf{0}_{2\times2} & \mathbf{0}_{2\times2} & \mathbf{0}_{2\times2} & \mathbf{0}_{2\times9} \\
\mathbf{0}_{1\times2} & \mathbf{0}_{1\times4} & -1 & 0 & \mathbf{0}_{1\times9} \\
\mathbf{0}_{1\times2} & [e_2^t - p^t]' & \mathbf{0}_{1\times3} & \|e_2^t - p^t\|^2 & \mathbf{0}_{1\times9} \\
\mathbf{0}_{9\times2} & \mathbf{0}_{9\times2} & \mathbf{0}_{9\times2} & \mathbf{0}_{9\times2} & \mathbf{0}_{9\times9}
\end{bmatrix}.$$

We now define the matrices $L_g \in \mathbb{R}^{17\times17}, \forall g \in \{1, \ldots, 10\}$. Let $L_g(k,l)$ denote an element at the kth row and the lth column of the matrix $L_g, g \in \{1, \ldots, 10\}$. Then,

$$L_1(k,l) = \begin{cases} 0.5, & \text{if } k=1, l=4, \\ 0.5, & \text{if } k=4, l=1, \\ -0.5, & \text{if } k=5, l=8, \\ -0.5, & \text{if } k=8, l=5, \\ 0 \text{ otherwise} \end{cases}, L_2(k,l) = \begin{cases} 0.5, & \text{if } k=2, l=3, \\ 0.5, & \text{if } k=3, l=2, \\ -0.5, & \text{if } k=6, l=8, \\ -0.5, & \text{if } k=8, l=6, \\ 0 \text{ otherwise} \end{cases},$$

$$L_3(k,l) = \begin{cases} 0.5, & \text{if } k=1, l=17, \\ 0.5, & \text{if } k=17, l=1, \\ -0.5, & \text{if } k=9, l=8, \\ -0.5, & \text{if } k=8, l=9, \\ 0 \text{ otherwise} \end{cases}, L_4(k,l) = \begin{cases} 0.5, & \text{if } k=2, l=17, \\ 0.5, & \text{if } k=17, l=2, \\ -0.5, & \text{if } k=10, l=8, \\ -0.5, & \text{if } k=8, l=10, \\ 0 \text{ otherwise} \end{cases},$$

$$L_5(k,l) = \begin{cases} 0.5, & \text{if } k=3, l=17, \\ 0.5, & \text{if } k=17, l=3, \\ -0.5, & \text{if } k=11, l=8, \\ -0.5, & \text{if } k=8, l=11, \\ 0 \text{ otherwise} \end{cases}, L_6(k,l) = \begin{cases} 0.5, & \text{if } k=4, l=17, \\ 0.5, & \text{if } k=17, l=4, \\ -0.5, & \text{if } k=12, l=8, \\ -0.5, & \text{if } k=8, l=12, \\ 0 \text{ otherwise} \end{cases},$$

$$L_7(k,l) = \begin{cases} 0.5, & \text{if } k=5, l=17, \\ 0.5, & \text{if } k=17, l=5, \\ -0.5, & \text{if } k=13, l=8, \\ -0.5, & \text{if } k=8, l=13, \\ 0 \text{ otherwise} \end{cases}, L_8(k,l) = \begin{cases} 0.5, & \text{if } k=6, l=17, \\ 0.5, & \text{if } k=17, l=6, \\ -0.5, & \text{if } k=14, l=8, \\ -0.5, & \text{if } k=8, l=14, \\ 0 \text{ otherwise} \end{cases},$$

$$L_9(k,l) = \begin{cases} 0.5, & \text{if } k=3, l=9, \\ 0.5, & \text{if } k=9, l=3, \\ -0.5, & \text{if } k=15, l=8, \\ -0.5, & \text{if } k=8, l=15, \\ 0 \text{ otherwise} \end{cases}, L_{10}(k,l) = \begin{cases} 0.5, & \text{if } k=4, l=10, \\ 0.5, & \text{if } k=10, l=4, \\ -0.5, & \text{if } k=16, l=8, \\ -0.5, & \text{if } k=8, l=16, \\ 0 \text{ otherwise} \end{cases},$$

References

1. AlDahak, A., Elnagar, A.: A practical pursuit-evasion algorithm: detection and tracking. In: Proceedings 2007 IEEE International Conference on Robotics and Automation, pp. 343–348. IEEE (2007)
2. Bajaj, S., Torng, E., Bopardikar, S.D.: Competitive perimeter defense on a line. In: 2021 American Control Conference (ACC), pp. 3196–3201. IEEE (2021)
3. Bhattacharya, S., Başar, T., Falcone, M.: Surveillance for security as a pursuit-evasion game. In: Poovendran, R., Saad, W. (eds.) GameSec 2014. LNCS, vol. 8840, pp. 370–379. Springer, Cham (2014). https://doi.org/10.1007/978-3-319-12601-2_23
4. Bishop, A.N., Fidan, B., Anderson, B.D., Doğançay, K., Pathirana, P.N.: Optimality analysis of sensor-target localization geometries. Automatica **46**(3), 479–492 (2010)
5. Blais, F.: Review of 20 years of range sensor development. J. Electron. Imaging **13**(1), 231–243 (2004)
6. Boyd, S., Boyd, S.P., Vandenberghe, L.: Convex Optimization. Cambridge University Press, Cambridge (2004)
7. Chang, C.B., Tabaczynski, J.: Application of state estimation to target tracking. IEEE Trans. Autom. Control **29**(2), 98–109 (1984)
8. Chung, T.H., Burdick, J.W., Murray, R.M.: A decentralized motion coordination strategy for dynamic target tracking. In: Proceedings 2006 IEEE International Conference on Robotics and Automation 2006, ICRA 2006, pp. 2416–2422. IEEE (2006)

9. Coleman, D., Bopardikar, S.D., Tan, X.: Observability-aware target tracking with range only measurement. In: 2021 American Control Conference (ACC), pp. 4217–4224. IEEE (2021)

10. English, J.T., Wilhelm, J.P.: Defender-aware attacking guidance policy for the target-attacker-defender differential game. J. Aerosp. Inf. Syst. **18**(6), 366–376 (2021)

11. Garcia, E., Casbeer, D.W., Pachter, M.: Active target defence differential game: fast defender case. IET Control Theory Appl. **11**(17), 2985–2993 (2017)

12. Garcia, E., Casbeer, D.W., Pachter, M.: Optimal target capture strategies in the target-attacker-defender differential game. In: 2018 Annual American Control Conference (ACC), pp. 68–73. IEEE (2018)

13. Hespanha, J.P.: Noncooperative Game Theory: An Introduction for Engineers and Computer Scientists. Princeton University Press, Princeton (2017)

14. Hung, N.T., Rego, F.F., Pascoal, A.M.: Cooperative distributed estimation and control of multiple autonomous vehicles for range-based underwater target localization and pursuit. IEEE Trans. Control Syst. Technol. **30**(4), 1433–1447 (2022)

15. Madani, R., Fazelnia, G., Lavaei, J.: Rank-2 matrix solution for semidefinite relaxations of arbitrary polynomial optimization problems. Constraints **21**, 25 (2014)

16. Martínez, S., Bullo, F.: Optimal sensor placement and motion coordination for target tracking. Automatica **42**(4), 661–668 (2006)

17. Miller, A., Miller, B.: Underwater target tracking using bearing-only measurements. J. Commun. Technol. Electron. **63**(6), 643–649 (2018). https://doi.org/10.1134/S1064226918060207

18. Murrieta-Cid, R., Ruiz, U., Marroquin, J.L., Laumond, J.P., Hutchinson, S.: Tracking an omnidirectional evader with a differential drive robot. Auton. Robots **31**(4), 345–366 (2011). https://doi.org/10.1007/s10514-011-9246-z

19. Polastre, J.: Design and implementation of wireless sensor networks for habitat monitoring. Ph.D. thesis, Citeseer (2003)

20. Ponda, S., Kolacinski, R., Frazzoli, E.: Trajectory optimization for target localization using small unmanned aerial vehicles. In: AIAA Guidance, Navigation, and Control Conference, p. 6015 (2009)

21. Quenzer, J.D., Morgansen, K.A.: Observability based control in range-only underwater vehicle localization. In: 2014 American Control Conference, pp. 4702–4707. IEEE (2014)

22. Rafieisakhaei, M., Chakravorty, S., Kumar, P.R.: On the use of the observability gramian for partially observed robotic path planning problems. In: 2017 IEEE 56th Annual Conference on Decision and Control (CDC), pp. 1523–1528 (2017). https://doi.org/10.1109/CDC.2017.8263868

23. Solodov, A., Williams, A., Al Hanaei, S., Goddard, B.: Analyzing the threat of unmanned aerial vehicles (UAV) to nuclear facilities. Secur. J. **31**(1), 305–324 (2018). https://doi.org/10.1057/s41284-017-0102-5

24. Spletzer, J.R., Taylor, C.J.: Dynamic sensor planning and control for optimally tracking targets. Int. J. Robot. Res. **22**(1), 7–20 (2003)

25. Tolić, D., Fierro, R.: Adaptive sampling for tracking in pursuit-evasion games. In: 2011 IEEE International Symposium on Intelligent Control, pp. 179–184. IEEE (2011)

26. Tsoukalas, A., Xing, D., Evangeliou, N., Giakoumidis, N., Tzes, A.: Deep learning assisted visual tracking of evader-UAV. In: 2021 International Conference on Unmanned Aircraft Systems (ICUAS), pp. 252–257. IEEE (2021)

27. Von Moll, A., Shishika, D., Fuchs, Z., Dorothy, M.: The turret-runner-penetrator differential game. In: 2021 American Control Conference (ACC), pp. 3202–3209. IEEE (2021)
28. Yang, C., Kaplan, L., Blasch, E.: Performance measures of covariance and information matrices in resource management for target state estimation. IEEE Trans. Aerosp. Electron. Syst. **48**(3), 2594–2613 (2012)
29. Zhang, J., Zhuang, J.: Modeling a multi-target attacker-defender game with multiple attack types. Reliab. Eng. Syst. Saf. **185**, 465–475 (2019)
30. Zhou, K., Roumeliotis, S.I.: Optimal motion strategies for range-only constrained multisensor target tracking. IEEE Trans. Robot. **24**(5), 1168–1185 (2008)
31. Zhou, K., Roumeliotis, S.I.: Multirobot active target tracking with combinations of relative observations. IEEE Trans. Robot. **27**(4), 678–695 (2011)
32. Zou, R., Bhattacharya, S.: On optimal pursuit trajectories for visibility-based target-tracking game. IEEE Trans. Robot. **35**(2), 449–465 (2018)

Adversarial Learning and Optimization

On Poisoned Wardrop Equilibrium
in Congestion Games

Yunian Pan[✉] and Quanyan Zhu

New York University, Brooklyn, NY, USA
{yp1170,qz494}@nyu.edu

Abstract. Recent years have witnessed a growing number of attack vectors against increasingly interconnected traffic networks. Informational attacks have emerged as the prominent ones that aim to poison traffic data, misguide users, and manipulate traffic patterns. To study the impact of this class of attacks, we propose a game-theoretic framework where the attacker, as a Stackelberg leader, falsifies the traffic conditions to change the traffic pattern predicted by the Wardrop traffic equilibrium, achieved by the users, or the followers. The intended shift of the Wardrop equilibrium is a consequence of strategic informational poisoning. Leveraging game-theoretic and sensitivity analysis, we quantify the system-level impact of the attack by characterizing the concept of poisoned Price of Anarchy, which compares the poisoned Wardrop equilibrium and its non-poisoned system optimal counterpart. We use an evacuation case study to show that the Stackelberg equilibrium can be found through a two-time scale zeroth-order learning process and demonstrate the disruptive effects of informational poisoning, indicating a compelling need for defense policies to mitigate such security threats.

Keywords: Congestion games · Adversarial attack · Stackelberg game · Sensitivity analysis

1 Introduction

With the rapid growth of the Internet-of-Things (IoT), there has been a significant number of vulnerable devices in the past decade, widening the cyber-physical attack surface of modern Intelligent Transportation Systems (ITS). For example, the adoption of IoT technologies for Vehicle-to-Vehicle (V2V), Vehicle-to-Infrastructure (V2I), and Infrastructure-to-Infrastructure (I2I) communications has enabled automated toll collection, traffic cameras and signals, road sensors, barriers, and Online Navigation Platforms (ONP) [9]. It, however, creates opportunities for attackers to disrupt the infrastructure by exploiting cyber vulnerabilities. A quintessential example of such attacks is the hijacking of traffic lights and smart signs. The recent work [2] demonstrates that due to lack of authentication, the wireless sensors and repeaters of the lighting control system can be accessed and manipulated through antenna, exposing serious vulnerabilities of the traffic infrastructure.

The impact of a local attack on the traffic systems propagates and creates a global disruption of the infrastructure. System-level modeling of cyber threats in traffic systems is crucial to understanding and assessing the consequences of cyber threats and the associated defense policies. One significant system-level impact is on the traffic conditions, including delays and disruptions. Attackers can launch a man-in-the-middle (MITM) on ONP systems to mislead the population to choose routes that are favored by the attackers. For instance, in 2014, two Israel students hacked the Google-owned Waze GPS app, causing the platform to report fake traffic conditions to its users; they used bot users to crowdsource false location information to the app, causing congestion [10]. A similar recent case happened in Berlin [6], where an artist loaded 99 smartphones in the street, causing Google-Map to mark that street as having bad traffic. It has been reported in [23] that real-time traffic systems can be deceived by malicious attacks such as modified cookie replays and simulated delusional traffic flows.

This class of attacks is referred to as *informational attacks* on traffic systems. They aim to exploit the vulnerabilities in the data and information infrastructures and strategically craft information to misguide users and achieve a target traffic condition. The advent of information infrastructures and ONP has made user decisions more reliant on services offered by Google and Apple. This reliance has made the attack easily influence the populational behaviors in a much faster and more direct way. Figure 1 illustrates an example attack scenario. The attack manipulates the information collected by an ONP, including traffic demand and travel latency, and misleads it to make false traffic prediction and path recommendations.

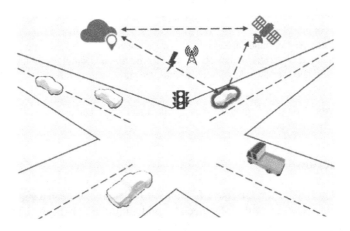

Fig. 1. An example attack scenario: a radio transmitter interferes the GPS communication channel, falsifying the user location information received by an ONP. ITS components, such as smart traffic signal and road cameras, can be hijacked to achieve the same goal.

Wardrop Equilibrium (WE) [26] has been widely used to predict the long-term behavioral patterns of the users and the equilibrium outcome of traffic conditions. It is a natural system-level metric for the impact assessment of informational attacks. Based on WE, we formulate a Stackelberg game as our attack model. In this model, the attacker, or the leader, aims to disrupt the traffic system by poisoning the traffic conditions in a stealthy manner with bounded capabilities. To capture this strategic behavior, we let the attacker's utility consist of the cost of modifying the traffic conditions and the payoff of disruption outcome. In addition, stealthy information falsification attacks seek to satisfy flow conservation constraints to evade inconsistency check. The best response of the users, or the followers, to such informational attacks is the path-routing equilibrium outcome subject to falsified traffic conditions, which are encapsulated by the poisoned traffic latency function and demand vector. We refer to the resulting behavioral pattern as the *Poisoned Wardrop Equilibrium* (PWE). The disruptive effects of such attack is measured by the *Poisoned Price of Anarchy* (PPoA), which is the ratio of the aggregated latency under PWE to its non-poisoned system-optimal counterpart. The local first-order stationary point is called differential Stackelberg equilibrium.

The sensitivity analysis of the PWE and PPoA shows that the attacker's utility function is sufficiently smooth under regularity assumptions of the latency functions. We characterize the implicit relation between the PWE and the attack parameters, based on which we give an explicit expression for the gradient of attack utility. By analyzing the attack gradient, we find that the existence of a differential Stackelberg equilibrium is determined by the weighting coefficient of attack payoff that captures the tradeoff between "disruption" and "stealthiness". We also uniformly characterize the locally Lipschitz parameters for both the attack utility and its gradient, which scale with a set of parameters, including the network size and topology, total traffic demand, and the smoothness level for the latency functions.

We propose a zeroth order two-time scale learning algorithm to find the differential Stackelberg equilibrium and study the iterative adversarial behavior. We approximate the attack gradient by sampling the aggregated latency outcome of PWE and give a polynomial sample efficient guarantee for gradient approximation. We test our algorithm using an evacuation case study on a Sioux Falls network, where the attacker consistently learns to manipulate the information during the evacuation process through bandit feedback. We show that after several iterations, the PPoA of the entire traffic network converges to a PWE where the traffic flow concentrates on several particular edges, causing congestion and low road utilization rates. As congestion games are ubiquitous not only in transportation networks but also in applications related to smart grid, distributed control, and wireless spectrum sharing, it is anticipated that similar attacks can occur in a broader range of scenarios, and there is a need for the development of secure and resilient mechanisms as future work.

Content Organization: We briefly introduce WE and some related works in Sect. 2. In Sect. 3, we present the model for WE and introduce two problem formulations corresponding to two fundamental principles, following which the attacker's problem is discussed. Section 4 provides several theoretical aspects for attack objective function. In Sect. 5, we explore the algorithmic development of the Stackelberg learning framework. We demonstrate the attack effects in Sect. 6.

2   Related Work

WE was introduced in 1952 [1, 26] as an equilibrium model to predict the traffic patterns in transportation networks. The equilibrium concept is related to the notion of Nash equilibrium in game theory that was developed separately. Rosenthal in [20] introduced the class of congestion games and showed its existence of a pure-strategy Nash equilibrium.

There have been an extensive and growing literature that studies congestion games and their variants, and they have been used to model and understand the various techno-logical impact on the transportation networks, including speed limits [17], road pricing [8] or direct ONP assignment [11]. In these works, congestion games are subsumed as a building block to formulate Stackelberg games [18] to design incentives, pricing, and policies. This work leverages the approach to create a formal framework to quantify and analyze the impact of the worst-case attack strategies on the transportation networks.

The learning of attack strategies is related to adversarial machine learning, which usually focuses on algorithm-poisoning, e.g., backdoor attack on deep reinforcement learning model [25]. To the best of our knowledge, we are the first to propose the con-cept of equilibrium-poisoning in transportation systems. Such poisoning happens when there are adversarial attacks on sensors, GPS devices in Cyber-Physical Systems (CPS). Some representative examples can be found in [12, 14].

PoA is commonly used as a metric and analytical tool for congestion games. Cominetti et al. in [4] have shown that PoA is a C^1 function of demand under cer-tain conditions, which coincides to our results showing the smoothness of attack utility w.r.t. the demand poisoning parameter. Aligned with our discussions on the latency cor-ruption, the effects of biased cost function have been investigated in [15], their results are based on the notion of (λ, μ)-smoothness [22], which differs from our methods. In general, PoA is sharply bounded by the condition number of the set of latency functions [21], called the Pigou-bound. We refer the readers to [5] for tighter analysis. Specifi-cally, for affine cost functions, this bound becomes $4/3$. Our numerical study shows that the inefficiency can be worse than the established results under informational attacks.

3   Problem Formulation

3.1   Preliminary Background: Congestion Game and Wardrop Equilibrium

Consider the traffic network as a directed graph $\mathscr{G} = (\mathscr{V}, \mathscr{E})$, with the vertices $\mathscr{V}$ rep-resenting road junctions, and edges $\mathscr{E}$ representing road segments. We assume that $\mathscr{G}$ is finite, connected without buckles, i.e., the edges that connect a vertex to itself. The network contains the following elements:

- $\mathscr{W} \subseteq \mathscr{V} \times \mathscr{V}$ is the set of distinct origin-destination (OD) pairs in the network; for $w \in \mathscr{W}$, $(o_w, d_w) \in \mathscr{V} \times \mathscr{V}$ is the OD pair;
- $\mathscr{P}_w \subseteq \mathscr{P}(\mathscr{E})$ is the set of all directed paths from o_w to d_w;
- $\mathscr{P} = \bigcup_{w \in \mathscr{W}} \mathscr{P}_w$ is the set of paths in a network, each $\mathscr{P}_w$ is disjoint;
- $Q \in \mathbb{R}_{\geq 0}^{|\mathscr{W}|}$ is the OD demand vector , Q_w represents the traffic demand between OD pair $w \in \mathscr{W}$;
- $q \in \mathbb{R}_{\geq 0}^{|\mathscr{E}|}$ is the edge flow vector, q_e is the amount of traffic flow that goes through edge $e \in \mathscr{E}$
- $\mu \in \mathbb{R}_{\geq 0}^{|\mathscr{P}|}$ is the path flow vector, μ_p is the amount of traffic flow that goes through path $p \in \mathscr{P}$.
- $\ell_e : \mathbb{R}_{\geq 0} \to \mathbb{R}_+$ $e \in \mathscr{E}$ is the cost/latency functions, determined by the edge flow. Let $\ell : \mathbb{R}_{\geq 0}^{|\mathscr{E}|} \to \mathbb{R}_+^{|\mathscr{E}|}$ denote the vector-valued latency function.

We assume that there is a set of infinite, infinitesimal players over this graph $\mathscr{G}$, denoted by a measurable space $(\mathscr{X}, \mathscr{M}, m)$. The players are non-atomic, i.e., $m(x) = 0 \; \forall x \in \mathscr{X}$; they are split into distinct populations indexed by the OD pairs, i.e., $\mathscr{X} = \bigcup_{w \in \mathscr{W}} \mathscr{X}_w$ and $\mathscr{X}_w \cap \mathscr{X}_{w'} = \varnothing \; \forall w, w' \in \mathscr{W}$. For each player $x \in \mathscr{X}_w$, we assume that the path is fixed at the beginning, and thus the action of player x is $A(x) \in \mathscr{P}_w$, which is $\mathscr{M}$-measurable. The action profile of all the players $\mathscr{X}$ induces the edge flows $q_e := \int_{\mathscr{X}} \mathbb{1}_{\{e \in A(x)\}} m(dx) \; e \in \mathscr{E}$, and a path flow $\mu_p := \int_{\mathscr{X}_w} \mathbb{1}_{\{A(x)=p\}} m(dx) \; p \in \mathscr{P}_w$, which are the fraction of players using edge e, and the fraction of players using $p \in \mathscr{P}_w$, respectively. The path flow can also be interpreted as a mixed strategy played by a single centralized planner. By definition, a feasible flow pattern $(q, \mu) \in \mathbb{R}^{|\mathscr{E}|} \times \mathbb{R}^{|\mathscr{P}|}$ is constrained by (1):

$$\Lambda \mu - Q = 0$$
$$\Delta \mu - q = 0 \qquad (1)$$
$$-\mu \preceq 0.$$

where $\Lambda \in \mathbb{R}^{|\mathscr{W}| \times |\mathscr{P}|}$, $\Delta \in \mathbb{R}^{|\mathscr{E}| \times |\mathscr{P}|}$ are the path-demand incidence matrix and the path-edge incidence matrix, respectively, which are defined in (2). The two matrices only depend on the topology of network $\mathscr{G}$.

$$\Lambda_{wp} = \begin{cases} 1 & \text{if } p \in \mathscr{P}_w \\ 0 & \text{otherwise} \end{cases} \quad \text{and} \quad \Delta_{ep} = \begin{cases} 1 & \text{if } e \in p \\ 0 & \text{otherwise} \end{cases}. \qquad (2)$$

The utility function for a single player is the aggregated cost for the path she selects, $\ell_p(\mu) = \sum_{e \in p} \ell_e(q_e)$. Note that the path latency, while being a function of q, can be also written as a function of μ, . We hereby impose the first assumption about the edge latency functions.

Assumption 1 ((ℓ-Regularity)). *For all $e \in \mathscr{E}$, the latency functions ℓ_e are l_0-Lipschitz continuous, twice differentiable with $\ell_e'(q_e) > 0$, and $\ell_e''(q_e) \geq 0$ for $q_e \geq 0$. In addition, ℓ_e' are l_1-Lipschitz continuous and ℓ_e'' is bounded by l_1.*

The path latency ℓ_p can be bounded by $D(\mathscr{G})c_0$, where $D(\mathscr{G})$ the diameter of the graph $\mathscr{G}$, and $c_0 := \|\ell\|_\infty = \max_{e \in \mathscr{E}} \ell_e(D)$. This congestion game $\mathscr{G}_c$ is thus encapsulated by the triplet $(\mathscr{X}, \ell, \mathscr{P})$.

3.2 System Optimum and Wardrop Equilibrium

In the seminar work [26], Wardrop proposed two different principles, leading to two solution concepts.

– *Wardrop's first principle (Nash equilibrium principle)*: Players aim to minimize their own travel cost, i.e., for a mixed strategy μ to be a Nash equilibrium, whenever a path $\mu_p > 0$ is chosen for the OD pair w, it holds that $\ell_p(\mu) \leq \ell_{p'}(\mu) \; \forall p' \in \mathscr{P}_w$, implying that every flow has the same latency.
– *Wardrop's second principle (social optimality principle)*: Players pick routes cooperatively such that the overall latency is minimized. The coordinated behaviors minimize the aggregated system performance $\sum_{e \in \mathscr{E}} q_e \ell_e(q_e)$ under proper constraints.

We hereby formalize the notion of *System Optimum* (SO) and WE. Definition 1 follows Wardrop's second principle, characterizing the cooperative behaviors of individuals that minimize the aggregated latency.

Definition 1 (System Optimum (SO)). *The socially optimal routing $(q^\star, \mu^\star)$ is a feasible flow pattern that optimizes the social welfare by minimizing the aggregated latency $S(q) = \sum_{e \in \mathcal{E}} q_e \ell_e(q_e)$, obtained from the optimization problem (3)*

$$\min_{q,\mu} \quad \sum_{e \in \mathcal{E}} q_e \ell_e(q_e)$$
$$\text{s.t.} \quad (q,\mu) \in F_Q \tag{3}$$

where $F_Q := \{(q,\mu) \in \mathbb{R}^{|\mathcal{E}|} \times \mathbb{R}^{|\mathcal{P}|} \,|\, (q,\mu) \text{ satisfies (1).}\}$

By assumption 1, problem (3) is strictly convex in $\mathbb{R}^{|\mathcal{E}|}$, admitting a strict global minimum edge flow $q^\star$, the corresponding path flow set $\mu^\star$ is generally the non-unique solution to the linear equation $\Delta\mu = q^\star$, satisfying (1). The optimal aggregated latency is denoted by $S^\star := S(q^\star)$.

The Nash equilibrium, on the other hand, exploits the self-interest nature of the individuals in a transportation network. Definition 2 follows Wardrop's first principle, characterizing the non-cooperative behaviors of individuals that minimize their own latency.

Definition 2 (Wardrop Equilibrium (WE)). *A flow pattern (q,μ) is said to be a Wardrop Equilibrium (WE), if it satisfies $(q,\mu) \in F_Q$, and for all $w \in \mathcal{W}$:*

– $\ell_p(\mu) = \ell_{p'}(\mu)$ *for all* $p, p' \in \mathcal{P}_w$ *with* $\mu_p, \mu_{p'} > 0$;
– $\ell_p(\mu) \geq \ell_{p'}(\mu)$ *for all* $p, p' \in \mathcal{P}_w$ *with* $\mu_p > 0$ *and* $\mu_{p'} = 0$.

Equivalently, WE can be characterized as the minimizer of the following convex program:

$$\min_{q,\mu} \quad \sum_{e \in \mathcal{E}} \int_0^{q_e} \ell_e(z)dz$$
$$\text{s.t.} \quad (q,\mu) \in F_Q, \tag{4}$$

where $\sum_{e \in \mathcal{E}} \int_0^{q_e} \ell_e(z)dz =: J(q)$ is called the Beckman potential.

Since, by assumption 1, ℓ_e is strictly increasing, the equilibrium edge flow q^* is uniquely defined; the corresponding equilibrium path flow set μ^* is generally the non-unique solution to the linear equation $\Delta\mu = q^*$, satisfying (1).

3.3 Stackelberg Congestion Security Game

This section formulates a Stackelberg congestion security game. We consider an attacker who manipulates latency and demand data to mislead the ONP and its users. To capture this malicious behavior, we introduce a pair of attack parameters $(\theta, d) \in (\Theta \times \mathcal{D})$ as the attack action, which parameterize two global traffic condition operators, $\Phi_\theta : \Theta \times \mathbb{R}^{|\mathcal{E}|} \times \mathbb{R}^{|\mathcal{P}|} \to \mathbb{R}^{|\mathcal{E}|} \times \mathbb{R}^{|\mathcal{P}|}$ and $\Phi_d : \mathcal{D} \times \mathbb{R}^{|\mathcal{W}|} \to \mathbb{R}^{|\mathcal{W}|}$. The flow operator Φ_θ

modifies the real-time traffic flow to poison the latency function; the demand opera-
tor Φ_d poisons the traffic demand prediction. Φ_θ and Φ_d are abstractions of the attack
behaviors illustrated in Fig. 1 and Sect. 1, they capture and unify how the attacker falsifies the traffic condition data by using the radio transmitters, Trojan, and ransomware
etc. to compromise the local devices.

After the poisoning, the demand prediction and latency function are corrupted to
be $\tilde{Q} := \Phi_d \cdot Q$ and $\tilde{\ell} = \ell \circ \Phi_\theta$, respectively. We hereby introduce the (θ,d)-*Poisoned
Wardrop Equilibrium* $((\theta,d)$-PWE$)$ as described in Definition 3.

Definition 3 $((\theta,d)$-**PWE**$)$. *A flow pattern (q,μ) is said to be a (θ,d)-PWE, if it is
a solution to the problem (4), with the latency function being $\tilde{\ell} = \Phi_\theta \circ \ell$ and the OD
demand vector being $\tilde{Q} = \Phi_d \cdot Q$. The equilibrium edge flow and path flow set are
denoted by $q^*(\theta,d)$, and $\mu^*(\theta,d)$, respectively.*

As illustrated in Fig. 2, the corruption of real-time traffic conditions, the poisoned
path recommendation by ONP, and the user path selection (the formation of PWE) form
a closed-loop system that is interfered by the attacker.

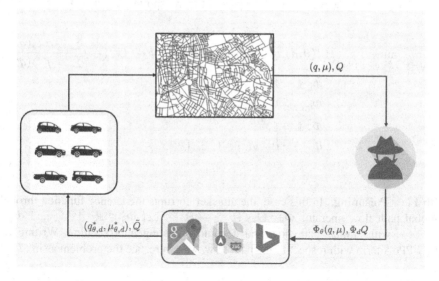

Fig. 2. An illustration of the (θ,d)-PWE-formation loop: the attacker stealthily intercepts the
communication channel that collects traffic conditions, forcing the formation of traffic flow that
is favored by the attacker.

To quantify the disruption caused by such informational attack, we introduce the
notion of (θ,d)-*Poisoned Price of Anarchy* $((\theta,d)$-PPoA$)$.

Definition 4. *The ratio of aggregated latency at (θ,d)-PWE to the aggregated latency
at non-poisoned SO is called (θ,d)-PPoA , i.e.:*

$$(\theta,d)\text{-PPoA} = \frac{\sum_{e \in \mathscr{E}} q_e^*(\theta,d)\ell_e(q_e^*(\theta,d))}{\sum_{e \in \mathscr{E}} q_e^\star \ell_e(q_e^\star)}. \tag{5}$$

Now, we are ready to define attacker's cost function and complete the attack model. We give two formulations in the sequel, based on the malicious manipulation of edge flow and path flow, respectively.

Edge Flow Poisoning. In this case, the attacker corrupts the latency function through a global edge flow operator $\Phi_\theta : \Theta \times \mathbb{R}^{|\mathcal{E}|} \mapsto \mathbb{R}^{|\mathcal{E}|}$. For simplicity, we consider the attack operators to be matrices of proper dimensions, i.e., $\Phi_\theta \in \mathbb{R}^{|\mathcal{E}| \times |\mathcal{E}|}$, and $\Phi_d \in \mathbb{R}^{|\mathcal{W}| \times |\mathcal{W}|}$.

The operators Φ_θ and Φ_d have the following interpretation. Through data manipulation, the fraction $\Phi_{\theta;i,j}$ of traffic flow in edge i is redistributed to edge j; the fraction $\Phi_{d,i,j}$ of demand between OD pair i is redirected to OD pair j. It is reasonable to let $\|\Phi_\theta\|_{op}$ and $\|\Phi_d\|_{op}$ be 1 such that the flow and demand corruption cannot be identified by checking the norm of the flow and demand vectors. The set of column-stochastic matrix satisfies such a constraint.

The problem (6) is to optimize the attack utility $\mathcal{L} : \Theta \times \mathcal{Q} \times \mathbb{R}^{|\mathcal{E}|} \mapsto \mathbb{R}$. The utility $\mathcal{L}$ contains two terms. The attack cost term is measured by the $\| \cdot \|_F$ norm of deviation from "no-attack" to "attack"; the attack payoff term is the (θ, d)-PPoA weighted by parameter γ, which measures the disruption of the transportation network.

$$\min_{(\theta,d)\in\Theta\times\mathcal{Q},\, q=q^*(\theta,d)} \mathcal{L}((\theta,d),q) := \frac{1}{2}(\|\Phi_\theta - I\|_F^2 + \|\Phi_d - I\|_F^2) - \gamma\frac{\sum_{e\in\mathcal{E}} q_e\ell_e(q_e)}{\sum_{e\in\mathcal{E}} q_e^\star\ell_e(q_e^\star)}$$

$$\text{s.t.} \quad \Phi_\theta^\top \mathbb{1} = \mathbb{1},$$

$$\Phi_{\theta;i,j} \geq 0 \quad \forall i,j \in 1,\ldots,|\mathcal{E}|,$$

$$\Phi_d^\top \mathbb{1} = \mathbb{1},$$

$$\Phi_{d;i,j} \geq 0 \quad \forall i,j \in 1,\ldots,|\mathcal{W}|.$$

$$(6)$$

Path Flow Poisoning. In this case, the attacker corrupts the latency function through a global path flow operator $\Phi_\theta : \Theta \times \mathbb{R}^{|\mathcal{P}|} \mapsto \mathbb{R}^{|\mathcal{P}|}$. Let $\Phi_\theta \in \mathbb{R}^{|\mathcal{P}| \times |\mathcal{P}|}$ and $\Phi_d \in \mathbb{R}^{|\mathcal{W}| \times |\mathcal{W}|}$, with similar path flow and demand operating interpretation. Writing the (θ, d)-PPoA term with respect to the path flow, we can restate the problem as in (7):

$$\min_{(\theta,d)\in\Theta\times\mathcal{Q}} \sup_{\mu\in\mu^*(\theta,d)} \mathcal{L}((\theta,d),\mu) := \frac{1}{2}(\|\Phi_\theta - I\|_F^2 + \|\Phi_d - I\|_F^2) - \gamma\frac{\sum_{p\in\mathcal{P}} \mu_p\ell_p(\mu)}{\sum_{p\in\mathcal{P}} \mu_p^\star\ell_p(\mu^\star)}$$

$$\text{s.t.} \quad \Phi_\theta^\top \mathbb{1} = \mathbb{1},$$

$$\Phi_{\theta;i,j} \geq 0 \quad \forall i,j \in 1,\ldots,|\mathcal{P}|,$$

$$\Phi_d^\top \mathbb{1} = \mathbb{1},$$

$$\Phi_{d;i,j} \geq 0 \quad \forall i,j \in 1,\ldots,|\mathcal{W}|,$$

$$(7)$$

where we take the supremum over the path flow set of (θ, d)-PWE. One can verify that the normalizing denominator $\sum_{p\in\mathcal{P}} \mu_p^\star\ell_p(\mu^\star) = \sum_{e\in\mathcal{E}} q_e^\star\ell_e(q_e^\star)$, i.e., while the one edge flow may correspond to multiple path flows, the aggregated latency remains the same.

Since in general the optimal path flow $\boldsymbol{\mu}^*(\theta,d)$ is a set-valued mapping, we focus on problem (6) for analytical convenience in the sequel. For the Stackelberg game defined in (6), we refer to the constraint set as $\mathscr{C}$. The convexity of the mathematical program (6) can not be determined due to the implicity of parameterization (θ,d)-PWE. Assuming that the parameterization yields sufficient smoothness conditions, we adopt the first-order local stationary point as the solution concept, called *Differential Stackelberg Equilibrium* (DSE), as described in Definition 5.

Definition 5 (Differential Stackelberg Equilibrium (DSE)). *A pair $((\theta^*,d^*),(q,\boldsymbol{\mu}))$ with $(\theta^*,d^*) \in \mathscr{C}$, $(q,\boldsymbol{\mu}) = (q^*(\theta^*,d^*),\boldsymbol{\mu}^*(\theta^*,d^*))$ being the (θ^*,d^*)-PWE, is said to be a Differential Stackelberg Equilibrium (DSE) for the Stackelberg game defined in (6), if $\nabla_{\theta,d}\mathscr{L} = 0$, and $\nabla^2_{\theta,d}\mathscr{L}$ is positive definite.*

Note that in defining DSE, we have inexplicitly assumed that the individuals have no knowledge of the poisoning. This modeling choice is valid when the attack is stealthy.

In practice, we consider the explicit case where $\boldsymbol{\Phi}_\theta$ is a matrix in $\mathbb{R}^{|\mathscr{E}|\times|\mathscr{E}|}$ (or $\mathbb{R}^{|\mathscr{P}|\times|\mathscr{P}|}$) and is parameterized by $\theta \in \Theta = \mathbb{R}^{|\mathscr{E}|^2}$ (or $\mathbb{R}^{|\mathscr{P}|^2}$) such that $vec(\boldsymbol{\Phi}_\theta) = \theta$, and $\boldsymbol{\Phi}_d$ is parameterized by $d \in \mathscr{D} = \mathbb{R}^{|\mathscr{W}|^2}$ such that $vec(\boldsymbol{\Phi}_d) = d$. In this case, $\mathscr{C}$ is a compact and convex set. Later on, we use the operator $\text{Proj}_{\mathscr{C}}(\theta,d)$ to represent the Euclidean projection onto $\mathscr{C}$, i.e., $\text{Proj}_{\mathscr{C}}(\theta,d) = \arg\min_{z\in\mathscr{C}} \|z - (\theta,d)\|^2$.

4 Sensitivity Analysis

4.1 Smoothness of (θ,d)-PWE

Let $\Theta, \mathscr{D}$ be open sets, for some fixed parameter $(\theta,d) \in \Theta \times \mathscr{D}$, a unique minimizer $q^*(\theta,d)$ of the parameterized Beckman program (8) is uniquely determined.

$$\min_{q,\mu} J((q,\mu)|\theta,d) := \sum_{e\in\mathscr{E}} \int_0^q (\ell \circ \boldsymbol{\Phi}_\theta)_e(z)d$$

$$\text{s.t.} \quad (\boldsymbol{\Phi}_\theta q,\mu) \in F_{\boldsymbol{\Phi}_d Q}. \tag{8}$$

To study the sensitivity of $\mathscr{L}$ and $q^*(\theta,d)$ to the perturbations of θ and d, we reduce the feasibility set for the parameterized version of Beckman program (4) to the q variable first. In doing so, we give Lemma 1.

Lemma 1. *Given attack parameter θ,d, define the feasible set of edge flow*

$$q_{\theta,d} := \{q \in \mathbb{R}^{|\mathscr{E}|} \mid \exists\mu \text{ such that } (\boldsymbol{\Phi}_\theta q,\mu) \in F_{\boldsymbol{\Phi}_d Q}\},$$

which has the following properties:

(a) There exists $A \in \mathbb{R}^{r\times|\mathscr{E}|}$ and $B \in \mathbb{R}^{r\times|\mathscr{W}|}$ of proper dimensions, with r depending only on $\mathscr{G}$, such that

$$q_{\theta,d} = \{q \in \mathbb{R}^{|\mathscr{E}|} \mid A\boldsymbol{\Phi}_\theta q \le B\boldsymbol{\Phi}_d Q\}.$$

(b) *Any $q \in \boldsymbol{q}_{\theta,d}$ is bounded by*

$$\|q\| \leq D\sqrt{|\mathscr{E}|}.$$

(c) *There exists a constant l_d such that for any $d',d \in \mathscr{D}$ and $q \in \boldsymbol{q}_{\theta,d}$ there exists $q' \in \boldsymbol{q}_{\theta,d'}$ satisfying*

$$\|q' - q\| \leq l_d \|d' - d\|.$$

By Lemma 1, the feasibility set $\boldsymbol{q}_{\theta,d}$ can be projected onto q-space as a linear inequality constraint on q-variable, which is bounded and local Lipschitz smooth w.r.t. d.

Lemma 2. *Let $q^*(\theta,d)$ be the unique minimizer of (8). Then, at each $(\bar{\theta},\bar{d}) \in \Theta \times \mathscr{D}$, there exists ε such that for all $(\theta,d) \in B_\varepsilon(\bar{\theta},\bar{d})$:*

(a) *The edge flow at (θ,d)-PWE, $q^*(\theta,d)$ is continuous, i.e., for any sequence $(\theta_n,d_n) \to (\bar{\theta},\bar{d}), n \in \mathbb{N}$, we have $q^*(\theta_n,d_n) \to q^*(\theta,d)$. In addition, there exists a Lipschitz constant $l_q > 0$ that is related to $\|B\Phi_d\|$ such that*

$$\|q^*(\theta,d) - q^*(\bar{\theta},\bar{d})\| \leq l_q \|(\theta,d) - (\bar{\theta},\bar{d})\| \tag{9}$$

(b) *The poisoned aggregated latency function $S(q^*(\theta,d))$ is locally Lipschitz continuous, i.e.,*

$$\|S(q^*(\theta,d)) - S(q^*(\bar{\theta},\bar{d}))\| \leq (c_0 + l_0 D) l_q \sqrt{|\mathscr{E}|} \|(\theta,d) - (\bar{\theta},\bar{d})\|.$$

The Lipschitz constant in 2 (b) has the following interpretation. The smoothness level of the poisoned aggregated latency function scales with three factors: the upper estimate scale of latency ($\|\ell\|_\infty$ and $l_0 D$), the network size ($\sqrt{|\mathscr{E}|}$), and the smoothness level of (θ,d)-PWE (l_q). This Lipschitz constant directly implies the smoothness level of (θ,d)-PPoA.

4.2 Differentiability of (θ,d)-PWE

By Lemma 1, the feasibility set can be reduced to a linear inequality constraint. Define the (θ,d)-poisoned Lagrangian:

$$L(q,\lambda,\theta,d) = \sum_{e \in \mathscr{E}} \int_0^{(\Phi_\theta q)_e} \ell_e(z)dz + \lambda^\top (A\Phi_\theta q - B\Phi_d Q). \tag{10}$$

The KKT condition states that a vector $\tilde{q} \in \mathbb{R}^{|\mathscr{E}|}$ is the solution $q^*(\theta,d)$ if and only if there exists $\tilde{\lambda} \in \mathbb{R}^r$ such that:

$$A\Phi_\theta \tilde{q} - B\Phi_d Q \preceq 0$$

$$\tilde{\lambda}_i \geq 0, \quad i = 1,\ldots,r$$

$$\tilde{\lambda}_i (A\Phi_\theta \tilde{q} - B\Phi_d Q)_i = 0, \quad i = 1,\ldots,r$$

$$\sum_{e' \in \mathscr{E}} \Phi_{\theta;e,e'}^\top \ell_{e'}((\Phi_\theta \tilde{q})_{e'}) + (\Phi_\theta^\top A^\top \tilde{\lambda})_e = 0, \quad e = 1,\ldots,|\mathscr{E}|,$$

To apply Implicit Function Theorem (IFT) to the poisoned Beckman program (4), we define the vector-valued function $g = \nabla_{(q,\lambda)} L$,

$$
g(\tilde{q}, \tilde{\lambda}, \theta, d) = \begin{bmatrix} \sum_{e' \in \mathcal{E}} \Phi_{\theta;e',1} \ell_{e'}((\Phi_\theta \tilde{q})_{e'}) + (\Phi_\theta^\top A^\top \tilde{\lambda})_1 \\ \cdots \\ \sum_{e' \in \mathcal{E}} \Phi_{\theta;e',|\mathcal{E}|} \ell_{e'}((\Phi_\theta \tilde{q})_{e'}) + (\Phi_\theta^\top A^\top \tilde{\lambda})_{|\mathcal{E}|} \\ \mathrm{diag}(\lambda)(A\Phi_\theta \tilde{q} - B\Phi_d Q) \end{bmatrix}, \tag{11}
$$

where $\mathrm{diag}(\cdot)$ transforms the vector λ into the matrix with λ_i being the diagonal entries. For a candidate WE solution $(\tilde{q}, \tilde{\lambda})$ such that $g(\tilde{q}, \tilde{\lambda}, \theta, d) = 0$, we define the partial Jacobian w.r.t. variable (q, λ):

$$
\mathrm{D}_{(q,\lambda)} g(\tilde{q}, \tilde{\lambda}, \theta, d) = \begin{bmatrix} \mathrm{D}_q \nabla_q L(\tilde{q}, \tilde{\lambda}, \theta, d) & \Phi_\theta^\top A^\top \\ \mathrm{diag}(\tilde{\lambda}) A \Phi_\theta & \mathrm{diag}(A\Phi_\theta \tilde{q} - B\Phi_d Q) \end{bmatrix}, \tag{12}
$$

where the first diagonal term

$$
\mathrm{D}_q \nabla_q L(\tilde{q}, \tilde{\lambda}, \theta, d) = [\sum_{e' \in [\mathcal{E}]} \Phi_{\theta;e',i} \Phi_{\theta;e',j} \ell'_{e'}((\Phi_\theta \tilde{q})_{e'})]_{i,j \in [\mathcal{E}]} = \Phi_\theta^\top \nabla_q \tilde{\ell},
$$

is positive definite according to assumption 1. By Shur's complement, one can verify that if $\{i \,|\, \tilde{\lambda}_i = 0 \text{ and } (A\Phi_\theta \tilde{q} - \Phi_d Q)_i = 0\} = \emptyset$, the partial Jacobian is non-singular. The partial Jacobian w.r.t. variable (θ, d) is

$$
\mathrm{D}_{(\theta,d)} g(\tilde{q}, \tilde{\lambda}, \theta, d) = \begin{bmatrix} \mathrm{D}_\theta \nabla_q L(\tilde{q}, \tilde{\lambda}, \theta, d) & \mathrm{D}_d \nabla_q L(\tilde{q}, \tilde{\lambda}, \theta, d) \\ \mathrm{diag}(\tilde{\lambda}) \mathrm{D}_\theta (A\Phi_\theta \tilde{q}) & -\mathrm{diag}(\tilde{\lambda}) \mathrm{D}_d (B\Phi_d Q) \end{bmatrix}. \tag{13}
$$

Lemma 3 gives the local differentiability result for (θ, d)-PWE.

Lemma 3 (IFT for (θ, d)-PWE). *Let $g(\tilde{q}, \tilde{\lambda}, \theta, d) = 0$, if the set $\{i \,|\, \tilde{\lambda}_i = 0 \text{ and } (A\Phi_\theta \tilde{q} - \Phi_d Q)_i = 0\} = \emptyset$, then $\mathrm{D}_{(q,\lambda)} g(\tilde{q}, \tilde{\lambda}, \theta, d)$ is non-singular, then the solution mapping for WE (4) has a single-value localization $q^*(\theta, d)$ around $(\tilde{q}, \tilde{\lambda})$, which is continuously differentiable in the neighbor of (θ, d) with partial Jacobian satisfying:*

$$
\mathrm{D}_\theta q^*(\theta, d) = -\mathrm{D}_{(q,\lambda)} g(\tilde{q}, \tilde{\lambda}, \theta, d)^{-1} \mathrm{D}_\theta g(\tilde{q}, \tilde{\lambda}, \theta, d) \qquad \forall \theta \in \Theta, \tag{14}
$$

and

$$
\mathrm{D}_d q^*(\theta, d) = -\mathrm{D}_{(q,\lambda)} g(\tilde{q}, \tilde{\lambda}, \theta, d)^{-1} \mathrm{D}_d g(\tilde{q}, \tilde{\lambda}, \theta, d) \qquad \forall d \in \mathcal{D}, \tag{15}
$$

where $\mathrm{D}_{(q,\lambda)} g(\tilde{q}, \tilde{\lambda}, \theta, d)$ is defined in (12), and $[\mathrm{D}_\theta g(\tilde{q}, \tilde{\lambda}, \theta, d), \mathrm{D}_d g(\tilde{q}, \tilde{\lambda}, \theta, d)]$ is defined in (13).

A similar derivation for the path flow case is given in Appendix A.

4.3 Characterizing Attacker Objective

Equipped with Lemma 3, we arrive at the explicit expression for $\nabla \mathcal{L}$ in Theorem 1.

Theorem 1. *For problem* (6), *the gradient of* $\mathscr{L}$ *w.r.t.* θ *is:*

$$\nabla_\theta \mathscr{L} = \theta - vec(I_{|\mathscr{E}|}) - \frac{\gamma}{S^\star} \sum_{e \in \mathscr{E}} \left(q_e^*(\theta,d) \frac{d\ell_e(z)}{dz}\Big|_{q_e^*(\theta,d)} + \ell_e(q_e^*(\theta,d)) \right) \nabla_\theta q_e^*(\theta,d),$$

(16)

where $\nabla_\theta q_e^*(\theta,d)$ *is the transpose of* $D_\theta q_e^*(\theta,d)$ *defined in* (14).
The gradient of $\mathscr{L}$ *w.r.t.* d *is:*

$$\nabla_d \mathscr{L} = d - vec(I_{|\mathscr{W}|}) - \frac{\gamma}{S^\star} \sum_{e \in \mathscr{E}} \left(q_e^*(\theta,d) \frac{d\ell_e(z)}{dz}\Big|_{q_e^*(\theta,d)} + \ell_e(q_e^*(\theta,d)) \right) \nabla_d q_e^*(\theta,d),$$

(17)

where $\nabla_d q_e^*(\theta,d)$ *is the transpose of* $D_d q_e^*(\theta,d)$ *defined in* (15).

Theorem 1 also indicates that the existence of a DSE can be controlled by the weighting factor γ. To see this, we first notice that the first-order condition $\nabla \mathscr{L}$ may not be achievable within $\mathscr{C}$ when γ is too large. For the second-order condition, observe that the Hessian $\nabla_\theta^2 \mathscr{L}$ takes the form similar to an M-matrix, i.e., $\nabla_\theta^2 \mathscr{L} = I - \gamma H$, where H is:

$$M = \frac{1}{S^\star} \nabla_\theta \sum_{e \in \mathscr{E}} \left(q_e^*(\theta,d) \frac{d\ell_e(z)}{dz}\Big|_{q_e^*(\theta,d)} + \ell_e(q_e^*(\theta,d)) \right) D_\theta q_e^*(\theta,d).$$

Under proper scaling of γ, the positive definiteness of $\nabla_\theta^2 \mathscr{L}$ can be guaranteed, given the spectral radius of M is strictly less than $\frac{1}{\gamma}$ everywhere in $\Theta \times \mathscr{D}$. The same analysis can be applied to $\nabla_d^2 \mathscr{L}$.

The weighting parameter γ also plays a role in balancing the local sensitivities of attack cost and payoff, as described in Theorem 2.

Theorem 2. *The attacker objective function* $\mathscr{L}$ *is* L_0-*locally Lipschitz continuous w.r.t. its argument* θ *and* d, *where* L_0 *is:*

$$L_0 = (\sqrt{2} + \gamma \frac{(c_0 + l_0 D)l_q}{S^\star})\sqrt{|\mathscr{E}|}.$$

(18)

L_0 consists of two terms: one is the smoothness level of quadratic cost that scales with the network size factor $\sqrt{|\mathscr{E}|}$; one is the smoothness level of (θ,d)-PPoA that scales with not only $\sqrt{|\mathscr{E}|}$, but also the ratio between Lipschitz constants of $S(q^*(\theta,d))$ and $S^\star$. It can be computed that $S^\star$ roughly scales with $c_0 D\sqrt{|\mathscr{E}|}$, hence γl_q must scale with $\sqrt{|\mathscr{E}|}$ to match the sensitivities of attack cost and payoff. This again indicates that the selection of weighting factor γ is non-trivial.

The gradient smoothness is an important condition for the convergence analysis of gradient-based algorithms. Determining the Lipschitz constant of $\nabla \mathscr{L}$ requires the upper estimates of $\|\nabla_{\theta,d} q_e^*(\theta,d)\|_{op}$, which in turn requires the lower eigenvalue estimates $\lambda_{\min}(D_{(q,\lambda)}g)$ and upper eigenvalue estimates $\lambda_{\max}(D_{\theta,d}g)$. Intuitively, the boundedness of the partial Jacobians of g can be guaranteed by the regularity assumption of ℓ and Φ_θ, which is already made in our context. We end this section with Lemma 4, which characterize the gradient smoothness under the regularity assumptions of $\|\nabla_{\theta,d} q_e^*(\theta,d)\|_{op}$.

Lemma 4. *Given* $\|\nabla_{\theta,d}q_e^*(\theta,d)\|_{op}$ *is bounded by* C_0 *and* C_1-*locally Lipschitz continuous, the attacker objective gradient* $\nabla_\theta\mathscr{L}$ *is* L_1-*locally Lipschitz continuous w.r.t. its argument* θ, *where* L_1 *is:*

$$L_1 = 1 + \frac{\gamma}{S^*}\left(C_0lq(l_0+\ell'(D)) + C_1c_0 + D\sqrt{|\mathscr{E}|}(C_0l_1l_q + C_1\ell'(D))\right)\sqrt{|\mathscr{E}|}. \quad (19)$$

5 Algorithmic Development

5.1 Consistent Attack as a Stackelberg Learning Process

Projected gradient-based method is a standard approach to find a first-order stationary point or a DSE. In the context of attack, the projected gradient dynamics can be captured by a two-time scale Stackelberg learning procedure, which requires the attacker to have access to the first-order oracle. The first-order oracle gives the zeroth and first-order information of the edge latencies, the traffic flow at PWE, and the partial Jacobians of g.

However, the first-order oracle is oftentimes unavailable in practice. A sophisticated attacker is able to approximately find the Stackelberg differential equilibria through bandit-feedback, i.e., the aggregated latency results of (θ,d)-PWE. To this end, we define two smoothed versions of attacker utility,

$$\begin{aligned} \mathscr{L}_r^\theta((\theta,d),q^*) &= \mathbb{E}_{u\sim\mathbb{B}_r^\theta}[\mathscr{L}((\theta+u,d),q^*)], \\ \mathscr{L}_r^d((\theta,d),q^*) &= \mathbb{E}_{v\sim\mathbb{B}_r^d}[\mathscr{L}((\theta,d+v),q^*)], \end{aligned} \quad (20)$$

where u,v are uniformly sampled from r-radius Frobenius norm balls $\mathbb{B}_r^\theta, \mathbb{B}_r^d$ with proper dimensions. As smoothed functions, $\mathscr{L}_r^\theta, \mathscr{L}_r^d$ have Lipschitz constants no worse than L for all $r > 0$, and their gradients, by standard volume argument from [7] Lemma 2.1,

$$\begin{aligned} \nabla_\theta\mathscr{L}_r^\theta((\theta,d),q^*) &= \frac{dim(\Theta)}{r^2}\mathbb{E}_{u\sim\mathbb{S}_r^\theta}[\mathscr{L}((\theta+u,d),q^*)u], \\ \nabla_d\mathscr{L}_r^d((\theta,d),q^*) &= \frac{dim(\mathscr{D})}{r^2}\mathbb{E}_{v\sim\mathbb{S}_r^\theta}[\mathscr{L}((\theta,d+v),q^*)v], \end{aligned} \quad (21)$$

where $\mathbb{S}_r^\theta, \mathbb{S}_r^d$ are r-radius spheres of proper dimensions.

Equipped with the smoothness results and (21), by standard concentration inequalities, we show that it suffices to use polynomial numbers of samples to approximate the gradients.

Proposition 1 (Gradient Approximation Efficiency). *Given a small* $\varepsilon > 0$, *one can find fixed polynomials* $h_r(1/\varepsilon)$, $h_{sample}(dim(\Theta),1/\varepsilon)$, $h_{sample}(dim(\mathscr{D}),1/\varepsilon)$, *for* $r \leq h_r(1/\varepsilon)$, *with* $m \geq \max\{h_{sample}(dim(\Theta),1/\varepsilon), h_{sample}(dim(\mathscr{D}),1/\varepsilon)\}$ *samples of* $u_1, \ldots, u_m$ *and* $v_1,\ldots,v_m$, *with probability at least* $1 - (d/\varepsilon)^{-d}$ *the sample averages*

$$\frac{dim(\Theta)}{mr^2}\sum_{i=1}^m\mathscr{L}((\theta+u_i,d),q^*)u_i, \quad \frac{dim(\mathscr{D})}{mr^2}\sum_{i=1}^m\mathscr{L}((\theta,d+v_i),q^*)v_i \quad (22)$$

are ε *close to* $\nabla_\theta\mathscr{L}$ *and* $\nabla_d\mathscr{L}$, *respectively.*

Leveraging the one-point gradient approximation technique, we propose the derivative-free Algorithm 1. This algorithm asynchronously perturbs the parameters θ and d to obtain the one-point gradient estimates.

Algorithm 1: Zeroth-Order Poisoning

Input: Admissible initial parameter θ, d, learning rate η, sample size m, radius r;

while *not done* **do**

    Attacker initiates attack Φ_θ, Φ_d;

    while *Attacking* **do**

        for $i = 1, \ldots, m$ **do**

            Sample (θ, d)-PWE for searching directions $u_i \sim \mathbb{S}_r^\theta$, $v_i \sim \mathbb{S}_r^d$, obtain:

$$\mathscr{L}_i^\theta = \mathscr{L}(\text{Proj}_{\mathscr{C}}(\theta + u_i, d), q^*), \quad \mathscr{L}_i^d = \mathscr{L}(\text{Proj}_{\mathscr{C}}(\theta, d + v_i), q^*).$$

        end

        Projected gradient updates:

$$\theta \leftarrow \text{Proj}_{\mathscr{C}}[\theta - \eta \frac{dim(\Theta)}{mr^2} \sum_{i=1}^{m} \mathscr{L}_\theta^i u_i] \quad d \leftarrow \text{Proj}_{\mathscr{C}}[d - \eta \frac{dim(\mathscr{D})}{mr^2} \sum_{i=1}^{m} \mathscr{L}_d^i v_i]. \quad (23)$$

    end

end

By projecting perturbed θ, d to the constraint set $\mathscr{C}$, we ensure the feasibility of the perturbed attack strategies when sampling $\mathscr{L}_i^\theta$ and $\mathscr{L}_i^d$. Algorithm 1 can proceed without the aid of first-order oracle, but it requires the number of samples to be polynomial w.r.t. the smoothness level of attack utility.

6 Case Study

Through an emergency evacuation case study [16], over the classical Sioux Falls, South Dakota Transportation Network [13] (Fig. 3 (b)), we test our Stackelberg learning algorithm and demonstrate the attack effects.

In our example, the evacuation lasts for one month. During each day, a total of 34200 individuals are transported from emergency locations (the red nodes) (14), (15), (22), and (23), to shelter places (the green nodes) (4), (5), (6), (8), (9), (10), (11), (16), (17), and (18). The transportation network data, including node attributes, free travel time, and road capacity, etc., are available at [19]. The edge latency is given by the standard Bureau of Public Roads (BPR) function:

$$\ell_e(q_e) = t_e^f \left(1 + \alpha \left(\frac{q_e}{C_e}\right)^\beta \right), \quad (24)$$

where t_e^f is the free time for edge e, C_e is the road capacity for edge e, and α, β are some parameters.

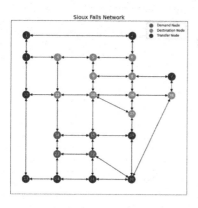

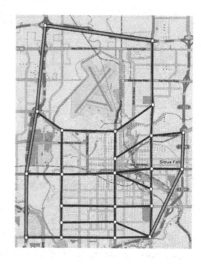

Fig. 3. The topological (left) and geographical layout [3] (right) of the Sioux Falls city, South Dakota transportation network. The red nodes represent the locations where people need to be evacuated, the green nodes represent the evacuation shelters, and the blue nodes represent transfer locations. (Color figure online)

The attacker's goal is to slow down the evacuation process through latency and demand poisoning. The attacker can launch multiple attacks during one day, for each attack, the aggregated latency at the corresponding PWE is revealed as an observation to the attacker. These observations are then used to update the attack strategy. The weighting factor γ and sample size m are both picked to scale with $\sqrt{|\mathcal{E}|}$, where $|\mathcal{E}| = 76$ is the total edge number. An annealing factor of 0.95 is used for the learning rate. We sample perturbations u_i and v_i from a standard normal distribution for practical purposes. The PPoA evolution curve is shown in Fig. 4.

Figure 4 shows that a stealthy attacker can decrease the efficiency of WE, pushing it far away from the SO. The convergence of the Stackelberg learning process implies the finding of a DSE.

We compare the edge efficiencies of SO and PWE in Fig. 5. Figure 5a shows the comparison of latency function values for each edge, given by (24) and the assigned edge flow; Fig. 5b shows the comparison of utilization ratio between the actual flow on that edge and its road capacity, q_e/C_e.

Figure 5a shows that at the end of the iteration, PWE assigns overwhelming traffic flow on several high-capacity edges, causing edge latencies to be higher than those of SO. It can be inferred that the congestion is likely to occur on those edges with the overwhelming flow. Figure 5b shows that those edges with significantly high traffic latencies are severely overloaded, which indicates that the evacuation process is highly disrupted.

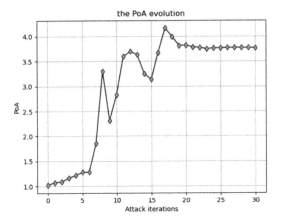

Fig. 4. The evolution of PPoA: after 15 days, the PPoA of this attack scenario reaches above 4; and the process is stabilized at day-20 and attains the PPoA around 3.6.

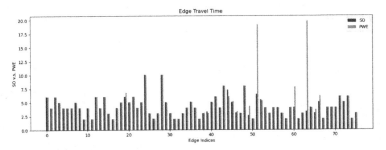

(a) This bar chart compares the edge travel time caused by SO and PWE of the last day. Edges indexed by 49, 51, 60, and 63 are experiencing significant traffic delays.

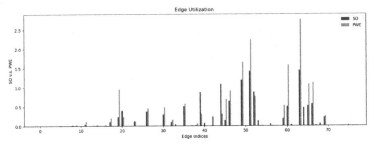

(b) This bar chart compares the edge utilization rate caused by SO and PWE of the last day. Corresponding to Fig. 5a, traffic flows in edges indexed by 49, 51, 60, and 63 are significantly larger than the edge capacities.

Fig. 5. Two edge efficiency comparison bar charts comparing the edge time and edge utilization rate caused by SO and PWE of the last attack.

7 Conclusion

In this paper, we have formulated a Stackelberg game framework to quantify and analyze the impact of informational attacks that aim to manipulate the traffic data to mislead the Online Navigation Platforms (ONP) to provide users with falsified route recommendations.

Through sensitivity analysis, we have shown the continuity and differentiability of the attack utility function and characterized its smoothness level. The result has shown that the PPoA is a C^1-function with respect to the poisoning attack parameters, and an optimal strategy of the attack model can be achieved by a consistent Stackelberg learning process. It reveals the vulnerabilities of the Wardrop Equilibrium (WE)-based flow planning systems and showcases the disruptive effects that an attacker can inflict on the entire traffic network.

Future research directions would include the investigation of the poisoning of transient equilibrium formation behavior and the development of effective defensive and detective strategies against this class of attacks.

A   Path Flow IFT

In the path flow poisoning scenario, the parameterized Lagrangian can be written as:

$$L(\mu,\lambda,\nu,\theta,d) = \sum_{e\in\mathscr{E}} \int_0^{(\Delta\Phi_\theta\mu)_e} \ell_e(z)dz - \lambda^\top\Phi_\theta\mu + \nu^\top(\Lambda\Phi_\theta\mu - \Phi_d Q).$$

Similarly for a candidate solution $\tilde{\mu},\tilde{\lambda},\tilde{\nu}$, write down the KKT conditions as:

$$-\Phi_\theta\mu \preceq 0$$
$$\Delta\Phi_\theta\mu - \Phi_d Q = 0$$
$$\tilde{\lambda}_p \geq 0, \quad p = 1,\ldots,|\mathscr{P}|$$
$$\tilde{\lambda}_p(\Phi_\theta\mu)_p = 0, \quad p = 1,\ldots,|\mathscr{P}|$$
$$\sum_{e\in\mathscr{E}}(\Delta\Phi_\theta)_{pe}^\top\ell_e((\Delta\Phi_\theta\mu)_e) - (\Phi_\theta^\top\lambda)_p + (\Phi_\theta^\top\Lambda^\top\nu)_p = 0, \quad p = 1,\ldots,|\mathscr{P}|$$

Again, we define the parameterized function $g(\tilde{\mu},\tilde{\lambda},\tilde{\nu},\theta,d)$

$$g(\tilde{\mu},\tilde{\lambda},\tilde{\nu},\theta,d) = \begin{bmatrix} \nabla_\mu L(\mu,\lambda,\nu,\theta,d) \\ -\operatorname{diag}(\lambda)\Phi_\theta\mu \\ \Delta\Phi_\theta\mu - \Phi_d Q \end{bmatrix} \tag{25}$$

The partial Jacobian of variable $(\tilde{\mu},\tilde{\lambda},\tilde{\nu})$ is

$$D_{(\tilde{\mu},\tilde{\lambda},\tilde{\nu})}g(\tilde{\mu},\tilde{\lambda},\tilde{\nu},\theta,d) = \begin{bmatrix} D_\mu\nabla_\mu L(\tilde{\mu},\tilde{\lambda},\tilde{\nu},\theta,d) & \Phi_\theta^\top & (\Delta\Phi_\theta)^\top \\ \operatorname{diag}(\tilde{\lambda})\Phi_\theta & \operatorname{diag}(-\Phi_\theta\mu) & 0 \\ \Delta\Phi_\theta & 0 & 0 \end{bmatrix}$$

And the partial Jacobian for θ and d is

$$D_{(\theta,d)}g(\bar{\mu},\tilde{\lambda},\tilde{\nu},\theta,d) = \begin{bmatrix} D_\mu \nabla_\mu L(\bar{\mu},\tilde{\lambda},\tilde{\nu},\theta,d) & \Phi_\theta^\top & (\Delta\Phi_\theta)^\top \\ \mathrm{diag}(\tilde{\lambda})\Phi_\theta & \mathrm{diag}(-\Phi_\theta\mu) & 0 \\ \Delta\Phi_\theta & 0 & 0 \end{bmatrix}. \tag{26}$$

We omit the explicit gradient calculation as there are diverse possibilities of parameterization. Note that in this formulation, the conditions for $D_{(\bar{\mu},\tilde{\lambda},\tilde{\nu})}g$ to be non-singular becomes $\mathrm{diag}(-\Phi_\theta\mu)$ and $(\Delta\Phi_\theta)$ being invertible. A result like Theorem 3 can be derived using a similar analysis.

B   Sketch of Proofs for Sensitivity Analysis

We omit the proofs of Lemma 1 and 2 (a), which is adapted from Lemma 8.3 and Corollary 8.1 of [24] by inserting Φ_θ and Φ_d. The following proofs are based on these preliminary results.

Proof (Lemma 2 ((b))). It suffices to show the smoothness of $\langle q^*(\theta,d)\ell(q^*(\theta,d))\rangle$, for $(\theta_1,d_1),(\theta_2,d_2) \in \Theta \times \mathscr{D}$, denote variable $z_1 = (\theta_1,d_1)$ and $z_2 = (\theta_2,d_2)$, by triangular inequality and Cauchy-Schwarz inequality,

$$\|\langle q^*(z_1)\ell(q^*(z_1))\rangle - \langle q^*(z_2)\ell(q^*(z_2))\rangle\|$$
$$\leq \|\langle q^*(z_1)\ell(q^*(z_1))\rangle - \langle q^*(z_1)\ell(q^*(z_2))\rangle\| + \|\langle q^*(z_1)\ell(q^*(z_2))\rangle - \langle q^*(z_2)\ell(q^*(z_2))\rangle\|$$
$$\leq \|q^*(z_1)\|\|\ell(q^*(z_1)) - \ell(q^*(z_2))\| + \|\ell(q^*(z_2))\|\|q^*(z_1) - q^*(z_2)\|$$
$$\leq \sqrt{|\mathscr{E}|}Dl_q l_0\|z_1 - z_2\| + \sqrt{|\mathscr{E}|}l_q c_0\|z_1 - z_2\|.$$

$\square$

Proof (Lemma 3). Immediately follows substituting the condition $H(x,t) = 0$ in general IFT with Stationarity KKT condition $g(q,\lambda,\theta,d) = 0$, and checking the Shur complement of partial Jacobian $D_{(q,\lambda)}g(\tilde{q},\tilde{\lambda},\theta,d)$. $\square$

Proof (Theorem 1). It suffices to show for variable θ. Taking derivative gives:

$$\nabla_\theta \mathscr{L} = \theta - vec(I_{|\mathscr{E}|}) - \frac{\gamma}{S^*}\langle\nabla_\theta q^*, \ell(q^*)\rangle + \langle q^*, \nabla_\theta q^* D\ell(q^*)\rangle$$

Rearranging the terms yields the results. $\square$

Proof (Theorem 2) For the attack cost term, we can compute the Lipschitz constant with respect to the two variables as $\sqrt{|\mathscr{E}|}\|\theta_1 - \theta_2\|$ and $\sqrt{|\mathscr{W}|}\|d_1 - d_2\|$, respectively. Thus the first part for the constant should be $\sqrt{2}\max\{\sqrt{|\mathscr{E}|}, \sqrt{|\mathscr{W}|}\} = \sqrt{2}\sqrt{|\mathscr{E}|}$. For the second part, multiplying the constant in Lemma 2 (b) with S^* and γ yields the result. $\square$

Proof (Lemma 4). We proceed under the assumption of boundedness and Lipschitz smoothness of $\|\nabla_\theta q^*\|_{op}$. We analyze two terms, $\langle \nabla_\theta q^*, \ell(q^*) \rangle$ and $\langle q^*, \nabla_\theta q^* D\ell(q^*) \rangle$. Write $q^*(\theta_1, d)$ and $q^*(\theta_2, d)$ as q_1^* and q_2^*, respectively. For the first term, we have

$$\|\langle \nabla_\theta q_1^*, \ell(q_1^*) \rangle - \nabla_\theta q_2^*, \ell(q_2^*) \rangle\|$$
$$\leq \|\langle \nabla_\theta q_1^*, \ell(q_1^*) \rangle - \nabla_\theta q_1^*, \ell(q_2^*) \rangle\| + \|\langle \nabla_\theta q_1^*, \ell(q_2^*) \rangle - \nabla_\theta q_2^*, \ell(q_2^*) \rangle\|$$
$$\leq (C_0 l_0 l_q \sqrt{|\mathcal{E}|} + C_1 c_0 \sqrt{|\mathcal{E}|}) \|\theta_1 - \theta_2\|.$$

For the second term, by the monotonicity of ℓ and the sensitivity results,

$$\|\langle q_1^*, \nabla_\theta q_1^* D\ell(q_1^*) \rangle - \langle q_2^*, \nabla_\theta q_2^* D\ell(q_2^*) \rangle\|$$
$$\leq \|\langle q_1^*, \nabla_\theta q_1^* D\ell(q_1^*) \rangle - \langle q_1^*, \nabla_\theta q_2^* D\ell(q_2^*) \rangle\| + \|\langle q_1^*, \nabla_\theta q_2^* D\ell(q_2^*) \rangle - \langle q_2^*, \nabla_\theta q_2^* D\ell(q_2^*) \rangle\|$$
$$\leq \left(\sqrt{|\mathcal{E}|} D(C_0 \sqrt{|\mathcal{E}|} l_1 l_q + C_1 \ell'(D) \sqrt{|\mathcal{E}|}) + l_q C_0 \sqrt{|\mathcal{E}|} \ell'(D) \right) \|\theta_1 - \theta_2\|$$

Summing the two terms together yields the result. □

C   Sketch Proof of Proposition 1

Proof. We show the sample bound for $\nabla_\theta \mathcal{L}$ approximation, the proof of sample bound for $\nabla_d \mathcal{L}$ follows the similar procedure. Let $\hat{V}$ denote the sample average in (22), the approximation error can be broken into two terms:

$$\hat{V} - \nabla_\theta \mathcal{L}((\theta, d), q^*) = \nabla_\theta \mathcal{L}_r^\theta((\theta, d), q^*) - \nabla_\theta \mathcal{L}((\theta, d), q^*) + \hat{V} - \nabla_\theta \mathcal{L}_r^\theta((\theta, d), q^*)$$

For the first term, choose $h_r(1/\varepsilon) = \min\{1/r_0, 2L_1/\varepsilon\}$, by Lemma 4 when $r < 1/h_r(1/\varepsilon) = \varepsilon/2L_1$, $\|\nabla_\theta \mathcal{L}((\theta + u, d), q^*) - \nabla_\theta \mathcal{L}((\theta, d), q^*)\| \leq \varepsilon/4$. Since

$$\nabla_\theta \mathcal{L}_r^\theta((\theta, d), q^*) = \nabla_\theta \mathcal{L}_r^\theta((\theta, d), q^*) = \frac{dim(\Theta)}{r^2} \mathop{\mathbb{E}}_{u \sim \mathbb{S}_r^\theta} [\mathcal{L}((\theta + u, d), q^*) u],$$

by triangular inequality, $\|\nabla_\theta \mathcal{L}_r^\theta((\theta, d), q^*) - \nabla_\theta \mathcal{L}((\theta, d), q^*)\| \leq \varepsilon/2$.

Select r_0 such that for any $u \sim \mathbb{S}_r$, it holds that $\mathcal{L}((\theta + u, d), q^*)$. By Theorem 2, one can select such a r_0 by examining related constants. Since $\mathbb{E}[\hat{V}] = \nabla_\theta \mathcal{L}_r^\theta((\theta, d), q^*)$, and each sampled norm is bounded by $2 dim(\Theta) \mathcal{L}/r$, by vector Bernstein's inequality, when $m \geq h_{sample}(d, 1/\varepsilon) \propto d(\frac{d\mathcal{L}^2}{\varepsilon r}) \log d/\varepsilon$, with probability at least $1 - (d/\varepsilon)^{-d}$, we have

$$\|\hat{V} - \nabla_\theta \mathcal{L}_r^\theta((\theta, d), q^*)\| \leq \varepsilon/2,$$

hence proving the claim. □

References

1. Beckmann, M., McGuire, C.B., Winsten, C.B.: Studies in the economics of transportation. Technical report (1956)
2. Cerrudo, C.: Hacking us traffic control systems. In: Proc. DEFCON **22**, 1–15 (2014)

3. Chakirov, A., Fourie, P.J.: Enriched sioux falls scenario with dynamic and disaggregate demand. Arbeitsberichte Verkehrs-und Raumplanung 978 (2014)
4. Cominetti, R., Dose, V., Scarsini, M.: The price of anarchy in routing games as a function of the demand. CoRR abs/1907.10101 (2019). https://arxiv.org/abs/1907.10101
5. Correa, J.R., Schulz, A.S., Stier-Moses, N.E.: On the inefficiency of equilibria in congestion games. In: Jünger, M., Kaibel, V. (eds.) IPCO 2005. LNCS, vol. 3509, pp. 167–181. Springer, Heidelberg (2005). https://doi.org/10.1007/11496915_13
6. Essers, L.: Hackers can cause traffic jams by manipulating real-time traffic data, researcher says. Computerworld. https://www.computerworld.com/article/2495379/hackers-can-cause-traffic-jams-by-manipulating-real-time-traffic-data-resea.html
7. Flaxman, A.D., Kalai, A.T., McMahan, H.B.: Online convex optimization in the bandit setting: gradient descent without a gradient. arXiv preprint. cs/0408007 (2004)
8. Groot, N., De Schutter, B., Hellendoorn, H.: Toward system-optimal routing in traffic networks: a reverse stackelberg game approach. IEEE Trans. Intell. Transp. Syst. **16**(1), 29–40 (2014)
9. Huq, N., Vosseler, R., Swimmer, M.: Cyberattacks against intelligent transportation systems. TrendLabs Research Paper (2017)
10. Khandelwal, S.: Popular navigation app hijacked with fake bots to cause traffic jam. The Hacker News. https://thehackernews.com/2014/04/popular-navigation-app-hijacked-with.html
11. Kollias, K., Chandrashekharapuram, A., Fawcett, L., Gollapudi, S., Sinop, A.: Weighted stackelberg algorithms for road traffic optimization. In: SIGSPATIAL (2021)
12. Laszka, A., Potteiger, B., Vorobeychik, Y., Amin, S., Koutsoukos, X.: Vulnerability of transportation networks to traffic-signal tampering. In: 2016 ACM/IEEE 7th International Conference on Cyber-Physical Systems (ICCPS), pp. 1–10. IEEE (2016)
13. LeBlanc, L.J., Morlok, E.K., Pierskalla, W.P.: An efficient approach to solving the road network equilibrium traffic assignment problem. Transp. Res. **9**(5), 309–318 (1975). https://doi.org/10.1016/0041-1647(75)90030-1. https://www.sciencedirect.com/science/article/pii/0041164775900301
14. Lou, J., Vorobeychik, Y.: Decentralization and security in dynamic traffic light control. In: Proceedings of the Symposium and Bootcamp on the Science of Security, pp. 90–92 (2016)
15. Meir, R., Parkes, D.: Playing the wrong game: smoothness bounds for congestion games with behavioral biases. ACM SIGMETRICS Perform. Eval. Rev. **43**(3), 67–70 (2015)
16. Ng, M., Park, J., Waller, S.T.: A hybrid bilevel model for the optimal shelter assignment in emergency evacuations. Comput.-Aided Civil Infrastruct. Eng. **25**(8), 547–556 (2010)
17. O'DEA, W.: Congestion pricing with an exogenously imposed speed limit. Int. J. Transp. Econ./Riv. Internazionale di economia dei trasporti, vol. 28(2), pp. 229–248 (2001). https://www.jstor.org/stable/42747597
18. Patriksson, M., Rockafellar, R.T.: A mathematical model and descent algorithm for bilevel traffic management. Transp. Sci. **36**(3), 271–291 (2002). https://www.jstor.org/stable/25769111
19. for Research Core Team., T.N.: Transportation networks for research, 01 July 2022. https://github.com/bstabler/TransportationNetworks
20. Rosenthal, R.W.: A class of games possessing pure-strategy nash equilibria. Internat. J. Game Theory **2**(1), 65–67 (1973)
21. Roughgarden, T.: The price of anarchy is independent of the network topology. J. Comput. Syst. Sci. **67**(2), 341–364 (2003)
22. Roughgarden, T.: Algorithmic game theory. Commun. ACM **53**(7), 78–86 (2010)
23. Schoon, B.: Google maps "hack" uses 99 smartphones to create virtual traffic jams. 9to5Google. https://9to5google.com/2020/02/04/google-maps-hack-virtual-traffic-jam/

24. Still, G.: Lectures on parametric optimization: an introduction. Optimization Online (2018)
25. Wang, Y., Sarkar, E., Li, W., Maniatakos, M., Jabari, S.E.: Stop-and-go: exploring backdoor attacks on deep reinforcement learning-based traffic congestion control systems. IEEE Trans. Inf. Forensics Secur. **16**, 4772–4787 (2021)
26. Wardrop, J.G.: Road paper. some theoretical aspects of road traffic research. Proceedings of the Institution of Civil Engineers, vol. 1, no. (3), pp. 325–362 (1952)

Reward Delay Attacks on Deep Reinforcement Learning

Anindya Sarkar[✉], Jiarui Feng, Yevgeniy Vorobeychik, Christopher Gill,
and Ning Zhang

Department of Computer Science and Engineering, Washington University in St. Louis,
St. Louis, MO 63130, USA
{anindya,feng.jiarui,yvorobeychik,cdgill,zhang.ning}@wustl.edu

Abstract. Most reinforcement learning algorithms implicitly assume strong synchrony. We present novel attacks targeting Q-learning that exploit a vulnerability entailed by this assumption by delaying the reward signal for a limited time period. We consider two types of attack goals: *targeted attacks*, which aim to cause a target policy to be learned, and *untargeted attacks*, which simply aim to induce a policy with a low reward. We evaluate the efficacy of the proposed attacks through a series of experiments. Our first observation is that reward-delay attacks are extremely effective when the goal is simply to minimize reward. Indeed, we find that even naive baseline reward-delay attacks are also highly successful in minimizing the reward. Targeted attacks, on the other hand, are more challenging, although we nevertheless demonstrate that the proposed approaches remain highly effective at achieving the attacker's targets. In addition, we introduce a second threat model that captures a minimal mitigation that ensures that rewards cannot be used out of sequence. We find that this mitigation remains insufficient to ensure robustness to attacks that delay, but preserve the order, of rewards.

Keywords: Deep reinforcement learning · Adversarial attack · Reward delay attack

1 Introduction

In recent years, deep reinforcement learning (DRL) has achieved super-human level performance in a number of applications including game playing [28], clinical decision support [24], and autonomous driving [18]. However, as we aspire to bring DRL to safety-critical settings, such as autonomous driving, it is important to ensure that we can reliably train policies in realistic scenarios, such as on autonomous vehicle testing tracks [1,13,29]. In such settings, reward signals are often not given exogenously, but derived from sensory information. For example, in lane following, the reward may be a function of vehicle orientation and position relative to the center of the lane, and these features are obtained from perception [14,32]. Since many such settings are also safety-critical, any adversarial tampering with the training process—particularly, with the integrity of the reward stream derived from perceptual information—can have disastrous consequences.

© The Author(s), under exclusive license to Springer Nature Switzerland AG 2023
F. Fang et al. (Eds.): GameSec 2022, LNCS 13727, pp. 212–230, 2023.
https://doi.org/10.1007/978-3-031-26369-9_11

A number of recent efforts demonstrated vulnerability of deep reinforcement learning algorithms to adversarial manipulation of the reward stream [3,15,20,22]. We consider an orthogonal attack vector which presumes that the adversary has compromised the *scheduler* and is thereby able to manipulate reward timing, but cannot modify rewards directly. For example, ROS 2.0 features modular design with few security checks and the ability to substitute different *executors* [5,6,8,9,30]. This means that once adversaries gain access to the ROS software stack, they can replace its scheduling policy readily, and as long as the executor behavior is not overtly malicious it can be a long time before the compromise has been discovered. Additionally, we assume that the adversary can infer (but not modify) memory contents using side channel attacks. This is a realistic assumption, since it has been demonstrated that it is feasible to leverage different types of system or architectural side channels, such as cache-based or proc-fs based side channels to infer secret information in other ROS modules [10,19,25]. However, write access to memory is often a lot more difficult to obtain due to existing process isolation [11,12].

Our attack exploits a common assumption of *synchrony* in reinforcement learning algorithms. Specifically, we assume that the adversary can delay rewards a bounded number of time steps (for example, by scheduling tasks computing a reward at time t after the task computing a reward at time $t + k$ for some integer $k \geq 0$). We consider two variations of such *reward delay* attacks. In the first, we allow the adversary to arbitrarily shuffle or drop rewards, assuming effectively that no security mechanisms are in place at all. Our second model evaluates the efficacy of the most basic security mechanism in which we can detect any rewards computed out of their arrival sequence, for example, through secure time stamping. Consequently, we propose the *reward shifting* attacks, where in order to remain undetected, the adversary can only drop rewards, or *shift* these a bounded number of steps into the future. Efficacy comparison between these two threat models will then exhibit the extent to which this simple security solution reduces vulnerability to reward delay attacks. In both attack variants, we consider two adversarial goals: untargeted attacks, which aim to minimize total reward accumulated at prediction time (essentially, eroding the efficacy of training), and targeted attacks, the goal of which is to cause the RL algorithm to learn a policy that takes target actions in specific target states.

We specifically study attacks on deep Q-learning algorithms. The adversarial model we introduce is a complex discrete dynamic optimization problem, even in this more narrow class of DRL algorithms. We propose an algorithmic framework for attacks that is itself based on deep Q learning, leveraging the fact that the current Q function, along with the recent sequence of states, actions, and rewards observed at training, provide sufficient information about system state from the attacker's perspective. The key practical challenge is how to design an appropriate reward function, given that the "true" reward is a property of the final policy resulting from long training, and only truly possible to evaluate at test time. We address this problem by designing proxy reward functions for both untargeted and targeted attacks that make use of only the information immediately available at training time.

We evaluate the proposed approach experimentally using two Atari games in OpenAI gym: Pong and Breakout. Our experiments demonstrate that the proposed attacks are highly effective, and remain nearly as effective even with the simple mitigation that ensures that rewards are not encountered out of order. Altogether, our results demonstrate the importance of implementing sound security practices, such as hardware and software-level synchrony assurance [21,27], in safety-critical applications of reinforcement learning.

2   Related Work

There are two closely related literature strands in attacks on reinforcement learning and multiarmed bandits: attacks that take place at decision time, and poisoning attacks.

Decision-Time attacks on Reinforcement Learning. Prior literature on adversarial attacks against RL has focused mainly on inference time attacks [3,15,20,22], where the RL policy π is pre-trained and fixed, and the attacker manipulates the perceived state s_t of the learner to s'_t in order to induce undesired actions, while restricting s'_t and s_t to be very similar to (or human-indistinguishable from) each other. For example, in video games the attacker can make small pixel perturbations to a frame to induce an action $\pi(s'_t) \neq \pi(s_t)$. [15] developed the uniform attack mechanism, which generates adversarial examples by perturbing each image the agent observes to attack a deep RL agent at every time step in an episode in order to reduce the agent's reward. [15] also introduced a decision time targeted attack strategy, i.e. enchanting attack tactic, which is a planning-based adversarial attack to mislead the agent towards a target state. [22] proposed a strategically timed attack, which can reach the same effect of the uniform attack by attacking the agent four times less often on average. [20] leverages the policy's value function as a guide for when to inject adversarial perturbations and shows that with guided injection, the attacker can inject perturbations in a fraction of the frames, and this is more successful than injecting perturbations with the same frequency but no guidance. [3] proposes an attack mechanism that exploits the transferability of adversarial examples to implement policy induction attacks on deep Q networks. Although test-time attacks can severely affect the performance of a fixed policy π during deployment, they do not modify the policy π itself.

Reward Poisoning Attacks on Reinforcement Learning. Reward poisoning has been studied in bandits [2,17,23,26], where the authors show that an adversarially perturbed reward can mislead standard bandit algorithms to suffer large regret. Reward poisoning has also been studied in batch RL where rewards are stored in a pre-collected batch data set by some behavior policy, and the attacker modifies the batch data [16,34–36]. [16] provides a set of threat models for RL and establishes a framework for studying strategic manipulation of cost signals in RL. [16] also provides results to understand how manipulations of cost signals can affect Q-factors and hence the policies learned by RL agents. [36] proposed an adaptive reward poisoning attack against RL, where the perturbation at time t not only depends on (s_t, a_t, s_{t+1}) but also relies on the RL agent's Q-value at time t. [35] presents a solution to the problem of finding limited incentives to induce a particular target policy, and provides tractable methods to elicit the desired policy after a few interactions. Note that all these previous works directly modify the value of the reward signal itself, by adding a quantity δ_t to the true reward $r(t)$, i.e. $r'(t) = r_t + \delta_t$. In contrast, we focus on delaying the reward signal with the aim to mislead a learner RL agent, but cannot directly modify the rewards. As such, our key contribution is the novel threat model that effectively exploits the common synchrony assumption in reinforcement learning.

3   Model

Consider a discounted Markov Decision Process (MDP) with a set of states S, set of actions A, expected reward function $r(s, a)$, transition function $P_{ss'}^{\alpha} = \Pr\{s_{t+1} = s'|s_t = s, a_t = a\}$, discount factor $\gamma \in [0, 1)$, and initial state distribution $D(s) = \Pr\{s_0 = s\}$. Suppose that we only know S and A, but must learn an optimal policy $\pi(s)$ from experience using reinforcement learning. To this end, we consider a Deep Q-Network (DQN) reinforcement learning framework; it is straightforward to extend our approach to other variants of deep Q learning. Let $Q(s, a; \theta)$ be a neural network with parameters θ representing the Q-function, and let $Q_t(s, a; \theta_t)$ denote an approximation of the Q-function at iteration t of RL (which we also denote by Q_t when the input is clear, and $Q_t(s, a; \theta)$ when we treat θ as a variable). In the DQN, parameters θ are updated after each iteration using the loss function $L(\theta) = (r_t + \gamma \max_{a'} Q_t(s_{t+1}, a'; \theta) - Q_t(s_t, a_t; \theta))^2$. Below, we omit the explicit dependence on θ. As this update rule makes evident, without experience replay the DQN training process itself is a Markov decision process (MDP) in which $\sigma_t = (Q_t, (s_t, a_t, r_t, s_{t+1}))$ constitutes state. Let T be the total number of DQN update iterations. This observation will be useful below. Given a Q function obtained at the end of T learning iterations, $Q_T(s, a)$, we assume that the learner will follow a deterministic policy that is optimal with respect to this function, i.e., $\pi(s) = \arg\max_a Q_T(s, a)$. For convenience, we abuse this notation slightly, using $\pi(s, a)$ as an indicator which is 1 if action a is played in state s, and 0 otherwise.

Suppose that the attacker has compromised the scheduler, which can delay a reward computed at any time step by a bounded number of time steps δ (for example, to prevent attacks from appearing too obvious). Attacks of this kind take advantage of the settings in which reward needs to be computed based on perceptual information. For example, the goal may be to learn a lane-following policy, with rewards computed based on vehicle location relative to lane markers inferred from camera and GPS/IMU data. A compromised scheduler can delay the computation associated with a reward, but cannot directly modify rewards (contrasting our attacks from prior research on reward poisoning [16, 34–36]). As a useful construct, we endow the attacker with a δ-sized disk $\mathcal{D}$ in which the past rewards are stored, and the attacker can utilize $\mathcal{D}$ to replace the original reward used to update the Q-function parameters at time t.

We consider two common attack goals: 1) *untargeted attacks* which simply aim to minimize the reward obtained by the learned policy, and 2) *targeted attacks*, which attempt to cause the learner to learn a policy that takes particular target actions. To formalize these attack goals, let $\mathbf{r}^{\alpha} = \{r_0^{\alpha}, \ldots, r_{T-1}^{\alpha}\}$ be an adversarial reward stream induced by our attack, resulting in the learned Q function $\tilde{Q}_T(s, a; \mathbf{r}^{\alpha})$. On the other hand, let $Q_T(s, a)$ be the Q function learned without adversarial reward perturbations.

Let $\tilde{\pi}(s; \mathbf{r}^{\alpha})$ be the policy induced by $\tilde{Q}_T$, with $\tilde{\pi}(s, a; \mathbf{r}^{\alpha})$ a binary indicator of which action is taken in which state. The goal of an untargeted attack is

$$\min_{\mathbf{r}^{\alpha}} \sum_a \tilde{\pi}(s, a; \mathbf{r}^{\alpha}) Q_T(s, a). \tag{1}$$

For a targeted attack, we define a *target policy* as a set-value function $f(s)$ which maps each state to a set of target actions, i.e., $f : S \to 2^A$, where $f(s) \subseteq A$ for each state $s \in S$. That is, the attacker aims to cause the learned policy $\tilde{\pi}$ to take one of a target actions $f(s)$, that is, $\tilde{\pi}(s; \mathbf{r}^{\alpha}) \subseteq f(s)$. A natural special case is when $f(s)$ is a singleton for each state s. This objective can be equivalently expressed in terms of the learned Q function $\tilde{Q}_T$ as the following condition in each state s:

$$\max_{a \in f(s)} \tilde{Q}_T(s, a; \mathbf{r}^{\alpha}) > \max_{a \notin f(s)} \tilde{Q}_T(s, a; \mathbf{r}^{\alpha}), \quad \forall s : f(s) \neq \pi(s). \tag{2}$$

We assume that the current state σ_t of the DQN algorithm is observed by the adversary at each time t. This assumption amounts to the compromised scheduler being able to read memory. This can be done either because the adversary has gained access to kernel space, or through a side-channel attack that recovers memory contents [10, 19, 25].

Our key observation is that whichever of the above goals the attacker chooses, since learning itself can be modeled as an MDP, the attacker's problem also becomes an MDP in which the state is $o_t = (\sigma_t, \mathcal{D}_t)$, where $\mathcal{D}_t$ is the state of the attacker disk (i.e., rewards saved, and their current delay length). The reward in this MDP is defined as above for both untargeted and targeted attacks. Let O denote the set of possible states in the attacker MDP. Next, we define two types of reward-delay attacks, which then determine the action space.

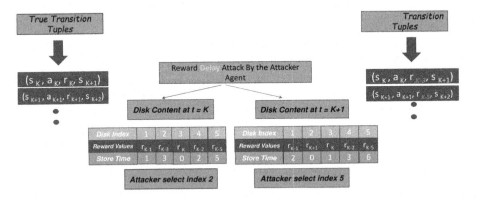

Fig. 1. Reward delay attack model.

We consider two variants of the reward delay attack. The first is a general *reward delay* variant in which rewards can be swapped arbitrarily or dropped, with the only constraint that if a reward is delayed, it is by at most δ time steps. The attacker also has the option of waiting at time t. In particular, at time t, the attacker can publish (e.g., by prioritizing the scheduling of) a reward $r_t^\alpha \in \mathcal{D}_t$ selected from disk at time t, $\mathcal{D}_t$; the implied set of attacker actions at time t is denoted by $A_t^\alpha = A^\alpha(o_t)$ (since it depends on the current state o_t). As a result, the learner receives the transition tuple $(s_t, a_t, r_t^\alpha, s_{t+1})$ in place of (s_t, a_t, r_t, s_{t+1}), where the current reward r_t is added to disk, obtaining the disk $\mathcal{D}_{t+1}$ for the next training step. We present an illustrative visualization of the *reward delay* attack model in Fig. 1.

A minimal level of security that a learner can easily implement is to securely time stamp incoming sensor data. Our goal is to evaluate how much impact this minimal level of protection has on the attack efficacy. To this end, we introduce a second significantly more constrained attack variant that only allows *reward shifting*: rewards can only be shifted forward (effectively, dropping some of these), but not arbitrarily swapped. In reward shifting attacks, since the sequence must be preserved, any time the attacker selects a reward $r_t^\alpha \in \mathcal{D}_t$ to publish, it must be the case that the time stamp on this reward exceeds that of the reward published at time $t - 1$. Consequently, the disc $\mathcal{D}_{t+1}$ is updated with the actual reward r_t, but all rewards in $\mathcal{D}_t$ with time stamp earlier than r_t^α are also removed (effectively, dropped). Additionally, the attacker has the option of waiting at time t, publishing a reward (or a sequence of rewards) at a later time point from the disk, which are then aligned in the corresponding temporal sequence with states and actions used for DQN updates. We present an illustrative visualization of the *reward shifting* attack model in Fig. 2. We denote the implied action space for the attacker in reward shifting attacks by $A_t^{\alpha,\text{shift}} = A^{\alpha,\text{shift}}(o_t)$. Next, we present our algorithmic approaches for implementing the attack variants above.

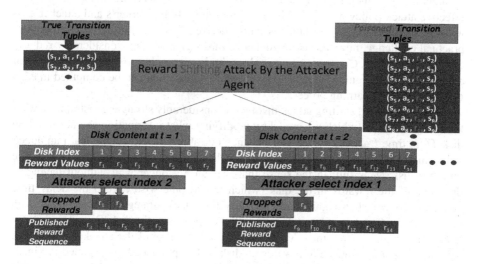

Fig. 2. Reward shifting attack model.

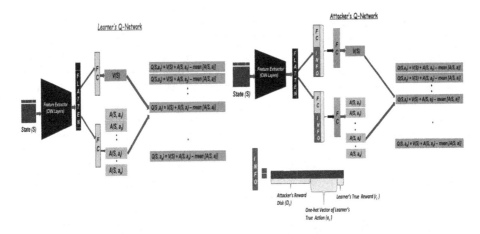

Fig. 3. Learner's and Attacker's Q-network.

4 Algorithmic Approaches for Reward-Delay Attacks

Recall that general reward-delay attacks can be represented by an attacker MDP with state space O and action sets $A^\alpha(o)$ for the general reward-delay attacks, and $A^{\alpha,\text{shift}}(o)$ for reward shifting attacks, where $o \in O$ is the current state. Since the state space is in general high-dimensional, it is natural to apply deep Q-learning attacks to learn an effective attack policy $\pi^\alpha(o)$. In Fig. 3 we present both the learner's and attacker's Q-network architecture (as the latter is partly derived from the former). An important practical challenge, however, is that delay reward signal so long considerably reduces efficacy of learning. Consequently, our algorithmic approaches to the different types of attacks involve designing effective proxy-reward signals that can be computed in each time step t of the learning process.

Since the reward shifting attack involves a considerably stronger constraint on what the attacker can do (which we model by modifying what information can be stored on disk $\mathcal{D}_t$ at time t above), we further enhance our ability to effectively learn an attack policy in two ways. First, we heavily leverage the *wait* option by delaying attack choice until the disk $\mathcal{D}_t$ is full, in the sense that we can no longer wait without having to drop one of the rewards in the disk (which would otherwise exceed the delay time constraint δ). We then significantly simplify the attack strategy by selecting a *drop index* i (where $0 \le i \le K$) and dropping all the rewards in the disk $\mathcal{D}_t$ with index $\le i$ from consideration. Note that, $K < d$, where d is the size of the attacker's disk. The residual temporal sequence of rewards on disk is then published (as depicted in Fig. 2) and used to train the learner's Q-network, and finally the attacker's disk is emptied. This reduces the policy consideration space to only the choice of an index of the reward to drop given a full disk.

At this point, the only remaining piece of the attack approach is the design of the proxy reward function, which we turn to next. Armed with appropriate proxy reward functions, we can apply any deep Q-network based algorithm for learning an attack policy for any of the attacks discussed above.

4.1 Proxy Reward Design for Untargeted Attacks

For untargeted attacks, suppose that Q_t is the *learner's* Q function in iteration t. Since DQN updates are deterministic, the learner's Q function Q_{t+1} can be precomputed for any reward r_t^α published by the attacker. Let s_t be the state observed by the learner at time t. We propose the following proxy reward for the attacker which is used for the *attacker's* DQN update:

$$\tilde{R}_t^{\text{att}} = \sum_{a \in A} -(\tilde{\pi}_{t+1}(s_t, a) \cdot Q_t(s_t, a)),$$

$$\text{where } \tilde{\pi}_{t+1}(s_t, a) = \frac{\exp(\tilde{Q}_{t+1}(s_t, a))}{\sum_{a' \in A} \exp(\tilde{Q}_{t+1}(s_t, a'))} \tag{3}$$

where $Q_t(s_t)$ is the *true* Q function vector and $\tilde{Q}_{t+1}(s_t)$ is the *proxy* Q function vector corresponding to all the learner's actions in step t and $t + 1$, respectively. Note that the learner's *true* $Q_{t+1}(s_t)$ is obtained by updating $Q_t(s_t)$ using randomly sampled batch data stored in the learner's replay buffer, whereas, the learner's *proxy* $\tilde{Q}_{t+1}(s_t)$ is obtained by updating $Q_t(s_t)$ using the recent transition tuples published by the attacker. The intuition for this proxy reward is that it accomplishes two things at once: first, by minimizing correlation between successive Q functions, the attacker minimizes the marginal impact of learning updates, thereby causing learning to fail, and second, if the learner happens to obtain a good estimate of the true Q function in iteration t, the quality of this function is actively reduced in iteration $t + 1$.

4.2 Proxy Reward Design for Targeted Attacks

The intuition for our proposed proxy reward function in the case of targeted attacks is to maximize similarity between the target policy $f(s)$ and the policy induced by the current Q function Q_t. However, since the policy induced by Q_t is not differential, we replace it with a stochastic policy $\pi_t(s_t) = \text{softmax}(Q_t(s_t))$, where

$$\pi_t(s_t, a) = \frac{\exp(Q_t(s_t, a))}{\sum_{a' \in A} \exp(Q_t(s_t, a'))}.$$

Further, we represent $f(s)$ as a vector $\hat{f}(s, a)$

$$\hat{f}(s, a) \leftarrow \begin{cases} 1, & \text{if } a \in f(s, a) \\ 0, & \text{o.w.} \end{cases} \tag{4}$$

$\hat{f}(s)$ then denotes the binary vector corresponding to $f(s)$. We then define the proxy reward for a targeted attack as follows:

$$\tilde{R}_t^{\text{att}} = \text{sign}\{\mathcal{L}_{CE}(\pi_t(s_t), \hat{f}(s_t)) - \mathcal{L}_{CE}(\tilde{\pi}_{t+1}(s_t), \hat{f}(s_t))\}, \tag{5}$$

where $\mathcal{L}_{CE}$ is the cross-entropy loss. The reward function in (5) suggests that, an attacker receives a positive reward, only if the performed actions of the attacker (i.e. choosing r_t^α from the disk $\mathcal{D}_t$) steers the learner's updated proxy Q-value distribution $\tilde{\pi}_{t+1}(s_t)$ to be more aligned with the target Q-table distribution corresponds to target policy $f(s)$ compared to the learner's previous true Q-value distribution $\pi_t(s_t)$.

4.3 Rule Based Targeted Reward Delay Attack

In addition to a targeted reward delay attack strategy that requires a proxy reward computation of the attacker as defined in Eq. (5), we also propose a simple rule based strategy in order to feed the attacker a reward at a given state as defined in Eq. (6). Note that the attacker's disk configuration at current time step (t) is represented as $\mathcal{D}_t$. According to (6), the attacker feeds back a high reward to the learner, if the learner acts in a way that is preferred by the attacker at any given target state.

$$\tilde{R}_t^{att} \leftarrow \begin{cases} Maximum \text{ Reward in } \mathcal{D}_t, & \text{if } \arg\max_a(Q_t(S_t, a)) \in a^T \text{ and } S_t \in S' \\ Minimum \text{ Reward in } \mathcal{D}_t, & \text{if } \arg\max_a(Q_t(S_t, a)) \notin a^T \text{ and } S_t \in S' \\ Random \text{ Reward in } \mathcal{D}_t, & \text{if } S_t \notin S' \end{cases}$$
(6)

5 Results

We evaluate the effectiveness of the proposed attack approaches on the Pong and Breakout Atari-2600 environments in OpenAI Gym [7] on top of the Arcade Learning Environment [4]. The states in those environments are high dimensional RGB images with dimensions (210 * 160 * 3) and discrete actions that control the agent to accomplish certain tasks. Specifically, we leverage the *NoFrameskip-v4* version for all our experiments, where the randomness that influences the environment dynamics can be fully controlled by fixing the random seed of the environment at the beginning of an episode. Please note that we used a standard computing server with 3 GeForce GTX 1080 Ti GPUs each of 12 GB for all the experiments in our work. We choose the Double DQN algorithm [31] with the Duelling style architecture [33] as the reference Q network for both the learner and attacker agents. Note that our proposed reward-delay attack and reward-shifting attack strategies can be easily applied to other DQN based learning algorithms without requiring further modifications. Unless noted otherwise, we set δ (i.e. the maximum number of time steps a reward can be delayed) to be 8. In the case of a *reward shifting* attack, we choose the maximum value of "drop-index"(K) to be 4, and attacker's maximum disk size (effectively, maximum wait time before implementing the attack) to be 8. We also perform experiments to show the impact of the reward delay attack for different choices of attack hyper-parameters.

We compare our approaches to two baselines: *random attack* and *fixed-delay attack*. In the random attack, an attacker chooses to publish a reward randomly from the disk at every time-step. In the fixed-delay attack, the attacker delays the reward signal by δ time steps. In addition, in the reward shifting attack setting, we use a *random reward*

Shift baseline, where in place of an attacker agent, we randomly select a value for "drop-index" (ranging from index 0 to K) to drop the reward. Apart from this step, the random baseline attack operates exactly as the *reward shifting* attack.

For untargeted attacks, our measure of effectiveness is the expected total reward at test time. In the case of targeted attacks, we evaluate the *success rate* of the attacks, measured as follows:

$$SuccessRate(SR) = \frac{\sum_{s \in S'} \mathbb{I}[a_t \in f(s)]}{No.\ of\ times\ agent\ visits\ target\ states}, \quad (7)$$

where $\mathbb{I}[.]$ is an indicator function and S' is a set of *target states* in which the attacker has a non-trivial preference over which action is played. Equation (7) yields the fraction of times the policy learned by the targeted RL agent chooses an action in the attacker's target set $f(s)$ in target states $s \in S'$.

In order to generate target policies $f(s)$, and in particular which states constitute target states S', we leverage an (approximately) optimal Q-network (learned without attacks), denoted by Q^*, which gives us a way to decide a subset of states that we target given the target action sets preferred by the attacker; for the remaining states, $f(s)$ allows any action, that is, the attacker is indifferent. Next, we define a state-independent set of target actions a^T; these will be target actions for a subset of target states, which we choose dynamically using the following rule:

$$s_t \leftarrow \begin{cases} \text{Is a Target State,} & \text{if } \arg\max_a(Q^*(S_t, a)) \notin a^T. \\ \text{Not a Target State,} & \text{otherwise.} \end{cases} \quad (8)$$

We describe our choice of the set a^T in the concrete experiment domains below. Note that at every time step in an episode, the learner interacts with the environment, but instead of receiving the true reward from the environment, the learner receives a poisoned reward published by the attacker. We train the learner's Q network with the modified reward sequence published by the attacker and also update the learner's Q network parameter following the Double DQN update rule. In parallel, we train and update the attacker's Q network following the Double DQN update rule as described above (see also Algorithms 1 and 2 in the Supplement). After the completion of each episode, we evaluate the learner's performance on test episodes. We report our results (cumulative rewards, etc.) obtained on these test episodes.

5.1 Untargeted Reward-Delay Attacks

We begin by evaluating the efficacy of the proposed approaches for accomplishing the goals of untargeted attacks. Figure 4 presents the total reward obtained during evaluation as a function of the number of training episodes in Atari Pong and Breakout, respectively. We observe that essentially all baselines perform nearly the same as each other and as our attack, with reward nearly zero in the case of Atari Breakout and nearly –21 in the case of Atari Pong. This clearly contrasts with normal training, which is highly effective. Consequently, in the untargeted setting, even if we limit considerably by how much rewards can be delayed, essentially any reshuffling of rewards entirely prevents effective learning.

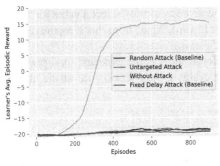
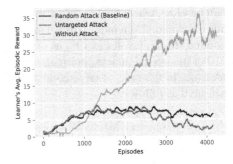

(a) Reward Comparison on Atari Pong.   (b) Reward Comparison on Atari Breakout.

Fig. 4. Effect of reward delay attack on minimizing reward.

We further investigate the efficacy of the untargeted reward delay attacks as we change δ, the maximum delay we can add to a reward (i.e., the maximum we can shift reward back in time relative to the rest of DQN update information), from 8 (the default value in experiments) to 16. As Fig. 5 shows, we see an improvement in the attack efficacy as would be expected intuitively; what is surprising, however, is that this improvement is extremely slight, even though we doubled the amount of time the reward can be delayed. Our results thus suggest that even a relatively short delay in the reward signal can lead DQN learning to be entirely ineffective.

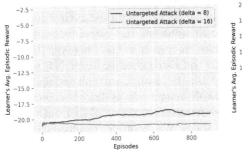
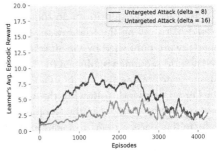

(a) Effect of δ on Untargeted Reward Delay At-   (b) Effect of δ on Untargeted Reward Delay Attack Strategy on Atari Pong environment.   tack Strategy on Breakout environment.

Fig. 5. Effect of δ.

We also examine the effectiveness of the untargeted reward delay attacks on a pre-trained Q network. Figure 6 depicts the net reward obtained by the pre-trained Q network during evaluation as a function of the number of training episodes in Atari Pong and Breakout, respectively. Our experimental finding indicates that, the reward decays exponentially as training progresses. We also notice that even naive baseline untargeted attacks are as effective as the untargeted reward delay attack in reducing the reward of the pretrained network. Such observations shows the importance of reward synchrony at every phase of deep reinforcement learning training.

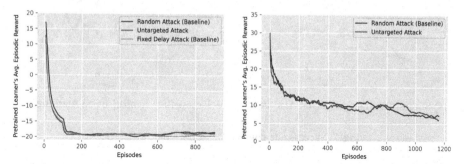

(a) Effect of Untargeted Reward Delay Attack Strategy on a Pre-trained Q network on Atari Pong environment.

(b) Effect of Untargeted Reward Delay Attack Strategy on a Pre-trained Q network on Breakout environment.

Fig. 6. Effect of reward delay attack on a Pre-trained Q network.

Next, we evaluate the efficacy of our approach in the context of the far more challenging targeted attacks.

5.2 Targeted Reward-Delay Attacks

In targeted attacks, we aim to achieve a particular target action (or one of a set of actions) in a subset of *target states*, with the attacker indifferent about which action is taken in the remaining states. In both Pong and Breakout environments, we chose *do not move* as the target action for this evaluation. Target states were defined using the condition in Eq. (8).

In Fig. 7, we compare the efficacy of our approach for targeted attacks compared to our baseline approach. Here we can see that the proposed targeted attack approaches are considerably more effective than the baseline, with success rate significantly higher than the best baseline in both Pong and Breakout. Interestingly, we can also see that while the proposed attack improves in efficacy with the number of training episodes, the baselines either have a constant success rate (essentially due entirely to chance), or the success rate of these may even decrease (we can see a mild decrease in the case of Pong, in particular). We also observe that the rule based reward delay targeted attack strategy is highly effective in achieving the targeted attack objective.

We further look into the effectiveness of targeted reward delay attacks as we vary δ, the maximum delay we can add to a reward. We present those results in Fig. 8. We observe that the *success rate* stays the same as we change the δ in both Atari Pong and Breakout environments.

Next, we assess the effectiveness of reward-shifting attacks, which are more constrained than reward delay attacks.

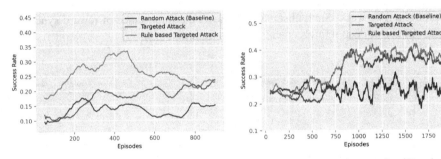

(a) Success Rate comparison on Atari Pong.   (b) Success Rate comparison on Atari Breakout.

Fig. 7. Success rate comparison of reward delay attack.

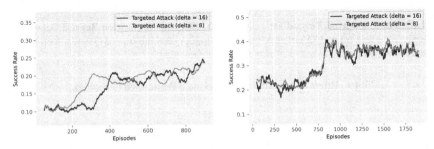

(a) Effect of δ on Targeted Reward Delay Attack   (b) Effect of δ on Targeted Reward Delay Attack
Strategy on Atari Pong environment.   Strategy on Breakout environment.

Fig. 8. Effect of δ.

5.3   Reward Shifting Attacks

We now turn to evaluating the effectiveness of a simple defense in which we ensure that rewards cannot be shuffled out of sequence. To this end, we evaluate the efficacy of the proposed reward shifting attacks, and compare that to our observations of the efficacy of reward delay attacks above.

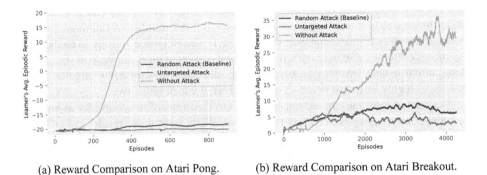

(a) Reward Comparison on Atari Pong.   (b) Reward Comparison on Atari Breakout.

Fig. 9. Effect of reward shifting attack on minimizing reward.

In Fig. 9, we present the results of the *reward shifting* attack in the Pong and Break-out environments. First, we observe that both the baseline and our untargeted reward shifting attacks are as effective as any of the attacks without the sequence-preserving constraint. Moreover, the proposed untargeted attack is now tangibly better than its baseline (random) counterpart, with the gap increasing with the number of episodes. In addition, Fig. 10 shows that the net episodic reward of a pre-trained Q network drops exponentially when trained with the untargeted reward shifting attack strategy. We also found that even a random reward shifting attack is highly capable of reducing the reward of a pre-trained Q network. Such findings indicate the adverse impact of incorrect reward timing on deep reinforcement learning. So, not only the *ordering of the reward sequence*, but the *precise timings of the reward sequence* are also very important for efficient deep reinforcement learning.

Nevertheless, the defense is clearly not effective in mitigating the untargeted reward shifting attacks. In the Pong environment, our proposed untargeted reward shifting attack yields reward near -20—that is almost what was achieved without any mitigation at all, but a far cry from the result of nominal training. Similarly, the reward after our attack in the Breakout environment is still far below what is achievable without attack.

Finally, we investigate the potency of the reward shifting attack in the context of the targeted attack. We report those results in Fig. 11. We observe that the targeted reward shifting attack actually yields a higher success rate compared to the baseline random reward shifting attack in both Atari Pong and Breakout environments, with the success rate gap increasing with the number of episodes.

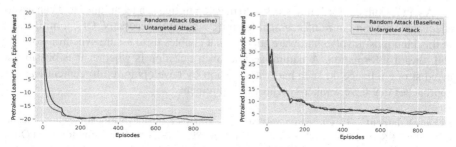

(a) Effect of Untargeted Reward Shifting Attack (b) Effect of Untargeted Reward Shifting Attack on a Pre-trained Q network on Pong environment. on a Pre-trained Q network on Breakout env.

Fig. 10. Effect of reward shifting attack on a Pre-trained Q network.

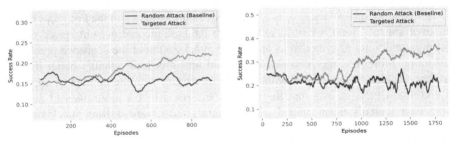

(a) Success Rate Comparison on Atari Pong.   (b) Success Rate Comparison on Atari Breakout.

Fig. 11. Success rate of reward shifting attack.

6   Conclusions

We study the problem of reward delay attacks against reinforcement learning agents. Our empirical findings suggest that it is possible to induce a sub-optimal policy, or even a specific target policy by strategically reshuffling the true reward sequence. Indeed, we find that even randomly shuffling rewards within relatively short time intervals is already sufficient to cause learning failure. This raises a potentially serious security threat to different downstream applications that rely on RL. Moreover, we showed that reward shifting attacks that assure that reward signals are not observed out of order, also have a disastrous effect on DQN learning. Our finding shows that current deep RL training strategy falls far short of ensuring adequate robustness to these in many cases.

A natural subject for future work is to develop mitigation techniques that can assure adequate synchrony in reinforcement learning when it is necessary. Often, mitigations of this kind must involve hardware support that enables us to assure synchrony of state and reward information. A natural second open question is whether it is possible to avoid strong reliance on such hardware support by developing reinforcement learning approaches that have weaker synchrony requirements.

Acknowledgments. This research was supported in part by the National Science Foundation (grants IIS-1905558, IIS-2214141, ECCS-2020289, CNS-2038995), Army Research Office (grant W911NF1910241), and NVIDIA.

7   Appendix

In this section, we present the end-to-end algorithmic approach of reward delay attack strategy and reward shifting attack strategy in Algorithm 1 and 2 respectively.

Algorithm 1. Reward Delay Attack Strategy

Input: $Q_t(s_t, a_t, \theta)$ - learner's ($\mathcal{A}$) current Q-network parameterized by θ; An attacker agent $\mathcal{A}'$ with corresponding MDP $\mathcal{M}' = (\Xi', \rho', \tau')$, Q-network($Q'$) parameterized by θ', disk $\mathcal{D}_0$ to store the rewards and attack constraint parameters $\{\delta, d\}$; Action set of the $\mathcal{A}'$, i.e. $A \in \{1,2,...,d\}$ where d is the disk size; T - No. of time-steps in an episode; $\mathcal{B}, \mathcal{B}'$ - Replay buffer of $\mathcal{A}$ and $\mathcal{A}'$;

1: **for** t=0, 1, ..., T **do**
2:     $\mathcal{A}$ interacts with the environment by taking an action a_t given a state s_t. Environment transits according to $P(s_{t+1}|s_t, a_t)$, and feeds back a reward signal r_t and a next state s_{t+1}.
3:     $\mathcal{A}$ extracts (s_t, a_t, r_t, s_{t+1}) and push r_t into $\mathcal{D}_t$.
4:     $\mathcal{A}'$ leverages the following information to act: $info_t = [s_t, a_t, r_t, \mathcal{D}_t]$ and learner's Q_t.
5:     $\mathcal{A}'$ takes action a'_t according to ϵ-greedy behavior policy

$$i \leftarrow \begin{cases} argmax_{a \in A} \ Q'_t(info_t, a, \theta'), & \text{If } 1 - \epsilon \\ \text{Randomly select from } A, & \text{else} \end{cases}$$

6:     r_t (the true reward) is exchanged with $r_i^{\mathcal{D}}$ (The reward stored at the i'th index in the disk $\mathcal{D}_t$). Accordingly, t'th transitional tuple data is updated as $(s_t, a_t, r_i^{\mathcal{D}}, s_{t+1})$ and stored into $\mathcal{B}$.
7:     Disk $\mathcal{D}_t$ is updated by removing $r_i^{\mathcal{D}}$ from the disk. We also *drop* the reward from $\mathcal{D}_t$ whose stored-time (i.e. delay duration) exceeds δ.
8:     $\mathcal{A}$ performs Q-learning given the poisoned mini-batch transition data sampled from $\mathcal{B}$, where t'th transition tuple of the mini-batch is represented as $(s_t, a_t, r_i^{\mathcal{D}}, s_{t+1})$:

$$y_j \leftarrow \begin{cases} r_i^{\mathcal{D}}, & \text{If } s_{t+1} \text{ is a Terminal State} \\ r_i^{\mathcal{D}} + max_{a'}(Q_t(s_{t+1}, a', \theta)), & \text{else} \end{cases}$$

Update the learner's ($\mathcal{A}$) Q-network parameters from Q_t to Q_{t+1} by minimizing the loss $\mathcal{L}(\theta) = (y_j - Q_t(s_t, a_t, \theta))^2$ following DQN update rule.
9:     $\mathcal{A}'$ computes reward r_t^{attacker} following the methods as described in section 4 and stores the transition tuple $(info_t, a'_t, r_t^{\text{attacker}}, info_{t+1})$ into its own replay buffer $\mathcal{B}'$.
10:     $\mathcal{A}'$ performs Q-learning given the attacker's mini-batch transition data sampled from $\mathcal{B}'$, where t'th transition tuple is denoted as $(info_t, a'_t, r_t^{\text{attacker}}, info_{t+1})$:

$$y_j \leftarrow \begin{cases} r_t^{\text{attacker}}, & \text{If } info_{t+1} \text{ is a Terminal State} \\ r_t^{\text{attacker}} + max_{a' \in A}(Q'_t(info_{t+1}, a', \theta')), & \text{else} \end{cases}$$

11:     $\mathcal{A}'$ also updates it's Q-network parameter θ' by minimizing $\mathcal{L}(\theta) = (y_j - Q'_t(info_t, a'_t, \theta'))^2$.
12: **end for**
13: **return** $\mathcal{A}$ and it's corresponding Q-network parameter θ;

Algorithm 2. Reward Shifting Attack Strategy

Input: $Q_t(s_t, a_t, \theta)$ - learner's ($\mathcal{A}$) current Q-network parameterized by θ; An attacker ($\mathcal{A}'$) with corresponding MDP $\mathcal{M}' = (\Xi', \rho', \tau')$, Q-network($Q'$) parameterized by θ', disk $\mathcal{D}_0$ to store the rewards and attack constraint parameters $\{l, d\}$; Action set of the $\mathcal{A}'$, i.e. $A \in \{1,2,...,K\}$; $\mathcal{B}, \mathcal{B}'$ - are Learner's and attacker's Replay Buffer respectively; T - The no. of time-steps in an episode.

1: **for** t=0, 1, ..., T **do**
2:    $\mathcal{A}$ interacts with the environment which results a transition tuple (s_t, a_t, r_t, s_{t+1}).
3:    $\mathcal{A}'$ Extract (s_t, a_t, r_t, s_{t+1}) and push reward r_t into $\mathcal{D}_t$.
4:    $\mathcal{A}'$ leverages the following information to act when $\mathcal{D}_t$ is full: $info_t = [s_t, a_t, r_t, \mathcal{D}_t]$ and Q_t.
5:    $\mathcal{A}'$ takes action a'_t according to ϵ-greedy behavior policy when $\mathcal{D}_t$ is full.

$$i \leftarrow \begin{cases} argmax_{a \in A} \ Q'_t(info_t, a, \theta'), & \text{If } 1 - \epsilon \\ \text{Randomly select from } A, & \text{else} \end{cases}$$

6:    $\mathcal{A}'$ publishes an updated reward sequence with the following modifications: Firstly, the rewards stored from index 0 to i are dropped, Secondly, the reward sequence ranging from index $(i + 1)$ to d is published in sequence. We denote the attacker's published reward sequence as $\{r_1^{\mathcal{D}}, r_2^{\mathcal{D}}, .., r_t^{\mathcal{D}}, ..\}$.
7:    $\mathcal{A}$ performs Q-learning given the poisoned mini-batch transition data sampled from $\mathcal{B}$, where t'th transition tuple of the mini-batch is represented as $(s_t, a_t, r_t^{\mathcal{D}}, s_{t+1})$:

$$y_j \leftarrow \begin{cases} r_t^{\mathcal{D}}, & \text{If } s_{t+1} \text{ is a Terminal State} \\ r_t^{\mathcal{D}} + max_{a'}(Q_t(s_{t+1}, a', \theta)), & \text{else} \end{cases}$$

Update the learner's ($\mathcal{A}$) Q-network parameters from Q_t to Q_{t+1} following DQN update rule.
8:    $\mathcal{A}'$ computes reward r_t^{attacker} following the methods as described in section 4 and stores the transition tuple $(info_t, a'_t, r_t^{\text{attacker}}, info_{t+1})$ into its own replay buffer $\mathcal{B}'$.
9:    $\mathcal{A}'$ performs Q-learning given the attacker's mini-batch transition data sampled from $\mathcal{B}'$, where t'th transition tuple is denoted as $(info_t, a'_t, r_t^{\text{attacker}}, info_{t+1})$:

$$y_j \leftarrow \begin{cases} r_t^{\text{attacker}}, & \text{If } info_{t+1} \text{ is a Terminal State} \\ r_t^{\text{attacker}} + max_{a' \in A}(Q'_t(info_{t+1}, a', \theta')), & \text{else} \end{cases}$$

10:    $\mathcal{A}'$ also updates it's Q-network parameter θ' by minimizing $\mathcal{L}(\theta) = (y_j - Q'_t(info_t, a'_t, \theta'))^2$.
11: **end for**
12: **return** $\mathcal{A}$ and it's corresponding Q-network parameter θ;

References

1. ACM: American center for mobility (2022). https://www.acmwillowrun.org/
2. Altschuler, J., Brunel, V.E., Malek, A.: Best arm identification for contaminated bandits. J. Mach. Learn. Res. **20**(91), 1–39 (2019)

3. Behzadan, V., Munir, A.: Vulnerability of deep reinforcement learning to policy induction attacks. In: Perner, P. (ed.) MLDM 2017. LNCS (LNAI), vol. 10358, pp. 262–275. Springer, Cham (2017). https://doi.org/10.1007/978-3-319-62416-7_19

4. Bellemare, M.G., Naddaf, Y., Veness, J., Bowling, M.: The arcade learning environment: an evaluation platform for general agents. J. Artif. Intell. Res. **47**, 253–279 (2013)

5. Blaß, T., Casini, D., Bozhko, S., Brandenburg, B.: A ROS 2 response-time analysis exploiting starvation freedom and execution-time variance. In: Proceedings of the 42nd IEEE Real-Time Systems Symposium (RTSS), pp. 41–53 (2021)

6. Blaß, T., Hamann, A., Lange, R., Ziegenbein, D., Brandenburg, B.: Automatic latency management for ROS 2: benefits, challenges, and open problems. In: Proceedings of the 27th IEEE Real-Time and Embedded Technology and Applications Symposium (RTAS), pp. 264–277 (2021)

7. Brockman, G., et al.: Openai gym. arXiv preprint arXiv:1606.01540 (2016)

8. Casini, D., Blaß, T., Lütkebohle, I., Brandenburg, B.: Response-time analysis of ROS 2 processing chains under reservation-based scheduling. In: Proceedings of the 31st Euromicro Conference on Real-Time Systems (ECRTS), pp. 6:1–6:23 (2019)

9. Choi, H., Xiang, Y., Kim, H.: PiCAS: new design of priority- driven chain-aware scheduling for ROS2. In: Proceedings of the 27th IEEE Real-Time and Embedded Technology and Applications Symposium (RTAS) (2021)

10. Chung, K., et al.: Smart malware that uses leaked control data of robotic applications: the case of Raven-II surgical robots. In: 22nd International Symposium on Research in Attacks, Intrusions and Defenses (RAID 2019), pp. 337–351. USENIX Association, Chaoyang District, Beijing, September 2019. https://www.usenix.org/conference/raid2019/presentation/chung

11. DeMarinis, N., Tellex, S., Kemerlis, V.P., Konidaris, G., Fonseca, R.: Scanning the internet for ROS: a view of security in robotics research. In: 2019 International Conference on Robotics and Automation (ICRA), pp. 8514–8521. IEEE (2019)

12. Dieber, B., Kacianka, S., Rass, S., Schartner, P.: Application-level security for ros-based applications. In: 2016 IEEE/RSJ International Conference on Intelligent Robots and Systems (IROS), pp. 4477–4482. IEEE (2016)

13. Dong, Y., et al.: Mcity data collection for automated vehicles study. arXiv preprint arXiv:1912.06258 (2019)

14. Garnett, N., Cohen, R., Pe'er, T., Lahav, R., Levi, D.: 3D-lanenet: end-to-end 3d multiple lane detection. In: IEEE/CVF International Conference on Computer Vision, pp. 2921–2930 (2019)

15. Huang, S., Papernot, N., Goodfellow, I., Duan, Y., Abbeel, P.: Adversarial attacks on neural network policies. arXiv preprint arXiv:1702.02284 (2017)

16. Huang, Y., Zhu, Q.: Deceptive reinforcement learning under adversarial manipulations on cost signals. In: Alpcan, T., Vorobeychik, Y., Baras, J.S., Dán, G. (eds.) GameSec 2019. LNCS, vol. 11836, pp. 217–237. Springer, Cham (2019). https://doi.org/10.1007/978-3-030-32430-8_14

17. Jun, K.S., Li, L., Ma, Y., Zhu, J.: Adversarial attacks on stochastic bandits. Adv. Neural Inf. Process. Syst. **31** (2018)

18. Kiran, B.R., et al.: Deep reinforcement learning for autonomous driving: a survey. IEEE Trans. Intell. Transp. Syst. (2021)

19. Kocher, P., et al.: Spectre attacks: exploiting speculative execution. In: 2019 IEEE Symposium on Security and Privacy (SP), pp. 1–19. IEEE (2019)

20. Kos, J., Song, D.: Delving into adversarial attacks on deep policies. arXiv preprint arXiv:1705.06452 (2017)

21. Li, A., Wang, J., Zhang, N.: Chronos: timing interference as a new attack vector on autonomous cyber-physical systems. In: Proceedings of the 2021 ACM SIGSAC Conference on Computer and Communications Security, pp. 2426–2428 (2021)
22. Lin, Y.C., Hong, Z.W., Liao, Y.H., Shih, M.L., Liu, M.Y., Sun, M.: Tactics of adversarial attack on deep reinforcement learning agents. arXiv preprint arXiv:1703.06748 (2017)
23. Liu, F., Shroff, N.: Data poisoning attacks on stochastic bandits. In: International Conference on Machine Learning, pp. 4042–4050. PMLR (2019)
24. Liu, S., et al.: Reinforcement learning for clinical decision support in critical care: comprehensive review. J. Med. Internet Res. **22**(7), e18477 (2020)
25. Luo, M., Myers, A.C., Suh, G.E.: Stealthy tracking of autonomous vehicles with cache side channels. In: 29th USENIX Security Symposium (USENIX Security 20), pp. 859–876 (2020)
26. Ma, Y., Jun, K.-S., Li, L., Zhu, X.: Data poisoning attacks in contextual bandits. In: Bushnell, L., Poovendran, R., Başar, T. (eds.) GameSec 2018. LNCS, vol. 11199, pp. 186–204. Springer, Cham (2018). https://doi.org/10.1007/978-3-030-01554-1_11
27. Mahfouzi, R., Aminifar, A., Samii, S., Payer, M., Eles, P., Peng, Z.: Butterfly attack: adversarial manipulation of temporal properties of cyber-physical systems. In: 2019 IEEE Real-Time Systems Symposium (RTSS), pp. 93–106. IEEE (2019)
28. Silver, D., et al.: A general reinforcement learning algorithm that masters chess, shogi, and go through self-play. Science **362**(6419), 1140–1144 (2018)
29. STII: Illinois autonomous and connected track (2022). https://ict.illinois.edu/i-act
30. Tang, Y., et al.: Response time analysis and priority assignment of processing chains on ROS2 executors. In: Proceedings of the 41st IEEE Real-Time Systems Symposium (RTSS) (2020)
31. Van Hasselt, H., Guez, A., Silver, D.: Deep reinforcement learning with double q-learning. In: Proceedings of the AAAI Conference on Artificial Intelligence, vol. 30 (2016)
32. Wang, Z., Ren, W., Qiu, Q.: LaneNet: real-time lane detection networks for autonomous driving. arXiv preprint arXiv:1807.01726 (2018)
33. Wang, Z., Schaul, T., Hessel, M., Hasselt, H., Lanctot, M., Freitas, N.: Dueling network architectures for deep reinforcement learning. In: International Conference on Machine Learning, pp. 1995–2003. PMLR (2016)
34. Zhang, H., Parkes, D.C.: Value-based policy teaching with active indirect elicitation. In: AAAI, vol. 8, pp. 208–214 (2008)
35. Zhang, H., Parkes, D.C., Chen, Y.: Policy teaching through reward function learning. In: Proceedings of the 10th ACM Conference on Electronic Commerce, pp. 295–304 (2009)
36. Zhang, X., Ma, Y., Singla, A., Zhu, X.: Adaptive reward-poisoning attacks against reinforcement learning. In: International Conference on Machine Learning, pp. 11225–11234. PMLR (2020)

An Exploration of Poisoning Attacks on Data-Based Decision Making

Sarah Eve Kinsey[1]([⊠]), Wong Wai Tuck[2], Arunesh Sinha[3],
and Thanh H. Nguyen[1]

[1] University of Oregon, Eugene, USA
{arbutler,thanhhng}@cs.uoregon.edu
[2] Singapore Management University, Bras Basah, Singapore
wt.wong.2020@msc.smu.edu.sg
[3] Rutgers University, New Brunswick, USA
arunesh.sinha@rutgers.edu

Abstract. Many real-world problems involve building a predictive model about an adversary and then determining a decision accordingly, including two-stage (predict then optimize) and decision focused (joint predict and optimize) approaches. The involvement of a predictive model learned from adversary's behavior data poses a critical threat that an adversary can influence the learning process, which will ultimately deteriorate the end-goal decision quality. In this paper, we study the problem of poisoning attacks in this data-based decision making setting. That is, the adversary can alter the training data by injecting some perturbation into the data to a certain limit that can substantially change the final decision outcome in the end towards the adversary goal. To our knowledge, this is the first work that studies poisoning attacks in such data-based decision making scenarios. In particular, we provide the following main contributions. We introduce a new meta-gradient based poisoning attack for various types of predict and optimize frameworks. We compare to a technique shown effective in computer vision. We find that the complexity of the problem makes attacking decision focused model difficult. We show that an attack crafted against a two-stage model is effectively transferable to a decision-focused model.

1 Introduction

As machine learning has been gaining a lot of adventions and interests from both research and industrial communities, the opportunities for and the potential cost of failure grow. Some sources of failure are well explored, such as poorly chosen models and biased datasets. More recently, research has also considered another avenue for failure: intelligent adversaries that wish to manipulate the results of machine learning models [10,17]. For example, adversaries can perform *evasion attacks* [5,15,22] to alter the classification of particular samples at test time; this requires access to some data that will be taken as input by a pre-trained model. Alternatively, with access to the training data, attackers can perform

F. Fang et al. (Eds.): GameSec 2022, LNCS 13727, pp. 231–252, 2023.
https://doi.org/10.1007/978-3-031-26369-9_12

poisoning attacks [6,12,26]. The goal of poisoning attack is to manipulate the training data such that the resulting model offers advantage to the adversary. *Adversarial machine learning* is the field that includes study of both evasion and poisoning attacks, as well as design of models resistant to these attacks.

Another emerging area of study is that of *data-based decision making*. Many machine learning applications involve a data to decision pipeline: first using known data construct a predictive model, then apply the predictive model to unknown data, and lastly make decisions based on those predictions. Traditional approaches here have been *two-stage*, with the predictive model being optimized solely for its prediction accuracy [8,19,28,29,33]. If the prediction model is perfect over the whole prediction space, the two-stage approach would be optimal. However, complicated prediction boundaries in high dimension spaces can never be modeled perfectly even with large but finite data; in fact, for data driven decision making the end goal is to make the best decisions possible, but the prediction model itself is not being optimized with that goal in mind. As a consequence of this observation, a method often referred to as *decision focused* learning seeks to directly integrate the decision optimizer into the prediction model during training. Hence, decision focused learning uses the decision quality to train the network. Updating the model via gradient descent, then, can be accomplished by differentiating *through* the solution to the decision optimization. This approach has proven more effective than corresponding two-stage models in some applications. However, this approach is significantly more computationally expensive, as each forward pass in the training process requires solving the optimization.

Our work lies at the intersection of data-based decision making and adversarial learning. We investigate the vulnerabilities of data-based decision making methods by developing poisoning attacks against these methods. To our knowledge, our work is the first one exploring this topic. Specifically, we look into using *end-to-end attacks* against both the aforementioned data-based decision methods designed for convex optimization, as well as a third model which we call the *simple joint* model. Here, the optimizer is itself approximated by a neural network. Furthermore, as it is important to understand the *transferability* of poisoning attacks between different models, we also investigate how effectively our generated attacks can be transferred beyond the originally targeted method (e.g. computing an attack against a two stage model and then also testing the generated poison on a decision focused model).

Our *first* contribution is to create a meta-gradient based poisoning attack. Put simply, we unroll the target model's training procedure (which consists entirely of differentiable steps) to differentiate through the training and calculate gradients of the attacker's loss function with respect to the training data itself. Then, we use these gradients to perform projected (into the feasible space defined by constraints on the attack) gradient descent.

Our *second* contribution is to demonstrate that existing state of the art methods in other domains (specifically Metapoison [11] in computer vision) may not be directly applicable to the field of data-based decision making. We accomplish this by attacking a simple data-based decision making learner (using Metapoison to solve the attack) as well as testing the found attack on both two-stage and decision focused learners. The ineffectiveness of this approach for our problem suggests that new techniques may have to be developed for poisoning attacks on data-based decision making models.

Our experiments yield several findings that should be of use to future research. Most notably, attacking a decision-focused learner directly is a particularly difficult ask due to the complexity of the learner's training process. Beyond the (significant) computational requirements of solving the attack, any stability or precision issues within the learner's gradient calculation are compounded when computing the meta-gradient. Common machine learning pitfalls such as exploding or vanishing gradients appear frequently and are harder to counteract. Furthermore, the complexity of the solution space (which scales with model size, optimization objective, and constraints) means that many optima of various quality exist, and finding a good one with gradient descent is not guaranteed. These effects are less noticeable when attacking the two-stage model or the simple joint model, as their training gradient updates do not involve backpropagating through an optimization problem.

Furthermore, we investigate the transferability of our method's attacks. Previous work has shown the transferability of meta-gradient based poisoning attacks [20]. Our experiments show that this property still applies, to varying degrees, across data-based decision making methods. This finding aligns with the general *transferability phenomenon* found in adversarial machine learning [21]. Primarily, we observe that poisons created against a two-stage learner effectively transfer to a decision-focused learner.

2   Related Work

Decision Focused Learning. Decision-focused learning is an approach that has been applied to discrete [30] and convex [31] optimization, as well as non-convex optimization in security games [23]. The key idea here is that, instead of a traditional two-stage "predict then optimize" approach to solving problems, the decision maker instead uses the decision quality itself as the training loss. This is done by backpropagating *through* the optimization problem, which can be accomplished by applying the implicit function theorem to the KKT conditions of that optimization [30]. Our proposed attack could be called a decision-focused attack; we differentiate through the entire data-based decision making problem to optimize our poison.

Adversarial Learning. Adversarial learning is a subfield of machine learning focused on attacking models. The attack formulated in this work is analogous to a *causative attack* (or poisoning attack) in adversarial learning [10,11,16,32,34]. A significant difference between our work and typical adversarial learning is that our attacker has end goals beyond minimizing prediction accuracy. While our attack does target the training process, the attacker's objective is to manipulate the decision outcome of the optimization problem.

Meta Learning. In machine learning, meta learning is an approach designed to optimize the training process itself. Historically, meta learning was focused on *improving* models, though more recently, meta learning based attacks have proven effective. Muñoz-González et al. used a metagradient method to optimize a poisoning attack by back-propagating *through* the learning process [20]. They demonstrated that this approach was effective against a variety of decision makers, for multiple different tasks. Interestingly, they found that these poisoning attacks could be effectively transferred to models other than the one against which they were optimized [20]. Zugner et al. utilized the metagradient method to attack graph learning problems, creating an attack capable of dramatically reducing global node classification accuracy [34]. MetaPoison uses shallow metagradients averaged over multiple models at each poison optimization step to produce a robust yet subtle attack on image classification that can be effectively transferred beyond the original target model [11]. Similar to these papers, our work focuses on a metagradient poisoning attack. Our contribution is in extending metagradient attacks to data based decision making models, and providing a detailed overview of the challenges in creating poisoning attacks in this setting.

3   Data-Based Decision Making

Data-based decision making refers to a common paradigm in artificial intelligence in which we are concerned with three related pieces of information: directly observable data (denoted by u), data that will be unobservable at test time (denoted by θ), and a *decision* that must be made (denoted by x). The decision, x, depends directly on θ, which in turn can be predicted based on u. The ultimate goal in a data-based decision making problem is to find an optimal decision to maximize a utility function, abstractly represented as follows:

$$\max_{x \in X} f(x, \theta)$$

where x is the decision variable and $X \subseteq \mathbb{R}^K$ is the set of all feasible decisions. Note that the objective, f, depends directly on the *unobservable* parameter θ, which must be inferred from the correlated observable data, u. In this work, we focus on the problem setting in which the decision space X can be represented as a set of linear constraints $X = \{x \in \mathbb{R}^K : Ax \leq b\}$ where (A, b) are constant.

In literature, there are two main approaches used to tackle the data-based decision making problem. The first approach, named **two-stage approach**, divides the problem into two separate phases. The first phase is the learning phase in which the unobserved parameter θ is learnt based on some training dataset $\mathcal{D} = \{(u_1, \theta_1), (u_2, \theta_2), \cdots, (u_n, \theta_n)\}$ in which each data point i is associated with a feature vector $u_i \in \mathbb{R}^d$ and a true label $\theta_i \in \mathbb{R}^K$ ($\theta_i \in \mathbb{N}^K$ if it is categorical). Then in the second phase which is called the decision-making phase, the decision x will be optimized based on the learning outcome θ. The second approach, named **decision-focused** learning, on the other hand, considers a single end-to-end pipeline (with an intermediate learning layer) that attempts to directly optimize the decision based on the training data $\mathcal{D}$. In addition to these two main approaches, in this paper, we create a third simple approach, named **simple joint approach** that formulates the data-based decision making

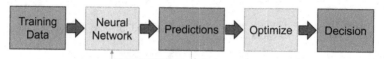

Fig. 1. Depiction of a two-stage learner

as a simple learning problem. We consider this approach as a baseline to study poisoning attacks in this data-based decision making setting.

In the following, we first describe in details all these three approaches. We then present our optimization formulations to compute poisoning attacks to these three approaches, which are challenging to solve. Our proposed methodology to solve these optimization problems will be presented in Sect. 4.

3.1 Two-Stage Approach

Learner Description. The traditional approach to data-based decision making is *two-stage* [8,28,29]. The first of these stages is predicting the unknown parameter θ from the observed feature vector u. The second stage, then, is to compute the optimal x given the predicted θ (Fig. 1). Predicting the *unknown* parameter θ can be done using a parametric model, denoted by $\hat{\theta} = g(u, w)$. Here, w is the model parameter that needs to be determined. Given a training dataset $\mathcal{D} = \{(u_1, \theta_1), (u_2, \theta_2), \cdots, (u_n, \theta_n)\}$ in which each data point i is associated with a feature vector $u_i \in \mathbb{R}^d$ and a true label $\theta_i \in \mathbb{R}^K$ ($\theta_i \in \mathbb{N}^K$ if it is categorical), the decision maker first trains a predictive model $g(u, w)$ to predict the label of a data point u. The learner seeks an optimal model parameter w^* that minimizes the training loss, abstractly formulated as follows:

$$\min_w \mathcal{L}(\mathcal{D}, w)$$

For example, one can use mean squared error as the training loss:

$$\mathcal{L}(\mathcal{D}, w) = \frac{1}{n} \sum_i (\theta_i - g(u_i, w))^2$$

Once the model has been trained (yielding w^*), the decision maker can use observed u values to predict θ value (i.e., $g(u, w^*)$), then use that prediction to find an optimal decision by solving the following optimization problem:

$$\max_{x \in X} f(x, g(u, w^*))$$

Poisoning Attack Formulation. In designing poisoning attacks, we assume an adversary can alter the training data by injecting a small perturbation to every data point. More specifically, each feature vector u_i can be altered by adding a small quantity ϵ_i with the constraint that $lb_i \leq \epsilon_i \leq ub_i$. Here, $lb_i < 0$

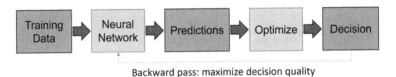

Fig. 2. Depiction of a decision focused learner

and $ub_i > 0$ represent the maximum perturbation the adversary can apply to the data point i. Intuitively, (lb_i, ub_i) captures the adversary's capability. The adversary attempts to optimize some goal, for example, minimizing the decision maker's utility in the test set or forcing the decision maker to produce a particular target decision output for some data points in the test set. We represent this poisoning attack on a two-stage model with the following general formulation:

$$\min \mathcal{L}^{adv}(x^*, \theta^{target}) \tag{1}$$

$$\text{s.t. } x^* \in \operatorname{argmax}_{x \in X} f(x, g(u^{target}, w^*)) \tag{2}$$

$$w^* \in \operatorname{argmin}_w \mathcal{L}(\mathcal{D}^{poison}, w) \tag{3}$$

$$\mathcal{D}^{poison} = \{(u_1 + \epsilon_1, \theta_1), \cdots, (u_n + \epsilon_n, \theta_n)\} \tag{4}$$

$$\epsilon_i \in [lb_i, ub_i], \forall i = 1, 2, \cdots, n \tag{5}$$

where $(u^{target}, \theta^{target})$ is the adversary's target element. Line 1 simply represents a general objective for the adversary. For example, if the adversary's goal is to minimize the decision maker's utility on this target, then $\mathcal{L}^{adv}(x^*, \theta^{target}) = f(x^*, \theta^{target})$. Line 2 is the optimization problem solved by the learner given the network output. Equation 3 then represents the optimal network weights as a function of the learner's training. Next, line 4 denotes the training dataset, altered by the attacker with poison values ϵ. Lastly, line 5 denotes the restrictions on the attacker's power, specifically a magnitude constraint on each poison element.[1] Solving the above optimization problem optimally is challenging since it has multiple connected levels of optimizations.

3.2   Decision Focused Approach

Learner Description. While the two-stage approach is straightforward and effective, its training process is disconnected from the end goal of the system. More specifically, the model is being trained for prediction accuracy, whereas the ultimate objective is to produce good decisions [31].

---

[1] Note that our formulation can be generalized to multiple targeted data points in the test set by taking the sum of losses over these data points. In addition, this can be also extended to incorporate perturbations on labels θ_i by introducing additional perturbation variables α_i to add to the labels.

A recent approach called *decision focused* learning seeks to bridge the disconnect between the training and the decisions produced, while still utilizing an explicit optimization solver (Fig. 2). In theory, this approach can improve final decision quality by concentrating the (inevitable) prediction errors in areas that will have the least detrimental effect. For each training data point, θ is predicted from u and the optimization problem is solved to produce x. Then, the network weights are updated via gradient descent to maximize the decision quality. Intuitively, we can think of this as incorporating a convex optimization layer as the last layer of a neural network. This method can give improved results over the two-stage approach, at the cost of training time [31]. Essentially, in a decision-focused approach, the loss function the learner minimizes is the negative mean decision quality:

$$\min_{w} \mathcal{L}(\mathcal{D}, w)$$

$$\text{where } \mathcal{L}(\mathcal{D}, w) = -\frac{1}{n} \sum_i f\left(\theta_i, x^*(\hat{\theta}_i)\right)$$

In this case, x^* is a result of solving the following optimization problem:

$$x^*(\hat{\theta}_i) \in \operatorname{argmax}_{x \in X} f(x, \hat{\theta}_i)$$

$$\text{where } \hat{\theta}_i = g(u_i, w) \text{ is the network output.}$$

Unlike the two-stage approach, here one must differentiate *through* the decision optimization problem to optimize the model parameters w. This can be accomplished by using the implicit function theorem on the KKT conditions of the optimization problem [2].

Poisoning Attack Formulation. Given the decision-focused formulation, we now can represent the problem of finding an optimal poisoning attack as the following optimization problem:

$$\min \mathcal{L}^{adv}(x^*, \theta^{target}) \tag{6}$$

$$\text{s.t. } x^* \in \operatorname{argmax}_{x \in X} f(x, g(u^{target}, w^*)) \tag{7}$$

$$w^* \in \operatorname{argmin}_w \left[\mathcal{L}(\mathcal{D}^{poison}, w) = -\frac{1}{n} \sum_i f\left(\theta_i, x^*(\hat{\theta}_i)\right) \right] \tag{8}$$

$$\text{given } x^*(\hat{\theta}_i) \in \operatorname{argmax}_{x \in X} f(x, \hat{\theta}_i) \tag{9}$$

$$\text{and } \hat{\theta}_i = g(u_i + \epsilon_i, w) \text{ is the network output.} \tag{10}$$

$$\mathcal{D}^{poison} = \{(u_1 + \epsilon_1, \theta_1), \cdots, (u_n + \epsilon_n, \theta_n)\} \tag{11}$$

$$\epsilon_i \in [lb_i, ub_i], \forall i = 1, 2, \cdots, n \tag{12}$$

At a high level, the general attack formulation in this setting is similar to the two-stage case. However, solving the above optimization problem is much more challenging since the learner's training Eq. (8–10) involves an inner optimization layer which depends on the decision optimizer for every training data point.

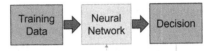

Fig. 3. Depiction of a learner using the simple joint approach

3.3   Simple Joint Approach

Learner Description. A naive approach to data based decision making is to train a parametric model using the features (u) to directly predict the optimal decision (x) (Fig. 3). Similar to the decision focused approach, we use negative mean decision quality as the loss function:

$$\min_w \; \mathcal{L}(\mathcal{D}, w)$$
$$\mathcal{L}(\mathcal{D}, w) = -\frac{1}{n} \sum_i f\left(\theta_i, \hat{x}(u_i)\right)$$

In this case, however, $\hat{x}$ itself is the network output: $\hat{x}(u_i) = g(u_i, w)$. This bypasses the need to directly predict the labels ($\hat{\theta}$). Intuitively, we can think of this as implicitly learning the predictive task "inside" of the network.

Alternatively, we could solve the optimization problem for each training set instance prior to training (producing x_i^* where $x_i^* \in \operatorname{argmax}_{x \in X} f(x, \theta_i)$) and then train the network to produce decisions as close as possible to these x^* values. In this method, we could use MSE as the loss function: $\mathcal{L}(\mathcal{D}, w) = \frac{1}{n} \sum_{i=1}^{n} (x_i^* - g(u_i, w))^2$. However, we found this approach less effective and more prone to overfitting than directly maximizing decision quality.

One complication when training a network to solve optimization problems is the constraints (if any exist) on the solution. Inspired by Shah et. al [27], we utilize a specially designed neural network layer to enforce constraints throughout the training process, ensuring valid decisions are made [27].

In practice, this naive approach is often ineffective as training networks to directly solve optimization problems is difficult. However, we investigate this simple model as a target for generating poisoning attacks that can then be transferred to the more sophisticated models.

Poisoning Attack Formulation. The attack formulation here is similar to the previous cases. The difference is in the second line; rather than producing predictions, this simple joint model simply treats the network output as the decision itself, and is trained accordingly:

$$\min \mathcal{L}^{adv}(x^*, \theta^{target})$$
$$\text{s.t. } x^* = g(u^{target}, w^*)$$

$$w^* \in \text{argmin}_w \left[\mathcal{L}(\mathcal{D}^{poison}, w) = -\frac{1}{n} \sum_i f\left(\theta_i, \hat{x}(u_i + \epsilon_i)\right) \right]$$

$$\mathcal{D}^{poison} = \{(u_1 + \epsilon_1, \theta_1), \cdots, (u_n + \epsilon_n, \theta_n)\}$$

$$\epsilon_i \in [lb_i, ub_i], \forall i = 1, 2, \cdots, n$$

4 Attack Generation Methodology

To solve the aforementioned optimization problems and determine poisoning attacks against each of these decision making approaches, we follow projected gradient descent. The core of gradient descent is to compute the gradient of the adversary loss $\mathcal{L}^{adv}$ with respect to the data perturbation ϵ, denoted by $\frac{d\mathcal{L}^{adv}}{d\epsilon}$. This gradient computation is challenging given that all the optimization problems involve multiple connected optimization levels.

Despite the differences among the aforementioned three data-based decision approaches, we employed two main computation techniques: (i) *computing gradients via meta gradient* [4]— the main idea of this technique is to differentiate through the gradient descent steps in solving inner optimization levels. The main advantage of this technique is that it can be can be applied for any non-convex optimization problems. One disadvantage of this technique is that it is generally computationally expensive; and (ii) *computing gradient via implicit function theorem* [7,30] — the main idea of this technique is to leverage convexity property, allowing us to differentiate through the KKT optimality condition. This technique is significantly less computationally expensive compared to the first technique. However, this technique is only applicable for convex optimization problem. Therefore, depending on the convexity of the problems, we then decide on one of these two techniques.

In the following, we first present in detail our proposed method to compute attacks to two-stage learning. Later, we will mainly highlight the differences or challenges regarding the decision-focused learning and the simple joint learning.

4.1 Attack to Two-Stage Approach

To solve the poisoning attack in this setting using gradient descent, the key is the gradient calculation of $\frac{d\mathcal{L}^{adv}}{d\epsilon}$, which can be decomposed into different gradient components via the chain rule:

$$\frac{d\mathcal{L}^{adv}}{d\epsilon} = \frac{d\mathcal{L}^{adv}}{dx^*} \frac{dx^*}{dg} \frac{dg}{d\epsilon} \qquad\qquad \frac{dg}{d\epsilon} = \frac{dg}{dw^*} \frac{dw^*}{d\epsilon}$$

Computing $\frac{d\mathcal{L}^{adv}}{dx^*}$ is straightforward, and $\frac{dg}{dw^*}$ is a result of the standard neural network back-propagation computation. On the other hand, computing the gradient components, $\frac{dx^*}{dg}$, the gradient of the optimal decision with respect to the label prediction $g(u^{target}, w^*)$, and $\frac{dw^*}{d\epsilon}$, the gradient of the optimal model parameter w^* w.r.t the perturbation ϵ, is not straightforward. This is because there is no explicit close-formed representation of x^* and w^* as a function of g and ϵ respectively, despite the fact that x^* depends on g and w^* depends on ϵ. In the following, we present our meta-gradient based method to approximate $\frac{dw^*}{d\epsilon}$ given the learning part (neural network function) is non-convex. We will then present the implicit function theorem based method to compute $\frac{dx^*}{dg}$ since the decision optimization part is convex.

Computing Decision Gradient via Implicit Function Theorem. We focus on the problem setting in which the decision optimization is convex (i.e., the utility function $f(x, \theta)$ is convex in the decision variable x). This convexity setting has been widely considered in previous studies on data-based decision making [1,7,30,31]. Based on this convexity characteristic, we leverage the implicit function theorem [14] to differentiate through the decision-optimization layer (i.e., computing $\frac{dx}{dg}$). Given the predicted value $\hat{\theta} = g(u^{target}, w^*)$, the decision-optimization component is formulated as a convex optimization problem:

$$\max_x \ f(x, \hat{\theta}) \ \text{s.t.} \ Ax \leq b$$

Since this is a convex optimization problem, any solution that satisfies the following KKT conditions is optimal:

$$-\nabla_x f(x, \hat{\theta}) + \lambda \cdot \nabla_x (Ax - b) = 0$$
$$\lambda \cdot (Ax - b) = 0$$
$$Ax \leq b, \lambda \geq 0$$

where λ is the dual variable. Observe that the first equation indicates that x and λ are functions of $\hat{\theta}$. Based on the implicit function theorem, we can differentiate through the first two equations to obtain the following gradient computation:

$$\begin{bmatrix} \frac{dx}{d\hat{\theta}} \\ \frac{d\lambda}{d\hat{\theta}} \end{bmatrix} = \begin{bmatrix} \nabla_x^2 f(x, \hat{\theta}) & A^T \\ diag(\lambda)A & diag(Ax - b) \end{bmatrix}^{-1} \begin{bmatrix} \frac{d\nabla_x f(x,\hat{\theta})}{d\hat{\theta}} \\ 0 \end{bmatrix} \tag{13}$$

Computing Learning Gradient via Meta Gradient. While we can leverage the convexity of decision optimization to compute the gradient of a decision with respect to the coefficients (as will be done when attacking the more complex models), we cannot apply the same approach for computing the learning gradient, $\frac{dw^*}{d\epsilon}$. This is because model learning is generally a non-convex optimization problem (as neural network models are non-convex in general). On the other hand, the implicit function theorem approach is most usefully applied to convex optimization. In order to tackle this challenge, we adopt the meta-gradient method [3].[2] This method works by assuming the model learning problem is solved via gradient descent. This is a reasonable assumption since neural network training typically relies on gradient descent method and its variants.

Based on this assumption, we can differentiate through the gradient descent steps. More specifically, we're concerned with the model's learning problem, abstractedly represented as follows:

$$\min_w \mathcal{L}(\mathcal{D}^{poison}, w)$$

$$\text{where } \mathcal{D}^{poison} = \{(u_1 + \epsilon_1, \theta_1), \cdots, (u_n + \epsilon_n, \theta_n)\}$$

At each gradient step t, given the previous value of the model parameters w_{t-1}, the gradient descent update is as follows: $w_t = w_{t-1} - \delta \frac{d\mathcal{L}}{dw_{t-1}}$, where δ is the learning rate. Note that $\mathcal{L}$ is a function of the perturbation variables $\epsilon = \{\epsilon_1, \cdots, \epsilon_n\}$. Therefore, w_t is also a function of ϵ (except for w_0 which is the initial value, a constant). As a result, we can differentiate through this gradient step as follows:

$$\frac{dw_t}{d\epsilon} = \frac{dw_{t-1}}{d\epsilon} - \delta \frac{dG}{d\epsilon}$$

where $G(w_{t-1}, \epsilon) = \frac{d\mathcal{L}}{dw_{t-1}}$. By applying the chain rule, we obtain:

$$\frac{dG}{d\epsilon} = \frac{\partial G}{\partial \epsilon} + \frac{\partial G}{\partial w_{t-1}} \cdot \frac{dw_{t-1}}{d\epsilon}$$

If we run gradient descent in T steps, we can approximate the gradient of the optimal w^* with respect to perturbations ϵ as follows: $\frac{dw^*}{d\epsilon} \approx \frac{dw_T}{d\epsilon}$.

Projected Gradient Descent Algorithm. Given this gradient computation, we illustrate our approach in Algorithm 1 where we run an iterative projected gradient descent process to compute an optimal attack. At each iteration j, given the current value of perturbation variables ϵ, Algorithm 1 first runs another inner gradient descent process to optimize the parameters w of the predictive model $g(u, w)$ based on the poison data $\mathcal{D}^{poison}$ (lines 5–13). At the end of this inner process, we obtain a trained model w^*. During this process, we simultaneously compute the learning gradient $\frac{dw^*}{d\epsilon}$.

Given the trained model w^*, Algorithm 1 proceeds into the decision optimization to compute the optimal decision x^* w.r.t the target u^{target} (line 14). Along with that computation, the gradient $\frac{dx^*}{dg}$ is computed (line 15). Finally, we update the value of ϵ based on the previous gradient computation (lines 16–17). This entire procedure (lines 5–17) is repeated until we reach a local optimal value of ϵ or reach the predetermined maximum number of iterations $nIter$.

---

[2] We can also apply this method to compute the decision gradient. However, meta-gradient is much more computationally expensive compared to the implicit function theorem method for convex problems.

Algorithm 1: Poisoning Attack Generation for Two-Stage Learning

---

1 Input: training data $\mathcal{D} = \{(u_1, \theta_1), (u_2, \theta_2), \cdots, (u_n, \theta_n)\}$;
2 Input: target $(u^{target}, \theta^{target})$;
3 Randomly initialize perturbation values $\epsilon = \{\epsilon_1, \cdots, \epsilon_n\}$.
4 **for** $j = 1 \rightarrow nIter$ **do**
  // Model learning
5   Initialize optimal learning loss $optL = \infty$;
6   **for** $r = 1 \rightarrow nRound$ **do**
7   Randomly initialize model parameter values w_0;
8   **for** $t = 1 \rightarrow T$ **do**
9   Update $w_t = w_{t-1} - \delta \frac{d\mathcal{L}}{dw_{t-1}}$;
10   Differentiate $\frac{dw_t}{d\epsilon} = \frac{dw_{t-1}}{d\epsilon} - \delta \frac{d\left(\frac{d\mathcal{L}}{dw_{t-1}}\right)}{d\epsilon}$;
11   **if** $\mathcal{L}(\mathcal{D}^{poison}, w_T) < optL$ **then**
12   Update optimal learning $w^* = w_T$;
13   Update learning gradient: $\frac{dw^*}{d\epsilon} = \frac{dw_T}{d\epsilon}$;

  // Decision optimizing
14   Compute optimal decision based on the learnt model w^*:
  $x^* \in \text{argmax}_{x \in X} f(x, g(u^{target}, w^*))$
15   Compute decision gradient w.r.t $\hat{\theta} = g(u^{target}, w^*)$ using Eq. (13)
  // Projected gradient step
16   Update perturbation variable $\epsilon = \epsilon - \delta \frac{d\mathcal{L}^{adv}}{d\epsilon}$ where:
  $\frac{d\mathcal{L}^{adv}}{d\epsilon} = \frac{d\mathcal{L}^{adv}}{dx^*} \frac{dx^*}{dg} \frac{dg}{dw^*} \frac{dw^*}{d\epsilon}$;
17   Project ϵ_i to feasible perturbation space: $[lb_i, ub_i]$ $\forall i$;
18 **return** ϵ;

4.2   Attack to Decision Focused Approach

Similar to the two-stage approach, in this setting, we aim to compute the gradient $\frac{d\mathcal{L}^{adv}}{d\epsilon}$, which can be decomposed into multiple components using chain rule:

$$\frac{d\mathcal{L}^{adv}}{d\epsilon} = \frac{d\mathcal{L}^{adv}}{dx^*} \frac{dx^*}{dg} \frac{dg}{d\epsilon} \qquad\qquad \frac{dg}{d\epsilon} = \frac{dg}{dw^*} \frac{dw^*}{d\epsilon}$$

However, as the two methods use different training processes, the details of the learning gradient calculation ($\frac{dw^*}{d\epsilon}$) differ significantly. In fact, it becomes much more complicated and computationally expensive due to the involvement of the optimizer in the training process itself.

Indeed, recall that for the calculation of the learning gradient ($\frac{dw^*}{d\epsilon}$), in general, we follow gradient descent at every to solve the model learning problem and then differentiate through the gradient steps as explained in the previous section. That is, we have the following differentiation update:

$$\frac{dw_t}{d\epsilon} = \frac{dw_{t-1}}{d\epsilon} - \delta \frac{d\left(\frac{d\mathcal{L}}{dw_{t-1}}\right)}{d\epsilon}$$

where $\mathcal{L}$ is the training loss. In two-stage approach, this training loss has a closed-formed representation as a function of ϵ. Therefore, the above gradient computation is straightforward. On the other hand, in decision-focused approach, the model training is represented in Eq. (8–10), in which multiple decision optimizations for every data point is involved. The gradient $\frac{d\mathcal{L}(\mathcal{D}^{poison},w)}{dw}$ now depends on the gradient of the optimal decision w.r.t the prediction outcomes $\frac{dx^*(\hat{\theta}_i)}{d\hat{\theta}_i}$ for all i, since we have according to the chain rule:

$$\frac{d\mathcal{L}}{dw} = \sum_i \frac{d\mathcal{L}}{dx^*(\hat{\theta}_i)} \frac{dx^*(\hat{\theta}_i)}{d\hat{\theta}_i} \frac{d\hat{\theta}_i}{dw}$$

Computing the gradient $\frac{dx^*(\hat{\theta}_i)}{d\hat{\theta}_i}$ for all data points can be done via implicit function theorem as discussed in Sect. 4.1, which already involves complex computations including inverse matrix computation and the second derivative computation, etc. As a result, it becomes very challenging to take a further gradient step of $\frac{d\left(\frac{d\mathcal{L}}{dw}\right)}{d\epsilon}$. We discuss this challenge in the experiment section.

4.3 Attack to Joint Simple Approach

Finally, solving the attack on the joint sample approach is the simplest:

$$\frac{d\mathcal{L}^{adv}}{d\epsilon} = \frac{d\mathcal{L}^{adv}}{dx^*} \frac{dx^*}{d\epsilon} \qquad\qquad \frac{dx^*}{d\epsilon} = \frac{dx^*}{dw^*} \frac{dw^*}{d\epsilon}$$

In this case, x^* is simply the output of the neural network. Computing $\frac{d\mathcal{L}^{adv}}{dx^*}$ is straightforward, and $\frac{dx^*}{dw^*}$ is a result of the standard neural network backpropagation computation. The only challenging component here is $\frac{dw^*}{d\epsilon}$ as w^* is a function of ϵ yet cannot be expressed in closed form. As when attacking the other models, we use the metagradient method to calculate this.

5 Experiment Setup

5.1 Attack Methods

For our experiments, we utilize three different methods to generate attacks and compare their effectiveness. Starting with the simplest model, the first method is based on MetaPoison [11] and is formulated against the naive end-to-end learner. More specifically, this attack utilizes multiple target models (each at a different stage of training) and *averages* their metagradients (limited to 2 training steps). Then, the attack is optimized alongside the target models. This method was found to produce effective, unnoticeable, and transferable attacks in the computer vision domain [11]. Our idea is to use this method against a simple learner in the data-based decision making domain to produce attacks that can then be leveraged against the more sophisticated learners (two-stage and decision-focused).

The second attack generation technique we consider involves attacking the two-stage learner directly. Here, rather than using the MetaPoison technique, we consider an attack trained against a single learner which is trained from scratch at each attack epoch, giving us a more complete metagradient (computed using Higher [9]). Unlike the previous method, this one requires differentiating through the solution to an optimization problem as the two-stage learner explicitly solves that optimization problem at test time. For this component, we use Qpth [2]. Once again, after an attack is generated, we further evaluate it by testing it against the decision-focused learner.

The third and most computationally complex attack we consider is one formulated directly against the decision focused learner. On the surface, this attack is nearly identical to the one against the two-stage learner. When considered in more depth, however, it's a significantly more difficult problem, for reasons previously discussed. Thus, we are motivated to investigate the feasibility of attacking this model directly.

5.2   Experiment Domains

Synthetic Data. For our synthetic data experiments, we consider the following decision optimization problem:

$$\min f(x, \theta) = \frac{1}{2}x^T Q x - \theta^T x \text{ s.t. } ||x|| \leq D, Ax \leq b \tag{14}$$

where Q is a diagonal positive-definite matrix, serving as a penalty parameter to make the problem convex, and θ is the unknown parameter that needs to be trained. $||x|| \leq D$ is simply a magnitude constraint on the decision variable, while $Ax \leq b$ represents some other constraints on the decision space. This decision optimization formulation is typically used for representing shortest path, maximum flow, bipartite matching, and a range of other domains [30].

In our experiments, in order to predict the unknown parameter θ, we consider a simple neural network and randomly (according to the normal distribution) generate synthetic data to train this predictive network. The labels are computed as a function of the features, plus a small amount of random noise. In addition, regarding the decision optimization, we randomly generate decision constraints. The amount of constraints used are varied across experiments to explore how this affects the attack generation. These constraints are added incrementally: an experiment with 9 constraints would include the same constraints as the corresponding experiment with 7 constraints, in addition to 2 new constraints.

Stock Market Portfolio Optimization. In addition to this simplified artificial problem, we demonstrate our attack in the portfolio optimization domain. This is naturally modeled via data-based decision making, where, prior to the optimization itself, future stock returns and the covariances between stocks must be predicted. This makes the domain a natural choice for our decision-focused attack. Similar to other recent work [29], we utilize the Markowitz model [18] to maximize expected return while encouraging a diverse portfolio. Overall, the objective function of the optimization problem combines maximizing immediate return at each time step with minimizing risk, formulated as follows:

$$f(x, \theta, p, Q) = p^T x - \lambda x^T Q x$$

where x is the investment decision made (a vector that sums to 1, representing percentage of investment in each stock), p is the expected immediate return, λ is a risk aversion parameter, and Q is a matrix capturing the covariance between the expected returns of all stocks. Intuitively, Q represents how correlated individual stocks are, and it is more risky to invest in correlated stocks. Thus, the penalty term incentivizes diverse investment.

The learning problem, then, is to utilize historical information about the stocks themselves to learn *both* the expected returns (p) as well as a 32 dimensional embedding for each stock. This embedding is then used to calculate the covariance between each pair of stocks, using cosine similarity. Specifically, we use the prices at the previous time step as well as rolling statistics as the input of the neural network to (separately) learn p and Q. As in [29] these statistics include a variety of sliding window means, as well as variances, of the historical stock prices. Loss functions for both the two-stage and the decision-focused models utilize ground-truth p and Q values directly computed from the dataset. Note that both p and Q depend on the price data from *future* timesteps: p is the next timestep's return, while Q is the cosine similarity of the returns over the next 10 timesteps.

We utilize real-world historical stock data, downloaded from the Quandl WIKI dataset, from 2004 to 2017 [24]. The stocks used belong to the SP500, giving us 505 potential stocks to work with. Attacking the features exclusively is not meaningful here, as the features are computed based on the raw price. Due to this, we target our attack on the *raw* historical stock market data, which affects the features, the labels (p), and the covariance matrix (Q). We restrict our experiments to a setting with 50 stocks and 500 timesteps.

6   Results

Now we present the results of our experiments. For all the graphs, the results are averaged over 5 random seeds which determine both the initial network weights as well as the randomized attack starting points. In the synthetic data domain, this also corresponds to 5 different data sets (generated using the same normal distribution). For supplemental results, see the linked appendix[3].

6.1   Synthetic Data

On the following graphs, a 'small dataset' refers to a setting with 250 instances in the training dataset, while a 'large dataset' refers to one with 750 elements.

---

[3] https://www.dropbox.com/s/6lznj4c1imk5qcm/DataBasedSupplemental.pdf.

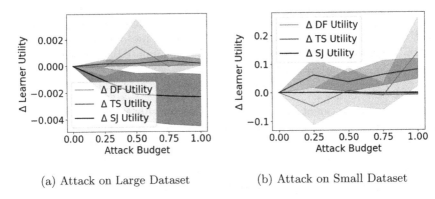

(a) Attack on Large Dataset   (b) Attack on Small Dataset

Fig. 4. Attacks generated against a simple joint model.

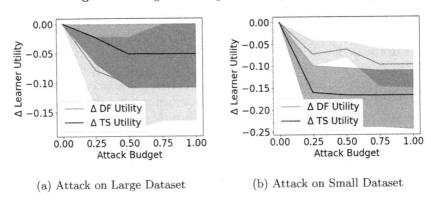

(a) Attack on Large Dataset   (b) Attack on Small Dataset

Fig. 5. Attacks generated against a two-stage learner

Simple Joint Model. In Fig. 4, we display the effectiveness of attacks generated against a simple joint learner. Both cases here demonstrate similar trends. First, that the found attacks are only minimally effective against the simple joint learner itself. Secondly, we observe that when transferring these attacks to the decision focused and the two-stage learners the effect on their utility is inconsistent and follows no clear trends. This finding stands in contrast to the results obtained by MetaPoison in the field of computer vision [11]. While this result may be surprising, the problems being solved in data-based decision making are notably different from computer vision tasks, and the models we utilize are significantly less complex.

Two-Stage Model. In Fig. 5 we show our results when generating an attack on the two-stage learner. Contrasted with the attacks in Fig. 4, we observe significantly higher effectiveness, both against the two-stage learner itself and when transferring the attack to the decision-focused learner. This contrast further suggests that methods from other domains (such as computer vision) may not be directly applicable when attacking data based-decision making models.

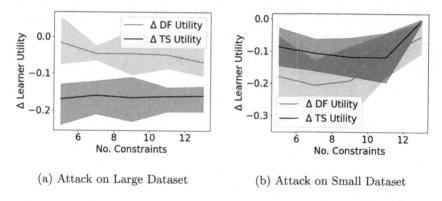

(a) Attack on Large Dataset   (b) Attack on Small Dataset

Fig. 6. Effect of adding constraints on attack results

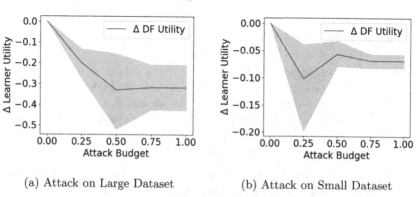

(a) Attack on Large Dataset   (b) Attack on Small Dataset

Fig. 7. Attacking a decision-focused model directly

Figure 6 demonstrates the effect of introducing more constraints to the optimization problem. What we observe here is that while the effectiveness of our attacks is dependent on the constraints, there is no simple trend when varying them. This makes it hard to predict how effective a metagradient based attack will be when attacking a new problem in data-based decision making.

Decision Focused Model. In Fig. 7 we examine the effectiveness of attacking a decision-focused learner directly. While our method is able to find good attacks in some scenarios, it is unreliable. Even in this simple setting, gradient descent often struggles to find a good optima, and this issue becomes even more apparent with a larger attack space. Combined with the prohibitive compute requirements of this attack, this is unlikely to be a practical approach in many data based learning settings.

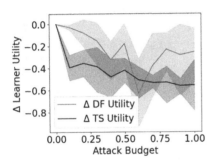
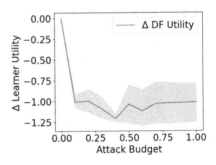

(a) Attack on two-stage learner   (b) Attack on decision focused learner

Fig. 8. Attacking a portfolio optimization model

6.2 Portfolio Optimization

Two-Stage Model. Figure 8a shows the results of attacking a two-stage model for portfolio optimization, as well as transferring that attack to a decision focused learner. Notably, we see that transferring the attack is often effective, though is inconsistent. This is likely due to the increased complexity of this domain compared to our synthetic setting, which includes both the transformation of raw prices into features as well as the objective of the optimization problem.

Decision Focused Model. In Fig. 8b, we display the results of attacking a decision-focused model directly. In this case, this attack is on average more effective than the attacks on the two-stage model. Most of this is likely due to the decision focused learner performing better when unattacked, getting an objective value of -0.005 to -0.094, compared to the two-stage learner that obtains objective values between -0.32 and -0.65. We also observe once again that higher 'budget' attacks (meaning a larger attack space) often lead to worse attacks (higher utility for the learner), further demonstrating the complexities of solving these attacks.

7 Conclusion

In this work, we formulated a generalized meta-gradient based poisoning attacks against two-stage models, decision focused models, and a simple joint model. We were able to provide insight into the difficulties of this attack by conducting extensive experiments in a synthetic domain as well as a real-world stock market portfolio optimization problem. These experiments show the following results. First, we observe that existing meta-gradient based techniques [11] may be ineffective here, despite being quite effective in the domain of computer vision. Next, we provide analysis showing that direct attacks on a decision-focused model are discouragingly difficult and problem dependent. Furthermore, despite the inherent training differences between two-stage and decision-focused learners, our results show that poisons crafted on a two-stage model can be effective against decision-focused models as well.

8 Appendix

8.1 Experiment Domain - Bipartite Matching

Bipartite matching is a well established problem in graph learning. In form, it is essentially identical to the synthetic data setting previously discussed:

$$\min f(x, \theta) = \frac{1}{2}x^T Q x - \theta^T x \text{ s.t. } ||x|| \leq D, Ax \leq b \tag{15}$$

In this case, however, the constraints enforced are that x must be *doubly stochastic*. Intuitively, x is a square matrix with continuous values. Each value x_{ij} represents the probability that node i on one side of the graph will be matched with node j on the other side. For the learning component of the problem, the goal is to predict the graph's edges from the nodes' features. This means that ϵ represents per-node features, while θ is the graph's adjacency matrix (relaxed to be continuous).

For these experiments, we utilize the Cora dataset [25] which consists of scientific papers. The features here are binary values indicating the presence of keywords in the paper, while the edges in the graph are citations. In total, there are 1433 features and 2708 nodes. Inspired by a recent paper [30], we split the dataset into 27 bipartite subgraphs, with 50 nodes on each side in each subgraph. This is accomplished using Metis [13] to partition the graph.

8.2 Supplementary Experiment Results

In Fig. 9, we display the results of using Metapoison [11] to solve attacks against a simple joint learner, and transferring the found attack to the two-stage and decision focused learners. Both domains display the same trends as observed

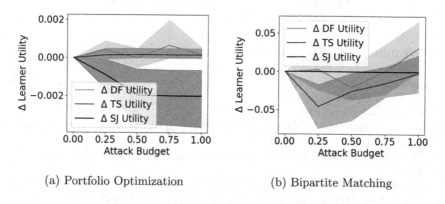

(a) Portfolio Optimization   (b) Bipartite Matching

Fig. 9. Attacks generated on simple joint models

in our synthetic domain - namely, that the attack is only nominally effective against the simple joint model, and not at all effective when transferred to the other two models. Once again, this suggests that techniques from domains such as computer vision may not be most appropriate for attacking data-based decision making models.

Figure 10 shows the results when attacking two-stage and decision focused models for bipartite matching. The trends are once again similar to the other domains: attacks trained against a two-stage learner can effectively transfer to a decision focused learner. Furthermore, as in portfolio optimization, we observe that the decision focused learner appears more susceptible to direct attack (Fig. 10b) than is the two-stage learner (Fig. 10a). Once again, this is likely due to the decision focused learner outperforming the two-stage counterpart in the absence of attack. Unattacked, the two-stage learner achieves utility values between 2.37 and 2.90 while the decision focused learner obtains utilities between 2.65 and 4.59. Particularly when attacking the decision focused learner (Fig. 10b) we can observe the recurring trend of increased attack budgets often leading to *worse* attacks and *higher* utility for the learner, demonstrating the difficulties of finding good attack optima via (meta)gradient descent.

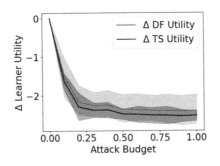

(a) Attack on two-stage learner

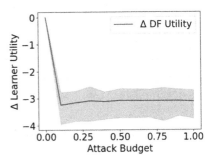

(b) Attack on decision focused learner

Fig. 10. Attacking a bipartite matching model

References

1. Agrawal, A., Amos, B., Barratt, S., Boyd, S., Diamond, S., Kolter, J.Z.: Differentiable convex optimization layers. In: Advances in Neural Information Processing Systems, vol. 32 (2019)
2. Amos, B., Kolter, J.Z.: OptNet: differentiable optimization as a layer in neural networks. arXiv preprint arXiv:1703.00443 (2017)
3. Andrychowicz, M., et al.: Learning to learn by gradient descent by gradient descent (2016)
4. Bengio, Y.: Gradient-based optimization of hyperparameters. Neural Comput. **12**(8), 1889–1900 (2000). https://doi.org/10.1162/089976600300015187

5. Biggio, B., et al.: Evasion attacks against machine learning at test time. In: Blockeel, H., Kersting, K., Nijssen, S., Železný, F. (eds.) ECML PKDD 2013. LNCS (LNAI), vol. 8190, pp. 387–402. Springer, Heidelberg (2013). https://doi.org/10.1007/978-3-642-40994-3_25

6. Biggio, B., Nelson, B., Laskov, P.: Poisoning attacks against support vector machines. arXiv preprint arXiv:1206.6389 (2012)

7. Donti, P., Amos, B., Kolter, J.Z.: Task-based end-to-end model learning in stochastic optimization. In: Advances in Neural Information Processing Systems, pp. 5484–5494 (2017)

8. Fang, F., et al.: Deploying paws: field optimization of the protection assistant for wildlife security. In: AAAI, vol. 16, pp. 3966–3973 (2016)

9. Grefenstette, E., et al.: Generalized inner loop meta-learning. arXiv preprint arXiv:1910.01727 (2019)

10. Huang, L., Joseph, A.D., Nelson, B., Rubinstein, B.I., Tygar, J.D.: Adversarial machine learning. In: Proceedings of the 4th ACM workshop on Security and artificial intelligence, pp. 43–58 (2011)

11. Huang, W.R., Geiping, J., Fowl, L., Taylor, G., Goldstein, T.: Metapoison: practical general-purpose clean-label data poisoning. In: Larochelle, H., Ranzato, M., Hadsell, R., Balcan, M.F., Lin, H. (eds.) Advances in Neural Information Processing Systems, vol. 33, pp. 12080–12091. Curran Associates, Inc. (2020). https://proceedings.neurips.cc/paper/2020/file/8ce6fc704072e351679ac97d4a9855 74-Paper.pdf

12. Jagielski, M., Oprea, A., Biggio, B., Liu, C., Nita-Rotaru, C., Li, B.: Manipulating machine learning: poisoning attacks and countermeasures for regression learning. In: 2018 IEEE Symposium on Security and Privacy (SP), pp. 19–35. IEEE (2018)

13. Karypis, G., Kumar, V.: Metis-a software package for partitioning unstructured graphs, partitioning meshes and computing fill-reducing ordering of sparse matrices (1997)

14. Krantz, S.G., Parks, H.R.: The Implicit Function Theorem: History, Theory, and Applications. Springer Science & Business Media, Cham (2002)

15. Kurakin, A., Goodfellow, I.J., Bengio, S.: Adversarial examples in the physical world. In: Artificial intelligence safety and security, pp. 99–112. Chapman and Hall/CRC (2018)

16. Li, J., Zhang, H., Han, Z., Rong, Y., Cheng, H., Huang, J.: Adversarial attack on community detection by hiding individuals. In: Proceedings of the Web Conference 2020, April 2020. https://doi.org/10.1145/3366423.3380171

17. Lowd, D., Meek, C.: Adversarial learning. In: ACM SIGKDD (2005)

18. Markowitz, H.: Portfolio selection. J. Finance **7**(1), 77–91 (1952) http://www.jstor.org/stable/2975974

19. Mukhopadhyay, A., Vorobeychik, Y.: Prioritized allocation of emergency responders based on a continuous-time incident prediction model. In: International Conference on Autonomous Agents and MultiAgent Systems (2017)

20. Muñoz-González, L., et al.: Towards poisoning of deep learning algorithms with back-gradient optimization. In: Proceedings of the 10th ACM Workshop on Artificial Intelligence and Security (2017)

21. Papernot, N., McDaniel, P., Goodfellow, I.: Transferability in machine learning: from phenomena to black-box attacks using adversarial samples. arXiv preprint arXiv:1605.07277 (2016)

22. Papernot, N., McDaniel, P., Jha, S., Fredrikson, M., Celik, Z.B., Swami, A.: The limitations of deep learning in adversarial settings. In: 2016 IEEE European Symposium on Security and Privacy (EuroS&P), pp. 372–387. IEEE (2016)

23. Perrault, A., Wilder, B., Ewing, E., Mate, A., Dilkina, B., Tambe, M.: Decision-focused learning of adversary behavior in security games (2019)
24. Quandl: WIKI various end-of-day data (2021). https://www.quandl.com/data/WIKI
25. Sen, P., Namata, G.M., Bilgic, M., Getoor, L., Gallagher, B., Eliassi-Rad, T.: Collective classification in network data. AI Mag. **29**(3), 93–106 (2008)
26. Shafahi, A., et al.: Poison frogs! targeted clean-label poisoning attacks on neural networks. In: Advances in Neural Information Processing Systems, vol. 31 (2018)
27. Shah, S., Sinha, A., Varakantham, P., Perrault, A., Tambe, M.: Solving online threat screening games using constrained action space reinforcement learning. CoRR abs/1911.08799 (2019). http://arxiv.org/abs/1911.08799
28. Wang, H., Xie, H., Qiu, L., Yang, Y.R., Zhang, Y., Greenberg, A.: Cope: traffic engineering in dynamic networks. In: Proceedings of the 2006 Conference on Applications, Technologies, Architectures, and Protocols for Computer Communications, pp. 99–110 (2006)
29. Wang, K., Wilder, B., Perrault, A., Tambe, M.: Automatically learning compact quality-aware surrogates for optimization problems. In: Advances in Neural Information Processing Systems, vol. 33, pp. 9586–9596 (2020)
30. Wilder, B., Dilkina, B., Tambe, M.: Melding the data-decisions pipeline: decision-focused learning for combinatorial optimization (2018)
31. Wilder, B., Ewing, E., Dilkina, B., Tambe, M.: End to end learning and optimization on graphs (2020)
32. Xue, M., He, C., Wang, J., Liu, W.: One-to-N amp; N-to-one: two advanced backdoor attacks against deep learning models. IEEE Trans. Dependable Secure Comput. **19**, 1562–1578 (2020). https://doi.org/10.1109/TDSC.2020.3028448
33. Xue, Y., Davies, I., Fink, D., Wood, C., Gomes, C.P.: Avicaching: a two stage game for bias reduction in citizen science. In: Proceedings of the 2016 International Conference on Autonomous Agents & Multiagent Systems, pp. 776–785 (2016)
34. Zügner, D., Günnemann, S.: Adversarial attacks on graph neural networks via meta learning. In: International Conference on Learning Representations (ICLR) (2019)

Novel Applications and New Game Models

A Network Centrality Game for Epidemic Control

Olivier Tsemogne[1,2](✉) [ID], Willie Kouam[1,2] [ID], Ahmed H. Anwar[3] [ID],
Yezekael Hayel[2] [ID], Charles Kamhoua[3] [ID], and Gabriel Deugoué[1] [ID]

[1] University of Dschang, Dschang, Cameroon
olivier.kamguia@alumni.univ-avignon.fr, kouamwillie00@gmail.com,
agdeugoue@yahoo.fr
[2] CERI/LIA, Avignon Université, Avignon, France
yezekael.hayel@univ-avignon.fr
[3] US Army Research Laboratory, Adelphi, USA
a.h.anwar@knights.ucf.edu, charles.a.kamhoua.civ@army.mil

Abstract. Many epidemic networks admit the partition of the population into three compartments of respective susceptible, infected, and removed individuals. These epidemics involve a conflict between the agent who is propagating the threat and the defender who tries to limit the importance of the propagation. In case of incapability of both agents to monitor the transitions of the network state, this conflict is generally modeled by a stochastic game. The resolution of this class of game is general enough, but remains unscalable. To overcome the curse of dimensionality, we propose a new framework that takes into account the network topology, and we show that the best strategy for each player at each period to optimize his/her overall outcome is to focus on the set of most influential nodes. That is, the use of players' memory is no longer necessary and, as a matter of result, the proposed algorithm is less time and memory consumptive than the value iteration-based algorithms.

Keywords: SIR Epidemic · Bayesian game · Network centrality

1 Introduction

The framework considered in this work is a network epidemic problem in which an attacker is trying to compromise computers in a network using a cyber-attack that propagates into the network following an epidemic process. Unlike in general problems in epidemiology, in our framework, the spread of an attack is controlled by a rational player who is called the attacker. Cyber-attacks have various goals among which are distributed denial of services (DDoSs), a threat inside an Internet of Things (IoT) or any other network of devices, a rumor in a social network, etc. In order to better mitigate the attacker's actions, it is usual to bring in an intelligent and rational defending agent. The resulting adversarial competition for control of a network between the defender and the attacker can be modeled as a game, where the defender is allocating defensive resources (e.g., honeypots), and the attacker is taking actions to gain greater control while remaining undetected. Game theory is becoming an increasingly important tool for optimizing the use of cyber-security resources, including strategic allocation of honeypots [9,17,18], allocating resources to perform the deep packet inspection, and modifying the structure or characteristics of the network [4,10]. We adopt a game-theoretic framework for optimizing honeypot deployments for detecting and defeating an adversary.

However, motivated by propagation scenarios involving two main agents, one of which aimed at compromising the network in the long term, we consider a richer class of games where the interactions between the attacker and the defender are dynamic, involve uncertainty, and may be long-lived. First, in realistic cases we want to model the interactions which are dynamic, in that the defender and attacker can react to new information and the moves of the other player, allowing them to update their strategies over time. Second, based on the fact that only one player, a cyber-attacker may illegally brutes force or use any other unauthorized techniques of scanning in order to get the state of each device on the network, the partial observation assumption is assumed to be true only for the defender. This is for example, what happens when a defender wants to protect a network under the threat of a botnet. Third, the interactions can be very long or very frequent. Finally, the goal of the defender correspond to the opposite of the attacker's one and then, our game is a zero-sum one. Therefore, [16] recently came out with one-sided partially observable stochastic game framework to determine an optimal strategy for the defender. The proposed value iteration (VI) algorithm presents a major problem related to scalability (number of nodes for which the solution is applicable). To try to overcome this problem, some authors have developed in [8] a so-called double oracle algorithm coupled with a compact representation of the defender belief. This approach allowed to increase the scalability of the solution up to 40 nodes in the context of lateral movement problems with lower dimensional state and belief spaces. Meanwhile, the epidemic control problem generally applies to networks with numerous devices and, henceforth, requires more efficient tools.

To try to overcome this problem, we always model our epidemic process using well-known compartmental framework like the Susceptible-Infected-Resistant (SIR) framework [14]; in this framework, each device can be in one of the three states at any time: vulnerable non-infected (or susceptible), infected or resistant (that at out of the reach of the threat). However, our model takes into account the topology of the network in the sense that the conflicting agents take their actions according to the importance of the nodes in the network; which importance is determined from some metrics called centrality measures and we can mention among others: the degree centrality, the eigenvalue centrality, the betweenness centrality, the centrality based on clustering coefficient, etc.

We model this problem as a two-player game on a graph between the attacker and the defender. The nodes of the graph correspond to hosts in the network, and the edges correspond to attacking another host using a particular vulnerability on the target host. The attacker sequentially chooses which hosts to attack to progress into the network in an untraceable way. The defender chooses edges that will act as honeypots (a honeypot is a computer security mechanism set to detect, deflect, or in some manner, counteract attempts at unauthorized use of information systems) which are able to detect certain moves by the attacker through the network and allow him to take additional mitigating actions. The defender can also change his honeypot deployment after any detection event to take into account the new piece of information about the attack. Moreover, our model takes into account several assumptions; first of all, the hypothesis that the attacker observes all the actions of the defender may not hold in our context and the importance of a node is determined from the same centrality measure for all agents; next, the detection of transmission implies the cure of the infected nodes and the attacker cannot infer such action from the defender and finally, even though nodes are not intelligent and rational, they may take some actions base on their state; more precisely after the action profile of players a node can go from the susceptible state to the resistant state or from the infected state to the susceptible state with certain probabilities. That is, no player can monitor the state transitions (i.e. the game framework is by construction partially observable). This assumes that a stage of our game consists of two phases: the first phase in which agents perform their actions and the second phase where there is a random internal transition for each node. In short, the problem considered in this paper of controlling an epidemic over a network can be seen a Bayesian zero-sum game between attacker and defender, where the different states of the network correspond to the types of the attacker.

Moreover, the different considerations constitute a real challenge for our Bayesian framework; thus, our paper aims to answer how to solve this Bayesian framework with unobservability assumptions for both players. The mains contributions of the paper are as follows:

- a zero-sum bayesian game is proposed to study optimal intrusion strategies against virus propagation,
- a two player zero-sum stochastic game is studied in which no player observes the opponent's action,
- a best strategies of both players for a one shot game case,
- our model involves a coupled system in which two players acting strategically and a set of devices reacting to their individual state.

The rest of paper is organized as follow. In the next section, some existing works in the literature on epidemics and game theoretical models. Further, in Sect. 3, we give a description of the model and the precise definition of our game, noting the defender's payoff associated with an action profile and taking into account the random transition of the nodes, the best response of each agent given this reward and the Nash equilibrium properties of this stage game. Then, in Sect. 4 we determine the equilibrium strategies for each agent at the end of a stage game.

2   Related Work

Connecting dynamic games and epidemic models offers a scientific foundation for rigorous and quantitative analysis and design of screening, containment, and mitigation strategies for large-scale dynamic and network systems.

2.1   Adversarial Study of Epidemics

The classification of epidemics in networks is like in biological systems [11], where the population is divided into compartments and the name of the epidemic derives from the possible compartments and the possible transitions of an individual between the compartments. Among them, we have a susceptible-infected-removed (SIR) epidemic model that admits three different compartments: the susceptible individuals (S) who can carry the virus, the infectious individuals (I) who carry the virus and can transmit it and the removed individuals (R) who are out of reach of an infection. Several authors have used this model to study the propagation process of an epidemic in a network.

In [12], the authors have developed new framework interconnecting human behaviors, decision-making, epidemic modeling, and systems and control. They propose a dynamic game model with a continuum of players to study the impact of social distancing behaviors on epidemics. The players have uncertainties on their infection state, which evolves according to a variant of SIR and choose actions based on limited information. This work first shows the existence of Nash equilibria of the proposed game framework and uses a class of nonlinear complementarity problems to characterize them. The authors exploit the monotonicity properties of the optimal policies and reduce the computation complexity of the Nash equilibrium using a low-dimensional optimization problem. It is observed from numerical experiments that homogeneous agents can have different behaviors and stringent constraints on the actions can benefit the more vulnerable agents at the expense of the less vulnerable ones.

In [2], the authors present a graphon-based mean-field model that captures the heterogeneous interactions of non-identical players over networks. This work creates a novel mathematical framework of epidemic processes over graphon-based networks and develops a new class of dynamic game models in which players make decisions by themselves. The authors show the exis- tence of Nash equilibrium solutions and provide sufficient conditions that characterize them. The equilibrium solutions rely on solving a continuum of fully coupled forward-backward ordinary differential equations.

In [1], the author studies the impact of social distancing using an SIR epidemic process with multiple types of subpopulations that interact over a network. This work establishes the epidemic reproduction number for different social distancing strategies as an important metric to identify network vulnerability and inform vaccination policies. An effective policy should result in the reproduction number smaller than one. Building on this result, the author further studies a social distancing game in which individuals choose their social distancing levels based on the global infection status. This work shows that there exists a performance gap between the voluntary social distancing solution and the social optimum solution. The author points out several research directions including the investigation of the individual choice of connectivity and social planning under a limited supply of vaccines.

In [17], based on SIR model, the authors investigate an information security application of the epidemic models. They design a novel zero-sum partially observable stochastic game to describe the interaction between a network defender and an attacker. It is formulated to investigate the optimal protective strategies against virus propagation, which is modeled by compartmental epidemic models. The main result of this work is a formal proof of convergence of the value backup operator. The main limitation of this paper is that the proposed value backup operator does not converge for a large number of nodes. The novel framework leads to several directions for future research, including the study of optimal attack and defense strategies, taking into account the properties of network structures.

2.2 Centrality Measures

A wide range of real-world phenomena, from social and information to technological and biological networks, can be described using complex networks which can be modeled using graphs for their performance analysis [7]. Diffusion, as a means of studying a complex network's dynamic behaviors, has been one of the most important topics in this area. Diffusion on the network is transferred from one node to another and it starts on a small scale and then affects more neighbors. Moreover, in diffusion scenario such as epidemic propagation, the goal is to find influential nodes which have a higher diffusion power in comparison with other nodes. Diffusion in complex networks has a lot of applications and based on the nature of a problem, specific influential nodes can be used to accelerate, control or prevent diffusion. For instance, in marketing on social networks, the highest amount of ads can be diffused with the least amount of time and resources using influential nodes. In computer networks, the spreading of viruses can be prevented by securing the most suitable nodes.

Since finding influential nodes is a NP-hard problem, some approximate methods called centrality measures are used and can be divided into three types: Local measures, global measures and semi-local measures [13].

– The first and simplest centrality measure in the category of local measures is the degree centrality. In this measure, only the first-degree neighbors of a node are considered important. In fact, a node is regarded as important if it has a higher degree. This measure can determine a node's importance to some extent but nodes with the same degree do not necessarily have the same essential role in the graph. This measure because of being local and ignoring the graph's global information, and with a linear time complexity of $O(n)$, does not have high accuracy [7]. One of the popular measures in the category of local measure is the degree centrality that Measures how many neighbors a node contains. There are two types of degree centrality (in-degree and out-degree) according to direction. It measures the immediate influence and it is used to calculate the central nodes in the simulation network, assesses how difficult it would be to isolate a given node (using edge disjoint k-path centrality), etc.

- In contrast, global measures need the entire graph's information to do so, and therefore have a higher accuracy and time complexity. As a result, they cannot be used for large-scale networks. One of the important measures in the category of global measures is the betweenness centrality. The goal of betweenness centrality is to determine the importance of a node based on the information flow existing within the graph. It is based on the number of times a node is located in the shortest paths among all the pairs of nodes in the graph. The high betweenness centrality of a node indicates that it is located between most of the shortest paths available in the graph [6].

- in recent years, due to increases in the size of real-life networks, a need for measures with high accuracy and low time complexity compared to global measures was felt. Measures in the semi-local category have been introduced for this reason. One of the most important and early semi-local measures is the LC measure. The LC centrality is an advanced version of the degree measure in which, in addition to the first-degree neighbors, second-degree neighbors are taken into consideration as well. Another measure recently developed in this category is measure based on clustering coefficient [20].

2.3 Bayesian Game

Chen [5] in his doctoral dissertation used game theoretic model to design the response for the importance-scanning Internet worm attack. The main idea is that defenders can choose how to deploy an application, that is the group distribution, when it is introduced to Internet to minimize the worm propagation speed. The attacker can choose the optimal group scanning distribution to maximize the infection speed. Thus a game would be played between the attacker and the defender. The attacker should choose so as to maximize the minimum speed of worm propagation, while defender wants to minimize the maximum speed of worm propagation. By framing the problem this way it turns out to be a zero sum game and a min-max problem. The optimal solution for this problem is that defender should deploy the application uniformly in the entire IP-address space or in each enterprise network, so that the best strategy that the attacker exploits is equivalent to random scanning strategy. This work gave a game theoretical framework to design the locations of vulnerable and high value hosts over a network.

Patcha et al. [15] proposed a game theoretic approach to model intrusion detection in mobile ad-hoc networks. The authors viewed intrusion detection as a game played between the attacker node and the IDS hosted on the target node. The objective of the attacker is to send a malicious message with the intention of attacking the target node. The modeled game is a basic signaling game which falls under the domain of multi-stage dynamic non-cooperative game.

Bloem et al. [3] modeled intrusion response as a resource allocation problem based on game theory. A cost is associated with attacks and responses. This problem, including imperfections in the sensor outputs, was first modeled as a continuous game. The strategies are discretized both in time and intensity of actions, which eventually leads to a discretized model. The reaction functions uniquely minimize the strictly convex cost functions. After discretization, this becomes a constrained integer optimization problem. To solve this they introduced their dynamic algorithm, Automatic or Administrator Response algorithm (AOAR). They classified attacks into those resembling previous attacks and those that do not, and many such intuitive classes with Kohonen self-organizing maps, a neural net, and the response cost is minimized. The simulations captured variation in vulnerability, value and cost of actions. Their results showed system performs improves after using AOAR.

3   Optimum Control of a Time-slot

To meet the optimal utility payoff, the number of infected nodes should be considered together with the influence of these nodes. This influence is captured by many centrality measures. Henceforth, for a given centrality measure, the players strategies should consist in controlling the nodes of maximum centrality values. In this section, we assume a fixed centrality measure, and we give the solution of both players trying to control the maximum total centrality value, call it the centrality game.

3.1   Model Definition

The interactions between the attacker and the defender as well as the epidemic spreading dynamics are described in detail in this section. The overall model is complex as it takes into account the conflicting nature of the two players, the dynamic spreading of a virus over a network, and the reaction of each node depending on their state. Note that node reaction is not strategically determined, but follows some specific rules. A strategic rational agent (the attacker) is spreading a virus inside a network. To this end, she silently propagates the malware from every infected node to adjacent ones. However, it may not be in the attacker's interest to transmit the virus from each infected node to all the susceptible neighbors, because it may expose the infected nodes and then alert about its presence. Perfect information is assumed for the attacker so that she has full knowledge about the state of each node of the network at every time slot. To mitigate this virus spreading, another strategic rational agent (the defender) observes, at each time slot, a limited number of edges using an Intrusion Detection System (IDS) tool as an honeypot and instantly cures the two nodes (source and destination nodes of the transmission) when a virus transmission is detected on an edge using a honeypot. The localization of the "honeypots/watchtowers" on edges is not reported to the attacker. These honeypots are available only for one time slot. This interaction between attacker and defender is repeated at each time slot.

3.2   Time Slot Description

Each time slot consists in two stages: the stage of strategic actions of the players (attacker and defender) and the stage of probabilistic moves/reaction of nodes depending on their state i.e. the internal state transition of nodes.

Strategic (first) Stage: The two players (attacker and defender) make their actions, which result in an intermediate state for each node of the network.

Probabilistic (second) Stage: Based on the intermediate state of the network, each node may change his own internal state from state I to S or from state S to R by applying self-restoration process. These decisions are free of charge and are performed randomly.

Node Reaction. At an intermediate state of a time-slot of the epidemic spreading process, each node can take an action which may result in a transition of his state. Any infected node can make an action such as updating software, virus scanning, etc. The virus is destroyed at this node and then the state of the node changes to the susceptible state in the second stage of the time-slot. Any susceptible node, which is not infected or protected, may install some specific protection/immunization mechanisms in order to become resistant. The state of this node then changes to resistant in the second stage of the time slot. These reaction processes are assumed to be random, and we denote by α the probability that any infected node becomes susceptible, and ρ the probability that any susceptible node becomes resistant at the second stage of the time slot. Finally, we assume that these internal transitions are known by the defender but not by the attacker. Therefore, the attacker cannot infer defender actions because an infected node can become susceptible because of a honeypot or an internal reaction.

Based on the previous description of one time slot, the next section is dedicated to the construction of the centrality game model that is used to determine how the defender and the attacker choose their best strategies at each time slot.

3.3   Definition of the Centrality Game

The *centrality game* is the zero-sum Bayesian game defined by a tuple $\mathcal{G} = (G, N, Z, A, \alpha, \rho, \mathcal{R}, b)$, where:

- $G = (V, E)$ is the network (a finite and directed graph) with $V = S \cup I \cup R$ set of nodes and E set of edges;
- The players are the defender (player 1) and the attacker (player 2);
- Z is the set of world's states, $Z = \mathcal{P}(I)$;
- The world is the sub-graph of the network consisting in non-resistant nodes, i.e., nodes in $N = V \setminus R = S \cup I$. The attacker knows the state of the world at each time t while the belief of the defender over this state at time t can be computed from his belief b^{t-1} over the state of the whole network at time $t - 1$. Nodes centrality values are those of the sub-graph restricted to N;

– A_1 is the set of defender's actions. An action for the defender consists in choosing at most h edges to watch. Strategically, in case the defender knows the network state, each such edge $\{i, j\}$ may be any one that links an infected to a susceptible nodes and an action for the defender thus-wise consists in choosing h couples $(i, j) \in I \times S$ of adjacent infected and susceptible nodes if there exists so much. Hence, in this case, by taking as effective stake zone,

$$\$_z = \{(i, j) \in I \times S : \{i, j\} \in E\},$$

the action space for the defender is $\begin{cases} \mathcal{P}_h\left(\$_z\right) \text{ if } |\$_z| > h \\ \{2^{\$_z}\} \quad\quad \text{otherwise} \end{cases}$, where $\mathcal{P}_h\left(A\right)$ and 2^A respectively denote the set of subsets of any set A with h elements and the power set of A. Now the defender does not know the state of the network, he plays over the rough stake $\$ = E \cap (N \times N)$ and his action space is accordingly $A_1 = \begin{cases} \mathcal{P}_h\left(\$\right) \text{ if } |\$| > h \\ \{2^{\$}\} \quad\quad \text{otherwise} \end{cases}$;

– A_2 is the set of attacker's actions. An action for the attacker consists in choosing from any infected node i a set T_i of adjacent, susceptible nodes to propagate the virus on it (call it target). Strategically, she will never target the same susceptible node from two distinct infected sources. In other words, the action space for the attacker is the set A_2 of tuples $T = (T_i)_{i \in I}$ that satisfy the properties: $\begin{cases} \forall i \in I, & T_i \subseteq S \\ \forall i \in I, \forall j \in T_i, & (i, j) \in \$_z \\ \forall k, l \in I, & k \neq l \implies T_k \cap T_l = \emptyset \end{cases}$;

– α is the probability that any infected node becomes susceptible;
– ρ is the probability that any susceptible node becomes resistant;
– $\mathcal{O}$ is the set of defender's observations at the end of each time slot;
– $\mathcal{R}$ is the defender's reward at each time slot;

When an action profile $(W, T) \in A_1 \times A_2$ is taken, the centrality value of any node is rewarded to the defender, if the node transits from infected to susceptible, or to the attacker, if the node transits from susceptible to infected. The expected partial reward of the defender is depicted in Table 1. The reward associated with an action profile $(W, T) \in A_1 \times A_2$ is

Table 1. The defender's expected reward resulting from a joint action (W, T) on one edge

		ATTACKER: Propagate $i \to j$?	
		Propagate ($j \in T_i$)	No propagate ($j \notin T_i$)
DEFENDER: Watch $\{i, j\}$?	Watch ($\{i, j\} \in W$)	$(1 - \rho)\, c_i$	0
	No watch ($\{i, j\} \notin W$)	$-(1 - \alpha)\, c_j$	0

$$\mathcal{R}\left(W,T\right) = \sum_{\substack{(i,j)\in\$_z \\ \{i,j\}\in W \\ j\in T_i}} (1-\rho)\,c_i - \sum_{\substack{(i,j)\in\$_z \\ \{i,j\}\notin W \\ j\in T_i}} (1-\alpha)\,c_j = \sum_{\substack{(i,j)\in\$ \\ \{i,j\}\in W \\ j\in T_i}} (1-\rho)\,c_i + \sum_{\substack{(i,j)\in\$ \\ \{i,j\}\notin W \\ j\in T_i}} (\alpha-1)\,c_j.$$

Indeed, for all $(i,j) \in \$ \setminus \$_z$, we never get $j \in T_i$.

Remark 1. *In case there are exactly or less than h edges in the stake, the centrality game is no worth termed so since the defender will actually have no more than one option. So, in the remaining of this section, we assume that the stake contains more than h edges.*

3.4   Reward Associated with a Strategy Profile

Players play strategies $\pi_1 \in \Delta(A_1)$ and $\pi_2 : Z \longrightarrow \Delta(A_2)$. Denote Π_i the strategy space for player i. The expected reward of the defender with belief $b \in \Delta(Z)$ when the strategy profile $\pi = (\pi_1, \pi_2)$ is $\mathcal{R}(\pi\,|b) = \sum_{z\in Z} b(z)\,\mathcal{R}(\pi\,|z)$,

where

$$
\begin{aligned}
\mathcal{R}\left(\pi\,|z\right) &= \sum_{(W,T)\in A_1\times A_2} \pi_1\left(W\right)\pi_2\left(T\,|z\right)\mathcal{R}\left(W,T\right) \\
&= \sum_{\substack{(i,j)\in\$ \\ (W,T)\in A_1\times A_2 \\ \{i,j\}\in W \\ j\in T_i}} \pi_1\left(W\right)\pi_2\left(T\,|z\right)(1-\rho)\,c_i + \sum_{\substack{(i,j)\in\$ \\ (W,T)\in A_1\times A_2 \\ \{i,j\}\notin W \\ j\in T_i}} \pi_1\left(W\right)\pi_2\left(T\,|z\right)(\alpha-1)\,c_j \\
&= \sum_{(i,j)\in\$} \sum_{\substack{(W,T)\in A_1\times A_2: \\ \{i,j\}\in W \\ j\in T_i}} \pi_1\left(W\right)\pi_2\left(T\,|z\right)(1-\rho)\,c_i \\
&\quad + \sum_{(i,j)\in\$} \sum_{\substack{(W,T)\in A_1\times A_2: \\ \{i,j\}\notin W \\ j\in T_i}} \pi_1\left(W\right)\pi_2\left(T\,|z\right)(\alpha-1)\,c_j \\
&= \sum_{(i,j)\in\$} \pi_1\left(i,j\right)\pi_2\left(i,j\,|z\right)(1-\rho)\,c_i + \sum_{(i,j)\in\$} (1-\pi_1\left(i,j\right))\pi_2\left(i,j\,|z\right)(\alpha-1)\,c_j \\
&= \sum_{(i,j)\in\$} \pi_1\left(i,j\right)\pi_2\left(i,j\,|z\right)\left((1-\rho)\,c_i + (1-\alpha)\,c_j\right) - \sum_{(i,j)\in\$} (1-\alpha)\,\pi_2\left(i,j\,|z\right)c_j \\
&= \sum_{(i,j)\in\$} \pi_2\left(i,j\,|z\right)\left(\pi_1\left(i,j\right)\left((1-\rho)\,c_i + (1-\alpha)\,c_j\right) - (1-\alpha)\,c_j\right),
\end{aligned}
$$

$\pi_1\left(i,j\right) = \displaystyle\sum_{\substack{W\in A_1 \\ \{i,j\}\in W}} \pi_1\left(W\right)$ and $\pi_2\left(i,j\,|z\right) = \displaystyle\sum_{\substack{T\in A_2 \\ j\in T_i}} \pi_2\left(T\,|z\right)$ being respectively the

probabilities that the defender watches edge $\{i,j\}$ and the attacker targets node j from node i when the network state is z.

So, the payoff associated with the strategy profile π under the defender belief b is

$$
\begin{aligned}
\mathcal{R}\left(\pi\,|b\right) &= \sum_{z\in Z}\sum_{(i,j)\in\$} \pi_1\left(i,j\right)\pi_2\left(i,j\,|z\right)b\left(z\right)\left((1-\rho)\,c_i + (1-\alpha)\,c_j\right) \\
&\quad - \sum_{z\in Z}\sum_{(i,j)\in\$} (1-\alpha)\,\pi_2\left(i,j\,|z\right)b\left(z\right)c_j \\
&= \sum_{z\in Z}\sum_{(i,j)\in\$} \pi_2\left(i,j\,|z\right)b\left(z\right)\left(\pi_1\left(i,j\right)\left((1-\rho)\,c_i + (1-\alpha)\,c_j\right) - (1-\alpha)\,c_j\right),
\end{aligned}
$$

or

$$\mathcal{R}\left(\pi \,|b\right) \;=\; \sum_{(i,j)\in \mathbb{S}} \pi_1\left(i,j\right) \pi_2\left(i,j\,|b\right) \left(\left(1-\rho\right)c_i + \left(1-\alpha\right)c_j\right) - \sum_{(i,j)\in \mathbb{S}} \left(1-\alpha\right)\pi_2\left(i,j\,|b\right)c_j$$

$$=\; \sum_{(i,j)\in \mathbb{S}} \pi_2\left(i,j\,|b\right) \left(\pi_1\left(i,j\right)\left(\left(1-\rho\right)c_i + \left(1-\alpha\right)c_j\right) - \left(1-\alpha\right)c_j\right).$$

One can also write

$$\mathcal{R}\left(\pi \,|b\right) = \sum_{(i,j)\in \mathbb{S}} \pi_1\left(i,j\right)\varphi_1\left(i,j\,|b\,,\pi_2\right) - \sum_{(i,j)\in \mathbb{S}} \psi_1\left(i,j\,|b\,,\pi_2\right) \tag{1}$$

$$=\; \sum_{(i,j)\in \mathbb{S}} \pi_2\left(i,j\,|b\right)\varphi_2\left(i,j\,|\pi_1\right), \tag{2}$$

where, for all nodes i and j, $\varphi_1\left(i,j\,|b\,,\pi_2\right) = \pi_2\left(i,j\,|b\right)\left(\left(1-\rho\right)c_i + \left(1-\alpha\right)c_j\right)$
is the defender's expected profit when he "asks for the cake and eat it too" in case of virus transmission from i to j, $\psi_1\left(i,j\,|b\,,\pi_2\right) = \left(1-\alpha\right)\pi_2\left(i,j\,|b\right)c_j$ is the marginal loss of the defender for a virus transmission from nodes i to j,

$$\varphi_2\left(i,j\,|\pi_1\right) = \pi_1\left(i,j\right)\left(\left(1-\rho\right)c_i + \left(1-\alpha\right)c_j\right) - \left(1-\alpha\right)c_j$$

$$=\; \pi_1\left(i,j\right)\left(1-\rho\right)c_i - \left(1-\pi_1\left(i,j\right)\right)\left(1-\alpha\right)c_j$$

is the expected reward of the defender in case the attacker targets node j from i and $\pi_2\left(i,j|b\right) = \sum_{(i,j)\in \mathbb{S}} \pi_2\left(i,j|z\right)b\left(z\right)$ is the marginal probability that the attacker spreads the virus from i to j knowing the defender's belief b.

Remark 2. 1. For all $z \in Z$ and all $(i,j) \notin \mathbb{S}_z$, we have $\pi_2\left(i,j\,|z\right) = 0$.
2. For all $(i,j) \notin \mathbb{S}_b = \bigcup_{z\in\text{supp}(b)} \mathbb{S}_z$, we have $\pi_1\left(i,j\right) = 0$, where $\text{supp}\left(b\right) = \{z \in Z : b\left(z\right) \neq 0\}$ is the support of the belief b.

3.5   Best Responses to Players' Strategies

Remember that the defender wishes to maximize the payoff, while the attacker wishes to minimize it. This subsection advices each player when the opponent's strategy is known.

Best Response of the Defender

A strategy π_1 for the defender is a best response to some strategy π_2 of the attacker when π_1 maximizes the reward $\mathcal{R}\left(\pi \,|b\right) =$

$\sum\limits_{(i,j)\in\$} \pi_1(i,j)\varphi_1(i,j\,|b\,,\pi_2) - \sum\limits_{(i,j)\in\$} \psi_1(i,j\,|b\,,\pi_2)$. And the maximum payoff

for a fixed attacker strategy π_2 and fixed coefficients $\varphi_1(i,j\,|b\,,\pi_2)$ and ψ_1 corresponds to the maximum of the $\sum\limits_{(i,j)\in\$} \pi_1(i,j)\varphi_1(i,j\,|b\,,\pi_2)$'s and is obtained

by taking $\pi_1(i,j)=0$ whenever (i,j) is not top ranked according to $\varphi_1(\cdot\,|b\,,\pi_2)$, i.e., the defender is not better off given that he will "ask for the cake and eat it too".

Note that the pseudo probability distribution π_1 over $\$$ should be consistent with some probability distribution over A_1, and this is true only if the number of edges to watch is important enough to receive all the honeypots. In other words, the defender should focus on the h top ranked $(i,j) \in \$$. To express this mathematically, define over the stake the rank $r(i,j\,|b\,,\pi_2) = 1+|\{(x,y)\in\$:\varphi_1(x,y\,|b\,,\pi_2)>\varphi_1(i,j\,|b\,,\pi_2)\}|$ that should guide the choice for the defender,

This done, π_1 best responds to π_2 if $\pi_1(i,j)=0$ whenever $r(i,j\,|b\,,\pi_2)>h$, i.e., if $\pi_1(i,j)=0$ for all (i,j) not in the set $\mathrm{SL}_1(\pi_2)=\{(x,y)\in\$:r(x,y\,|b\,,\pi_2)\leqslant h\}$ of the h top ranked in the stake according to $\varphi_1(\cdot\,|b\,,\pi_2)$. However, for all $(i,j)\in\$$, $\pi_1(i,j)=0$ iff

$$\forall W \in A_1, \quad \{i,j\} \in W \implies \pi_1(W)=0.$$

Practically, this means that the defender focuses on edges $\{i,j\}$ with maximal values of $\varphi_1(i,j\,|b\,,\pi_2)$ and ignores the other edges, which is always possible. $\mathrm{SL}_1(\pi_2)$ is the short list for the defender best responding to π_2 attacker strategy. The effective probability distribution over this short list should meet some probability distribution over A and it is not excluded that $\pi_1(i,j)=0$ for some $(i,j) \in \mathrm{SL}_1(\pi_2)$.

Best Response of the Attacker

Similarly, a strategy π_2 for the attacker best responds to some strategy π_1 of the defender when π_2 minimizes the reward $\mathcal{R}(\pi\,|b) = \sum\limits_{(i,j)\in\$}\sum\limits_{z\in Z} \pi_2(i,j\,|z)\,b(z)\,\varphi_2(i,j\,|\pi_1)$. And the minimum reward for a fixed

defender strategy π_1 and fixed coefficients $\varphi_2(i,j\,|\pi_1)$ and $b(z)$ is realized if $\pi_2(i,j\,|z)=0$ in any possible state z $(b(z)\neq 0)$ in which $\varphi_2(i,j\,|\pi_1)$ is not minimal, i.e., if, for all possible state $z \in Z$, $\pi_2(i,j\,|z)=0$ whenever (i,j) is not in the set $\mathrm{SL}_2(\pi_1)=\{(x,y)\in\$:\forall(u,v)\in\$,\varphi_2(u,v\,|\pi_1)\geqslant\varphi_2(x,y\,|\pi_1)\}$ of $\varphi_2(\cdot\,|\pi_1)$-minimally valued possibilities in the stake. However, for all $(i,j)\in\$$, $\pi_2(i,j\,|z)=0$ iff

$$\forall T \in A_2, \quad j \in T_i \implies \pi_2(T\,|z)=0.$$

Practically, this means that when the network state is z, from each infected node i, the attacker may transmit the virus to some susceptible neighbor j only if $\varphi_2(i,j\,|\pi_1)$ is minimal over the stake. $\mathrm{SL}_2(\pi_1)$ is the short list for the attacker best responding to the defender's strategy π_1 when the network state is z, i.e., from node i, the attacker transmits the virus to nodes of lower expected reward for the defender.

3.6 Nash Equilibria

At Nash equilibrium (NE) $\pi^* = (\pi_1^*, \pi_2^*)$, each player best responds to his/her opponent's strategy and therefore, for all $(i, j) \notin \mathrm{SL}_n(\pi_{-n})$, player n assigns the probability 0 to (i, j).

Lemma 1. *If $\mathrm{SL}_1(\pi_2^*) \neq \$$, then $\mathrm{SL}_1(\pi_2^*) \subseteq \mathrm{SL}_2(\pi_1^*)$.*

i.e., At NE, unless the short list for the defender extends to the hole stake, all member of this short list is in the short list for the attacker. In other words, unless the defender wishes to watch all edges, he does not care attacker's a priori irrelevant targets.

Proof. Suppose that $\mathrm{SL}_1(\pi_2^*) \neq \$$ and take any $(i, j) \notin \mathrm{SL}_2(\pi_1^*)$. It comes successively:

$(i, j) \notin \mathrm{SL}_2(\pi_1^*)$;

for all $z \in Z$, if $b(z) \neq 0$, then $\pi_2^*(i, j \,|\, z) = 0$, so,

for all $z \in Z$, $\varphi_1(i, j \,|\, b, \pi_2^*) = \pi_2^*(i, j \,|\, z) b(z) \Big((1 - \rho) c_i + (1 - \alpha) c_j \Big) =$

0. In this case, (i, j) is minimally ranked according to $\varphi_1(\cdot \,|\, b, \pi_2^*)$ because $\varphi_1(u, v \,|\, b, \pi_2^*) \geqslant 0, \forall (u, v) \in \$$.

Since $\mathrm{SL}_1(\pi_2^*) \neq \$$, at least one $(x, y) \in \$$ is not h top ranked according to $\varphi_1(\cdot \,|\, b, \pi_2^*)$. As $\varphi_1(x, y \,|\, b, \pi_2^*) \geqslant 0$, we conclude that, $(i, j) \notin \mathrm{SL}_1(\pi_2^*)$. ∎

Lemma 2. *1. For all $(i, j) \in \mathrm{SL}_1(\pi_2^*)$, all $(k, l) \in \mathrm{SL}_2(\pi_1^*) \setminus \mathrm{SL}_1(\pi_2^*)$ and all $(u, v) \in \$ \setminus \mathrm{SL}_2(\pi_1^*)$, it holds: $\begin{cases} c_j \geqslant c_l > c_v \\ c_j > c_l \iff \pi_1^*(i, j) > 0 \end{cases}$.*
2. For all couples $(k, l), (k', l')$ in $\mathrm{SL}_2(\pi_1^*) \setminus \mathrm{SL}_1(\pi_2^*)$, it holds: $c_l = c_{l'}$.

i.e., at NE: (1) the defender protects centrality values down to a certain threshold θ_1 while the attacker targets centrality values down to a not more important threshold θ_2; (2) all possible attacker target nodes that the defender should not protect have the same centrality value. Note that this lemma does not state that $\mathrm{SL}_2(\pi_1^*) \setminus \mathrm{SL}_1(\pi_2^*)$ is a non-empty set.

Proof. From $(k, l) \notin \mathrm{SL}_1(\pi_2^*)$, it comes $\pi_1^*(k, l) = 0$. From $(k, l) \in \mathrm{SL}_2(\pi_1^*)$, it comes that $\varphi_2(k, l \,|\, \pi_1^*) = -(1 - \alpha) c_l$ is minimal. This point witnesses the second statement of the lemma. Note that $(u, v) \notin \mathrm{SL}_2(\pi_1^*)$, and from Lemma 1, $(u, v) \notin \mathrm{SL}_1(\pi_2^*)$. So, $\pi_1^*(u, v) = 0$. Then $\varphi_2(u, v \,|\, \pi_1^*) = -(1 - \alpha) c_v$ and, since $\varphi_2(k, l \,|\, \pi_1^*) = -(1 - \alpha) c_l$ is minimal, it comes $-(1 - \alpha) c_l < -(1 - \alpha) c_v$ and, consequently, $c_l > c_v$.

In addition, the minimality of $\varphi_2(k, l \,|\, \pi_1^*)$ also applies to (i, j) and, therefore $\pi_1^*(i, j) \Big((1 - \rho) c_i + (1 - \alpha) c_j \Big) - (1 - \alpha) c_j = -(1 - \alpha) c_l$. Then,

$\pi_1^* (i,j) \left((1-\rho) c_i + (1-\alpha) c_j \right) = (1-\alpha)(c_j - c_l)$. The positivity of $c_j - c_l$ relies on that of $(1-\rho) c_i + (1-\alpha) c_j$.   ∎

Theorem 1. *For some centrality values θ_1 and θ_2, it holds:*

1. $SL_1(\pi_2^*) = \{(i,j) \in \$: c_j \geqslant \theta_1\}$, $SL_2(\pi_1^*) = \{(i,j) \in \$: c_j \geqslant \theta_2\}$;
2. *For some $(i,j) \in SL_p$, $p = 1,2$, it holds $c_j = \theta_p$ and $\pi_p^* (i,j) \neq 0$;*
3. $\theta_2 \leqslant \theta_1$;
4. *If $\theta_2 < \theta_1$, then no centrality value can lie in the space (θ_2, θ_1).*

Proof. Consider $\theta_p = \min\limits_{(\text{source,target}) \in SL_p} c_{\text{target}}$, for $p = 1,2$.

By this definition, $c_j \geqslant \theta_p$ for any $(i,j) \in SL_p$. Conversely, on the one hand, take any $(k,l) \in \$$ such that $c_l \geqslant \theta_2$. The minimum value θ_2 is attained for some $(k',l') \in SL_2$. Then, from the inequality $c_l \geqslant c_{l'}$ and Lemma 2.1, it comes $(k,l) \in SL_2(\pi_2^*)$ (Indeed, suppose $(k,l) \in \$ \setminus SL_2(\pi_2^*)$, we have, $c_l < c_{l'}$)). On the other hand, take any $(i,j) \in \$$ such that $c_j \geqslant \theta_1$. With a similar reasoning, we get $(i,j) \in SL_1$. Point 1 is proven.

For the proof of point 2, since $\theta_p = \min\limits_{(\text{source,target}) \in SL_p} c_{\text{target}}$, for $p = 1,2$, they are attained for some $(i,j) \in SL_1$ and $(k,l) \in SL_2$ respectively.

Since $SL_1(\pi_2^*) \subseteq SL_2(\pi_1^*)$ and the definition of θ_p, $p = 1,2$, we have $\theta_2 \leq \theta_1$ (and more specifically $\theta_2 < \theta_1$ iff $SL_1(\pi_2^*) \subset SL_2(\pi_1^*)$). Point 3, is proven.

For the proof of point 4, let's assume that there is $(u,v) \in SL_2(\pi_1^*)$ and $(i,j) \in \$$ such that $\theta_2 = c_v$ and c_j is in the space (θ_2, θ_1); in this case, $(i,j) \in SL_2(\pi_1^*) \setminus SL_1(\pi_2^*)$. Therefore, $(i,j), (u,v) \in SL_2(\pi_1^*) \setminus SL_1(\pi_2^*)$, by Lemma 2.2, $c_j = \theta_2$ which is absurd. Point 4 is proven.

4   Computation of the Nash Equilibria

We assume that the players are playing an NE strategy profile π. That is, the supports $\text{supp}(\pi_i)$, $i = 1,2$ of their strategies π_i are included in their respective shortlists $SL_i(\pi_{-i})$ that depends upon respective thresholds θ_i.

4.1   Shortlists Exploitation

In this subsection, we note s the minimum value of φ_2 under the NE, i.e., $s = \min\limits_{(i,j) \in \$} \varphi_2(i,j | \pi_1)$.

Proposition 1. *1.* $s = -(1-\alpha) \dfrac{\left(\sum\limits_{\substack{(i,j) \in \$_b \\ c_j \geqslant \theta_1}} \dfrac{c_j}{(1-\rho) c_i + (1-\alpha) c_j} \right) - \dfrac{h}{1-\alpha}}{\sum\limits_{\substack{(i,j) \in \$_b \\ c_j \geqslant \theta_1}} \dfrac{1}{(1-\rho) c_i + (1-\alpha) c_j}}.$

2. *For all* $(i, j) \in \mathbb{S}$,

$$
\begin{cases}
(i, j) \in \mathrm{SL}_2 (\pi_1) \implies \varphi_2 (i, j \,|\, \pi_1) = s \text{ and } \pi_1 (i, j) = \dfrac{s + (1 - \alpha) \, c_j}{(1 - \rho) \, c_i + (1 - \alpha) \, c_j} \\
(i, j) \notin \mathrm{SL}_2 (\pi_1) \implies \varphi_2 (i, j \,|\, \pi_1) > s \text{ and } \pi_1 (i, j) = 0
\end{cases}
$$

3. $$
\sum_{\substack{(i,j) \in \mathbb{S}_b \\ c_j \geqslant \theta_1}} \frac{c_j - \theta_1}{(1 - \rho) \, c_i + (1 - \alpha) \, c_j} \leqslant \frac{h}{1 - \alpha}.
$$

If $\theta_1 > \theta_2$, *then* $$
\sum_{\substack{(i,j) \in \mathbb{S}_b \\ c_j \geqslant \theta_1}} \frac{c_j - \theta_2}{(1 - \rho) \, c_i + (1 - \alpha) \, c_j} = \sum_{\substack{(i,j) \in \mathbb{S}_b \\ c_j \geqslant \theta_2}} \frac{c_j - \theta_2}{(1 - \rho) \, c_i + (1 - \alpha) \, c_j} =
$$

$$
\frac{h}{1 - \alpha}.
$$

4. *If* $\mathrm{Last}_h \subseteq \{(i, j) \in \mathbb{S}_b : c_j \geqslant \theta_1\}$ *is any set of* h *last ranked elements of the plausible stake according to* $\pi_1 (i, j)$, *then:*

$$
\sum_{(i,j) \in \mathrm{Last}_h} \pi_1 (i, j) \geqslant \frac{(h - 1) \, h}{|\mathbb{S}_b| - 1}.
$$

5. *If* $s \geqslant 0$ *then* $\theta_1 = \min\limits_{(i,j) \in \mathbb{S}_b} c_j$.

   If $s < 0$ *then the attacker infects a susceptible node* j *if and only if that for some infected node* i, *it holds* $\varphi_2 (i, j \,|\, \pi_1) = s$.

Proof. The comparison of $\varphi_2 (i, j \,|\, \pi_1)$ and s comes from the definition of the attacker's shortlist; in case $(i, j) \in \mathrm{SL}_2 (\pi_1)$, the value of $\pi_1 (i, j)$ comes from this comparison. The point 2 is proven. Point 1 comes from the facts that the probabilities $\pi_1 (i, j)$ sum to the number h of edges the defender chooses, and $\pi_1 = 0$ out of the defender's shortlist. The non-negativeness of π_1 implies $(1 - \alpha) \, c_j \geqslant s$ then $(1 - \alpha) \, \theta_1 \geqslant s$ on the defender's shortlist. In case $\theta_1 > \theta_2$, for some $(i, j) \in \mathrm{SL}_2 \setminus \mathrm{SL}_1$, it holds $c_j = \theta_2$ and $\pi_1 (i, j) = \dfrac{s + (1 - \alpha) \, c_j}{(1 - \rho) \, c_i + (1 - \alpha) \, c_j} = 0$. So, we get $s = (1 - \alpha) \, \theta_2$. Thus, $(1 - \alpha) \, c_j \geqslant s$ in the general case, and $s = (1 - \alpha) \, \theta_2$ in case $\theta_1 > \theta_2$. This witnesses the to point 3. Point 4 is a condition that comes from [19]. Note that it is equivalent to

$$
\sum_{(u,v) \in \mathrm{Last}_h} \frac{-(1 - \alpha) \dfrac{\left(\displaystyle\sum_{\substack{(i,j) \in \mathbb{S}_b \\ c_j \geqslant \theta_1}} \dfrac{c_j}{(1 - \rho) \, c_i + (1 - \alpha) \, c_j} \right) - \dfrac{h}{1 - \alpha}}{\displaystyle\sum_{\substack{(i,j) \in \mathbb{S}_b \\ c_j \geqslant \theta_1}} \dfrac{1}{(1 - \rho) \, c_i + (1 - \alpha) \, c_j}} + (1 - \alpha) \, c_v}{(1 - \rho) \, c_u + (1 - \alpha) \, c_v} \geqslant \frac{(h - 1) \, h}{|\mathbb{S}_b| - 1}.
$$

$$(3)$$

For the proof of 5, suppose $s \geqslant 0$. That is, for any $(i,j) \in \$$, we get successively: $\varphi_2(i,j \,|\pi_1) \geqslant 0$, $\pi_1(i,j)\,((1-\rho)\,c_i + (1-\alpha)\,c_j) - (1-\alpha)\,c_j \geqslant 0$,

$$\pi_1(i,j) \geqslant \frac{(1-\alpha)\,c_j}{(1-\rho)\,c_i + (1-\alpha)\,c_j} > 0, \; (i,j) \in \$, \; c_j \geqslant \theta_1.$$ Suppose on the

other hand that $s < 0$. From the definition of the attacker'r shortlist, it comes:

$$\mathcal{R}(\pi \,|b) = \sum_{\substack{(i,j)\in\$ \\ \varphi_2(i,j|\pi_1) \text{ is minimal}}} \pi_2(i,j \,|b)\,\varphi_2(i,j \,|\pi_1) = s \sum_{\substack{(i,j)\in\$ \\ \varphi_2(i,j|\pi_1)=s}} \pi_2(i,j \,|b).$$

The minimization of this result imposes maximization of the $\pi_2(i,j \,|b)$'s whenever $\varphi_2(i,j \,|\pi_1)$ is minimal.

5   Numerical Illustrations

We consider the case of total observation, where the defender knows the network state and as the centrality we take the node's degrees. A simulation of the result of the centrality game on the epidemic dynamics is presented in this section. Even though our model is general enough to handle any centrality measure, the simulation uses the degree centrality. We consider an Erdös-Réyni random graph with 2000 nodes and an expected degree value of 10 for each node. 50 nodes, chosen randomly, are infected at time-slot 1 and all the other nodes are susceptible. The simulation run 100 times with $\alpha = 0.1$, $\varrho = 0.7$ and 20 honeypots. After the 100 simulations, the program reported from each edition the value of the following metrics

- The epidemic peak (EP), which is the maximum number of infected nodes available in the network;
- The time this peak is attained (TP);
- The time for the control of the epidemic (TC), i.e., the first period at which the number of edges in the stake is not greater than the number of honeypot. From that period onward, the defender prevents any infection;
- The time for the virus extinction, i.e., the first period at which no infected node exists in the network.

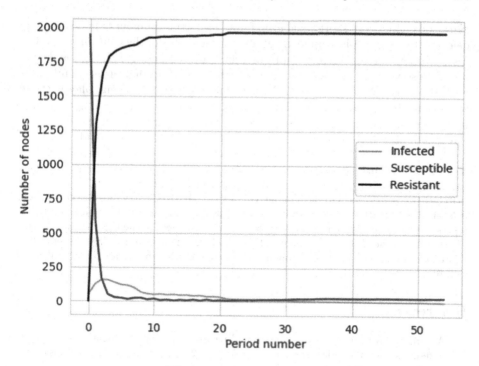

Fig. 1. Epidemic evolution

The program also return the most relevant result (see Fig. 1) by considering the distance of each simulation to the mean of the preceding simulations, from the perspective of the above last metrics. Each simulation elapsed 0.97 second in average.

In average, the epidemic reached its peak, of 142 or 143 nodes at the period 3. The defender took control of the epidemic after 54 periods and the epidemic died out after 55 periods. The confident intervals (at 95%) for those metrics is [142.44, 143.20] (EP), [3.13, 3.15] (TP), [54.29, 54.75] (TC), [55.29, 55.75] for the TE.

6   Conclusions and Further Work

In order to circumvent the hardness of the value iteration algorithm, we propose a game theoretic framework based on nodes' centrality. At each period, each player optimize the centrality measures of nodes under his/her control. The attacker and the defender are therefore involved in a bayesian game in which the type of attacker correspond to the state of the network. The NE correspond to a situation where each player has fixed a threshold and protect/attack only nodes of centrality bounded from below by this threshold, the defender being at least equal to that of the attacker. This property yield equations that allow a computational resolution determination of the NE. Experiments prove that the game solved in a very short time, even for an important number of nodes, and the defender takes control of epidemic at the earlier stages of the confrontation. Our framework applies to any centrality measure, and we adopted the nodes degree. We have solved the problem in the case where the information is complete for both the defender and the attacker and assuming that the agents play with the same centrality measures. Our future work will consist in extending this game to a game with incomplete information on the one hand and in assuming that the agents play with different centrality measures on the other hand.

Acknowledgments. Research was sponsored by the U.S. Army Research Office and was accomplished under Cooperative Agreement Numbers W911NF-19-2-0150, W911NF-22-2-0175 and Grant Number W911NF-21-1-0326. The views and conclusions contained in this document are those of the authors and should not be interpreted as representing the official policies, either expressed or implied, of the U.S. Army Research Laboratory or the U.S. Government. The U.S. Government is authorized to reproduce and distribute reprints for Government purposes notwithstanding any copyright notation herein.

References

1. Amini, H., Minca, A.: Epidemic spreading and equilibrium social distancing in heterogeneous networks. Dyn. Games Appl. **12**(1), 258–287 (2022). https://doi.org/10.1007/s13235-021-00411-1
2. Aurell, A., Carmona, R., Dayanıklı, G., Laurière, M.: Finite state graphon games with applications to epidemics. Dyn. Games Appl. **12**(1), 49–81 (2022). https://doi.org/10.1007/s13235-021-00410-2
3. Bloem, M., Alpcan, T., Basar, T.: Intrusion response as a resource allocation problem. In: Proceedings of the 45th IEEE Conference on Decision and Control, pp. 6283–6288. IEEE (2006)
4. Cai, G., Wang, B., Hu, W., Wang, T.: Moving target defense: state of the art and characteristics. Front. Inf. Technol. Electron. Eng. **17**(11), 1122–1153 (2016). https://doi.org/10.1631/FITEE.1601321
5. Chen, Z.: Modeling and defending against internet worm attacks. Ph.D. thesis, Georgia Institute of Technology (2007)
6. Freeman, L.C.: A set of measures of centrality based on betweenness. Sociometry **40**, 35–41 (1977)
7. Freeman, L.C.: Centrality in social networks conceptual clarification. Soc. Netw. **1**(3), 215–239 (1978)
8. Horák, K., Bosansky, B., Kiekintveld, C., Kamhoua, C.: Compact representation of value function in partially observable stochastic games, pp. 350–356 (2019). https://doi.org/10.24963/ijcai.2019/50
9. Horák, K., Bošanský, B., Pěchouček, M.: Heuristic search value iteration for one-sided partially observable stochastic games. In: International Joint Conference on Artificial Intelligence, vol. 31, pp. 558–564 (2017)
10. Jajodia, S., Ghosh, A.K., Subrahmanian, V., Swarup, V., Wang, C., Wang, X.S.: Moving Target Defense II: Application of Game Theory and Adversarial Modeling, vol. 100. Springer, Cham (2012)
11. Kiss, I.Z., Miller, J.C., Simon, P.L., et al.: Mathematics of Epidemics on Networks, vol. 598. Springer, Cham (2017)

12. Kordonis, I., Lagos, A.R., Papavassilopoulos, G.P.: Dynamic games of social distancing during an epidemic: analysis of asymmetric solutions. Dyn. Games Appl. **12**(1), 214–236 (2022)
13. Lü, L., Chen, D., Ren, X.L., Zhang, Q.M., Zhang, Y.C., Zhou, T.: Vital nodes identification in complex networks. Phys. Rep. **650**, 1–63 (2016)
14. Pastor-Satorras, R., Castellano, C., Van Mieghem, P., Vespignani, A.: Epidemic processes in complex networks. Rev. Mod. Phys. **87**(3), 925 (2015)
15. Patcha, A., Park, J.M.: A game theoretic approach to modeling intrusion detection in mobile ad hoc networks. In: Proceedings from the Fifth Annual IEEE SMC Information Assurance Workshop, 2004, pp. 280–284. IEEE (2004)
16. Tsemogne, O., Hayel, Y., Kamhoua, C., Deugoue, G.: Partially observable stochastic games for cyber deception against network epidemic. In: GameSec 2020. LNCS, vol. 12513, pp. 312–325. Springer, Cham (2020). https://doi.org/10.1007/978-3-030-64793-3_17
17. Tsemogne, O., Hayel, Y., Kamhoua, C., Deugoue, G.: A partially observable stochastic zero-sum game for a network epidemic control problem. Dyn. Games Appl. **12**(1), 82–109 (2022)
18. Tsemogne, O., Hayel, Y., Kamhoua, C., Deugoué, G.: Game theoretic modeling of cyber deception against epidemic botnets in internet of things. IEEE Internet Things J. **9**(4), 2678–2687 (2021)
19. Zaman, A., Marsaglia, G.: Random selection of subsets with specified element probabilities. Commun. Stat.-Theory Methods **19**(11), 4419–4434 (1990)
20. Zhao, X., Liu, F., Wang, J., Li, T., et al.: Evaluating influential nodes in social networks by local centrality with a coefficient. ISPRS Int. J. Geo-Inf. **6**(2), 35 (2017)

Optimizing Intrusion Detection Systems Placement Against Network Virus Spreading Using a Partially Observable Stochastic Minimum-Threat Path Game

Olivier Tsemogne[1,3]($\boxtimes$) (iD), Yezekael Hayel[1] (iD), Charles Kamhoua[2] (iD),
and Gabriel Deugoué[3] (iD)

[1] CERI/LIA, Avignon Université, Avignon, France
`olivier.kamguia@alumni.univ-avignon.fr`, `yezekael.hayel@univ-avignon.fr`
[2] US Army Reseach Laboratory, Adelphi, USA
`charles.a.kamhoua.civ@army.mil`
[3] University of Dschang, Dschang, Cameroon
`agdeugoue@yahoo.fr`

Abstract. Intrusion Detection Systems (IDS) are security tools that aim to detect tentative of virus propagation between two interconnected devices. As the propagation of a virus or malware is dynamic and can be strategically controlled by the attacker, we model the problem of optimally determining IDS position in a network as a partially observable zero-sum stochastic Minimum-Threat path game (POSMPG). The goal of the attacker is to infect a maximum number of nodes at a given instant, and then a state-extended stochastic game framework is proposed in order to get optimality equations. We are then able to determine optimal solutions of the POSMPG and to apply our result to an adversarial control of virus propagation on a network.

Keywords: Partially observable stochastic minimum-threat path game · Partially observable stochastic shortest-path game · Epidemic control

1 Introduction

By comparison, many scenarios can be analyzed as epidemic propagation. Henceforth, the study of epidemic enters the scope of mathematics [13], with the division of the population into compartments like S (susceptible), I (infected) and R (removed) in the case of SIR epidemic model for instance. Unlike in biology, an epidemic in a network is generally a token (worm, virus, rumor, etc.) strategically propagated by an intelligent, rational agent. So the control of the propagation involves one or many rational, intelligent agents with mutually exclusive goals. Hence, game theoretic models are widely used to optimize this control. In realistic situations where nodes of the network (IoT users, for example) may not

© The Author(s), under exclusive license to Springer Nature Switzerland AG 2023
F. Fang et al. (Eds.): GameSec 2022, LNCS 13727, pp. 274–296, 2023.
https://doi.org/10.1007/978-3-031-26369-9_14

meet these characteristics of intelligence and rationality, recent articles [23] suggest a protection by a single defender trying to mitigate attacker's goal. Instead of optimizing players' one-stage strategies like in [24], which may not help to obtain the overall optimum payoffs, authors optimize strategies based on the history available to the player. The resulting game theoretic model is a zero-sum one-sided partially observable stochastic game (POSG).

In Markov decision processes as in stochastic games, the importance of the payoff is captured by the utility. Among the utilities presented in [16] is the one that corresponds to extremum component of a sequence, which gives better reward than any other utility captures the peak of an epidemic in a propagation scenario. However, to the best of our knowledge, there is no framework that tackles the optimization of the epidemic peak assuming an infinite attack-defense scenario with system transitions that no player can monitor. This obsolescence of the extremum-utility is witnessed by the non-interchangeability of the mean with the maximum or the minimum. So, in the literature, frameworks that tackle the epidemic control from the perspective of stochastic games assume the non-realistic sum or discounted sum of players reward. In this article, we make the realistic assumption of players trying to optimize the epidemic propagation, and we propose an algorithm for the optimal behavior for each player.

Our contribution is threefold:

- We propose a new game model for adversarial epidemic control;
- We study extremum-utility function for two-player zero-sum POSGs, and we set an algorithm for optimal strategies;
- We prove the convergence of this algorithm in the context of adversarial SIR epidemic control. In fact, we prove this convergence for the more general case two-player zero-sum POSG where the utility for one player is the overall maximum of the rewards.

The rest of the article is organized as follows. In the next section, we discuss some existing work on the epidemic control and the utility function considered. Next, we present a new game theoretic model, namely the partially observable stochastic minimum-threat path game. Then, in section Sect. 4, we discuss the solution of this model. Section 5 presents an algorithmic resolution of SIR epidemic model and, finally, we conclude our work in Sect. 6 and we give some perspectives.

2   Related Work

In mathematics and computer science, a broad scale of epidemic study addresses the issue of virus propagation as in biology, i.e., without consideration of the virus goal. In this scope, [13] uses terms from mathematical modelling of infectious diseases, classifies epidemics and study their propagation in a network through deferential analysis. Intractable differential equations that apply not only in the domain of computer network study put in relations the proportion of each compartments and their evolution. Focusing on network diseases and attempting to immunize network systems, [5], as well as [3] and [26], presents the Analytical Active Worm Propagation (AAWP) model, which characterizes the propagation of worms that employ random scanning. This model differs from the epidemiological model, which uses continuous time and never considers the patching rate nor the time it takes to a worm to infect a machine. Long before attacker releases the worm, she scans the system to find out vulnerable machines and establish a "hitlist" of machines that she will further infect and use as "stepping stones" to infect other vulnerable machines. With random scanning, if there are m_i vulnerable machines and n_i infected ones with a scanning rate of s, then the number of newly infected machines at the following stage will be $(m_i - n_i) \left[1 - \left(1 - \dfrac{1}{2^{32}} \right)^{sn_i} \right]$ in average. For many authors, there exists an epidemic threshold under which the epidemic dies out. However, the description via Markov chain shows that every state tends to be absorbent. This paradox suggested [26], an application of mean field approximation, which apply in the [26]'s N-intertwined model. For the sake of effectiveness, an important aspect of the virus study is the immunization strategies among which the targeted immunization strategy, which is based on immunizing the highest betweenness centrality nodes or links which could be thought effective up to 2011. However, taking possible size of the network that could be infected serves as the performance measure of the immunization procedure. [18] outlines a method which is significantly more efficient in preventing disease spreading. Another type of immunization, namely random immunization, also presents some weaknesses that [6] overcomes. On the one hand, almost all of the nodes need to be immunized before an epidemic is arrested; on the other hand, when the most highly connected nodes are targeted first, removal of just a small fraction of the nodes results in the network's disintegration. [6] presents an effective strategy based on the immunization of a small fraction of random acquaintances of randomly selected nodes.

Unlike in Biology, network viruses, among which botnets (which are used in DDoS) have targets and are discussed in the literature ([14] and [2] for instance). The Mirai botnet was first found in 2016 and has been used in some of the largest and most DDoS, including an attack in September 2016 on computer security journalist Brian Krebs' web site, an attack on French web host OVH, and the October 2016 Dyn cyber attack. Studying DDoS activities from August 2016 to February 2017, Antonakakis et al. noticed a capability to infect more than 60,000 IoT devices in its first 20 h and the existence of a steady state. Left apart a frequent check for network status and new prospective target victims, the Mirai attack consists in six steps including a brute-force attack to discover the default credentials of weakly configured IoT devices, the report to the "report server", the issuing of an infected command, the loading in the target devices of an instruction to download the malware (which protects the new recruited bot instances from other malware), (after a sufficient number of hosts is achieved) an instruction to commence an attack against a target server, the attack against the server. The victims range from game servers, telecoms, and anti-DDoS providers, to political websites and relatively obscure Russian sites ([2], p. 104).

Epidemics in networks are classified like in biological systems (see [3]). The population is divided into compartments, and the name of the epidemic derives from the possible compartments and the possible transitions of an individual between the compartments. For example, a Susceptible-Infected-Susceptible (SIS) epidemic model [12] admits two different compartments: the susceptible (S) individuals who can carry the virus but do not currently carry it; the infectious individuals (I) who carry the virus and can transmit it. Propagation of the virus implies transitions of individual state from S to I and from I to S. The NE concept is used in [21, 22] and [1] to stop the spread of SIS epidemics in a decentralized manner and to optimize influence in competitive contexts. To compare the advantages of centralized and decentralized protection of a network against threats, Trajanovski, Hayel et al. [21] discuss the price of anarchy (PoA) in single community, bipartite and multi-community networks. They prove the existence of the Nash equilibrium and outline a reinforcement learning algorithm to find the NE in pure strategies. They bounded the PoA (particularly in single community and bipartite networks) analytically and in concrete examples. The upper bound relies on the costs of possible individual decisions (to invest for protection or not), on the number of individuals in the communities and on the spreading rate. To address the issue of designing an optimal network topology while balancing multiple, possibly conflicting objectives such as cost, performance, and resiliency to viruses, Trajanovski, Kuipers et al. [22] model the SIS epidemic with the N-intertwined mean field approximation and use the network formation game model. As result, they give a new upper bound of PoA, show that the prize of stability is equal to 1 and the NE is achieved only if the graph is a star or a path graph. The decentralized protection is encouraged by [11] that regrettably does not consider the intervention of an actor who cares for the health of the whole network, which contradicts the selfishness of players in real situations.

In order to handle this selfishness, the literature also pay importance on the decentralized protection. [15], for example, optimizes the action of a defender monitoring normal nodes against the action of an attacker monitoring attack nodes towards a target server. [4] on its side addresses the following problem: the outbreak of propagation process is dynamic and the outbreak detection time is uncertain. It designs a Stackelberg game model for adversarial outbreak detection and outlines an algorithm that approximates the optimal response under the assumption that the detection of one infected node inhibits further attacks.

When studied under the scope of decentralized protection, epidemic dynamics generally involve an infinite horizon attack-defense scenario and the optimization of the overall process may not correspond to the optimization of each step. Furthermore, the foreseeability of the transition of individuals in epidemic dynamics suggests the use of stochastic games defined in [17, 19]. This category of game is used in [7–9] in the context of partial observability to defeat an attacker performing a lateral movement, while [23, 25] uses it in a context of epidemic control. The underlined results are obtained under the assumption that the overall reward for each player is the overall sum of his/her rewards corresponding to each period with a discount factor. Since [25] with its general case overall reward function does not prove that some particular overall reward function is suitable enough for the epidemic peak minimization, to be realistic, the utility function to use for each player should be the extremum (maximum or minimum) of his/her overall reward.

3   Partially Observable Stochastic Minimum-Threat Path Game

Since an objective of the defender in an epidemic is to reach a state corresponding to the death of the epidemic, this article focuses on games with goal state, i.e., a state from which the defender can no longer be charged any cost. However, the definitions are general enough to apply to games without goal state.

3.1   Two-Player Zero-Sum Partially Observable Stochastic Game

A two-player zero-sum partially observable stochastic game (POSG) is any tuple

$$\mathcal{G} = \left(Z, O, A, T, r, b^0, Z_{\text{goals}}\right)$$

that, with the assumptions of common knowledge and rationality, represents the following scenario infinitely repeated in the time divided in periods: two intelligent and rational individuals, call them players 1 and 2, act simultaneously and independently upon a system. Their actions induce opposite rewards to both players and probabilistically result in a transition of the state of the system. However, for some particular state values called goal states, from the period the state of the system takes any of these values onward, no effective transition will happen and players will not be rewarded. The state is always known to player 2 while player 1 may be unable to infer it, unless it is a goal one. In the above notation:

- Z is the finite set of possible states of the system; $Z_{\text{goals}} \subseteq Z$ is the set of goal states;
- A_i, $i = 1, 2$, is the finite action space of player i, and $A = A_1 \times A_2$ is the set of action profiles;
- O is the finite set of possible observations for player 1;
- $T : Z \times A \longrightarrow \Delta(Z \times O)$, with $\Delta(Z \times O)$ denoting the set of probability distributions over the set $Z \times O$, is the transition function;
- $r : Z \times Z \times A \longrightarrow \mathbb{R}$ is the reward function for player 1;
- $b^0 \in \Delta(Z)$ is the belief of player 1 over the state of the system at the beginning of the game.

In the rest of the article, we use the pronouns "he" for the player 1 and "she" for the player 2. At the beginning of every period $t \in \{1, 2, \ldots\}$, each player i selects an action a_i^t from his action space A_i. As a result of the action profile $a^t = (a_1^t, a_2^t)$ taken in state z^t, the state of the system transitions into a state z^{t+1} at the end of the period and generates an observation o^t to player 1, according to a probability distribution P that satisfies: $P\left(z^{t+1} = z', o^t = o \,|\, z^t = z, a^t = a\right) = T\left(z', o \,|\, z, a\right)$; the system also a generates reward $r^t = r\left(z^{t+1} \,|\, z^t, a^t\right)$ to player 1 and a reward $\mu^t = -r^t$ to player 2. Only one player, player 2, is always aware of the transition; player 1 only makes an observation $o^t \in O$ and consequently updates his belief from current value b^{t-1} to a new value b^t. Without any loss of generality, we assume that this scenario is repeated at infinite horizon. However, for all $z \in Z_{\text{goals}}$ and $z' \in Z$, the player 1's reward is $r(z'|z,a) = 0$ and for a fixed observation $o_{\text{reach}} \in O$, the transition probability is $T(z',o|z,a) = \mathbb{1}_{o=o_{\text{reach}}} \cdot \mathbb{1}_{z'=z}$.

The sequences $\text{out}_1 = (r^t)_{t=1}^{\infty}$, $\text{out}_2 = (\mu^t)_{t=1}^{\infty}$, $\theta = (z^t, a^t, o^t)_{t=1}^{\infty}$, $\theta_1 = (a_1^t, o^t)_{t=1}^{\infty}$ and $\theta_2 = (z^t, a_2^t)_{t=1}^{\infty}$ are random variables respectively equal to the players 1 and 2's *outputs*, the *path* of the play and the players 1 and 2's *paths*. For all period $n \geqslant 2$, the prefix $\theta^n = \left((z^t, a^t, o^t)_{t=1}^{n-1}, z^n\right)$, $\theta_1^n = (a_1^t, o^t)_{t=1}^{n-1}$ and $\theta_2^n = \left((z^t, a^t)_{t=1}^{n-1}, z^n\right)$ are random variables representing the history of the play, and the histories available to players 1 and 2 respectively at period n. At period $n = 1$, the history of player 1 is "no observation", that we denote $\theta_1^1 = \phi$, and player 2's history is the state of the system, i.e., $\theta_2^1 = z^1$. The set of possible histories (respectively possible histories for players 1 and 2) at period n is denoted H^n (respectively H_1^n, H_2^n) while the overall set of possible histories is

$$H = \bigcup_{t=1}^{\infty} H^t \text{ (respectively } H_1 = \bigcup_{t=1}^{\infty} H_1^t, \ H_2 = \bigcup_{t=1}^{\infty} H_2^t).$$

3.2 Minimum-Threat Path and Shortest-Path Games

The aim of each player is to realize the optimum output. However, the comparison criterion, named the *utility*, widely depends on the situation. In the context of malware propagation by player 2 trying to take control of the largest number of devices in a network, for example, the reward of player 2 can be seen as the current number of devices under the control of the malware. In this context, the utility of the attacker's output, out_2, is the overall maximum level $u_2 = \max_{t \geqslant 1} \mu^t$ of the threat and the corresponding defender reward $u_1 = \min_{t \geqslant 1} r^t$ is the utility of the defender. That is, our utility function is the application $(x_t)_{t=1}^{\infty} \longmapsto \sup_{t=0,\dots,\infty} x_t$. Note that $\mu^t \geqslant 0$ and $r^t \leqslant 0$. We refer to such game as a *partially observable stochastic minimum-threat path game (POSMPG)*.

The case in which the player 2 reward is non-negative and the utility function is the application $(x_t)_{t=1}^{\infty} \longmapsto \sum_{t=0}^{\infty} x_t$ is called *partially observable stochastic shortest path game (POSSPG)*.[1]

3.3 Decision Rules and Strategies

At each period t, player 2 observes the state z^t of the system and takes a decision $\pi_2^t(\cdot|z^t) \in \Delta(A_2)$ that consists in a probability distribution over the possible actions; player 1 takes a decision (which is also a decision rule) $\pi_1 \in \Delta(A_1)$. The application π_i^t is termed *decision rule* of player i at period t. The set of possible decision rules for player i is denoted Π_i. Note that $\Pi_1 = \Delta(A_1)$ while

---

[1] The reward of player 2 is assumed positive in [20].

$\Pi_2 = \Delta(A_2)^Z$. A behavioral *strategy* for player i is a rule that maps a history to its decision, i.e., an application $\sigma_i : H^i \longrightarrow A_i$. The set of possible strategies for player i is Σ_i. With some initial system state z, the expected utilities of players 1 and 2 associated with the strategy profile $\sigma = (\sigma_1, \sigma_2)$ are respectively $U^\sigma(z) = \mathbb{E}^z_\sigma(\mathfrak{u}_1) = \mathbb{E}^z_\sigma\left(\min_{t \geqslant 1} r^t\right) = \mathbb{E}_\sigma\left(\min_{t \geqslant 1} r^t \mid z^1 = z\right)$ and

$U^\sigma_2(z) = \mathbb{E}^z_\sigma(\mathfrak{u}_2) = \mathbb{E}^z_\sigma\left(\max_{t \geqslant 1} \mu^t\right) = \mathbb{E}_\sigma\left(\max_{t \geqslant 1} \mu^t \mid z^1 = z\right)$. Clearly, these utilities are opposite numbers, so U^σ stands for the utility of strategy profile σ. Note that $U^\sigma(z) = \lim_{n \mapsto \infty} U^{\sigma,n}(z)$, where $U^{\sigma,n}(z) = \mathbb{E}^z_\sigma\left(\max_{t=1,\dots,n} \mu^t\right)$ is the utility at the end of period n. This definition of the utility function is extended to the belief of the defender over the network state by $U^{\sigma,n}(b) = \sum_{z \in Z} b(z) U^{\sigma,n}(z)$ and

$U^\sigma(b) = \sum_{z \in Z} b(z) U^\sigma(z)$.

If player 1 decides to rule a strategy σ_1, player 2 will rule a strategy σ_2 such that the expected utility is minimal. Therefore, this minimal expected utility, $\text{val}^{\sigma_1}(b) = \min_{\sigma_2 \in \Sigma_2} U^{(\sigma_1,\sigma_2)}(b)$ is referred to as the *value* of the strategy σ_1. So, the optimum utility, termed *optimum value function*, for player 1 is $V^*(b) = \max_{\sigma_1 \in \Sigma_1} \text{val}^{\sigma_1}(b) = \max_{\sigma_1 \in \Sigma_1} \min_{\sigma_2 \in \Sigma_2} U^{(\sigma_1,\sigma_2)}(b) = \min_{\sigma_2 \in \Sigma_2} \max_{\sigma_1 \in \Sigma_1} U^{(\sigma_1,\sigma_2)}(b)$.

The objective is to find out a Nash equilibrium (NE) strategy profile, i.e., a palyer 1's strategy σ_1 that maximizes val^{σ_1} and a player 2's best response to it. An NE is any strategy profile σ such that $U^\sigma = V^*$.

4   Nash Equilibrium for a Partially Observable Stochastic Minimum-Threat Path Game (POSMPG)

Due to the non-interchangeability of the mean with the maximum, the resolution of a POSG when the utility is the maximum remains a challenge. However, the case the utility is the sum of rewards is solved for discounted sum and for POSSPGs. In order to leverage the resolution of this second type of POSGs, we extend the state of the system with a memory that contains the updated overall maximum reward of player 2 and we derive a POSSPG whose NE is that of the initial POSMPG $\mathcal{G} = (Z, A, T, r, b^0)$.

4.1   State-Extended Game

In the remainder of this article, we denote $\mathcal{M} = \{\mu(z'|z,a) : (z',z,a) \in Z \times Z \times A\}$ the set of possible rewards in game $\mathcal{G}$. For all application $\varphi : Z \longrightarrow \mathcal{M}$,[2] we call *state φ-extended game* or simply *extended game*, the POSSG $\widetilde{\mathcal{G}} = \left(\widetilde{Z}, O, A, \widetilde{T}, \widetilde{r}, \widetilde{b}^0, \widetilde{Z}_{\text{goals}}\right)$ defined as follows:

---

[2] In the case of epidemic for example, $\varphi(z)$ is the number of infected nodes in state z.

- The extended state space and set of goal states

$$\widetilde{Z} = Z \times \mathcal{M} \qquad \text{and} \qquad \widetilde{Z}_{\text{goals}} = Z_{\text{goals}} \times \mathcal{M}; \tag{1}$$

- The reward function due to the increase of memory and defined by $\widetilde{r} = -\widetilde{\mu}$ and, for all $(z, m), (z', m') \in Z \times \mathcal{M}$ and $a \in A$:

$$\widetilde{\mu}\left(z', m' \mid z, m, a\right) = \begin{cases} 0 & \text{if } z \in Z_{\text{goals}} \\ \max\left(m' - m, 0\right) & \text{otherwise} \end{cases}, \tag{2}$$

where $\mu = -r$;
- The initial belief defined by:

$$\widetilde{b}^0\left(z, m\right) = \begin{cases} b^0\left(z\right) \text{ if } m = \varphi\left(z\right) \\ 0 \qquad \text{otherwise} \end{cases}; \tag{3}$$

- The extended transition function defined for all $\widetilde{z} = (z, m)$ and $\widetilde{z}' = (z', m')$ with $z, z' \in S$, $m, m' \in M$, and for all $a \in A$ and $o \in O$ by:

$$\widetilde{T}\left(z', m', o \mid z, m, a\right) = \begin{cases} T\left(z', o \mid z, a\right) \text{ if } \begin{cases} \mu\left(z' \mid z, a\right) \leqslant m \\ m' = m \end{cases} \text{ or } \begin{cases} \mu\left(z' \mid z, a\right) > m \\ m' = \mu\left(z' \mid z, a\right) \end{cases} \\ 0 \qquad\qquad\qquad\quad \text{otherwise} \end{cases} \tag{4}$$

A state of the POSSPG is a state of the POSMPG together with a number that represents a memory of the last maximum reward attained by player 2. For such, at the end of each period, the memory is incremented with the eventual additional reward as the current reward is compared to the last maximum reward attained and this incremented reward is the reward for the POSSPG.

The following propositions respectively witness the straightforwardness and the importance of the above definition of the extended POSG.

Proposition 1.(a) $\widetilde{Z}$ is a finite set.
(b) For all $(\widetilde{z}, a) \in \widetilde{Z} \times A$, $\widetilde{T}\left(\cdot \mid \widetilde{z}, a\right)$ is a probability distribution on $\widetilde{Z} \times A$.
(c) All state in $\widetilde{Z}_{\text{goals}}$ is a goal state.

Proof. From $\mathcal{M}$ is the image set of the function μ defined on the finite set $S \times S \times A$, it comes that the sets $\mathcal{M}$ then $\widetilde{Z}$ are finite. The proof of (b) is the following: (1) the obvious non-negativity of T and (2): for all $\widetilde{z} = (z, m) \in \widetilde{Z}$ and all $a \in A$, we get:

$$\sum_{(\widetilde{z}', o) \in \widetilde{Z} \times O} \widetilde{T}\left(\widetilde{z}', o \mid \widetilde{z}, a\right) = \sum_{(z', m', o) \in Z \times \mathcal{M} \times O} \widetilde{T}\left(z', m', o \mid z, m, a\right)$$

$$= \sum_{\substack{(z', o) \in Z \times O \\ \mu\left(z' \mid z, a\right) \leqslant m}} \widetilde{T}\left(z', m, o \mid z, m, a\right) + \sum_{\substack{(z', o) \in Z \times O \\ \mu\left(z' \mid z, a\right) > m}} \widetilde{T}\left(z', \mu\left(z' \mid z, a\right), o \mid z, m, a\right)$$

$$= \sum_{\substack{(z', o) \in Z \times O \\ \mu\left(z' \mid z, a\right) \leqslant m}} T\left(z', o \mid z, a\right) + \sum_{\substack{(z', o) \in Z \times O \\ \mu\left(z' \mid z, a\right) > m}} T\left(z', o \mid z, a\right) = 1.$$

For the proof of (c), if $(z, m) \in \tilde{Z}_{\text{goals}}$ and $m' \neq m$, from (4), $\tilde{T}(z, m', o_{\text{reach}} \,|\, z, m, a) \neq 0$ only if $\mu(z \,|\, z, a) > m$. Since $\mu(z \,|\, z, a) = 0$, this last statement would contradict the non-negativeness of the values in $\mathcal{M}$. ∎

Furthermore, the state extension makes the POSMPG a POSSPG as it is shown in the following proposition.

Proposition 2. *If the path $h = (z^t, a^t, o^t)_{t=1}^{\infty}$ is realized in game $\mathcal{G}$ and generates the output $(\mu_t)_{t=1}^{\infty}$ for player 2, then, by taking $\mu_0 = m_1 = \tilde{\mu}_0$, the associated path $\tilde{h} = (\tilde{z}^t, a^t, o^t)_{t=1}^{\infty}$ in game $\tilde{\mathcal{G}}$ (with $\tilde{z}_t = (z_t, m_t)$) and the resulting output $(\tilde{\mu}_t)_{t=1}^{\infty}$ satisfy for all period $t \geqslant 1$:*

$$m_t = \sum_{n=0}^{t-1} \tilde{\mu}_n = \max_{n=0,\ldots,t-1} \mu_n. \tag{5}$$

Proof (by induction). The equations clearly hold for $t = 1$.

From Proposition 1.(c), if the equations hold until a goal state is reached, then it hold onward.

Suppose it holds for some $t \geqslant 1$ and no goal state is reached. Note that from (4), it comes:

$$m_{t+1} = \begin{cases} m_t & \text{if } \mu(z_{t+1} \,|\, z_t, a_t) \leqslant m_t \\ \mu(z_{t+1} \,|\, z_t, a_t) & \text{if } \mu(z_{t+1} \,|\, z_t, a_t) > m_t \end{cases}, \tag{6a}$$

then

$$m_{t+1} = \max(m_t, \mu_t). \tag{6b}$$

So, $m_{t+1} = \max_{n=0,\ldots,t} \mu_n$.

From 2, if $z_t \notin Z_{\text{goals}}$, then

$$\tilde{\mu}_t = m_{t+1} - m_t. \tag{7}$$

In case $z_t \in Z_{\text{goals}}$, for all state $z' \in Z$ and action profile $a \in A$, we get $\mu(z' \,|\, z_t, a) = 0 \leqslant m$, which from (4) implies $m_{t+1} = m_t$. We also get $\mu_{t+1} = 0$. So, Eq. (7) holds in any case, and $m_{t+1} = m_t + \tilde{\mu}_t = \sum_{n=0}^{t} \tilde{\mu}_n$. ∎

Then, based on the previous result, we have that the supremum of rewards earned in the POSMPG is the sum of the rewards earned in the POSSPG and, at the same time, the value in memory.

4.2   Relation Between the POSMPG and the POSSPG

We closely examine the relation between the two games, and we prove that their resolutions are equivalent.

Proposition 3. *The POSSPG uniquely depends on the POSMPG.*

Proof. Suppose games $\mathcal{G} = (Z, O, A, T, \mu, b^0)$ and $\mathcal{G}' = (Z', O', A', T', \mu', b'^0)$ are equally sate-extended to $\overline{\mathcal{G}} = (\overline{Z}, \overline{O}, \overline{A}, \overline{T}, \overline{\mu}, \overline{b}^0)$. Immediately, we get $O = \overline{O} = O'$ and $A = \overline{A} = A'$, and from Eq. 3 it comes $b^0 = \overline{b}^0 = b'^0$. So, from Eq. 1, we get $Z = Z'$ and the equality of image sets $\mathcal{M} = \{\mu(z' | z, a) : (z, z', a) \in Z \times Z \times A\}$ and $\mathcal{M}' = \{\mu'(z' | z, a) : (z, z', a) \in Z \times Z \times A\}$, which, coupled to Eq. 6b, imply the equality of the reward functions of both POSMPGs. From this equality and Eq. 4, we get the equality of the transition functions T and T'. ∎

Respectively denote $\widetilde{\text{out}}_1$, $\widetilde{\text{out}}_2$ and $\widetilde{\theta}$ the players 1 and 2 outputs ant the history in game $\widetilde{\mathcal{G}}$ and consider the natural projection $s\colon (z, m) \longmapsto z$ of the state space $\widetilde{Z}$ of the POSSPG onto the state space Z of the POSMPG, that consists in relaxing the memory. This projection induces other projections, that we also denote s, of the history set $\widetilde{H}$ and player 2 history set $\widetilde{H}_2$ in the POSSPG onto the corresponding history sets in the POSMPG, defined by $s\left((z^t, m^t, a^t, o^t)_{t=1}^{n-1}, z^n, m^n\right) = \left((z^t, a^t, o^t)_{t=1}^{n-1}, z^n\right)$ and $s\left((z^t, m^t, a_2^t)_{t=1}^{n-1}, z^n, m^n\right) = \left((z^t, a_2^t)_{t=1}^{n-1}, z^n\right)$. Note that player 1 has the same history in both games. That is, each strategy σ_2 for player 2 in the POSMPG induces the strategy $\sigma_2 \circ s$. The converse is established in the following proposition:

Proposition 4. *For any period $n \geqslant 2$ and any two histories $\widetilde{h}_1 = \left((z^t, m_1^t, a^t, o^t)_{t=1}^{n-1}, z^n, m_1^n\right)$ and $\widetilde{h}_2 = \left((z^t, m_2^t, a^t, o^t)_{t=1}^{n-1}, z^n, m_2^n\right)$ in the POSSPG, if the equality $m_1^t = m_2^t$ holds for $t = 1$, then it holds for all period $t \in \{1, \ldots, n\}$.*

In other words, a history h in the POSSPG is uniquely determined by its projection $s(h)$ onto the POSMPG and its first value in memory $m^1(h)$. This is, the application $\overline{s}\colon \widetilde{h} \longmapsto \left(s\left(\widetilde{h}\right), m^1\left(\widetilde{h}\right)\right)$ is an injection from $\widetilde{H}$ to H. It is a bijection by (6).

Proof (By induction). Equation (6a) implies that at time t where the system is in state z_t with memory m_t, if action a_t is taken and makes the system state transition to z_{t+1}, the new value m_{t+1} in memory is known. ∎

In a mater of consequence, since a strategy profile $\widetilde{\sigma}$ in the POSSPG maps a decision profile to any extended history, which is nothing but a couple (h, m) composed of a history h, and its first value in memory $m = m^1(h)$, for any m, the partial application $\widetilde{\sigma}(\cdot, m)$ is a strategy profile in the POSMPG. Note that $m^1 = \varphi(z^1)$. That is, one strategy profile exactly in the POSMPG, note it $\varphi(\widetilde{\sigma}) = \widetilde{\sigma}(\cdot, m)$, is associated with the strategy profile $\widetilde{\sigma}$ of the POSSPG.

Theorem 1. *The two strategy profiles $\widetilde{\sigma}$ and $\varphi(\widetilde{\sigma})$ share the same utility value.*

Proof. Suppose the initial state in the POSMPG is z. The initial state is the POSSPG is $\widetilde{z} = (z, \varphi(z))$. The utility value of player 2 is:

$$\widetilde{U}_2^{\widetilde{\sigma}}(z, \varphi(z)) = \mathbb{E}_{\widetilde{\sigma}}\left(\sum_{t=1}^{\infty} \widetilde{\mu}_t \middle| z^1 = z, m^1 = \varphi(z)\right) = \mathbb{E}_{\widetilde{\sigma}}\left(\max_{t \geqslant 1} \mu_t \middle| z^1 = z, m^1 = \varphi(z)\right) = U_2^{\sigma}(z).$$

∎

The operator φ is a bijection from the strategies of the POSSPG to the strategies of the POSMPG. That is, the two games are played concurrently with equivalent outputs for equivalent strategies and therefore for same actions.

An NE $\widetilde{\sigma}^*$ of the POSSPG exists and is associated with the optimal value function $V^* = U^{\widetilde{\sigma}}$ defined by $V^*(b) = \max_{\widetilde{\sigma}_1} \min_{\widetilde{\sigma}_2} U^{(\widetilde{\sigma}_1, \widetilde{\sigma}_2)}(b)$. From the above theorem, V^* is also the optimal value function of the POSMPG, and $V^* = U^{\varphi(\widetilde{\sigma})}$. Therefore, the resolution of the state POSSPG is mathematically equivalent to the resolution of the POSMPG. We choose the computational resolution of the first one. Each player will play in the POSMPG the NE strategy corresponding to the POSSPG NE.

4.3   Solving POSSPGs

An algorithm for POSSPGs is provided in [20] with the assumption that the reward of player 2 is strictly positive until a goal state is reached. We prove that this assumption can be relaxed when the POSSPG is the state-extension of game in which the utility is the maximum. In the remaining of this section, we note

$$\widetilde{R}(\widetilde{z}, a) = \sum_{(\widetilde{z}', o) \in \widetilde{Z} \times O} \widetilde{T}(\widetilde{z}', o | \widetilde{z}, a) \times \widetilde{r}(\widetilde{z}' | \widetilde{z}, a). \tag{8}$$

In [20] the authors propose an algorithm that converges only when the instantaneous reward admits some negative bound before a goal state is reached, i.e., for some $\widetilde{R}_{\max}$, the inequality $\widetilde{R}(\widetilde{z}, a) \leqslant \widetilde{R}_{\max}$ holds for all action profile $a \in A$ taken in all non-goal state $z \in Z \setminus Z_{\text{goals}}$. For all period $k \geqslant 1$, they define the *k-cutoff game* as the k-period prefix of the POSSPG with the recommendation that player 1 is forced to play uniform strategy $\widetilde{\sigma}_{\text{unif}}$ from period $k + 1$ onward. The utility of a strategy $\widetilde{\sigma}$ is defined by

$$U^{\widetilde{\sigma}, k-}(\widetilde{b}) = \mathbb{E}_{\widetilde{b}}^{\widetilde{\sigma}}\left(\sum_{t=1}^{k} \widetilde{R}(\widetilde{z}^t, a^t) + \text{val}^{\widetilde{\sigma}_{\text{unif}}}(\widetilde{b}^{(k)})\right), \tag{9}$$

where $\widetilde{b}^{(k)}$ is the result of the successive updates of player 1's belief at the end of each of the k first periods. Authors prove the following results in the general case and use the strict negativity of the reward of player 1 while no goal state is reached to bound $V^* - V^{*,k-}$.

Theorem 2 ([20]). *For arbitrary period $k \geqslant 1$, it holds:* $\text{val}^{\widetilde{\sigma}_{\text{unif}}} \leqslant V^{*,k-} \leqslant V^*$.

Keeping in mind that V^* is bounded, consider the *k-horizon limited game* of the POSSPG, for which the utility of any strategy $\widetilde{\sigma}$ is defined by

$$U^{\widetilde{\sigma},k+}\left(\widetilde{b}\right) = \mathbb{E}_{\widetilde{b}}^{\widetilde{\sigma}}\left(\sum_{t=1}^{k}\widetilde{R}\left(\widetilde{z}^t, a^t\right)\right). \tag{10}$$

We then get the following result:

Theorem 3. *For an arbitrary period $k \geqslant 1$, it holds: $V^* \leqslant V^{*,k+}$.*

Proof. Take any belief $\widetilde{b}$ and consider any strategy profile $\widetilde{\sigma}$ of the infinite horizon POSSPG and its restriction, also noted $\widetilde{\sigma}$ on the set of histories before period $k+1$. The negativity of the function $\widetilde{R}$ implies $U^{\widetilde{\sigma}}\left(\widetilde{b}\right) \leqslant U^{\widetilde{\sigma},k+}\left(\widetilde{b}\right)$, then $U^{\widetilde{\sigma}}\left(\widetilde{b}\right) \leqslant V^{*,k+}\left(\widetilde{b}\right)$. So, for the NE $\widetilde{\sigma}^*$, it comes $V^*\left(\widetilde{b}\right) = U^{\widetilde{\sigma}^*}\left(\widetilde{b}\right) \leqslant V^{*,k+}\left(\widetilde{b}\right)$.   ∎

This result yields the bounding $V^{*,k-} \leqslant V^* \leqslant V^{*,k+}$.

4.4   Algorithm for the Extended Game

Algorithm for the POSSPG with Discounted Sum. The algorithm for the resolution of the extremum-utility POSSPGs is adapted from the algorithm for the resolution of sum-utility POSSPGs proposed in [10]. This algorithm in its turn is adapted from the algorithm designed for discounted sum-utility POSGs (Algorithm 1), with discount factor any $\gamma \in (0, 1)$, which approaches the optimal

---

Algorithm 1: HSVI algorithm for Discounted OS-POSGs [20]

1 **while** $\overline{V}\left(\widetilde{b}^0\right) - \underline{V}\left(\widetilde{b}^0\right) > \varepsilon$ **do**

2   Explore($\widetilde{b}^0$, 1)

3 **procedure** Explore($\widetilde{b}^{t-1}$, t)

4   **if** excess$_t\left(\widetilde{b}^{t-1}\right) > 0$ **then**

5         $\widetilde{\pi}_1^t \leftarrow$ optimal strategy of player 1 in $\left[H\overline{V}\right]\left(\widetilde{b}^{t-1}\right)$

6         $\widetilde{\pi}_2^t \leftarrow$ optimal strategy of player 2 in $\left[H\underline{V}\right]\left(\widetilde{b}^{t-1}\right)$

7         $\widetilde{b}^t \leftarrow \underset{(a_1,o)\in A_1\times O}{\arg\max}\ \mathbb{P}_{\widetilde{b}^{t-1},\widetilde{\pi}_1^t,\widetilde{\pi}_2^t}(a_1,o) \times \text{excess}_{t+1}\left(\tau\left(\widetilde{b}^{t-1}, a_1, \widetilde{\pi}_2^t, o\right)\right)$

8   Explore($\widetilde{b}^t$, $t+1$)

9   Perform point-based update of $\overline{V}$ and $\underline{V}$ in $\widetilde{b}^{t-1}$

value V^* as the fixed point of the backup function H defined for all function $V \colon \Delta\left(\widetilde{Z}\right) \longrightarrow \Delta\left(\widetilde{Z}\right)$ by

$$[HV]\left(\widetilde{b}\right) = \max_{\widetilde{\pi}_1 \in \widetilde{\Pi}_1} \min_{\widetilde{\pi}_2 \in \widetilde{\Pi}_2} \left(\mathbb{E}_{\widetilde{b}, \widetilde{\pi}_1, \widetilde{\pi}_2} \left[\widetilde{R}\left(z, a_1, a_2\right)\right]\right.$$
$$\left. + \gamma \times \sum_{(a_1, o) \in A_1 \times O} \mathbb{P}_{\widetilde{b}, \widetilde{\pi}_1, \widetilde{\pi}_2}[a_1, o] \times V\left(\tau\left(\widetilde{b}, a_1, \widetilde{\pi}_2, o\right)\right)\right).$$

The backup value, HV, is the result of the computation of the NE (lines 5 and 6) of the game termed *stage game* $[HV]\left(\widetilde{b}\right)$. Suppose that currently the belief of player 1 is $\widetilde{b}$ and the optimal value function of the sub-game that begins at next period is V. If players have to run decision rules $\widetilde{\pi}$ of their choices, then player 1 is immediately rewarded $\mathbb{E}_{\widetilde{b}, \widetilde{\pi}_1, \widetilde{\pi}_2}\left[\widetilde{R}\left(z, a_1, a_2\right)\right]$ in expectation. Also, he will play some action a_1 and make some observation o at probability

$$\mathbb{P}_{\widetilde{b}, \widetilde{\pi}_1, \widetilde{\pi}_2}[a_1, o] = \sum_{(\widetilde{z}', \widetilde{z}, a_2) \in \widetilde{Z} \times \widetilde{Z} \times A_2} \widetilde{T}\left(\widetilde{z}', o \mid \widetilde{z}, a_1, a_2\right) \times \widetilde{b}\left(\widetilde{z}\right) \times \widetilde{\pi}_2\left(a_2 \mid \widetilde{z}\right)$$

and update his belief to $\tau\left(\widetilde{b}, a_1, \widetilde{\pi}_2, o\right)$ defined by

$$\tau\left(\widetilde{b}, a_1, \widetilde{\pi}_2, o\right)\left(\widetilde{z}'\right) = \frac{1}{\mathbb{P}_{\widetilde{b}, \widetilde{\pi}_1, \widetilde{\pi}_2}[a_1, o]} \sum_{(\widetilde{z}, a_2) \in \widetilde{Z} \times A_2} \widetilde{T}\left(\widetilde{z}', o \mid \widetilde{z}, a_1, a_2\right) \times \widetilde{b}\left(\widetilde{z}\right) \times \widetilde{\pi}_2\left(a_2 \mid \widetilde{z}\right).$$

Authors of [20] assume optimistic players 1 and 2 respectively and simultaneously performing over time a point-based update of upper and lower bounds $\overline{V}$ and $\underline{V}$ (line 9) of the optimal value V^* by the application of the backup operator. Player 2 starts with a point-wise maximum $\underline{V} \colon \widetilde{b} \longmapsto \max_{\alpha \in \Gamma} \langle \alpha, \widetilde{b} \rangle = \max_{\alpha \in \Gamma} \sum_{\widetilde{z} \in \widetilde{Z}} \alpha\left(\widetilde{z}\right) \times \widetilde{b}\left(\widetilde{z}\right)$ over some set Γ of linear functions α termed α-vectors. The update of $\underline{V}$ adds an α-vector $\mathcal{L}\Gamma\left(\widetilde{b}\right)$ corresponding to an NE strategy of player 1 in the game $[H\underline{V}]\left(\widetilde{b}\right)$ and expands the set Γ of α-vectors to $\Gamma \cup \left\{[H\underline{V}]\left(\widetilde{b}\right)\right\}$. Player 1 starts from an upper bound $\overline{V}$ of a restriction of the optimal value V^* on a finite set Υ of beliefs. The update of $\overline{V}$ at some belief $\widetilde{b}''$ consists in (1) updating the definition of $\overline{V}$ by $\overline{V}\left(\widetilde{b}\right) \leftarrow \inf_{\widetilde{b}' \in \Upsilon}\left\{\overline{V}\left(\widetilde{b}'\right) + (U - L) \times \|\widetilde{b} - \widetilde{b}'\|_2\right\}$, where $U = \max_{(\widetilde{z}, a) \in \widetilde{Z} \times A} \widetilde{R}\left(\widetilde{z}, a\right)$, $L = \min_{(\widetilde{z}, a) \in \widetilde{Z} \times A} \widetilde{R}\left(\widetilde{z}, a\right)$ and $\|\cdot\|_2$ is the euclidean norm, and in (2) expanding Υ to $\Upsilon \cup \left\{\widetilde{b}''\right\}$.

The gap $\overline{V} - \underline{V}$ converges to the zero function. However, due to the propagation of errors on the beliefs, The authors suggest that one assumes the algorithm has reached the optimal value at some period t at which the belief is $\tilde{b}$ with precision ε when the excess defined by

$$\text{excess}_t\left(\tilde{b}\right) = \overline{V}\left(\tilde{b}\right) - \underline{V}\left(\tilde{b}\right) - \varrho(t)$$

does not exceed ε. The function ϱ is defined on integer, positive numbers by

$$\varrho(1) = \varepsilon \qquad \varrho(t+1) = \frac{\varrho(t) - 2 \times \delta \times D}{\gamma},$$

where $\delta = \dfrac{\max \tilde{R}(\cdot) - \min \tilde{R}(\cdot)}{2 \times (1-\gamma)}$ and D is any parameter that satisfy $0 < D < \dfrac{(1-\gamma) \times \varepsilon}{2 \times \delta}$, i.e., ϱ is monotonically increasing and unbounded.

Algorithm for the POSSPG. The boundedness of the value of the POSSPG established in Theorems 2 and 3 suggests that one can iteratively apply the value iteration algorithm on the upper and lower bounds of $V^{*,k+}$ and $V^{*,k-}$ to bound V^*. However, the Algorithm 1 applies only for discounted infinite horizon POSGs while the k-cutoff and the k-horizon limited games are finite, and the reward is not discounted. To adapt this algorithm to a N-horizon POSG with not discounted sum $\mathcal{G}^{(N)} = (S, A, O, T, R, b^0)$, authors of [20] make the problem an infinite-horizon POSG with γ-discounted sum $\mathcal{G}^\gamma = (S^\gamma, A, O, T^\gamma, R^\gamma, b^0)$. For $\gamma \in (0,1)$, the game $\mathcal{G}^\gamma$ are defined as follows:

- Games $\mathcal{G}^{(N)}$ and $\mathcal{G}^\gamma$ have the action and observation sets;
- The set S_n^γ of possible states of $\mathcal{G}^\gamma$ when n periods remain to be played in $\mathcal{G}^{(N)}$, $n \in \{0, \ldots N\}$ can be iteratively obtained as follows:[3]

$$\begin{cases} S_N^\gamma = \text{supp}(b^0) \times \{N\} = \{(s, N) \,|\, s \in S \text{ and } b^0(s) > 0\} \\ S_n^\gamma = \left\{(s', n) \,\middle|\, \text{for some } (s, n+1) \in S_{n+1}^\gamma \text{ the transition from } s \text{ to } s' \text{ is possible in } \mathcal{G}^{(N)} \right\} \end{cases}.$$

- The transition function in $\mathcal{G}^\gamma$ respects the transition probabilities in $\mathcal{G}^{(N)}$, i.e.:
  - $T^\gamma(o, s', n \,|\, s, n+1, a) = T(o, s' \,|\, s, a)$
  - $T^\gamma(\hat{o}, s, 0 \,|\, s, 0, a) = 1$ for an arbitrary fixed observation $\hat{o}$, i.e., there is no effective transition in $\mathcal{G}^\gamma$ when it remains no period to play in $\mathcal{G}^{(N)}$;
- About the reward function: $\begin{cases} R^\gamma(s, n, a) = \dfrac{R(s, a)}{\gamma^{N-n}} \text{ if } n \in \{1, \ldots, N\} \\ R^\gamma(s, 0, a) = 0 \end{cases}.$

Both games have the same value function. So, the value iteration algorithm applies for the k-cutoffs and the k-horizon limitations of the POSSPG.

Algorithm 2 leverages the boundedness of the value function of the POSSPG between the finite horizon games to iteratively approach the value of this first value function. Therein, players 1 and 2 respectively play the successive cutoff

---

[3] One can take $S_N^\gamma = S \times \mathbb{N}$.

Algorithm 2: HSVI algorithm for the POSSPG

---

1 $k \leftarrow 1$

2 $\underline{V}^{k-} \leftarrow \text{val}^{\widetilde{\sigma}_{\text{unif}}}$

3 $\overline{V}^{k+} \leftarrow V^{*0+}$ ▷ the zero function

4 **while** $\overline{V}^{k+}\left(\widetilde{b}^0\right) - \underline{V}^{k-}\left(\widetilde{b}^0\right) > \varepsilon$ and $k \leqslant K$ **do**

5 $\quad$ Explore$(\widetilde{b}^0, 1)$

6 $\quad$ $k \leftarrow k + 1$

7 **procedure** Explore$(\widetilde{b}^{t-1}, t)$

8 $\quad$ **if** excess$_t\left(\widetilde{b}^{t-1}\right) > 0$ **then**

9 $\quad\quad$ $\widetilde{\pi}_1^t \leftarrow$ optimal strategy of player 1 in $\left[H\overline{V}^{(k-t)+}\right]\left(\widetilde{b}^{t-1}\right)$

10 $\quad\quad$ $\widetilde{\pi}_2^t \leftarrow$ optimal strategy of player 2 in $\left[H\underline{V}^{(k-t)-}\right]\left(\widetilde{b}^{t-1}\right)$

11 $\quad\quad$ $\widetilde{b}^t \leftarrow \underset{(a_1,o)\in A_1 \times O}{\arg\max} \; \mathbb{P}_{\widetilde{b}^{t-1},\widetilde{\pi}_1^t,\widetilde{\pi}_2^t}(a_1,o) \times \text{excess}_{t+1}\left(\tau\left(\widetilde{b}^{t-1},a_1,\widetilde{\pi}_2^t,o\right)\right)$

12 $\quad\quad$ Explore$(\widetilde{b}^t, t+1)$

13 $\quad\quad$ Perform point-based update of $\overline{V}^{(k-t)+}$ and $\underline{V}^{(k-t)-}$ in $\widetilde{b}^{t-1}$

---

and limited games (lines 9, 10 and 13). When a precision ε and a number K of periods are given, the algorithm terminates at the K-th period, unless the precision ε is reached before (line 4). The lower and upper bounds are respectively initialized in lines 2 and 3 at the value of uniform strategy of player 1 and the zero function.

We cannot guarantee the convergence of Algorithm 2 but at least we can state the monotonicity of the value of the uniform strategy, i.e.,

Theorem 1. *For all belief $\widetilde{b}$ in the POSSPG, the sequence* $\left(\text{val}^{\widetilde{\sigma}_{\text{unif}}}\left(\widetilde{b}^{(n)}\right)\right)_{n=0}^{\infty}$ *increases in n.*

So, either the sequence is stationary or it converges.

Proof. Recall $b^{(0)} = b$. Take lowermem$_n = \min\left\{m \,\middle|\, (z,m) \in \text{supp}\left(\widetilde{b}^{(n)}\right)\right.$ for some $z \in Z\Big\}$, i.e., lowermem$_n$ is the minimum possible value in memory at period n. Player 1 knows that the memory cannot decrease, so, lowermem$_{n+1} \geqslant$ lowermem$_n$ for all n. ∎

In case $\left(\text{val}^{\widetilde{\sigma}_{\text{unif}}}\left(\widetilde{b}^{(n)}\right)\right)_{n=0}^{\infty}$ is constant from some period N onward, the uniform strategy achieves the maximum expected value of $\lim_{n\to\infty} m^t$ and is therefore the optimal strategy for player 1 from period N onward.

5   Adversarial Control of Epidemics

In this section, we are interested into the act of a malicious rational, intelligent agent (*the attacker*) spreading a malware inside a network with the aim to obtain the highest number of currently infected nodes. This is the case for example in a botnet attack with the intention to launch a distributed denial of service.

5.1   An *SIR* Epidemic on Network

The malicious agent can propagate the malware from every infected node to adjacent ones but, for the sake of discretion, she may decide not to expose the infected nodes, and it may not be of her interest to transmit the virus from each infected node to all the susceptible neighbors. This transmission may be successful towards some nodes (susceptible ones) while it surely results in failure towards other nodes (resistant ones). We assume perfect information for the attacker, so that she has full knowledge about the state of each node of the network at every period. In addition, each infected (respectively susceptible) node may decide to become susceptible (respectively resistant) and let the defender know if it does it. To mitigate this spreading, another rational agent (*the defender*) deploys on edges a limited number of one period-availability traps that have the property of detecting any transmission and instantly curing the two sides of the edge, i.e., source and destination nodes of the transmission.

The time is divided into periods consisting each one in two stages: the stage of strategic moves of the players (the defender and the attacker) and the stage of probabilistic moves of nodes. Both stages are described as follows and depicted on Fig. 1.

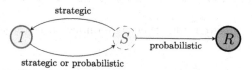

Transition $S \to R$ is endogenously determined by the node itself in a random manner and not strategically whereas transition $S \to I$ is a result of an attack from an infected neighbor node and determined by the attacker's action. Transition $I \to S$ either results from the detection of a transmission or is of the formal nature.

Fig. 1. Possible effective state transitions for each node.

First (strategic) Stage: Both players make their actions, which results in an intermediate state for each node of the network. The defender's action consists in reallocating a limited number of traps on edges of the graph; the attacker's action consists in choosing a set of neighbors of each infected devices to propagate the worm from it. The so determined action profile result in an in intermediate state for each node.

Second (probabilistic) Stage: Based on the intermediate state of the network, each node may change its own internal state: from state I to S by applying self restoration process, or from S to R by becoming resistant/protected to the virus. These decisions are free of charge, but are performed in a random manner. Moreover, these decisions and known by the defender and makes the attacker unable to infer the defender's actions.

The dynamics in this situation are basically those of an SIR variant epidemic on the network (a non-directed graph) $G = (V, E)$ where $V = \{1, 2, \ldots, |V|\}$ is the finite set of nodes, and $E \subseteq \mathcal{P}_2(V) = \{e \in 2^V : |e| = 2\}$ is the set of edges. Indeed: (a) the population (set of nodes) can be divided into 3 compartments: *infected* nodes (I), *susceptible* nodes (S), that are vulnerable and non-infected, and *resistant* (or removed) nodes (R), that cannot be successfully contaminated; (b) 3 possible effective transitions for each node state at each stage: $S \to I$, $S \to R$ and $I \to S$ where $A \to B$ means the node transits from A compartment to B compartment as depicted in Fig. 1.

5.2   Game Model Description

From a perspective that should take into account the various interactions, this scenario presents the following features:

– It involves two types of actors:
  • The attacker and the defender are strategical actors. The attacker observes everything, while the defender has a limited observation over the network's state;
  • The decision of a node is basically unpredictable. Therefore, nodes are probabilistic actors. We assume that the respective probabilities α and ϱ at which an infected node become susceptible and a susceptible node become resistant are positive and constant in the node, and in the time (see Fig. 2);
– The scenario is repeated until there is no infected node, and the underlined state is a target one.

We assume that the defender and the attacker are intelligent and rational, i.e., they are players 1 and 2 respectively, and we model the interactions by the POSMPG $\mathcal{G} = (Z, O, A, T, r, b^0, Z_{\text{goals}})$ defined as follows:

The system is the network G and the state of all nodes define the network state $z = (z_i)_{i=1}^{|V|}$. In other words, $Z = \{S, I, R\}^V$. We also denote $K^t \subseteq V$, or more simply K, where $K \in \{S, I, R\}$, the set of nodes that are in state K at the beginning of the period t.
There is exactly one goal state, corresponding to the situation $z_{\text{goal}} = (R, \ldots, R)$ where all nodes are resistant;

Attacker's action space. An action for player 2 (the attacker) consists in choosing from any infected node i a set T_i of adjacent, susceptible nodes to propagate the virus on it (call it target). Strategically, she will never target the same susceptible node from two distinct infected sources. In other words, the action space for the attacker is the set A_2 of sequences $T = (T_i)_{i \in I}$

that satisfy the properties:
$$\begin{cases} T_i \subseteq S, & \forall i \in I \\ (i,j) \in \mathbb{S}_z, & \forall i \in I, \forall j \in T_i \\ T_k \cap T_l = \emptyset \Longleftarrow k \neq l, & \forall k, l \in I \end{cases}, \text{ where}$$

$\mathbb{S}_z = I \times S$ is the set of possible infections and will be referred to as the *stake* related to the state z.

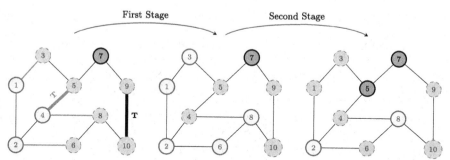

The defender places 2 traps, on edges $4 \leftrightarrow 5$ and $9 \leftrightarrow 10$; the attacker launches contamination $1 \rightarrow 3$, $2 \rightarrow 6$, $4 \rightarrow 5$ and $4 \rightarrow 8$; the first three ones are undetected while the last one is detected.

The propagation over nodes 3, 6 and 8 is not detected and therefore results in two new infected nodes, whereas defender has intercepted an infection crossing the edge $4 \leftrightarrow 5$. Then, nodes 4 and 5 states becomes susceptible.

With respect to probabilities α and ρ, nodes 1, 3 and 6 transit $I \rightarrow S$, node 5 transits $S \rightarrow R$ and the other nodes do not change their states.

⊙ = susceptible node; ⊘ = infected node; ● = resistant node; —— = edge; —— = edge
chosen by attacker; T = trapped edge.

Fig. 2. One period of the game: a possible scenario with 10 nodes.

Defender's action space. The defender chooses h edges (or less) on which he deploys the traps. He may not know the stake and will therefore act regarding the set $\mathbb{S}_b = \bigcup_{z \in Z} \mathbb{S}_z$ of likely transmissions. So, strategically, his action consists in a subset $W \subseteq \mathbb{S}_b$ of edges that he watches, such that $\begin{cases} W = \mathbb{S}_b \text{ if } |\mathbb{S}_b| \leqslant h \\ |W| = h \text{ if } |\mathbb{S}_b| > h \end{cases}$ The defender acts before the attacker, but the attacker cannot infer his action.

The transitions. The state transition of a node between the beginning and the end of a period, call it *period state transition*, is composed of two *stage state transitions* associated with each stages of the period.

When an action profile $a = (a_1, a_2) = (W, T)$ has been taken in the network state z, the network state $a(z)$ resulting from the deterministic stage state transition relies on the action and the state (see the first four lines of Table 2); the probabilities of the second stage state transition are recalled in Table 1.

The observations. The defender observation is his information on each node states at the end of each period. In the general case, if the defender is aware of the final state z_i', the observation is $o_i = z_i'$. Otherwise, there is no actual observation for the defender, and we denote $o_i := X$. As shows Table 2, 13

Table 1. Probabilities of nodes probabilistic state transitions

		z_i'		
		S	I	R
$a(z)_i$	S	$1-\rho$	0	ρ
	I	α	$1-\alpha$	0
	R	0	0	1

Table 2. Observation of the defender at the end of the period

	1, 1'	2, 2'	3	4	5	6	7	8	9	10	11
z_i	I	I	I	I	S	S	S	S	S	S	R
a	NT or UT		TT	TT	NT	NT	UT	UT	TT	TT	NT
$a(z)_i$	I	I	S	S	S	S	I	I	S	S	R
z_i'	I	S	S	R	S	R	I	S	S	R	R
o_i	X	S	S	R	X	R	X	S	S	R	R

UT = the node is involved in an untrapped transmission and is not involved in any trapped transmission, TT = the node is involved in a trapped transmission, NT = the node is not involved in any trapped transmission, X = the defender cannot infer the node's state

case figures exist and the observation o_i generated about a node i relies on the action profile a and the state transition $z_i \rightarrow z_i'$ of the node. The difference between cases numbers 5 and 9 for example resides only in the action involving the nodes. For a susceptible node whom state has not got changed, the defender observes the final state only in case of trapped transmission. Case number 5 is that of nodes 9 and 10 of Fig. 2, while case number 9 is the one of node 5. In cases 1 and 1', the node remain infected during the period (nodes 1 and 2) and the defender cannot infer the final state.

Finally, we note $\omega(z'|z,a)$ the observation generated to the defender at the end of a period at which action profile a was taken in state z and the network transitioned to state z'.

The transition function. With the natural assumption that nodes transit independently of each other, Table 1 makes possible to calculate the probability $\mathbb{P}(z'|z,a)$ at which the system transitions to state z' when action a was taken in state z. The transition function is defined by $T(z',o|z,a) =$
$$\begin{cases} \mathbb{P}(z'|z,a) & \text{if } o = \omega(z'|z,a) \\ 0 & \text{otherwise} \end{cases}.$$

The rewards. The threat $\mu(z'|z,a)$ is the number $\varphi(z') = |\{i \in V : z_i' = I\}|$ of infected nodes at the end of the period.

5.3 Algorithm for Defender Optimal Strategy

We extend the POSMG with the above function φ. So, the number of infected nodes at the beginning of the game is the first value in memory. The game needs not reach the goal state for the algorithm to terminate. Indeed, it is possible to check out if the uniform strategy is stationary and from the underlined period onward, the defender should run this strategy. Note that the defender might be not aware his strategy $\widetilde{\pi}_1$ is already stationary. So, the algorithm terminates anyway. This verification is made in line 4 of algorithm 2 through function *ShouldContinue* (see Algorithm 3). To know if the value cannot be improved, the algorithm checks if the POSMPG has returned to visited state while the maximum number of infected nodes has not been improved (lines 9 to 18). From the finitude of the state space, it comes that the algorithm converges. In case needed to force the algorithm to terminate before the convergence, we keep the control $k \leqslant K$.

Algorithm 3: HSVI algorithm for Adversarial Epidemic Control

---

1   $k \leftarrow 1$

2   $\underline{V}^{k-} \leftarrow \mathrm{val}^{\widetilde{\sigma}_{\mathrm{unif}}}$

3   $\overline{V}^{k+} \leftarrow V^{*0+}$ ▷ the zero function

4   StuckStates $\leftarrow \emptyset$ ▷ in the POSMG

5   CheckMemory $\leftarrow -1$

6   **while** $\overline{V}^{k+}\left(\widetilde{b}^0\right) - \underline{V}^{k-}\left(\widetilde{b}^0\right) > \varepsilon$ *and* $k \leqslant K$ *and* ShouldContinue() **do**

7 | Explore($\widetilde{b}^0$, 1)

8 | $k \leftarrow k + 1$

9   **Function** ShouldContinue()

10   **if** new maximum number of infected nodes = CheckMemory **then**

11   **if** state $\in$ StuckStates **then**

12 | **return** false

13   **else**

14   StuckStates $\leftarrow$ StuckStates $\cup$ {state}

15   **return** true

16   **else**

17   CheckMemory $\leftarrow \emptyset$

18   **return** true

19   **procedure** Explore($\widetilde{b}^{t-1}$, t)

20   **if** excess$_t\left(\widetilde{b}^{t-1}\right) > 0$ **then**

21       $\widetilde{\pi}_1^t \leftarrow$ optimal strategy of player 1 in $\left[H\overline{V}^{(k-t)+}\right]\left(\widetilde{b}^{t-1}\right)$

22       $\widetilde{\pi}_2^t \leftarrow$ optimal strategy of player 2 in $\left[H\underline{V}^{(k-t)-}\right]\left(\widetilde{b}^{t-1}\right)$

23       $\widetilde{b}^t \leftarrow \underset{(a_1,o) \in A_1 \times O}{\arg\max} \ \mathbb{P}_{\widetilde{b}^{t-1}, \widetilde{\pi}_1^t, \widetilde{\pi}_2^t}(a_1, o) \times \mathrm{excess}_{t+1}\left(\tau\left(\widetilde{b}^{t-1}, a_1, \widetilde{\pi}_2^t, o\right)\right)$

24   Explore($\widetilde{b}^t$, $t + 1$)

25   Perform point-based update of $\overline{V}^{(k-t)+}$ and $\underline{V}^{(k-t)-}$ in $\widetilde{b}^{t-1}$

---

6   Conclusions and Perspectives

The control of strategic SIR epidemic spread with opposite decision makers can be studied as POSMPGs with infinite horizon two-player zero-sum POSGs with goal states. The outcome of any player is captured by the overall extremum value in the instantaneous utility. The overall maximum value in the outcome of the attacker is the peak of the threat, and the defender aim to minimize it. To circumvent the non-interchangeability of the mean and the maximum, we derive a POSSPG from the POSMPG that admits the same optimal strategy profiles. Henceforth, the resolution of the first game may be done through the resolution of the latest one. However, unlike in [20], our POSSPG may generate zero reward while a goal state is not yet reached and, consequently, the boundedness of the optimal solution determined by the previous authors is not proved in our context. Nevertheless, we iteratively bound the optimal value of our POSMPG between the optimal values of two fine horizon POSGs. In order to obtain the algorithm for our inferred POSSPG, we first transform the finite horizon POSGs into infinite horizon discounted sum POSG by applying a technique proposed in [20], then the optimal value of the infinite horizon game is iteratively approximated by the point-based update of the finite bounds. We finally propose an algorithm that converges in the particular case of epidemic control. As perspectives, we plan to study the scalability of our algorithm, which is a serious issue when a cyber security problem is targeted from the perspective of POSGs. The epidemiological nature of the threat analyzed in this paper makes this scalability issue more intricate. However, taking into account some special features like the possibility of playing many periods with zero reward implies a much more specific algorithm and scales down the issue.

Acknowledgments. Research was sponsored by the U.S. Army Research Office and was accomplished under Cooperative Agreement Number W911NF-22-2-0175 and Grant Number W911NF-21-1-0326. The views and conclusions contained in this document are those of the authors and should not be interpreted as representing the official policies, either expressed or implied, of the U.S. Army Research Laboratory or the U.S. Government. The U.S. Government is authorized to reproduce and distribute reprints for Government purposes notwithstanding any copyright notation herein.

References

1. Ansari, A., Dadgar, M., Hamzeh, A., Schlötterer, J., Granitzer, M.: Competitive influence maximization: integrating budget allocation and seed selection. https://www.researchgate.net/profile/Masoud-Dadgar-2/publication/338228670_Competitive_Influence_Maximization_Integrating_Budget_Allocation_and_Seed_Sel ection/links/5e177f904585159aa4c2d628/Competitive-Influence-Maximization-Int egrating-Budget-Allocation-and-Seed-Selection.pdf
2. Antonakakis, M., et al.: Understanding the Mirai botnet. In: 26th USENIX Security Symposium, pp. 1093–1110 (2017). https://www.usenix.org/conference/usenixsecurity17/technical-sessions/presentation/antonakakis

3. Chakrabarti, D., Wang, Y., Wang, C., Leskovec, J., Faloutsos, C.: Epidemic thresholds in real networks. ACM Trans. Inf. Syst. Secur. **10**(4), 1–26 (2008). https://doi.org/10.1145/1284680.1284681

4. Chen, L., Wang, Z., Li, F., Guo, Y., Geng, K.: A stackelberg security game for adversarial outbreak detection in the internet of things. Sensors **20**, 804 (2020). https://doi.org/10.3390/s20030804

5. Chen, Z., Gao, L., Kwiat, K.: Modeling the spread of active worms. In: IEEE INFOCOM, vol. 3, pp. 1890–1900. IEEE (2003)

6. Cohen, R., Havlin, S., Ben-Avraham, D.: Efficient immunization strategies for computer networks and populations. Phys. Rev. Lett. **91**, 247901 (2013)

7. Garg, N., Grosu, D.: Deception in honeynets: a game-theoretic analysis. In: 2007 IEEE SMC Information Assurance and Security Workshop, pp. 107–113 (2007)

8. Horák, K.: Scalable algorithms for solving stochastic games with limited partial observability. Ph.D. thesis, Czech Technical University in Prague (2019)

9. Horák, K., Bosansky, B., Tomášek, P., Kiekintveld, C., Kamhoua, C.: Optimizing honeypot strategies against dynamic lateral movement using partially observable stochastic games. Comput. Secur. **87**, 101579 (2019). https://doi.org/10.1016/j.cose.2019.101579

10. Horák, K., Bošanský, B., Pěchouček, M.: Heuristic search value iteration for one-sided partially observable stochastic games. In: International Joint Conference on Artificial Intelligence, vol. 31, pp. 558–564 (2017). ISBN 978-1-57735-780-3

11. Huang, Y., Zhu, Q.: Game-theoretic frameworks for epidemic spreading and human decision-making: a review. Dyn. Games Appl. 1–42 (2022)

12. Kephart, J., White, S.: Directed-graph epidemiological models of computer viruses. In: Proceedings of IEEE Symposium Research Security and Privacy (1991)

13. Kiss, I.Z., Miller, J.C., Simon, P.L., et al.: Mathematics of Epidemics on Networks, vol. 598. Springer, Cham (2017). https://doi.org/10.1007/978-3-319-50806-1

14. Kolias, C., Kambourakis, G., Stavrou, A., Voas, J.: DDoS in the IoT: Mirai and other botnets. Computer **50**(7), 80–84 (2017)

15. Kumar, B., Bhuyan, B.: Using game theory to model DoS attack and defence. Sādhanā **44**(12), 1–12 (2019). https://doi.org/10.1007/s12046-019-1228-4

16. Puterman, M.L.: Markov Decision Processes: Discrete Stochastic Dynamic Programming. Wiley, Hoboken (2014)

17. Raghavan, T.: Stochastic games-an overview. In: Stochastic Games and Related Topics, pp. 1–9 (1991)

18. Schneider, C., Mihaljev, T., Havlin, S., Herrmann, H.: Suppressing epidemics with a limited amount of immunization units. Phys. Rev. E **84**, 061911 (2011). https://doi.org/10.1103/PhysRevE.84.061911

19. Shapley, L.S.: Stochastic games. Proc. Natl. Acad. Sci. **39**, 1095–1100 (1953)

20. Tomášek, P., Horák, K., Aradhye, A., Bošanskỳ, B., Chatterjee, K.: Solving partially observable stochastic shortest-path games (2021). https://www.ijcai.org/proceedings/2021/0575.pdf

21. Trajanovski, S., Hayel, Y., Altman, E., Wang, H., Mieghem, P.: Decentralized protection strategies against sis epidemics in networks. IEEE Trans. Control Netw. Syst. **2**, 406–419 (2015). https://doi.org/10.1109/TCNS.2015.2426755

22. Trajanovski, S., Kuipers, F., Hayel, Y., Altman, E., Mieghem, P.: Designing virus-resistant, high-performance networks: a game-formation approach. IEEE Trans. Control Netw. Syst. **5**(4), 1682–1692 (2017). https://doi.org/10.1109/TCNS.2017.2747840

23. Tsemogne, O., Hayel, Y., Kamhoua, C., Deugoue, G.: Partially observable stochastic games for cyber deception against network epidemic. In: 11th International Conference GameSec (2020)
24. Tsemogne, O., Hayel, Y., Kamhoua, C., Deugoué, G.: Game-theoretic modeling of cyber deception against epidemic botnets in internet of things. IEEE Internet Things J. **9**(4), 2678–2687 (2021)
25. Tsemogne, O., Hayel, Y., Kamhoua, C., Deugoue, G.: A partially observable stochastic zero-sum game for a network epidemic control problem. Dyn. Games Appl. **12**(1), 82–109 (2022)
26. Van Mieghem, P., Omic, J., Kooij, R.: Virus spread in networks. IEEE/ACM Trans. Netw. **17**(1), 1–14 (2009)

Voting Games to Model Protocol Stability and Security of Proof-of-Work Cryptocurrencies

Sanjay Bhattacherjee[1]([✉])[iD] and Palash Sarkar[2][iD]

[1] Institute of Cyber Security for Society and School of Computing, Keynes College, University of Kent, Canterbury CT2 7NP, UK
s.bhattacherjee@kent.ac.uk

[2] Applied Statistics Unit, Indian Statistical Institute, 203, B.T. Road, Kolkata 700108, India
palash@isical.ac.in

https://www.kent.ac.uk/computing/people/3156/bhattacherjee-sanjay,
https://www.isical.ac.in/~palash/

Abstract. We model the *protocol stability* and the *security* of proof-of-work cryptocurrencies using voting games. The first game, which we call the Rule Game, pertains to the scenario where the cryptocurrency miners engage in a voting procedure to accept or reject a proposal for change of the cryptocurrency protocol. The second game, which we call the Attack Game, refers to the scenario where a group of miners can form a coalition to launch a 51% attack on the system and consequently change a portion of the history of the underlying blockchain, thus defeating its promise of immutability. For the Attack Game, we define progressively granular notions of security all of which are based on the key concept of minimal winning coalitions from voting game theory. For both the Rule Game and the Attack Game, we show practical applicability of tools from voting game theory using a snapshot of real world data for Bitcoin. In particular, this highlights the fragile nature of the security of Bitcoin with respect to 51% attacks.

Keywords: Voting games · Cryptocurrency · Bitcoin (BTC) · Preventive power · Protocol change · 51% attack · Security

1 Introduction

Since the proposal of Bitcoin (BTC) by the eponymous Satoshi Nakamoto [29], many cryptocurrencies have been proposed. Bitcoin though, remains the most popular and valuable cryptocurrency. The underlying blockchain technology has found numerous applications as well. There are multiple dimensions to research on blockchains. In this work, we model (1) the procedure to change the protocol and (2) the security of proof-of-work cryptocurrencies using voting games. The ensuing analysis shows the practical applicability of tools from voting game theory in the scrutiny of cryptocurrency systems.

F. Fang et al. (Eds.): GameSec 2022, LNCS 13727, pp. 297–318, 2023.
https://doi.org/10.1007/978-3-031-26369-9_15

Voting Games

Voting Games are typically used to model and analyse the decision-making procedure in scenarios that involve several entities or players. Of practical interest are weighted majority voting games. In such games, each player has a preassigned weight. A coalition of players wins if the sum of the weights of all the players in the coalition is at least a certain pre-specified fraction q of the total sum of the weights of all the players.

Voting Games in Proof-of-Work Cryptocurrencies

A proof-of-work cryptocurrency has an underlying linear blockchain data structure. Blocks are added to this structure by individual miners and mining pools who find the proof-of-work for a new block as a solution to a computational puzzle. For simplicity, we use the name *miner* for any mining entity - an individual or a pool. The more the computational power or the "hash rate" (explained in [3]) invested by a miner, more are its chances to succeed in mining a new block. This feature indicates the presence of an implicit voting game in cryptocurrencies.

In this work, we model two key functional aspects of a proof-of-work cryptocurrency system using voting games. By adding new blocks to the system, a miner participates as a player in both these games. The weight of a miner in these games is proportional to the fraction of the total network's hash rate that it controls. The winning threshold q is fixed depending upon the functional aspect that is being modelled.

The first functional aspect that we model is the procedure to change the *rules governing the cryptocurrency* described as *protocols*. The miners and other participating entities of the system follow the protocols. Being a decentralised and distributed system, the protocols are not determined or distributed by any central authority. They are initially agreed upon by the miners at the time of inception and as part of the specification, there is a well-defined procedure to change the protocols through consensus of the miners.

In the context of Bitcoin, a protocol modification happens through a Bitcoin Improvement Proposal (BIP). We show that a BIP [7] can be viewed as a weighted majority voting game among the miners where the winning threshold q is 0.95 (although there are instances of lower thresholds being used as well [6]). More generally, we use the term Rule Game to denote the voting games arising in the context of protocol change of any cryptocurrency (details in [3]). The purpose of having a high winning threshold in a Rule Game is to achieve near unanimity for a protocol change to take place. From the viewpoint of voting games, having a high winning threshold results in several miners becoming blockers.

The core principles of the Bitcoin blockchain have been emulated to varied extents by perhaps all cryptocurrencies that have been developed thereafter. Just like BIP, protocol changes requiring consensus are a very common phenomenon in Ethereum [16] and other proof-of-work blockchains [26, 30].

It is perhaps natural that a procedure to achieve consensus among multiple agents gives rise to situations of cooperation and conflict and hence is a topic of certain game theoretic interest. When the miners are in agreement over the protocols, we say that the cryptocurrency is *stable*. Proposals for protocol change that lead to conflicts among miners make the system less stable. An extreme consequence of disagreement between the miners over protocol changes is the *forking* of the cryptocurrency into two separate ones. A fork splits the network and even though some of the miners may continue to mine on both the chains, it certainly reduces the hash rate invested in both cryptocurrencies as compared to the original one. This makes both chains more vulnerable to attacks compared to the original chain. There are of course other socio-economic implications of rifts between miners over protocol changes leading to reduced stability. Some of the highly debated cryptocurrency protocol changes include SegWit [5] that led to a new cryptocurrency Bitcoin Cash (BCH) forked from the BTC chain, and the split between Ethereum and Ethereum Classic [37] after the DAO attack. This shows that protocol stability is a major challenge for proof-of-work cryptocurrencies. We use the Coleman preventive power measure (as argued in [3]) to capture the influence of a miner in a Rule Game for protocol stability.

The second functional aspect that we model is the immutability of the underlying blockchain data structure ensured by the miners not attacking the system. If a coalition of miners acquire at least 51% of the hash rate of the system, then with non-negligible probability, such a coalition can engage in changing a substantial part of the blockchain and consequently double spending of the currency. At any point of time, some of the miners may be attempting to attack the system while the others are preventing it. We model this as a voting game between the miners with the winning threshold $q = 0.51$. We call this an Attack Game.

There have been several instances of 51% attacks [1] on various cryptocurrencies, including Bitcoin [36], Bitcoin Gold [9], Ethereum Classic [13], Bitcoin SV [8], Verge [10], Litecoin Cash [27], Vertcoin [28], and many more. These attacks have led to owners of the respective cryptocurrencies suffer huge losses. The Attack Game and its detailed characterisation and analysis is thus extremely important for the cryptocurrency space.

Our analysis of the Attack Game is based on questions formulated around the crucial notion of minimal winning coalitions. For example, one may wish to know the minimum cardinality of any minimal winning coalition; another relevant question would be the minimum cardinality of any minimal winning coalition containing a particular miner. We define related notions of security to provide concrete answers to such questions.

The top level security notion that we introduce is that of the cryptocurrency being c-secure, where c is the maximum integer such that there is no minimal winning coalition for the Attack Game of size c or lower. In other words, this means that no coalition of c or lesser number of miners will be able to attack the cryptocurrency. Starting from this security notion, we define progressively granular notions of security finally leading to the following security consideration. Suppose L is a set of 'large' miners, i.e., miners who control a significant amount of the network hash rate. Let (S_1, S_2) be a partition of L. We consider the scenario where the miners in S_1 are trying to compromise the system, but, the miners in S_2 are not doing so. Then the question is how much support do the miners in S_1 require from miners outside L to attack the system. We define the cryptocurrency to be (L, c_1, c)-secure if for any subset S_1 of L of size c_1, more than c miners outside of L are required to form a coalition with S_1 and successfully attack the system.

To the best of our knowledge, the game theoretic modelling, the definitions of security and the mechanisms for analysing the stability of a cryptocurrency that we introduce have not appeared before either in the voting game or in the cryptocurrency literature.

Snapshot Analysis

To actually compute the power measures and the minimal winning coalitions in a cryptocurrency game, it is required to obtain the weights of the miners which are their hash rates. The values of the hash rates are not directly available. Instead, they need to be estimated. A simple estimate can be obtained based on the assumption that the hash rate is proportional to the number of blocks mined by a miner in a given interval of time. This provides a snapshot estimate of the actual hash rate of the miners.

For Bitcoin, we use such a snapshot estimate and show how to perform a meaningful analysis of the Rule and the Attack Games. The results for the Attack Game throw light on the vulnerability of Bitcoin. For example, in the time interval that we have considered, there were 8 different coalitions each consisting of 5 known miners such that any of these coalitions could have won the Attack Game. Given that the Bitcoin market is worth billions of dollars, it is a disconcerting thought that there can be several coalitions of a small number of parties who can disrupt the whole system. While a cryptocurrency does not have any central authority, the power to compromise the system residing in the hands of a few parties certainly detracts from the purposed goal of a completely decentralised system.

Related Works: An introduction to voting games can be found in [11] and an extensive overview of the topic is provided in [18]. The idea of measuring power in a voting game was introduced in [34, 35]. The use of swings to measure voting power of players was suggested in [2, 33]. Later work by [14] provided alternative proposals for capturing the notions of preventive and initiative powers of players. Voting power measures based on the idea of minimal winning coalitions were suggested in [15, 20, 21]. We refer to [24, 31] for surveys on voting games.

There is a fairly large and growing literature on cryptocurrencies. Some game theoretic aspects of cryptocurrencies have already been studied [19, 22, 23, 25]. To the best of our knowledge, the applications of weighted majority voting games to model protocol stability and security of cryptocurrencies have not been considered earlier.

2   Background and Preliminaries

In this section we provide a high level overview of proof-of-work cryptocurrencies and voting games to help understand how voting games arise in these cryptocurrencies. For further details on blockchains, the reader may consult [12,32]. More details on voting games can be found in [11,18].

2.1   Blockchain Basics

A typical *blockchain* is fundamentally a linear data structure that is built and maintained by a distributed system of computing nodes connected through peer-to-peer networking. The data structure is composed of a "chain of blocks" $\mathbf{B} = \{B_0, B_1, \ldots\}$. Each block B_i is made up of a header h_i and a body b_i. For $i \in \{1, 2, \ldots\}$, the header h_i of every block B_i contains a digest of the body b_i and the hash value $\mathcal{H}(h_{i-1})$ where $\mathcal{H}$ is a cryptographically secure hash function and h_{i-1} is the header of the previous block B_{i-1} in the chain. A cryptocurrency system $\mathfrak{C}$ is a blockchain where the information on the creation and transfer of the currency is stored in the body of each block.

In Bitcoin, a key criteria for validity of a new block B_r is that the hash of its header $\mathcal{H}(h_r)$ should have a certain number of leading zeros also called the *difficulty*. The node that produced B_r is called the *miner* of that block. The Bitcoin protocol allows the miner to include a random number or *nonce* η_r in the header h_r of B_r so that its hash $\mathcal{H}(h_r)$ has the required difficulty. The nonce thus found through mining is called *proof-of-work*. Finding the proof-of-work is a computational challenge, and the probability of success is proportional to the number of hashes that the miner can compute per second (called its *hash rate*). Miners may increase their individual hash rates to increase the number of blocks they are able to mine and thus their profits thereof. Multiple miners may come together to *pool* their computing resources and mine blocks together. This increases the probability of successfully mining the block and results in more profits within a specified time frame. For the purpose of this paper, we do not distinguish between miners and mining pools.

In general for any blockchain system, we use the name *miner* to denote an entity that creates a block, and the term *weight* to denote the amount of computational resource (hash rate) they have invested in the system. The weight is their contribution of resources in running and maintaining the system.

Blockchain Security. The primary security promise offered by a blockchain system is the immutability of its history. As new blocks are appended to $\mathbf{B}$, the existing blocks get farther away from the last block of $\mathbf{B}$. If a block $B_i \in \mathbf{B}$ is altered to B_i' by an attacker, its header h_i and the hash $\mathcal{H}(h_i)$ will change. The new hash $\mathcal{H}(h_i')$ will not tally with the hash value $\mathcal{H}(h_i)$ stored in the header h_{i+1} of B_{i+1}.

To alter a proof-of-work blockchain, the attacker will have to find a new proof-of-work η_i' for this altered block B_i'. To make the system consistent, $\mathcal{H}(h_i')$ will then have to be saved in B_{i+1} changing it to B_{i+1}'. So now the attacker has to find a new proof-of-work η'_{i+1} for B'_{i+1} to be saved in the header of B_{i+2} and so on. Thus a single change in B_i will result in a cascade of changes to all subsequent blocks in the chain until the last block in the blockchain. If an attacker controls *more than half* of the (computational) resources of the network, it can launch such an attack on **B**. Such an attack is thus called the "*51% attack*". As mentioned in Sect. 1, there are many known instances of such attacks on cryptocurrencies.

Blockchain Protocol Stability. A decentralised blockchain system is completely maintained by its miners. The maintainability of a blockchain includes the ability to change the blockchain protocol itself. Typically, a protocol change is proposed on some off-chain forum like a common web-portal, mailing list, etc. that is popularly followed. The block headers contain a set of bits that are mapped to a change proposal though an off-chain mechanism as well. For every new block created, its creator denotes their support/opposition to the currently active protocol change proposals by setting/unsetting the corresponding bits. Only when an overwhelming majority of the blocks added to **B** within a predetermined period of time have support in favour of a change, it is incorporated into the protocol. As discussed in Sect. 1, protocol change proposals have resulted in several debates between contending groups of miners and in the worst case of disagreements have even led to the forking of blockchains.

2.2   Voting Game Basics

Let $N = \{A_1, A_2, \ldots, A_n\}$ be a set of n players. A subset of N is called a coalition and the power set of N, i.e., the set of all possible coalitions is denoted by 2^N. A voting game G comprising of the players in N is given by its characteristic function $\Psi_G : 2^N \rightarrow \{0, 1\}$ where a winning coalition is assigned the value 1 and a losing coalition is assigned the value 0. The set of all winning coalitions is denoted by $W(G)$ and the set of all losing coalitions is denoted by $L(G)$. For a finite set S, $\#S$ will denote the cardinality of S.

For any $S \subseteq N$, $A_i \in N$ is called *swing* in S if $A_i \in S$, $\Psi_G(S) = 1$ but $\Psi_G(S \setminus \{A_i\}) = 0$. The number of subsets $S \subset N$ such that A_i is a swing in S will be denoted by $m_G(A_i)$. A coalition $S \subseteq N$ is called a *minimal winning coalition* if $\Psi_G(S) = 1$ and there is no $T \subset S$ for which $\Psi_G(T) = 1$. A coalition $S \subseteq N$ is called a *minimal blocking coalition* [4] in G if $\Psi_G(N \setminus S) = 0$ and for any non-empty $T \subset S$, $\Psi_G(N \setminus T) = 1$. A player A_i is called a blocker if $\{A_i\}$ is a minimal blocking coalition.

Definition 1. *Consider a triplet* $(N, \mathbf{w}, q)$, *where* $N = \{A_1, \ldots, A_n\}$ *is a set of players,* $\mathbf{w} = (w_1, w_2, \ldots, w_n)$ *is a vector of non-negative weights with* w_i *being the weight of* A_i *and* q *is a real number in* $(0, 1)$. *Let* $w_S = \sum_{A_i \in S} w_i$ *denote the sum of the weights of all the players in the coalition* $S \subseteq N$. *Then,*

$w_N = \sum_{A_i \in N} w_i$. A weighted majority voting game $G = (N, \mathbf{w}, q)$ is defined by the characteristic function $\Psi_G : 2^N \to \{0, 1\}$ as follows.

$$\Psi_G(S) = \begin{cases} 1 & \text{if } w_S/w_N \geq q, \\ 0 & \text{otherwise.} \end{cases}$$

3   Voting Games Arising from Proof-of-Work Cryptocurrencies

Proof-of-work cryptocurrencies give rise to at least two weighted majority voting games. We first describe the common features of both the games.

The Players, Their Weights and the Winning Threshold: The miners and the mining pools are the players in the game. We will simply write miner to mean either an individual miner or a mining pool. Intuitively, the weight of a player is its ability to mine a new block. In a proof-of-work based system, suppose there are k miners having hash rates $h_1, \ldots, h_k$ with the total hash rate h of the system being equal to $h = h_1 + \cdots + h_k$. The weights of the miners are the hash rates $h_1, \ldots, h_k$. For any positive real number λ, it is possible to use $\lambda h_1, \ldots, \lambda h_k$ as the weights without changing the characteristic function of the game. The winning threshold depends on the game as explained in Sects. 3.1 and 3.2.

Approximations of the Hash Rates of the Players: Being a decentralised and distributed system, the hash rates of the miners of a proof-of-work cryptocurrency system are not directly available. However, the proportion of blocks contributed by a miner to the system should indicate its proportion of the total hash rate.

Several Internet sites provide the number of blocks mined by various miners in a given time period. From this, it is possible to obtain an estimate of the hash rate of the miners. Suppose that for a given time period, a list $(A_1, b_1), \ldots, (A_k, b_k)$ is available indicating that the miner A_i has mined b_i blocks in that time period. It is reasonable to assume that the fraction of blocks mined by A_i in a given time period is proportional to h_i/h. Under this assumption, an estimate of the proportional hash rate of the miner A_i can be taken to be b_i/b where $b = b_1 + \cdots + b_r$. Since for a particular time period, b is constant, the weight of a miner can be taken to be the number of blocks it has mined in the given time period. The choice of this time period is not definite. It should not be too long since then miners who had been active earlier, but are no longer active will get positive weights. Neither should it be too short as then the estimate would not be accurate.

The suggested method of approximating the weights of the miners has a limitation. The actual weight of a miner is its hash rate while the approximate weight of a miner vote is taken to be the number of blocks that it is able to mine in the given time interval. While this number is expected to be proportional to the hash rate of the miner, it is not an exact correspondence. For example, it is possible that miners with low weights are unable to mine any block in the required time interval. As a result, the approximate weights of these miners will be zero, even though they have positive hash rates. While this is indeed an issue, for the miners with high hash rates, the proportion of mined blocks would be quite close to the proportional hash rates.

We note that the theoretical aspects of our work are not dependent on the method employed to obtain estimates of the hash rates of the miners. The theory that we develop could be equally well applied to hash rates estimated using some other method.

3.1   The Rule Game

The procedure for protocol change in a proof-of-work cryptocurrency has been briefly described in Sects. 1 and 2. For Bitcoin, this is done through a BIP. The Rule Game arising from a BIP occurs as follows. The difficulty (minimum number of leading zeros) of the hash value for a valid Bitcoin block is fixed for every 2016 blocks. Such a window of 2016 blocks is called the *target period* that typically lasts for 2 weeks. A BIP has to be decided upon within 26 consecutive target periods (around a year's time). Once started and before time-out, each of the 26 target periods creates a new Rule Game for the BIP. The winning threshold for a BIP is typically 95%. So at least 95% of the 2016 blocks in a target period must indicate support for the BIP (by setting the respective bit for the BIP in the block header) for it to be considered as accepted and active. So BIP games are played during fixed time intervals which are the periods of constant difficulty. Coalitions of players can form for the activation (or blocking) of a BIP. The interests of the members of such a coalition would be aligned, i.e., all of them would benefit (or suffer) in the same manner if a BIP is activated.

Simultaneous Voting Games: Several BIPs could be under consideration at the same point of time. In any target period, a miner who mines a new block has to indicate its preference for all of these BIPs. So in each time period a number of voting games are being simultaneously played. If the outcomes of the BIPs are unrelated, then the effect of simultaneous voting games can be captured by considering the voting games to be played sequentially. While some BIPs can indeed be unrelated, it is unlikely that BIPs under consideration will always be unrelated. The interaction between the outcomes can create complex voting and coalition strategies among the miners. For example, a miner may indicate support for a BIP only if some other miners indicate support for some other BIP.

Repeated Voting Games: Voting for a BIP takes place in at most 26 consecutive target periods. A BIP may not receive adequate support in a particular target period. However, this does not mean that the BIP has failed. It will again be open for voting in the subsequent target period. This process continues until the BIP gets locked-in, or, it times out after the 26 target periods. This feature is again very different from conventional voting game scenarios where once a motion fails, it is not taken up for voting any more.

A miner may mine several blocks in the time period over which voting takes place. We have assumed that the miner indicates its support or opposition to a protocol change proposal in all the blocks in a consistent manner. This seems to be a reasonable assumption. We do not know if there is any situation where a miner in a given time interval may indicate support to a proposal in some of the mined blocks and indicate opposition to the same proposal in the other mined blocks.

3.2   The Attack Game

In this game, the goal of a player or a coalition of players is to get control of the network by ensuring that the total sum of their hash rates is at least 51% of the entire hash rate of the network. So the winning threshold in this game is 51%.

A set of miners may form a coalition whereby they pool their computational resources so that the combined hash rate of the coalition becomes 51%. Such a coalition can attempt to launch a double spending attack on the network and agree to divide the income from the double spending among themselves in accordance with some criterion. It is possible that different coalitions of players can achieve the 51% threshold.

Continuously Playable Game: The Attack Game has the potential of being played at any point of time. There is no fixed time when the game is to be played. If we assume that the players are constantly trying to maximise their profits, then they are potentially exploring coalitions which will increase the hash rate. The aspect of the Attack Game whereby it is always possible to be played is not present in more conventional weighted majority voting games which are played at certain points of time and with adequate notice.

Remark: We have taken 51% as the winning threshold for the Attack Game. It has been suggested that the Bitcoin system can be attacked with even lower threshold [17]. The actual value of the winning threshold is not important for the method of analysis outlined in this work. So even though we later work with only the 51% threshold, a similar analysis can be done with other thresholds.

4   Security Notions for Analysis of the Attack Game

Let $\mathfrak{C}$ be a cryptocurrency system and let G be an Attack Game for $\mathfrak{C}$. For users of $\mathfrak{C}$ a basic question is whether $\mathfrak{C}$ is secure against the 51% attack, or, more formally whether the pair $(\mathfrak{C}, G)$ is secure. The question that arises is how to define security for the pair $(\mathfrak{C}, G)$? Of course, if there is a single miner in G having weight 51% or more of the total weight, then $\mathfrak{C}$ is clearly insecure. A single miner, however, may not have sufficient hash rate to be able to compromise the system. Then one needs to consider a coalition of miners who may wish to attack $\mathfrak{C}$. So any minimal winning coalition in the Attack Game G can mount a successful attack on $\mathfrak{C}$. Consequently, the number of minimal winning coalitions in G provide the number of ways in which $\mathfrak{C}$ can be attacked. It is unlikely that all possible minimal winning coalitions can actually form. More granular information provides better understanding of the security of $\mathfrak{C}$.

Denoting mw_c to be the number of minimal winning coalitions of size c, we are essentially looking for the distribution (c, mw_c) for $c = 1, \ldots, n$. For example, if $\mathsf{mw}_1 > 0$, then a single miner can win the Attack Game. So one measure of security is the maximum value of c such that $\mathsf{mw}_c = 0$. This would ensure that $(\mathfrak{C}, G)$ is secure against a coalition of c or less number of miners. This leads to the following definition.

Definition 2. *Let $\mathfrak{C}$ be a cryptocurrency system and $G = (N, \mathbf{w}, q)$ be an Attack Game for $\mathfrak{C}$. Then $(\mathfrak{C}, G)$ is said to be $\mathfrak{c}$-secure if $\mathfrak{c} = \max\{c : \mathsf{mw}_c = 0\}$. Equivalently, $(\mathfrak{C}, G)$ is said to be $\mathfrak{c}$-secure if $\mathsf{mw}_c = 0$ for all $c \leq \mathfrak{c}$ and $\mathsf{mw}_{\mathfrak{c}+1} \neq 0$.*

It is perhaps intuitive that $(\mathfrak{C}, G)$ provides the maximum security against the Attack Game if all miners in G have equal weights. We prove a formalisation of this statement in [3]. For a cryptocurrency $\mathfrak{C}$, one may ask for the maximum $\mathfrak{c}$ such that $(\mathfrak{C}, G)$ is $\mathfrak{c}$-secure where the maximum is taken over all possible Attack Games G having n players and the sum of the weights of the players is w_N. Elementary arguments show that when the players have the same weight, the maximum value of $\mathfrak{c}$ is $\lceil nq \rceil - 1$.

It is possible to consider the Attack Game from the viewpoint of a particular player A. Suppose A wishes to win the Attack Game. Then a relevant question for A is the minimum number of other players it needs to form a coalition with. This is captured by considering minimal winning coalitions containing A. More generally, instead of a single miner A, one can consider a coalition S and ask how many other miners are required to win the Attack Game.

For any subset S, denote by $\mathsf{mw}_c(S)$ the number of minimal winning coalitions of cardinality c which contain all elements of S. The distribution $(c, \mathsf{mw}_c(S))$ is of interest. The maximum value of c such that $\mathsf{mw}_c(S) = 0$ is a measure of security of $(\mathfrak{C}, G)$ with respect to the subset S. It indicates the minimum number of other miners that the coalition S will need to collude with to compromise the system. This leads to the following definition.

Definition 3. *Let $\mathfrak{C}$ be a cryptocurrency system and $G = (N, \mathbf{w}, q)$ be an Attack Game for $\mathfrak{C}$. Then $(\mathfrak{C}, G)$ is said to be $\mathfrak{c}$-secure with respect to S if $\mathfrak{c} = \max\{c : \mathsf{mw}_c(S) = 0\}$. Equivalently, $(\mathfrak{C}, G)$ is said to be $\mathfrak{c}$-secure with respect to S if $\mathsf{mw}_c(S) = 0$ for all $c \leq \mathfrak{c}$ and $\mathsf{mw}_{\mathfrak{c}+1}(S) \neq 0$.*

If $S = \{A\}$ is a singleton set consisting of a single player A, then we can talk about $(\mathfrak{C}, G)$ to be $\mathfrak{c}$-secure with respect to the player A. If $(\mathfrak{C}, G)$ is $\mathfrak{c}$-secure, then it is not difficult to argue that $\mathfrak{c} = \min_{A \in N} \max\{c : \mathsf{mw}_c(A) = 0\}$.

So far, we have assumed that all coalitions are possible. In a realistic setting, it is reasonable to postulate that not all coalitions will form. There could be two competing miners who will not be part of any coalition. More generally, one can consider two disjoint coalitions S_1 and S_2 and consider the scenario where the miners in S_1 wish to win the Attack Game but, the miners in S_2 do not wish to compromise $\mathfrak{C}$.

For a positive integer c, we define $\mathrm{mw}(S_1, S_2, c)$ to be the number of minimal winning coalitions in G of cardinalities c containing all elements of S_1 and no element of S_2.

Definition 4. *Let $\mathfrak{C}$ be a cryptocurrency system and $G = (N, \mathbf{w}, q)$ be an Attack Game for $\mathfrak{C}$. Let S_1 and S_2 be two subsets of N. Then $(\mathfrak{C}, G)$ is said to be c-secure with respect to the pair (S_1, S_2) if $c = \max\{c : \mathrm{mw}(S_1, S_2, c) = 0\}$.*

Remarks:

1. For the pair $(\mathfrak{C}, G)$, $\mathrm{mw}(\emptyset, \emptyset, c) = \mathrm{mw}_c$.
2. For any miner A, $\mathrm{mw}(\{A\}, \emptyset, c)$ is the number of minimal winning coalitions in G containing A and having cardinalities equal to c. Consequently, $(\mathfrak{C}, G)$ is c-secure with respect to A if and only if $(\mathfrak{C}, G)$ is c-secure with respect to the pair $(\{A\}, \emptyset)$.
3. For any subset S of miners, $\mathrm{mw}(\emptyset, S, c)$ is the number of minimal winning coalitions in G not containing any element of S and having cardinalities equal to c. Consequently, $(\mathfrak{C}, G)$ is c-secure with respect to the pair $(\emptyset, S)$ if the size of any minimal winning coalition in G not containing any element of S is at least $c + 1$. By leaving out a set of miners, we ask for the possibility of the system being compromised by some coalition of the other miners. The maximum value of c such that G is c-secure with respect to the pair $(\emptyset, S)$ provides a measure of security of the system against coalitions of miners who are not in S.

Definition 5. *Let $\mathfrak{C}$ be a cryptocurrency system and $G = (N, \mathbf{w}, q)$ be an Attack Game for $\mathfrak{C}$. We say that $(\mathfrak{C}, G)$ is (c_1, c_2, c)-secure, if*

$$c = \max\{c : \mathrm{mw}(S_1, S_2, c) = 0 \text{ for all subsets } S_1, S_2 \subseteq N \text{ with } \#S_1 \leq c_1, \ \#S_2 \leq c_2\}.$$

Remarks:

1. If $S_1 = S_2 = \emptyset$, then there are no constraints and in this case $\mathrm{mw}(S_1, S_2, c) = \mathrm{mw}_c$. $(\mathfrak{C}, G)$ is $(0, 0, c)$-secure if the size of any minimal winning coalition in G is at least c.
2. If $S_1 = \{A_i\}$ and $S_2 = \emptyset$, then $\mathrm{mw}(S_1, S_2, c)$ is the number of minimal winning coalitions of cardinality c containing A_i in G.
   $(\mathfrak{C}, G)$ is $(1, 0, c)$-secure if for any miner A_i, the size of any minimal winning coalition containing A_i is at least c.
3. $(\mathfrak{C}, G)$ is $(0, 0, c)$-secure if and only if the cardinality of any minimal winning coalition in G is at least $c + 1$. On the other hand, $(\mathfrak{C}, G)$ is $(1, 0, c)$-secure if and only if the cardinality of any minimal winning coalition in G containing at least one miner is at least $c + 1$. Since a minimal winning coalition must contain at least one miner, it follows that G is $(0, 0, c)$-secure if and only if $(\mathfrak{C}, G)$ is $(1, 0, c)$-secure.

4. If $S_1 = \{A_i\}$ and $S_2 \neq \emptyset$, then $\mathsf{mw}(S_1, S_2, c)$ is the number of minimal winning coalitions of cardinality c in G containing A_i, but, not containing any element of S_2.

$(\mathfrak{C}, G)$ is $(1, 1, \mathfrak{c})$-secure if for any two miners A_i and A_j, the size of any minimal winning coalition containing A_i but not containing A_j is at least $\mathfrak{c}$.

5. If $S_1 = \emptyset$ and $S_2 \neq \emptyset$, then $\mathsf{mw}(S_1, S_2, c)$ is the number of minimal winning coalitions of cardinality c in G not containing any element of S_2.

$(\mathfrak{C}, G)$ is $(0, \mathfrak{c}_2, \mathfrak{c})$-secure if for any set S_2 of size at most $\mathfrak{c}_2$, the size of any minimal winning coalition not containing any element of S_2 is at least $\mathfrak{c}$.

Typically, in a cryptocurrency system the set of miners can be roughly divided into two sets, those having "large" hash rates and those have significantly smaller hash rates. Let L be such a set of "large" miners. Any successful attack is likely to involve the miners in L. On the other hand, it is also quite unlikely that all the miners in L will collude. So one can consider a partition (S_1, S_2) of L where the miners in S_1 are part of the coalition attacking the system while the miners in S_2 are not part of this coalition, i.e., $L = S_1 \cup S_2$ and $S_1 \cap S_2 = \emptyset$. The relevant question is what is the minimum number of miners outside L (i.e., in $N \setminus L$) who need to form a coalition with the miners in S_1 to win the Attack Game?

Let N be a set of miners and L be a subset of N. For any subset S of L, by $\mathsf{mw}_L(S, c)$ we will denote the number of minimal winning coalitions in G containing S which are disjoint from $L \setminus S$ and have cardinalities equal to c.

Definition 6. *Let $\mathfrak{C}$ be a cryptocurrency system and $G = (N, \mathbf{w}, q)$ be an Attack Game for $\mathfrak{C}$. Let L be a subset of N. We say that $(\mathfrak{C}, G)$ is $(L, \mathfrak{c}_1, \mathfrak{c})$-secure if*

$$\mathfrak{c} = \max\{c : \mathsf{mw}_L(S, c) = 0 \text{ for all subsets } S \subseteq L \text{ with } \#S = \mathfrak{c}_1\}.$$

If $(\mathfrak{C}, G)$ is $(L, \mathfrak{c}_1, \mathfrak{c})$-secure, then the following is ensured. Consider any partition of L into S and $L \setminus S$ with $\#S = \mathfrak{c}_1$ and suppose that the coalition S does not collude with any miner in $L \setminus S$. Then to win the Attack Game the coalition S must collude with at least $\mathfrak{c} - \#S$ miners from $N \setminus L$.

Remark: Suppose $\mathfrak{C}$ is a cryptocurrency and G is an Attack Game for $\mathfrak{C}$. Suppose B is any minimal blocking coalition in G. Then any winning coalition for G must contain at least one miner from B. This has practical implications. Suppose that at some point of time $\mathfrak{C}$ is indeed attacked, then it is certain that at least one of the miners in B must have been involved in the attack. Given the pseudonymity of participants in a blockchain network, identifying attackers is a challenge. The above formalisation of the Attack Game could be a useful tool to either reduce the set of suspects or in certain cases even pin-point the set of attackers. We leave the details for future work.

5   A Snapshot Analysis of Bitcoin

For the snapshot analysis, we consider the blocks mined during the period July 2021 to June 2022 as shown in Table 1. For both the Rule Game and the Attack

Game, the players are the miners and as explained in Sect. 3, the weight of a miner is its hash rate estimated from the number of blocks mined by it during this one-year period. We have obtained the data from https://blockchair.com/. Our analysis can be applied equally well if the hash rates are estimated using some other methods, for any other meaningful time period and for any proof-of-work cryptocurrency.

Table 1. Miners (22 known) and the number of blocks they are known to have mined during July 2021 to June 2022.

Miner#	Miner Name	#blocks	Miner#	Miner Name	#blocks
01	Unknown	13808	02	AntPool	8287
03	F2Pool	7454	04	ViaBTC	6078
05	Binance	5645	06	Poolin	4810
07	Foundry USA Pool	3204	08	SlushPool	2955
09	Huobi	331	10	SBICrypto	325
11	EMCD	261	12	Bitdeer	212
13	MaraPool	142	14	OKEX	139
15	BTC.com	113	16	SpiderPool	34
17	Solo CKPool	9	18	50BTC	6
19	SigmaPool	6	20	OKKONG	5
21	mmpool	3	22	BTC.TOP	3
23	KanoPool	1			

The data in Table 1 attributes the highest number of blocks to "Unknown". This means that the identities of the miners of these blocks are not known. It is most likely that it is not a single entity which mined these blocks. So in the computation of the voting powers, it is not appropriate to consider "Unknown" as a player. Let U be the set of all miners in the group "Unknown". We handle the miners in U in the following manner.

Suppose the total weight of the components $\mathbf{w}$ is w_N out of which the miners in U have a total weight of w. Suppose that a fraction p of the total weight of the miners in "Unknown" play to win the game while the other $(1-p)$ fraction of the total weight of the miners in "Unknown" try to block the winning. By considering different values of p in $[0,1]$, it becomes possible to study the effect of the "Unknown" miners on the game. To capture this idea we make the following definition.

Definition 7. *Given the game $G = (N, \mathbf{w}, q)$, a player U with weight w and $p \in [0,1]$, we define the game $G^{(p)}$ with respect to U as $G^{(p)} = (N \setminus \{U\}, \mathbf{w}_{\overline{U}}, q^{(p)})$ where $q^{(p)} = (q \cdot w_N - p \cdot w)/(w_N - w)$ and w_N is the sum of the weights of all the players in the original game G. Here $\mathbf{w}_{\overline{U}}$ denotes the weight vector obtained from $\mathbf{w}$ by leaving out the entry corresponding to U.*

The miners in "Unknown" are not present in $G^{(p)}$ so the total weight of the miners in $G^{(p)}$ is $w_N - w$. To win, a coalition in the original game G needed to have weight at least $q \cdot w_N$. So in $G^{(p)}$, to win a coalition needs to have weight at least $q \cdot w_N - p \cdot w$.

In the game $G = (N, \mathbf{w}, q)$ obtained from Table 1, there are a total of $n = 23$ miners with the weight vector $\mathbf{w}$ as given in Table 1 and $q = 0.95$. The value of w_N is 53831 and "Unknown" miners have total weight of $w = 13808$. In the game $G^{(p)}$, the group U is removed from the game while the threshold $q^{(p)}$ is modified depending upon the value of p.

5.1   Computation of Voting Powers in the Rule Game

There is a large literature suggesting a variety of indices on how to measure the power or influence of a player in a voting game. We refer to [18] for discussions on this vast subject and to [11] for a textbook level introduction. We consider the Coleman preventive power measure which has been defined in [14]. Under this measure, the power of a player A_i in a game G is defined as follows.

$$\mathsf{CP}_G(A_i) = \frac{m_G(A_i)}{\#W(G)}.$$

The value of $\mathsf{CP}_G(A_i)$ is at least 0 and at most 1. We get $\mathsf{CP}_G(A_i) = 0$ if and only if A_i is not a swing in any coalition (a dummy player with $m_G(A_i) = 0$). We have $\mathsf{CP}_G(A_i) = 1$ if and only if A_i is present in every winning coalition (a blocker with $m_G(A_i) = \#W(G)$). Further, $\mathsf{CP}_G(A_i)$ is monotonically non-decreasing with the weight of A_i. For the Rule Game, the property of a miner being a blocker is of crucial interest. To the best of our knowledge, among the various power measures available in the literature, CP is the only power measure which assigns the maximum value of 1 to a blocker and is monotonically non-decreasing with the weights of the players. Due to these two reasons, we suggest that CP is an appropriate measure for measuring the power of a player in the Rule Game.

Let $G = (N, \mathbf{w}, q)$ where the sum of the weights of all the players in G is w_N. Let U be a player with weight w. For $p \in [0, 1]$ consider the game $G^{(p)}$ with respect to U. A player A_i in $G^{(p)}$ of weight w_i is a blocker if and only if $w_i > (1 - q)w_N + (p - 1)w$. So whether a player is a blocker depends on the value of p. It may happen that for a certain value of p, the player is a blocker, but, fails to be a blocker for a different value of p. For a specified value of p, the set of blockers in $G^{(p)}$ is fixed.

We consider the game $G^{(p)}$ for various values of p. The power profile given by CP for $G^{(p)}$ for various values of p is shown in Table 2. In Table 2 a value of 1 in the (i, p) cell indicates that player number i is a blocker in $G^{(p)}$. For $p = 0$, when none of the "Unknown" miners support the protocol change, the largest 7 miners are blockers (the protocol cannot be changed without their support) while the remaining 15 miners are all dummies with no say in the matter. As p increases, the number of blockers decreases. In Table 2, the numbers of blockers are 7, 5, 5, 2, and 1 corresponding to the values of $p = 0, 0.1, 0.2, 0.3$ and 0.4. For the other values of p, none of the known players are blockers. As the fraction of miners in "Unknown" who support the protocol change increases, the blocking capability of the other players go down. More generally, in Table 2, with increase in p, the power of any particular player decreases monotonically.

Table 2. Values of the Coleman preventive power index of the different players in the Rule Game for July 2021 to June 2022 and for various values of p.

Player#	Player	wt	p										
			0	0.1	0.2	0.3	0.4	0.5	0.6	0.7	0.8	0.9	1
02	AntPool	8287	1	1	1	1	1	0.941	0.864	0.876	0.759	0.731	0.641
03	F2Pool	7454	1	1	1	1	0.998	0.799	0.864	0.711	0.719	0.603	0.621
04	ViaBTC	6078	1	1	1	0.996	0.716	0.797	0.635	0.625	0.560	0.548	0.409
05	Binance	5645	1	1	1	0.913	0.713	0.783	0.593	0.580	0.527	0.457	0.408
06	Poolin	4810	1	1	1	0.536	0.713	0.494	0.591	0.488	0.478	0.383	0.364
07	Foundry USA Pool	3204	1	0.959	0.335	0.518	0.435	0.465	0.354	0.338	0.242	0.282	0.244
08	SlushPool	2955	1	0.780	0.332	0.518	0.435	0.405	0.328	0.308	0.241	0.252	0.222
09	Huobi	331	0	0.117	0.001	0.044	0.007	0.061	0.018	0.049	0.023	0.042	0.017
10	SBICrypto	325	0	0.117	0.001	0.043	0.007	0.060	0.018	0.048	0.023	0.042	0.016
11	EMCD	261	0	0.094	0.001	0.038	0.007	0.047	0.014	0.037	0.017	0.032	0.013
12	Bitdeer	212	0	0.076	0.001	0.031	0.007	0.039	0.012	0.030	0.015	0.026	0.011
13	MaraPool	142	0	0.057	0.001	0.022	0.005	0.026	0.007	0.020	0.009	0.017	0.007
14	OKEX	139	0	0.056	0.001	0.022	0.005	0.025	0.007	0.019	0.009	0.017	0.007
15	BTC.com	113	0	0.045	0.001	0.017	0.004	0.020	0.006	0.016	0.008	0.014	0.006
16	SpiderPool	34	0	0.017	0.001	0.008	0.001	0.007	0.001	0.005	0.002	0.004	0.001
17	Solo CKPool	9	0	0.002	0	0.001	0	0.002	0.001	0.001	0.001	0.001	0.001
18	50BTC	6	0	0.001	0	0.001	0	0.001	0	0.001	0.001	0.001	0
19	SigmaPool	6	0	0.001	0	0.001	0	0.001	0	0.001	0.001	0.001	0
20	OKKONG	5	0	0.001	0	0.001	0	0.001	0	0.001	0	0.001	0
21	mmpool	3	0	0.001	0	0	0	0.001	0	0	0	0	0
22	BTC.TOP	3	0	0.001	0	0	0	0.001	0	0	0	0	0
23	KanoPool	1	0	0	0	0	0	0	0	0	0	0	0
#blockers			7	5	5	2	1	0	0	0	0	0	0

5.2   Computation of Security in the Attack Game

As in the Rule Game, the role of the miners in the group marked "Unknown" is tackled by considering the game $G^{(p)}$ for various values of p. This indicates that a fraction p of the total weight of the miners in "Unknown" are trying to attack the system while a fraction $1 - p$ of the total weight of the miners in "Unknown" do not form part of any such attack coalition.

The cardinality wise number of minimal winning coalitions in $G^{(p)}$ for different values of p are shown in Table 3. The value of 0 means that there is no minimal winning coalition for the particular values of c and p. There is, however, a nuance in the interpretation of this condition. For $c \leq 3$, the value 0 denotes that there is actually no winning coalition in the game while for $c \geq 16$, the value 0 denotes that the winning coalitions are not minimal, i.e., dropping any miner from the coalition does not convert it into a losing coalition. We have the following observations from Table 3.

1. There is no winning coalition of cardinality 1 of known miners. So a coalition of at least 2 known miners along with more than 80% of the unknown miners' weight is required to win the Attack Game.
2. If 50% of the weight of the "Unknown" miners can be roped in then there are 3 minimal winning coalitions of the other 22 miners of cardinality 3.
3. There are several minimal winning coalitions of cardinalities 4 (or more) that do not require any unknown miner to win the Attack Game. So the system is vulnerable if 4 miners collude. In fact, there are 22 different ways of forming a set of 7 miners (without the "Unknown" miners) which can compromise the system. Given that the Bitcoin market is worth billions of dollars, the thought that there are multiple ways to form a malicious coalition of only 7 miners (all mining pools) is disconcerting.
4. In general, as p increases, the number of minimal coalitions initially increases and then decreases. The increase indicates that the number of winning coalitions itself goes up while the decrease indicates that some of the winning coalitions fail to remain minimal.

Table 3. Cardinality wise number of minimal winning coalitions in $G^{(p)}$ for the time period July 2021 to June 2022 of Table 1.

c	p										
	0.0	0.1	0.2	0.3	0.4	0.5	0.6	0.7	0.8	0.9	1.0
1	0	0	0	0	0	0	0	0	0	0	0
2	0	0	0	0	0	0	0	0	0	1	3
3	0	0	0	0	0	3	6	11	18	19	24
4	1	3	6	11	25	15	17	12	20	10	25
5	8	8	15	13	17	13	26	17	53	44	48
6	3	0	23	19	47	30	38	47	44	29	36
7	22	0	18	5	45	15	59	53	31	58	33
8	41	17	50	50	44	37	48	50	64	65	7
9	63	64	40	61	55	63	43	80	50	88	18
10	76	72	74	101	107	110	77	102	43	99	17
11	85	97	120	108	146	126	63	97	35	65	4
12	95	84	94	108	117	96	70	58	26	14	1
13	73	51	40	48	45	88	41	45	9	13	1
14	26	64	3	31	22	52	11	31	1	18	7
15	14	34	5	36	8	10	9	5	1	5	1
16	4	20	1	9	0	9	1	0	0	1	0
17	1	8	0	0	0	0	0	0	0	0	0
19	0	0	0	0	0	0	0	0	0	0	0
20	0	0	0	0	0	0	0	0	0	0	0
21	0	0	0	0	0	0	0	0	0	0	0
22	0	0	0	0	0	0	0	0	0	0	0
23	0	0	0	0	0	0	0	0	0	0	0
Total	512	522	489	600	678	667	509	608	395	529	225

In Table 4, we provide the cardinality wise number of minimal winning coalitions containing the largest miner AntPool. It is possible to compute similar data for all the individual players and their subsets. From the totals of the first columns of Tables 3 and 4 we see that there are $512 - 362 = 150$ minimal winning coalitions of miners other than the largest miner AntPool and the "Unknown" miners in the Attack Game. Table 4 shows that if 50% of the "Unknown" miners can be roped in, then AntPool can form possible coalitions consisting of itself and just 2 of the other 22 miners to win the Attack Game. On the other hand, if coalitions of size 4 or more are considered, then AntPool can form several winning coalitions in the Attack Game without involving any of the miners in "Unknown". Again, this is not a very comfortable scenario. Note that for $p = 0$, $\mathsf{mw}_5(\{Antpool\}) = 0$ although $\mathsf{mw}_4(\{Antpool\}) > 0$. This means that the winning coalitions of cardinality 5 are *not minimal*.

(L, c_1, c)-**Security:** For a set L of large miners, we consider (L, c_1, c)-security in $G^{(p)}$ for different values of p. We have considered several options for L, namely, L consists of the miners with i of the largest weights where we have taken $i = 1, 2, 3, 4, 5$ and 6. The value of c_1 is in the set $\{0, 1, \ldots, i\}$. In each case, we have computed the corresponding value of c. Table 5 provides values of ∂ such that $G^{(p)}$ is $(L, c_1, c_1 + \partial - 1)$-secure for different values of p and c_1. This means that c_1 largest miners in L need to collude with at least ∂ miners outside of L to win the Attack Game. In the table, a '$-$' denotes that there is no winning coalition for the corresponding condition whereas a '$*$' denotes that any coalition of size c_1 of L is already a winning coalition in $G^{(p)}$. Based on Table 5, we make the following observations.

Table 4. Cardinality wise number of minimal winning coalitions containing the largest miner AntPool for Table 1 in $G^{(p)}$.

c	p										
	0.0	0.1	0.2	0.3	0.4	0.5	0.6	0.7	0.8	0.9	1.0
0	0	0	0	0	0	0	0	0	0	0	0
1	0	0	0	0	0	0	0	0	0	1	3
2	0	0	0	0	0	3	5	8	12	9	3
3	1	3	6	10	22	8	9	6	8	0	3
4	8	6	12	10	14	12	26	17	35	25	20
5	0	0	19	19	32	30	36	47	34	27	15
6	2	0	2	4	22	11	33	43	20	35	25
7	26	10	16	21	2	3	15	21	30	44	2
8	35	36	17	28	11	17	9	18	31	53	0
9	41	46	16	40	18	34	21	22	18	64	8
10	57	64	25	43	7	26	4	19	7	33	3
11	75	49	25	43	2	11	0	18	3	4	1
12	72	24	18	24	0	17	1	10	0	6	0

(continued)

Table 4. (*continued*)

$\mathfrak{c}$	p										
	0.0	0.1	0.2	0.3	0.4	0.5	0.6	0.7	0.8	0.9	1.0
13	26	45	1	17	9	12	0	0	0	1	0
14	14	29	5	21	8	2	0	0	0	0	0
15	4	13	1	9	0	4	0	0	0	0	0
16	1	2	0	0	0	0	0	0	0	0	0
17	0	0	0	0	0	0	0	0	0	0	0
18	0	0	0	0	0	0	0	0	0	0	0
19	0	0	0	0	0	0	0	0	0	0	0
20	0	0	0	0	0	0	0	0	0	0	0
21	0	0	0	0	0	0	0	0	0	0	0
Total	362	327	163	289	147	190	159	229	198	302	83

1. Case $\#L = 4$ and $\mathfrak{c}_1 = 0$. All corresponding entries in the table are '–'. This means that if the largest four miners are left out, then there is no way to win the Attack Game. In other words, the set of four largest miners form a minimal blocking coalition. So any attack on the system certainly involves one of the four largest miners. As mentioned earlier, this fact contains useful information. If an attack is detected in the future, then one can be sure that at least one of the four largest miners was certainly part of the attack.

2. Case $\#L = 5$ and $\mathfrak{c}_1 \geq 5$. All corresponding entries in the table are marked by '$*$'. Similarly, for $\#L = 6$. This means that if five (or more) of the largest miners collude, then the Attack Game is immediately won.

3. Case $\#L = 3$ and $\mathfrak{c}_1 = 0$, i.e., the three largest miners are left out. The entries for $p \leq 0.6$ are '–'. This means that if less than 60% of the hash rate of "Unknown" miners are involved in the attack, then the attack cannot be successful. On the other hand, the entry for $p = 0.7$ is 9. This means that if 70% of the hash rate of the "Unknown" miners are involved in the attack, then leaving out the three largest miners, a coalition of 9 of the other $23 - 1 - 3 = 19$ miners is both necessary and sufficient to win the Attack Game.

4. Case $\#L = 4$ and $\mathfrak{c}_1 = 3$ and $p = 0.4$. The corresponding entry in the table is 1. The condition $\#L = 4$ and $\mathfrak{c}_1 = 3$ means that out of the four largest miners, one is left out. If 40% of the miners in "Unknown" can be roped in, then out of the 19 other miners, it is necessary and sufficient to have only 1 miner to win the Attack Game.

5. Case $\#L = 5$, $\mathfrak{c}_1 = 1$ and $p = 0.9$. The corresponding entry in the table is 4. The condition $\#L = 5$ and $\mathfrak{c}_1 = 1$ means that out of the five largest miners, four are left out. If 90% of the miners in "Unknown" can be roped in, then out of the 7 other miners, it is necessary and sufficient to have only 4 miners to win the Attack Game.

6. Consider the cases ($\#L = 5$, $c_1 = 3$, $p = 0$) and ($\#L = 6$, $c_1 = 3$, $p = 0$). The corresponding entries in the table are 2 and '$-$'. This may appear to be surprising, since in both cases $c_1 = 3$. The explanation is that in the first case, out of the five largest miners, two are left out, while in the second case, out of the six largest miners, three are left out. Since in the second case, more miners are left out, that leads to the absence of any (minimal) winning coalition.

Table 5. The entries in the table are $\mathfrak{d}$ such that $G^{(p)}$ is $(L, c_1, c_1+\mathfrak{d}-1)$-secure where L consists of the miners with the i largest weights as given in Table 1 for $i = 1, 2, 3, 4, 5, 6$.

		p										
		0.0	0.1	0.2	0.3	0.4	0.5	0.6	0.7	0.8	0.9	1.0
$\#L = 1$	$c_1 = 0$	6	5	5	4	4	4	3	3	3	3	3
	$c_1 = 1$	3	3	3	3	3	2	2	2	2	1	1
$\#L = 2$	$c_1 = 0$	-	-	-	7	5	5	4	4	3	3	3
	$c_1 = 1$	4	4	3	3	3	3	2	2	2	2	1
	$c_1 = 2$	2	2	2	2	2	1	1	1	1	*	*
$\#L = 3$	$c_1 = 0$	-	-	-	-	-	-	-	9	4	4	3
	$c_1 = 1$	-	9	4	4	3	3	3	2	2	2	1
	$c_1 = 2$	3	2	2	2	2	1	1	1	1	*	*
	$c_1 = 3$	1	1	1	1	1	*	*	*	*	*	*
$\#L = 4$	$c_1 = 0$	-	-	-	-	-	-	-	-	-	-	-
	$c_1 = 1$	-	-	-	-	-	9	3	3	3	2	2
	$c_1 = 2$	6	3	3	2	2	1	1	1	1	*	*
	$c_1 = 3$	2	1	1	1	1	*	*	*	*	*	*
	$c_1 = 4$	*	*	*	*	*	*	*	*	*	*	*
$\#L = 5$	$c_1 = 0$	-	-	-	-	-	-	-	-	-	-	-
	$c_1 = 1$	-	-	-	-	-	-	-	-	-	4	2
	$c_1 = 2$	-	-	-	9	3	2	2	1	1	*	*
	$c_1 = 3$	2	2	1	1	1	*	*	*	*	*	*
	$c_1 = 4$	*	*	*	*	*	*	*	*	*	*	*
	$c_1 = 5$	*	*	*	*	*	*	*	*	*	*	*
$\#L = 6$	$c_1 = 0$	-	-	-	-	-	-	-	-	-	-	-
	$c_1 = 1$	-	-	-	-	-	-	-	-	-	-	-
	$c_1 = 2$	-	-	-	-	-	-	3	1	1	*	*
	$c_1 = 3$	-	7	1	1	1	*	*	*	*	*	*
	$c_1 = 4$	*	*	*	*	*	*	*	*	*	*	*
	$c_1 = 5$	*	*	*	*	*	*	*	*	*	*	*
	$c_1 = 6$	*	*	*	*	*	*	*	*	*	*	*

6   Conclusion

Protocol stability and security play extremely important roles in the socio-economic dynamics of any proof-of-work cryptocurrency. In this work, we have modelled these two key functional aspects using weighted majority voting games. Our modelling immediately allows the rich tools from the theory of voting games to be used for analysis of cryptocurrency systems. As a practical contribution, we have shown how to perform concrete snapshot analysis on the games using such tools. We suggest that such analysis be performed at regular intervals to build a good understanding of the socio-economic dynamics of proof-of-work cryptocurrencies like Bitcoin. Wide dissemination of the results of such periodic analysis will help the general public to understand and appreciate the risks involved in using and investing in cryptocurrencies. This will also place the usually small number of parties who can compromise the system under intense public scrutiny and hopefully prevent any malicious behaviour. We also hope that this work will stimulate interest in the connection between cryptocurrencies and voting games leading to further interesting work on the intersection of these two topics.

Acknowledgements. We would like to thank the anonymous reviewers for their comments and suggestions. Majority of this work was done while Sanjay Bhattacherjee was visiting the Turing Laboratory, Applied Statistics Unit, Indian Statistical Institute.

References

1. 51% Attacks (Digital Currency Initiative, MIT Media Lab). https://dci.mit.edu/51-attacks. Accessed 8 Sept 2022
2. Banzhaf, J.F.: Weighted voting doesn't work: a mathematical analysis. Rutgers Law Rev. **19**, 317–343 (1965)
3. Bhattacherjee, S., Sarkar, P.: Cryptocurrency voting games. Cryptology ePrint Archive, Paper 2017/1167 (2017). https://eprint.iacr.org/2017/1167
4. Bhattacherjee, S., Sarkar, P.: Weighted voting procedure having a unique blocker. Int. J. Game Theory **50**(1), 279–295 (2021)
5. BIP 141: Segregated Witness (Consensus layer). https://github.com/bitcoin/bips/blob/master/bip-0141.mediawiki. Accessed 8 Sept 2022
6. BIP 91: Reduced threshold Segwit MASF. https://github.com/bitcoin/bips/blob/master/bip-0091.mediawiki. Accessed 8 Sept 2022
7. BIP Github page. https://github.com/bitcoin/bips. Accessed 8 Sept 2022
8. Bitcoin Magazine article on a 51% attack on Bitcoin SV (2021). https://bitcoinmagazine.com/markets/bitcoin-sv-sees-51-attack. Accessed 8 Sept 2022
9. Bitcoin.com article on a 51% attack on Bitcoin Gold (2020). https://news.bitcoin.com/bitcoin-gold-51-attacked-network-loses-70000-in-double-spends/. Accessed 8 Sept 2022
10. Bitcoin.com article on a 51% attack on Verge (2021). https://news.bitcoin.com/privacy-coin-verge-third-51-attack-200-days-xvg-transactions-erased/. Accessed 8 Sept 2022
11. Chakravarty, S.R., Mitra, M., Sarkar, P.: A Course on Cooperative Game Theory. Cambridge University Press, Cambridge (2015)

12. Chakravarty, S., Sarkar, P.: An Introduction to Algorithmic Finance, Algorithmic Trading and Blockchain. Emerald Group Publishing, Bingley (2020)
13. CoinDesk article on a 51% attack on Ethereum Classic (2020). https://www.coindesk.com/markets/2020/08/29/ethereum-classic-hit-by-third-51-attack-in-a-month/. Accessed 8 Sept 2022
14. Coleman, J.S.: Control of collectives and the power of a collectivity to act. In: Lieberma, B. (ed.) Social Choice, pp. 269–298. Gordon and Breach, New York (1971)
15. Deegan, J., Packel, E.W.: A new index of power for simple n-person games. Int. J. Game Theory **7**(2), 113–123 (1978)
16. EIP Github page. https://github.com/ethereum/EIPs. Accessed 8 Sept 2022
17. Eyal, I., Sirer, E.G.: Majority is not enough: bitcoin mining is vulnerable. In: Financial Cryptography and Data Security - 18th International Conference, FC 2014, Christ Church, Barbados, 3–7 March 2014, pp. 436–454 (2014)
18. Felsenthal, D.S., Machover, M.: The Measurement of Voting Power. Edward Elgar, Cheltenham (1998)
19. Fisch, B., Pass, R., Shelat, A.: Socially optimal mining pools. In: Devanur, N.R., Lu, P. (eds.) WINE 2017. LNCS, vol. 10660, pp. 205–218. Springer, Cham (2017). https://doi.org/10.1007/978-3-319-71924-5_15
20. Holler, M.J.: Forming coalitions and measuring voting power. Political Stud. **30**(2), 262–271 (1982)
21. Holler, M.J., Packel, E.W.: Power, luck and the right index. J. Econ. **43**(1), 21–29 (1983)
22. Kiayias, A., Koutsoupias, E., Kyropoulou, M., Tselekounis, Y.: Blockchain mining games. In: Proceedings of the 2016 ACM Conference on Economics and Computation, EC 2016, Maastricht, The Netherlands, 24–28 July 2016, pp. 365–382 (2016)
23. Kroll, J., Davey, I., Felten, E.W.: The economics of Bitcoin mining, or Bitcoin in the presence of adversaries. In: Workshop on the Economics of Information Security (2013)
24. Kurz, S., Maaser, N., Napel, S., Weber, M.: Mostly sunny: a forecast of tommorow's power index research. Homo Oecon. **32**, 133–146 (2015)
25. Lewenberg, Y., Bachrach, Y., Sompolinsky, Y., Zohar, A., Rosenschein, J.S.: Bitcoin mining pools: a cooperative game theoretic analysis. In: Proceedings of the 2015 International Conference on Autonomous Agents and Multiagent Systems, AAMAS 2015, Istanbul, Turkey, 4–8 May 2015, pp. 919–927 (2015)
26. LIP Github page. https://github.com/litecoin-project/lips. Accessed 8 Sept 2022
27. Livebitcoinnews.com article on a 51% attack on Litecoin Cash (2018). https://www.livebitcoinnews.com/litecoin-cash-51-attack-highlights-insecurity-of-smaller-pow-coins/. Accessed 8 Sept 2022
28. Medium.com article on a 51% attack on Vertcoin (2018). https://medium.com/coinmonks/vertcoin-vtc-is-currently-being-51-attacked-53ab633c08a4. Accessed 8 Sept 2022
29. Nakamoto, S.: Bitcoin: a peer-to-peer electronic cash system (2008)
30. Namecoin (IFA) Proposals Github page. https://github.com/namecoin/proposals. Accessed 8 Sept 2022
31. Napel, S.: Voting power. In: Congleton, R., Grofman, B., Voigt, S. (eds.) Oxford Handbook of Public Choice. Oxford University Press, Oxford (2016)
32. Narayanan, A., Bonneau, J., Felten, E.W., Miller, A., Goldfeder, S.: Bitcoin and Cryptocurrency Technologies: A Comprehensive Introduction. Princeton University Press, Princeton (2016)

33. Penrose, L.S.: The elementary statistics of majority voting. J. Roy. Stat. Soc. **109**(1), 53–57 (1946)
34. Shapley, L.S.: A value for n-person games. In: Kuhn, H.W., Tucker, A.W. (eds.) Contributions to the Theory of Games II (Annals of Mathematics Studies), pp. 307–317. Princeton University Press, Princeton (1953)
35. Shapley, L.S., Shubik, M.J.: A method for evaluating the distribution of power in a committee system. Am. Polit. Sci. Rev. **48**, 787–792 (1954)
36. The Guardian article on a 51% attack on Bitcoin (2014). https://www.theguardian.com/technology/2014/jun/16/bitcoin-currency-destroyed-51-attack-ghash-io. Accessed 8 Sept 2022
37. Why Ethereum Classic? (2022). https://ethereumclassic.org/why-classic. Accessed 8 Sept 2022

Author Index

A

Anwar, Ahmed H.   44, 255
Araujo, Frederico   87

B

Bajaj, Shivam   168
Bhambri, Siddhant   87
Bhattacherjee, Sanjay   297
Bilinski, Mark   23
Bopardikar, Shaunak D.   168
Bosansky, Branislav   44

C

Chauhan, Purv   87

D

Deugoué, Gabriel   255, 274
Doupé, Adam   87

F

Feng, Jiarui   212
Fu, Jie   67
Fugate, Sunny   23

G

Gabrys, Ryan   23
Gill, Christopher   212

H

Hayel, Yezekael   255, 274

K

Kambhampati, Subbarao   87
Kamhoua, Charles   44, 255, 274
Kiekintveld, Christopher   44
Kinsey, Sarah Eve   231
König, Sandra   129
Kouam, Willie   255
Kroupa, Tomáš   149

L

Li, Henger   107

M

Mauger, Justin   23

N

Nguyen, Thanh Hong   3, 231

P

Pan, Yunian   191

R

Rass, Stefan   129

S

Sarkar, Anindya   212
Sarkar, Palash   297
Sayed, Md Abu   44
Silva, Daniel   23
Sinha, Arunesh   231

T

Tsemogne, Olivier   255, 274
Tuck, Wong Wai   231

V

Vorobeychik, Yevgeniy   212
Votroubek, Tomáš   149

Y

Yadav, Amulya   3

Z

Zhang, Ning   212
Zheng, Zizhan   107
Zhu, Quanyan   191

F. Fang et al. (Eds.): GameSec 2022, LNCS 13727, p. 319, 2023.
https://doi.org/10.1007/978-3-031-26369-9

Printed in the United States
by Baker & Taylor Publisher Services